Elements in
Political Science

Elements in Political Science

Frank Bealey, Richard A. Chapman and Michael Sheehan

Edinburgh University Press

We dedicate this book to

Jan Hus Educational Foundation
Association Jan Hus
Vzdělávací Nadace Jana Husa
Vzdelávacia Nadácia Jana Husa

© Frank Bealey, Richard A. Chapman and Michael Sheehan, 1999

Edinburgh University Press
22 George Square, Edinburgh

Typeset in 10 on 12½ Stone Serif
by Hewer Text Limited, Edinburgh, and
printed and bound in Great Britain by
MPG Books, Bodmin, Cornwall

A CIP record for this book is available
from the British Library

ISBN 0 7486 1197 5 (hardback)
ISBN 0 7486 1109 6 (paperback)

Contents

Section Four **Public Administration**
Richard A. Chapman

Section Five **International Relations**
Michael Sheehan

Preface

Sections Two to Five of this book were originally delivered as lectures at universities in Slovakia between 1993 and 1995. They were part of the Support for Higher Education (SHE) programme of the Jan Hus Educational Foundation. The authors wish to thank the Foundation and its Director, Dr Miroslav Pospišil, for their support which enabled the lectures to be given. Thanks are also owing to the Komensky University at Bratislava and the P. J. Šafárik University at Prešov for hosting lecture courses and providing accommodation.

The Jan Hus Educational Foundation was established in 1980 in order to support the Charter 77 dissidents in Czechoslovakia, most of whom were suffering from loss of employment, official harassment and imprisonment or the threat of it. In these circumstances they lacked information about cultural and intellectual trends in the rest of the world. The Jan Hus Educational Foundation and its sister organisation in France, Association Jan Hus, in the 1980s provided visiting lecturers to attend seminars organised by leading dissidents. Since 1989 both organisations have assisted in the rehabilitation of university education in what are now two republics. In 1990 it was decided gradually to transfer all activities as an educational foundation to the headquarters of a Czech and Slovak body at Brno in Moravia.

The authors would like to thank Pamela Strang, Janet Michaelsen, Chris Mcleod and William Bealey who assisted greatly with typing and printing, and Alasdair McLean and Andrew Campbell who never failed to unravel computer problems. Derek Urwin read the whole work in draft and drew our attention to shortcomings in fact and presentation. Nicola Carr of Edinburgh University Press made useful suggestions about revising the scope of the book. Any errors that remain are, of course, the responsibility of the authors.

Frank Bealey, Richard A. Chapman and Michael Sheehan

April 1998

Section One

Introduction

Frank Bealey

1

Politics and political science

Political science is the study of politics in all its aspects. Occasionally politics is used as a synonym for political science: sometimes as the title of university departments of political science. This may be confusing. Although a few political scientists have become politicians, and even more rarely politicians have become political scientists, the activities of the two, despite impinging on each other, are quite different.

1.1 What is politics?

Politics can be regarded in at least four ways.

1.1.1 Politics as an activity

Politics is an activity indulged in, either full-time or part-time, by politicians. They are concerned with some or all of the collective decisions that affect the political unit they live in. It could be a small sub-unit like a parish, or it could be the central government. In most societies there is a divide between politicians and the rest of the citizenry who choose to play only a minimal part in decision-making for the collectivity. The politicians have become professionalised – they are professional politicians. But hypothetically there is no reason why there should be such a divide. There are small communities in existence where all adults participate in making decisions for the whole body politic.

Yet to say 'politics is an activity' is merely the beginning of wisdom. The activity is pursued quite variously in different contexts. In some it is the occasion of great antagonisms. Not all politicians, by any means, want every proposal adopted: on the contrary, they may try to prevent most of them succeeding. In some societies policies will be imposed by rulers and opposition may not be allowed. Here there will be only a few politicians imposing their own decisions. Hence there are numerous types of political regime (see Chapter 4 below) and numerous kinds of political activity.

1.1.2   Politics as 'current affairs'

To much of the non-political public, politics is a part of life with which they do not want to be involved. Indeed, to some it is disreputable and dangerous. Contention must be avoided: 'politics and religion are two things one should not talk about' is a much-quoted adage. But some citizens are quite interested and view political goings-on as they might a spectator sport. They support political parties as they support football teams, cheering from the sidelines. Students who take up political science often start from the angle of current affairs, a very useful approach to the subject. Another compendious and similar term is 'political life'. Foreign wars, what politicians do and say, praise and abuse of them, commentaries in the papers and on radio and television about their personal lives, gladiatorial argument between them, elections and party politics – all these may be included under the rubric of politics as current affairs.

1.1.3   Politics as what the government does

To govern is to control and all communities at an early stage of development will be concerned with the problem of control. The actions of those who control – the rulers, the incumbent government – may be perceived as politics. Where dissent is not possible this will be the only manifestation of politics.

1.1.4   Politics as conflict and the resolution of conflict

Conflict is here used in a wide sense to mean contestation, including any form of disagreement. Indeed, all group interrelationships will be involved with differences, even when compromise between the parties is regularised and institutionalised. Physical contestation is an extreme form of conflict. An initial assumption is that disagreement is very common. People disagree about objectives to be reached and they disagree about how to reach them. If there were no disagreement there would be no need for politics: to use old-fashioned terms, people disagree about ends and they disagree about means. Problems are likely to be resolved sooner or later and the role of the politician is to participate in the resolution.

Disagreement, of course, may occur at a personal level about quite trivial matters. Indeed, S. E. Finer, Professor of Political Institutions at

Keele, used to begin his lectures with the parable of two dogs fighting over an indivisible bone. One would eventually get it and the other dog would be dissatisfied with the outcome. But combat is not the only method of resolving disagreement. Brian Barry also lists contests (running a race or a boxing match), drawing lots, authoritative determination by setting up an arbitrator, bargaining, discussion on merits and voting.[1] While most of these are not appropriate to dogs they are all possible with human beings. Collective social objectives are not analogous to bones and people who disagree about them can choose several other methods of resolving their disputes.

This does not rule out combat, but many will feel that this is a risky and unpleasant way of resolving conflict. Foes defeated in war may replenish their arsenals, reinvigorate their morale and attempt revenge. Thus a victor in war should perhaps kill all enemies to be secure, which is not always very practical. Hence a sensible way of settling conflict may be one that maintains a certain stability, peace and order in society. Many see this as the basic problem in politics. It is also the best justification for politics – that it is concerned with the resolution of conflict with as little disorder as possible. As Bernard Crick points out, this is something that Aristotle was aware of when he said politics was the 'master science'.[2] It is an activity that calls for great skill, flair, experience and knowledge to be used in the service of resolving social conflicts that will destroy society if they are not resolved. This also includes, in the last resort, dealing with the allocation of scarce material resources. Markets cannot do this if people draw guns in them. A framework of law must be maintained if markets are to allocate freely. Thus political activity determines the continuation or discontinuation of all other activities and studies. That politics may be a necessary activity for a decent existence is something only anarchists will disagree with, though some forms of political activity may end in a very indecent existence.

If conflict is to be resolved rationally and peaceably on a regular basis, conditions must be devised allowing discussion and consultation with compromise, possibly, as the final end. Once such procedures are stabilised we have a set of institutions – a political system. (see Chapter 6) Structures of this kind can only exist within a framework of order. For them to exist for long, rules must be drawn up – at first they may be accepted customs but later they will be written and promulgated – and steps taken to see they are observed. Law can only be sustained where there is a framework of order. This explains why the term 'international society' (see Chapter 25) is only a hope and an aspiration: international law cannot be enforced because there are no effective forces of order.

To sum up: politics is a term with several usages. Fundamentally, however, political activity is concerned with conflictual activity and its resolution in the widest sense.

1.2   What is political science?

Political science is the study of politics in all its dimensions. At least four can be distinguished.

1.2.1   Political science as philosophy and theory

Early study of politics took place in small communities. The ancient Greeks who asked many of the important questions (and answered some of them well enough to satisfy many people today) lived in city states where rulers and decision-making were not remote. Their primary concern was with the nature of the good and just society and what the attitude of the citizen should be towards authority. The nature of our obligation to our rulers became an important theme in the early study of politics. Why do we obey the state? (see Chapter 3).

The easy answer to this question is that people obey out of habit. It does not occur to them to disobey. In modern times the question might be answered by anthropologists studying primitive societies, or by psychologists studying small groups of people and their response to leadership in laboratory situations. The ancient philosophers believed the answer lay in the nature of man. Aristotle perceived man as an animal of the *polis*: outside society people could not attain true happiness. The real nature of man could only be realised by associating with others. He assumed that the good life lay in the polity and that legally constituted government was the natural form, so that corruptions of good government were aberrations. Hence harmony was more natural than conflict. Neither Plato nor Aristotle seems to have conceived that disagreement could be irreconcilable. Christian philosophers believed that authority came from God and, therefore, should be obeyed. Later dynastic rulers transformed this into the claim that hereditary rulers were appointed by divine law and so disobeying them was unthinkable.

Once the acknowledgement of basic disagreement arose the question of political obligation either disappeared or became far more complicated. The Scientific Revolution, the Renaissance, the Reformation and finally the eighteenth-century Enlightenment removed many of the old certainties. Machiavelli (1469–1527), who had been imprisoned and tortured by rulers' commands, believed people were fickle and prone to evil. He was the holder of high office at the period of the expulsion, and then reinstatement, of the Medici in Florence. Instability, he held, could always be round the corner. When the safety of the country is ultimately in question, he wrote, there must be no question of justice or injustice, of mercy or cruelty, of praise or ignominy. It was not a matter of obligation, but of success or failure. Similarly Hobbes (1588–1679), writing in the period of the English Civil War and religious intolerance, perceived man's nature as fearful in consequence of the struggle for survival. People battled against one another to achieve their ends and in consequence life was 'nasty, brutish and short'. Hence a sovereign was needed to enforce law and order. We obey the sovereign because if people start disobeying everyone will be miserable in a state of mutual conflict. It is not a moral obligation, it is a necessity.

From the late seventeenth century onward the question of the relationship between the individual and the state generally shifted from the obligation to obey to the circumstances in which one could disobey. It was argued by John Locke (1632–1704) that rulers rule with the consent of their people with whom they have a contract. If the ruler breaches their individual rights the people have a right to replace him. This justification of the English Revolution of 1688, when Parliament replaced a hereditary monarch it disapproved of, became an inspiration for the American Revolutionaries. Thus the study of political thought turned to constitutional liberalism and the need to control powerful government. Montesquieu (1689–1755) believed that this could only be done by separating the powers of the judiciary, legislature and executive from each other. Rousseau (1712–1778), with his belief in equality and sovereignty belonging to the people, challenged all previous ideas about authority.

After the American and French Revolutions obedience was no longer either a habit or an accepted and expected pattern of behaviour. Conflict among the people, who were rarely even 90 per cent in favour of any proposal, had to be assumed. The arrival of the Common Man and the pluralistic society meant that philosophic thinking about politics could no longer be the simple matter of the relationship between the individual and the state.

This is only the briefest summary of that part of most political science syllabuses known as political philosophy or political theory. (In Chapters 2 and 3 more recent developments are discussed.) It is possible to make a distinction between these two rubrics. Political philosophy is more concerned with implicit assumptions and internal logic, while political theory tends to be more related to intellectual influences and to cultural and historical environments, but the terms are sometimes used interchangeably.

1.2.2   Political science as the study of conflict

At its core political science is concerned with the study of conflict. This can take place at several levels. Personal conflict, usually studied by psychologists, can be of service to political scientists. The study of aggressive instincts, for example, or the ability to compromise are obvious examples and these themes can also apply to group conflict.

Collective conflict is obviously the main field of investigation. It is of a different order from personal conflict because it involves all sorts of considerations about group coherence and group fragmentation. Political sociologists investigate for what reasons and to what extent people identify with others and to what degree they emphasise their distinction from those in other groups. When a group achieves a level of continuous existence, develops rules and decision-making procedures and systematically begins to recruit members, it is called an 'association'.

The part of the subject variously called political institutions or comparative institutions (see below) is involved with the study of conflict within the framework of a set of institutions. A political institution is a public body with formally designated structures and functions intended to regulate defined activities applying to the whole population. Governments, parliaments and the law courts are political institutions. Their interrelationships are defined in constitutions.

Collective conflict may take place at three levels – at that of local associations, at that of national associations and at that of nation-states. Often collective conflict takes the form of a clash between those associations and interests involved in the government and those outside it. In authoritarian regimes (see Chapter 4), however, where governments rule virtually unchallenged, conflict at the first two levels is submerged or likely to be repressed. Unless there is one-man rule, however, there will be conflict in private cabals. Such situations are not easy for the researcher to examine. Conversely, the study of politics in democracies, where conflict is permitted and even encouraged and where it often takes place publicly, is so much easier.

The study of conflict between local groups may be made at the community level. It may be about the building of a new bypass or the closing of a footpath. Increasingly nationwide groups associate themselves with such matters, but there may be other local issues, such as a dispute between travellers and local landowners, which proceed no further than local government. In the Western world physical conflict at this level is rare, but there are areas where internal disputes, especially ethnic rivalries, deteriorate into armed conflict.

A very large proportion of the literature of political science is concerned with conflict between nationally organised associations. There are two kinds of political association: pressure groups and political parties (see Chapter 10). Pressure groups do not want to participate in governing, although they do want to obtain access to the decision-making process and to influence its outcome. Unlike parties they usually have a specific political objective. Parties tend to be coalitions of interests with many objectives concerned to govern or share in the task of governing. Political scientists sometimes study one of these organisations separately as a political system in itself: usually within large pressure groups and parties there are factions in conflict. At other times relationships between different groups are examined.

It should be said that increasingly pressure groups operate on an international scale and lobby at international conferences – the so-called non-governmental groups (NGOs). This is particularly the case with women's and environmental groups. (see Chapter 5).

Collective group conflict of this kind would usually be included in the study of comparative institutions where the role of associations in relation to political institutions, especially legislatures and executives, is clearly a necessary component (see Chapters 6–10) Wider study of the social and cultural backgrounds of association memberships and leaderships is likely to be dealt with under the heading of political sociology.

1.2.3   Political science as international relations

Conflict between states is the core of international relations (see Chapter 21). This is sometimes taught in departments separate from political science. It can be argued that the subject matter is quite different because there is no such thing as international society (see Chapter 25) or world government. A world system does not exist: world society is an unregulated state of nature. On the other hand, as Michael Sheehan argues, some societal elements – international courts of law and world declarations of human rights – can be seen and are growing in importance.

1.2.4   Political science as the study of institutions

Political scientists are also involved with the resolution of conflict in policy-making and decision-making and the imposition of decisions once they are finalised. Here there is scope for numerous fields of study.

In most developed states a good deal of decision-making, certainly the most visible part, is standardised by procedural rules, institutional processes and constitutions. The study of political institutions is a major part of the discipline. Frequently the political institutions of one country are studied, but quite as often countries and their political institutions are compared under the heading of comparative institutions. The subject may require knowledge of constitutional law, historical background and social and cultural environment. It is the framework which shapes the political life of countries and within which decision-making takes place.

The imposition, or implementation, of decisions once they are made is another wide field of study. The modern state has a large apparatus of administrators concerned with applying the numerous laws which modern legislatures produce (see Chapter 4). This apparatus, or bureaucracy, needs coordination and supervision. As its officials are often appointed for life while the incumbency of democratic politicians is transitory, the bureaucracy may also wield some power. All these themes come under the heading of public administration (see Section Four) which was one of the early foundations on which university political science was built. It has always been concerned with management and in recent years management studies has partly developed from it. In addition, the study of policy-making has become important because of the increasing degree to which specialised administrators, or technocrats, have moved away from the role of the neutral administrator as a mere implementer of policy.

Political scientists are also concerned to study reasons for the maintenance and breakdown of political systems. Rebellions and revolutions are, after all, not uncommon and even apparently stable regimes have been known to collapse. The Russian Revolution in 1917 and the dramatic and sudden collapse of the Soviet Union in 1989–90 are both evidence of political forces erupting in authoritarian states. Even more alarming to liberals are instances of the collapse of democracy as in Germany in the late 1920s and early 1930s and, more recently, in Greece in 1967. Thus the conditions underlying stability are a natural subject of study. This leads to the investigation of social and other cleavages within states – their depth and intensity – and how to deal with them. Surprisingly, political scientists have not been active in studying political skills. The art of diplomacy in both domestic and international settings has been somewhat neglected. Only in the area of international relations has crisis management received any attention.

In recent years attention has turned to the environments which affect conflict and its resolution. Especially the economic and social environments of the political system have interested political scientists, leading them to study the areas where the polity overlaps with the economy and society. These two areas are known repectively as political economy and political sociology.

Political economy

This was a seventeenth-century term meaning the public management of the affairs of the state. The contemporary mercantilist doctrine implied that those with political power controlled the economy. There are several reasons why interest in relations between politics and the economy have revived in recent decades. The most obvious is the importance of the economy for democratic politicians. A perception of prosperity is a great help towards winning elections and the reverse is true: a feeling of depression is bad for incumbent governments at the polls. Consequently governments are bound to be tempted to manipulate the economy. Political scientists have identified a 'political business cycle' showing that boosts to the economy are often administered in the months before elections.

The influence, however, is not all one way. An unstable political system can ruin an economy. Visible examples from the developing world are not difficult to find. Political scientists who study development perceive political development as part of the process of modernisation. For the political system this implies the development of specialisation, structural differentiation, accommodation with pluralism and secularisation. It presumes the growth of a bureaucracy and, perhaps, democracy in the end.

There have also been attempts by political scientists to borrow economists' models. (Models are dealt with in Chapter 6). One well-known example is the analogy between oligopoly, a market with few sellers, and a state with only a few political parties. Another more fundamental one is the claim that the individual voter, faced with an array of policy options to choose from, is in an analogous situation with the sovereign consumer in the market.

Political sociology

The relationship between political science and sociology proceeded in rather the same fashion, from empiricism towards model-building. It was the study of electorates and their motives which led to the conceptualisation of political culture (culture is a term whose origins are in anthropology – see Chapter 6). This is the set of beliefs, attitudes and values which people hold towards their political system. Then the concept of socialisation, the process through which people are prepared to participate in social systems, was borrowed to construct the concept of political socialisation, the process by which people become aware of their political systems. Other political scientists studying public opinion became interested in propaganda and mass behaviour (on the margins of psychology, though political psychology, as yet, is an infant social science).

A further borrowing from sociology relates to social systems as integrating and stabilising agents, a notion first advanced by Talcott Parsons.[3] David Easton produced a more sophisticated model with input and output functions that owed much to computer systems (see Chapter 6).

1.3   Is political science a science?

Natural scientists sometimes complain about the description of the study of politics as a science. They argue that it cannot be a science because, unlike the natural sciences:

1. The variables in political science are not all subject to measurement. Its elements are not like matter whose weight, volume, temperature and so on can be quantified.
2. Unlike natural scientists, political scientists cannot set up experiments with what are apparently the same ingredients, in the same conditions and produce the same results. Environments cannot be controlled as in a laboratory. The ingredients change because they are human. For example, there can be contagion in that they can learn from each other. They also learn from their experiences and may behave quite differently from one situation to another that appears to be similar.
3. Therefore political scientists can never accurately predict. (Of course, this may also apply to some natural sciences such as meteorology, seismology, zoology.)

Most political scientists accept these objections. They believe the best reason for calling their subject political science is to distinguish it from politics. (Incidentally, no one seems to object to domestic science as a term to cover the culinary and home-building arts.) Science is merely a derivation of the Latin word for knowledge. The argument began with the political behaviouralists who saw numeracy as the key to science and believed quantification of data and analysis by statistical testing would allow them to test the validity of hypotheses. Unfortunately although hypotheses can be presented the results only have validity within a small space and a short time. Moreover, much political data cannot be quantified and the number of variables, anyway, is enormous. Political scientists may claim they are value-free – there *is* objectivity in their approach – but they cannot make authoritative statements of the same universal validity as natural scientists.

Notes

1. B. Barry, *Political Argument* (London: Routledge, 1965), pp. 89–90.
2. B. Crick, *In Defence of Politics* (Harmondsworth: Penguin, 1962), p. 164.
3. T. Parsons, *The Social System* (London: Routledge, 1951).

Questions

1. 'Man is a political animal.' Discuss.
2. 'If there were no disagreement there would be no politics.' Discuss.

2

Power, legitimacy and authority

2.1 Power

Power is the central concept in political science. Yet it cannot be measured: there is no unit of power. We speak of people having less power or more power or no power, but these are all assessments and they may be guesses. One has to assess power – and assess it well – in order to understand political situations. Politicians who make mistakes in estimating power are not likely to be successful. Political scientists could be judged on their ability to identify where power lies, how it is exerted and how it is divided. (It is rare for anyone to have total power.) One reason why power is elusive is that much exertion of power goes on behind the scenes. It is often in the interests of power-holders not to reveal how much power they possess. Perceptions may deceive. Some may appear to have power when they do not possess it. Paradoxically, the perception of holding power may in fact confer power.

2.1.1 Definitions of power

It is therefore difficult to define power. Three recent attempts illustrate the problem.

Weber

Probably the best known definition is that of Max Weber (1864–1920) who characterised power as the chance of a man or number of men to realise their own will in a communal action even against the resistance of others who are participating in the action.[1] Two comments that spring to mind about this definition are that it puts an emphasis on opportunity and will, and that it assumes that the exertion of power takes place within a formal context. Hence power is visible and can be located by empirical investigation and evaluated in terms of Lasswell's characterisation of politics, 'Who gets what, when, how?'[2] Robert Dahl (1915–), adopting the Weberian definition, investigated the decision-making process in New Haven, Connecticut and came to the conclusion that power-wielders' preferences were realised only partially in contested situations.[3] In the democratic context, structures of power were pluralistic (see Chapter 4) and a situation he called 'polyarchy' prevailed.

Others have defined power as the ability and capacity to achieve desired ends. Bertrand Russell said power was the production of intended effects.[4] Like Weber's definition, these neglect the need to want to exert power. Unless one has the will to use power all the resources and skills will be of little avail. It does not require much research to discover that most people do not appear to want power to any great degree.

Bachrach and Barantz

Hence later commentators were concerned as much with the powerless as the wielders of power in the formal decision-making process. Bachrach and Baratz pointed to the neglect of the study of non-decisions.[5] Was it not likely that the real wielders of power were those who prevented decisions being taken because they did not allow issues they considered embarrassing to appear on the 'political agenda'? This suggested power was much more complex than the simple pluralists had implied. Moreover, some issues were more important than others. Perhaps political scientists who studied visible decision-making and assessed the achievement of 'intended effects' were deceiving themselves. Much more powerful people were preventing the most important issues from being discussed and from entering the decision-making arena. Therefore people's preferences were being ignored for the benefit of the interests of a ruling group or class. What political scientists should be studying was the way political agendas were drawn up. As the implication was that many of these agendas were hidden, this task appeared far from easy.

Lukes

Lukes took the problem of power into a further dimension of complexity.[6] He argued that power was being exercised by hegemonies whose interest was to maintain the status quo by fashioning people's perceptions, beliefs and values so that their stated 'preferences' (Dahl's term) were contrary to their interests. Consequently, in order to understand a political situation one needed to know the strategies underlying the decision-making processes, including the agenda-setting procedures and the way in which the perceptions of the powerless are shaped. This three-dimensional insight into the complexities of power puts a premium on the study of deception and the manipulation of minds.

People's conceptions of their interests are not the real ones. They suffer from 'false consciousness'.

Various implications stem from Lukes's radical view of power. One is that the pluralistic democratic process as described by Dahl is a fraud. We have to accept either the classical elitist theories of inevitable oligarchic rule as portrayed by Mosca[7] and Pareto[8] (see Chapter 15), or some other hegemony which can be overthrown by the powerless seizing the levers of power by which their consciousness has been distorted, as in Marxist theory (see Chapter 13). Lukes moved the problem of power from an empirical to a theoretical and normative plane.

The implication for political scientists is that they should be concerned with the identification of the real consciousnesses of people and not with their false ones as indicated by their statements of their preferences and voting records. It is not clear how this can be done by empirical method. It assumes colossal presumption on someone's part – to be prepared to judge what people's actual interests are even when they say they are otherwise.

Alford and Friedland have conceived a typology of power at three levels.[9] The *situational* corresponds to Weber's notion of power being a situation of command and obedience; the *institutional* level of power refers to the features of institutional frameworks which bias decision-making in the interests of certain groups; and the *systemic* level concerns the characteristics of society which help certain people, classes or groups to realise their aspirations. This last level is what Lukes called the 'third face of power'.

2.1.2   Resources of power

While some of the resources of power are material and easily identified, others are more subtle.

Weaponry

Everyone knows Mao Tse-tung's (see Chapter 4) remark, 'Power grows out of the barrel of a gun.' The death threat is clearly a good way of making people do what they do not wish to do. All arms from knives to nuclear missiles deserve respect, especially from the unarmed. They are very important in the evaluation of power in relationships between states, but they can also be used by military dictatorships to cow populations. 'Why are they not in power everywhere,' Finer enquires; 'they have all the guns?'[10] It is a rhetorical question. Guns are not appropriate in some contexts. The President of the USA is a powerful international figure who is commander-in-chief of the US armed forces, yet he cannot use arms to make Congress pass his proposals. Nor do the big guns always win. The heavily armed USA could not, after many years' fighting, defeat the guerrilla armies of the Vietcong.

Wealth

Wealth is a power resource in most circumstances. In primitive societies it will not be wealth measured in money. Wealth will be most effective where law and order is enforced. Wealthy people hold power because they can use it to buy people and politicians in order to achieve their ends. In modern democratic politics money is particularly important in election campaigns when it is used for publicity purposes. Political parties and pressure groups may depend on wealthy donors for a good deal of their income. Industrialists and financiers are often perceived as manipulating markets and stock exchanges in order to obtain the sort of government they want. Left-wing governments tend to suspect them of this intention. Socialist parties saw the 1931 financial crisis as a 'bankers' ramp'.

Numbers

Other things being equal (which frequently they are not), it is better to be supported by more people than less. In democracies it is clear that more than 50 per cent support at elections usually confers power: at least the power to assume office. But one can overestimate the power of numerical majorities. Stein Rokkan, a Norwegian political scientist, said 'Votes count: resources decide',[11] meaning resources other than numbers of people. Organised numbers, whose support is unconditional, confer more power than disorganised supporters with ephemeral allegiance. In the field of international relations large armies confer power on states. Stalin, whose view of power was brutally cynical, summed it up when he enquired 'How many divisions has the Pope?'

Strategic location

Position may be a power resource in all senses of the word. A small country in a strategically important position may find its bargaining strength a help even in terms of international trade. People who hold strategic positions in organisations may acquire power. They may be in situations where they can control the flow of resources, including information and access to a power hierarchy. Such people are known as 'gatekeepers'.

Information

The amount of information (or 'intelligence' in diplomatic terms) one has about a situation is clearly a power factor. Rational decision-making depends on complete information, a rare position. Without knowing the 'background' of an issue or piece of policy-making one is at a disadvantage. One's opponents are likely to withhold as much information as possible. They may bluff and pretend they have information they do not possess: in fact, information about the amount of information opponents have will be an asset. Those in power, in particular, will have a tendency to keep information secret: hence campaigns for open government by opposition groups. It is not easy to make governments accountable if one does not know what they are doing or proposing to do.

Skills

The capacity to attain desired ends will also depend on the skills of those leading enterprises with policy goals. Various types of skills may be important. Personal attributes of democratic politicians tend to shade into political skills because they depend on public support: an attractive personality wins votes. An important political skill is the ability to persuade. This may involve not just oratory, a gift for stating an argument, but also an ability to explain and a willingness to listen. Less public political skills are those concerned with negotiation, mastering details and striking a compromise. Some of these skills are learnt; others are inherited.

Reputation

A reputation for good judgement and success in making decisions gives a political leader power. Sometimes reputations are unjustified. In some circumstances, especially where people are gullible or unused to assessing their political leaders, reputations may be artificially created by the image-makers. Sometimes the reputation of one's family will confer power – as with the Kennedys or Gandhis. Conversely a reputation for failure will deny one power.

Hence the resources of power are many and heterogeneous. Their scope and range vary greatly as do the contexts in which they are likely to be deployed. The ways in which power is deployed are also varied.

2.1.3   Styles of exercising power

The style varies between crude and brutal oppression and sophisticated persuasion. Very much depends on the regime (see Chapter 4). Absolutist rulers act in an arbitrary and suppressive manner: democratic leaders rely on the force of law.

Coercion

All states whether democratic or authoritarian in the last resort have to rely on coercion. This may not be physical compulsion. Power is exerted through sanctions of all kinds. Death is the most extreme sanction and quite popular as a way of silencing opponents in some regimes. Almost as effective is imprisonment. But in many political contexts the desired outcome of controlling people may result from threat of a fine, loss of promotion or even public ridicule.

Manipulation

This can include manipulation of the masses or of individuals and is a form of control without sanctions or the threat of sanctions. Clever politicians can outwit and use other politicians in negotiating processes – what one might call the committee level of politics. Manipulation of the masses can depend on the ability to control information and that involves controlling the media in order to influence people's beliefs and values. If one accepts Lukes's view of power, a belief in a process of this kind is inevitable.

Influence

This may be used to manipulate but it can never be associated with coercion. Influence is behind the scenes. Those holding formal power may seek the ideas and opinions of people held to be well-informed, wise and experienced. Such people are influential. Others may approach formal power-holders and convey the wishes, blandishments and threats of pressure groups and other interests. The extent to which influence is important will depend on a country's political culture and the values of its decision-makers. Thus the influence of intellectuals is held to be more important in France than Britain. (Like all statements about power this one is hard to verify.) Many of the factors affecting influence are the same as for power. Strategic location, reputation, skills and the possession of information are clearly important in this respect.

2.1.4 Summary

Power is the central concept in political science and yet it is the most difficult to grasp. It cannot be measured in units: there is no currency of power. Russell's desire for power to be like energy in physics was always unattainable.

Dahl's was the first attempt to systematise the assessment of power and he set out four ways of studying power distribution.

1. By observing those holding formal positions – chairpersons, secretaries, etc. – in official hierarchies. This neglects indirect behind-the-scenes power where it exists.
2. By using 'judges' – shrewd people in positions where they can observe the political scene and evaluate each actor's contribution. But who judges the judges?
3. By studying participation in decisions. Yet participation can hardly be equated with power-holding. Moreover, what about the non-decisions, perhaps the result of the real power-holders keeping issues off political agendas?
4. By attempting to overcome the problem of quantification by assigning scores or marks to the political actors and thus making a league table of power-holders – as carried out by Dahl in his New Haven study of power. Yet there are, as Dahl admits, arbitrary elements in this method. However, beyond that obvious objection is the one that none of the decisions studied were identical and therefore not even the probability tests of the statisticians could be applied.[12]

Mackenzie observes that power has and can be studied by two different methodologies. One is the situational. For example, we can look at the structure of power in a particular country or community. Here political scientists often are asking the question: 'Is power here oligarchic or (in Dahl's terms) polyarchic?' The second methodology is relational. Power is a form of interactivity between people. This leads Mackenzie into a consideration of forms of systems analysis.[13] Suppose, however, we ask a question about the relationship between democratic politicians and their electorate. Who holds more power and how do politicians get formal power positions? When the latter win elections can it be attributed to their control of material resources such as money and party organisation? Or to their personal magnetism? Or to their shrewd assessment of what the voters want? Do incumbent politicians stay in power by not doing what they perceive would be unpopular with the voters? This would be an invisible inter-action leading to non-decisions being taken! Is it the electorate that holds the power and hands it to the politicians to exert it?

As Allison argues the problem of evaluating power begins with the question of attributability. 'If a person has power, the consequences of that power must be attributable to that person who is responsible for those consequences.'[14] There is often great difficulty in assessing who is ultimately responsible for outcomes. Rumours about secret power-holders are rife, giving rise to stories about conspiracies.

Power is a nebulous concept and attempts to define and measure it have not been very successful.

2.2 Legitimacy

A political regime is legitimate when it is accepted as right and proper by most of its members. It is bound to be a relative concept: no regime will be accepted as right and proper by all its members and it is likely that some aspects of a regime will have more legitimacy than others. The concept raises questions about any type of political system.

2.2.1 How do we know whether a regime is legitimate or not?

It is not enough to cite compliance with a regime's rules and its intermediaries as evidence for legitimacy. Empirically we learn from both distant and recent history that people for the most part comply with the orders of an occupying army, but they hate it. They think its rule wrong and improper. Hence the successful exercise of power does not make it legitimate. Research that set out to discover whether a regime was legitimate or not would proceed through observation and interrogation. A regime that had persisted for a long period would suggest an assumption of legitimacy, but it could not be taken for granted. In 1987 the Soviet Union might have seemed a legitimate regime. Yet by 1990 it had disintegrated, largely from internal pressures. This leads to a second question for political scientists.

2.2.2 How do regimes lose their legitimacy?

We have numerous examples from history of regimes collapsing. Empires are especially prone to collapse. The Roman, Spanish, Austro-Hungarian, Turkish, British, French, Dutch, Portuguese and Soviet empires all disintegrated. Both outside and inside pressures seem to have contributed to their downfalls. It is doubtful whether empires are ever accepted as legitimate by their subject peoples. Sooner or later they cease to respect the rules and orders of their rulers who find policing them increasingly exhausting, both physically and financially.

Frequently political regimes begin to lose legitimacy when their rulers start to doubt the beliefs and values justifying their rule. New generations of power-holders begin to lose faith in what has been called the 'legitimating myth' – perhaps, in the case of empires, the conviction that they are bringing peace, progress, enlightenment and civilisation. The loss of confidence leads to instability. Legitimacy is then threatened. Where the imperial masters have liberal values they will find it difficult, in the end impossible, to deny the same democratic rights and procedures to their subject peoples that they accord to their own people.

Dahl explains legitimacy with the metaphor of a reservoir. As long as it stays at a certain level stability is maintained, but if it falls below that level it is endangered.[15] In the 1970s some political scientists began to question the sustainability of 'Western democracy'. Dunleavy and O'Leary have summarised the main arguments.[16] One was that the success of capitalism had created a consumer society in which affluence had produced values contrary to the Protestant work ethic which had been fundamental to capitalism. Another was that democratic governments had become too ambitious in their policies and had 'overloaded' themselves with too many functions. They should divest themselves of many of them. A third was that democracy had never been properly extended to people. Both decentralisation and greater political participation were needed.

2.2.3   Can a regime bolster up, or even increase, its legitimacy?

Although the legitimacy of regimes is ultimately determined by the attitudes of its citizens, subjects or non-elite (to use various terms to describe them), the rulers, governments or elites are likely to ensure that their legitimacy is not declining. They will try to secure compliance by introducing policies that increase rewards and decrease penalties. Democracies with procedures and institutions, such as elections and a free press, enabling them to monitor the reactions of their citizens will be in a much better position to do this than authoritarian regimes (see Chapter 4).

Whether a regime is legitimate or not is a matter for investigation. Researchers need to discover whether its members believe compliance with its rules right and proper. Basically it is not a moral question: some quite brutal and corrupt regimes, like Tsarist Russia, appear to have been legitimate.

2.3 Authority

It is usual to say authority confers legitimacy on power. It may not be correct to say, however, that 'authority is legitimised power' because there are some forms of authority which are not concerned with the exercise of power: for example, the authority of the priest over his flock, or the authority of parents over children. Others would argue that these two instances are illustrations of the exercise of power. If this is the case it may be necessary in political science discourse to separate the concept of power into political power and non-political power.

Here we are concerned with political power, as was the German social and political theorist, Max Weber, when he concluded that legitimacy was conferred upon power-holders in three different ways. These types of authority were distinguished by different characteristics. Each is an 'identikit' – what he called an 'ideal-type' – a set of features helping in identification. In reality every form of government is a mixture of these ideal-types. Thus an ideal-type is a characterisation of features which helps expounding, explaining, investigating and learning.

2.3.1 Traditional authority

This is based upon a belief in the sanctity of age-old rules and practice of power. Weber divided it into three sub-types:

1. A belief that the oldest in the community should exercise authority. One might call this gerontocracy.
2. Patriarchalism, which is a form of simple dynastic rule, under which authority is passed down in succeeding generations to the male head of one particular family.
3. Patrimonialism, which occurs where patriarchal rule begins to develop an administrative apparatus as was typical of medieval Europe emerging from feudalism, and of Oriental despotisms.

In all forms of traditional authority government is exercised personally and often arbitrarily. There is no clear definition of the rules. Values underlying judgements by the rulers possess, or are given, the quality of 'revealed truth'.

2.3.2 Legal/rational authority

In contrast with traditional authority this refers to a situation where power is held to be legitimate because authority is conferred by rules which have been drawn up in a rational framework. Thus a society in which legal/rational authority prevails is one in which laws are obeyed. This applies to the rulers and their apparatus for ruling. They are also subject to the laws. Hence the society is characterised by norms of impersonality and lack of arbitrariness. The exercise of power is clearly defined and loyalty is accorded by subordinates because they perceive it to be based on rationality.

Weber implies, though he does not assert, that legal/rational authority is the best. It was the most rational and it is a feature of the way the world was developing. More and more the world was becoming subject to organisational forms and the salient feature of this organisation was bureaucracy, the administrative apparatus by which the laws are implemented (See Chapter 17 for an examination of this concept).

2.3.3   Charismatic authority

This is quite different from the other two types. Weber defines charisma as 'a certain quality of an individual personality by virtue of which he is . . . treated as endowed with supernatural, superhuman, or at least exceptional powers or qualities'. Legitimacy is thus based upon the claim of such a leader to have the qualities essential for leadership, and the acceptance of this claim by his followers. The ruler reinforces his authority by the performance of actions, seen to be heroic and, perhaps, near-miraculous.

The emergence of charismatic authority is associated with the breakdown of an established order and a change in systems of values. It may destroy the customs of traditional authority and the laws of legal/rational authority. Essentially it is a revolutionary force and is bound to be temporary and transitional. Charismatic rule will either revert to traditional rule through a charismatic ruler establishing a dynasty, or it will be 'routinised' and regularised and become legal/rational authority.

The nebulous nature of the notions of power and legitimacy, their resistance to empirical investigation and yet their obvious importance is, as noted above, fertile soil for the growth of conspiracy theories about the location and thrust of political power-wielders in society. Elitists see power as impossible to wrest from consolidated oligarchies. Marxists see power as almost invisibly exerted by the capitalist class. They prevent the working class from realising its true revolutionary role and knowing its own interests by bribing them with consumer goods and/or manipulating their minds with propaganda. Thus the capitalists hold on to power.

Notes

1. H. H. Gerth and C. W. Mills, *From Max Weber* (London: Routledge, 1948), p. 180.
2. H. D. Lasswell, *Politics: Who Gets What, When, How* (New York: Meridian Books, 1958).
3. R. A. Dahl, *Who Governs?* (New Haven, Conn.: Yale University Press, 1961).
4. B. Russell, *Power: a New Social Analysis*, 2nd edn (London: Allen & Unwin, 1969; first edn, 1938).

5. P. Bachrach and M. S. Baratz, 'Two Faces of Power', *American Political Science Review*, vol. 56, 1962, pp. 947–52.
6. S. Lukes, *Power: a Radical View* (London: Macmillan, 1974).
7. G. Mosca, *The Ruling Class*. (Westport, Conn.: Greenwood Press, 1980.
8. S. E. Finer, (ed.), *Vilfredo Pareto: Sociological Writings* (London: Pall Mall, 1966).
9. R. Alford and R. Friedland, *The Powers of Theory* (Cambridge: Cambridge University Press, 1985).
10. S. E. Finer, *Man on Horseback*, 2nd. edn (Harmondsworth: Penguin, 1976).
11. S. Rokkan, 'Numerical Democracy and Corporate Pluralism' in R. A. Dahl, (ed.), *Political Oppositions in Western Democracies* (New Haven, Conn.: Yale University Press, 1966), p. 106.
12. R. A. Dahl, *Modern Political Analysis* (Englewood Cliffs, NJ: Prentice Hall, 1963), p. 52f.
13. W. J. M. Mackenzie, *Power, Violence, Decision* (Harmondsworth: Penguin, 1975), p. 56.
14. L. Allison, 'Power', in I. McLean (ed.), *Oxford Concise Dictionary of Politics* (Oxford: Oxford University Press, 1996), p. 397.
15. R. A. Dahl, *Polyarchy* (New Haven, Conn.: Yale University Press, 1971), p. 279.
16. P. Dunleavy and B. O'Leary, *Theories of the State* (London: Macmillan, 1987), pp. 65–70.

Questions

1. 'Authority is legitimised power.' Discuss.
2. How would you assess the relative effectiveness of the different forms of state sanctions?

3

The state

The concept of the state is one of great complexity. The term state is used in at least three different contexts – philosophical, legal and political – and each of these three streams of thought provides us with a history of the development of the concept which has also been a response to the social and political environment.

There are three common perceptions of what is meant by the term 'the state'.

3.1   The state as an apparatus of control

This is the image of the state with which most people are familiar. It is concerned with policy-making and policy-implementation. It means much more, therefore, than the government or any other group of politicians who may control the administrative apparatus at the centre. It consists also of all other public servants including the armed forces, the police and administrators in local government.

It may help in envisaging the scope of the modern state to examine the broad functions of the contemporary British state, though the catalogue which follows would apply to nearly all modern industrialised states. The functions can be grouped under five headings.

3.1.1   Guardian of law, order and property

This is the oldest function of the state. It includes:

1.   policing – backed up if necessary by the armed forces;
2.   punishing and imprisoning;
3.   interpreting the laws – the function of the judiciary.

3.1.2 Treasurer

This takes two forms.

1. *Tax gatherer.* This is another ancient function. Today more than two-thirds of annual British revenue is collected by the Board of Inland Revenue and Customs and Excise. Schumpeter called the modern state the 'tax state' because of its scope and range.[1] Taxes make a great impact on the public as they emphasise the punitive role of the state.
2. *Accountant.* This is a more recent function in a professional sense. The Comptroller and Auditor General and his department examine the details of the national accounts. He is independent of the executive and responsible to Parliament.

3.1.3 Inspector

This is a more recent function, dating from the nineteenth century. Factory inspection began in 1833 and sanitary inspection in 1866. Vehicle licensing and safety checks are twentieth-century functions and food inspection is even more recent. The state with its inspectors is enforcing standards in numerous fields.

3.1.4 Allocator of values

Because of its activities in rewarding some sections of society and penalising others the modern state is very much involved in making value-judgements. This is especially so with the redistribution of income, collected through the state's function as tax gatherer, taking place under the umbrella of what is called the 'Welfare State'. Some of these functions go back to the late nineteenth century.

1. *Provider for the poor.* This is the oldest social function, beginning with the Elizabethan Poor Law. Money is paid, though often with increasing reluctance, to people not able to provide for themselves.
2. *Educator.* Education is compulsory between the ages of 5 and 16 and is largely administered by local governments though, increasingly, central government has intervened as inspector and regulator.
3. *Insurance agent.* The state makes provision for people in work against sickness and unemployment. Contributions by citizens to these schemes helps to provide benefit after retirement in the form of old age pensions.

4. House builder and landlord. In Britain this function dates from the 1920s when 'homes fit for heroes to live in' were provided for ex-servicemen of the First World War. Provision was delegated to local governments who rented them out and so became landlords.
5. *Doctor and nurse.* Since 1947 British governments have administered a National Health Service, providing free medical care to the population.

3.1.5 Coordinator

The modern state is a coordinator in three ways: it coordinates functions, resources and policies.

1. To coordinate functions governments have increasingly structured themselves on hierarchical lines. In parliamentary government there is a tendency to ranking among ministers with not all departmental ministers being in the cabinet. There is what S.E. Finer called the 'cone of command' with the prime minister at the top.[2] The increase in the functions of the state which has gradually taken place has led to more layering of power, and this is bound to lead to more coordination.
2. The coordination of resources takes place in national treasuries which vet the annual estimates of expenditure of all government departments. A process of evaluation and prioritisation takes place with treasuries arbitrating between different claims. Demands from sections of the electorate and pressure groups are great, and these tend to be passed on to appropriate government departments.
3. The coordination of policies is necessary because of the proliferation of policy-making. In Britain the trend is for more of it to proceed in committees and sub-committees of the Cabinet and especially in inter-departmental committees of civil servants. Ultimate synchronisation, at one time achieved through the Cabinet Office, has in recent years passed increasingly to the Prime Minister's Office. As economic policy and the management of it has become more and more important, the necessity for a position giving national direction and supervising the steering has correspondingly increased.

To sum up: the state as an apparatus of control has passed through several stages in the last three centuries, usefully summarised under four headings. The early or 'primitive state' was characterised by rudimentary law and order, some legal recognition of claims to property, and a currency and a taxation system that required the beginnings of bureaucracy. Industrialisation and the advent of democracy made this type of state obsolete. It was succeeded by the 'collectivist state' with many more functions, a much larger bureaucracy and a much greater impact on its people, largely in response to their pressures. In the twentieth century the 'interventionist state' emerged as a result of experiences of wartime control of economies, intellectual teachings of economists like Keynes and the growing strength of left-wing ideas and political parties. Over the last twenty years a fourth type, the 'managerial state', has arisen. It is dedicated to efficient management, decentralisation of decision-making within a framework of centrally devised guidelines, and a brisk assertion of centralised power without too much attention to the niceties of constitutional conventions and civilised behaviour.

3.2 The state as an international actor

This follows from the assertion of state sovereignty (see Chapter 25). In its relations with the outside world – with other states – sovereignty means the capacity of a state to maintain its integrity by ensuring that its frontiers and its nationals are respected by other states. Indeed, a state only becomes one when it is recognised as such by other states and, today, by the United Nations Organisation. The sovereignty of a state may be impaired when another state has military installations on its territory, or by another state dominating economic investment within its borders. Very small states can scarcely feel they possess sovereignty when, like Honduras or Liberia, they have a large multinational corporation within their borders employing a large part of the national labour force.

States are quick to protest when their sovereignty is under threat. They like to preserve the myth that being a state implies 100 per cent sovereignty, and this may be important in international law. But in practice the world today is so interdependent that no state has 100 per cent sovereignty. A complete absence of relationships with other states would be disastrous.

3.3 The state as an abstract concept

3.3.1 Classical perceptions of the state

This was the province of legal theorists and philosophers before political science existed as a discipline. Their central concern was with the relationship between human beings and political authority (see Chapter 1). Early precursors of the term state came from Aristotle (384–322 BC) who used the term *polis* meaning both a city and a form of society and Cicero (106–43 BC) who spoke of *res publica* (public affairs) in which he believed there was a mixture of *populo* (the people), the source of power, and *auctoritas* (authority) which stemmed from the Senate, the ruling body of the Roman republic. Usually, however, it is Machiavelli (1469–1527)who is credited with the first use of the term 'state' in his work, *The Prince*. Although he is only writing about the small Italian states, he uses the term in its recognised modern sense to describe a political authority with the monopoly of ultimate coercion within a territory with defined borders. Clever diplomacy and statecraft were necessary to sustain a state and morality was not a consideration. He first used the phrase 'reason of state'.[3]

The idea of independent, autonomous territories with governments with supreme power over their peoples and single sources of law was widely recognised towards the end of the Middle Ages. Bodin (1529–96) called this characteristic 'sovereignty'. Without sovereignty there is no power and without power there can be no state. Laws are the emanation of the sovereign state and to maintain the laws sanctions are needed – penalties for those breaking laws. Sovereignty also means complete independence in the international context. Hence with Machiavelli and Bodin there develops the concept of the state as a political association different in its nature from other forms of organisation in society.

By the seventeenth century political philosophers for the first time were beginning to consider the impact of the individual upon the state. Hobbes conceived the state as made by men through fear of themselves. Because all men sought to gratify their desires they were aggressive and destructive, yet for that reason fearful. Recognising their nature they made a compact and set up Leviathan, a ruler to ensure compliance. John Locke (1632–1704) asserted that individuals had basic rights which could be enshrined in a contract with the state. These rights were broadly expressed in the American Declaration of Independence of 1776 as 'Life, Liberty and the pursuit of Happiness'. It went on to proclaim 'That to secure these rights, Governments are instituted among Men, deriving their just powers from the consent of the governed.' The French Declaration of the Rights of Man and of Citizens 1789, promulgated by the new National Assembly, similarly declared 'Men are born and always continue free and equal in respect of their rights', and 'The end of all political associations is the preservation of the natural and imprescriptible rights of man.'

The American and French Revolutions cast the problem of the state in new terms. The effect of popular emancipation was to bring the people into the ambit of political theory for the first time. The relationships between the state and the people, and the state and groups of people, especially concerned Jean Jacques Rousseau (1712–78) whom many consider to be the main intellectual force contributing to revolutionary sentiment in nineteenth-century Europe. For him the major problem was how to obtain a kind of association, allowing everyone to be as free as in a state of nature and at the same time protecting the property and person of each individual member. How could collectivity be reconciled with individuality? Could one devise an association in which each, while uniting himself with all, may still obey himself alone and remain as free as before? Rousseau answered the question with the Social Contract by which men entered into a civil association and gave up their individual rights in order to find true freedom in obedience to the rule of law. Liberty was freedom to obey laws prescribed by ourselves. For Rousseau the sovereignty of the people meant the sovereignty of the General Will. We realise our individual rights by obeying the General Will.

The General Will, however, was not the Will of all which could change from time to time as it expressed different interests. Cleavages in society (see Chapter 10) were harmful. Legislative institutions were unable to express will: this could only be done by referendums. Nor would debates and discussions help to identify the General Will whose true expression lay in unanimity. Consequently parties and sects, the manifestations of particular wills, should not be allowed. They were in error and it was necessary to restrain them and to guide their followers, the 'blind multitude' as Rousseau puts it, towards the perception of what was willed by the General Will. People had to be 'forced to be free'. Thus Rousseau, who some still see as the harbinger of democracy, rejected pluralism and representative democracy. He has been described paradoxically as the prophet of 'totalitarian democracy'.[4]

From the beginning of the nineteenth century onwards the relationships between collective forces and the state becomes far more complicated. Industrialisation and urbanisation produced new social groups with compelling demands upon political authority. To the freedoms promised by the French and American Revolutions were added the individualistic ideas of the liberal economists and nationalistic demands of ethnic groups for statehood. The former theme, as far as state theory is concerned, was classically expressed by Herbert Spencer (1820–1903) who argued that the state had no right to interfere in the economy. The state should be a 'night watchman' concerned only to safeguard property and the sanctity of business contracts. From the latter trend arose, especially among the new nations, a reaction against the fragmented pluralism already visible in the fledgling democracies. The outstanding interpreter of this theme was G. W. F. Hegel (1770–1831) who pointed out that the modern state was distinctive in that it possessed a large sector given over to the activities of independent individuals. He called this *die bürgerliche Gesellschaft*, usually translated as 'civil society'. Hegel saw the state as encompassing civil society as well as cultural, legal and ethical spheres. Consequently the state should further the quest for perfection in rational and moral values, uphold solidarity and correct the phases of instability to which civil society was prone.

Kenneth Dyson sums up the theory of the state until recent times in two ways.[5] First, he makes a historical analysis, perceiving the state at three different periods of social and economic development.

1. *The state as a reflection of a hierarchic social order.* It would be incorrect to speak of a 'feudal state', but where feudal relics linger and there is a society with fairly well-defined status differences this type can be identified. Nineteenth-century European states were of this nature and the collaborationist Vichy regime in France (1940–44) was an attempt at its restoration.

2. *The state as a reflection of an individualistic social order.* This is a reaction against 1. above. It is consequent upon the emergence of a market economy and entrepreneurial capitalism and assumes a non-interventionist state with people being allowed greater freedom to pursue their own course of action. No state has ever approached an absolute position on this. It remains an ideal.

3. *The state as an embodiment of the community.* This is a reaction against the individualistic state and its alleged lack of coherence. The state is needed to assert 'public good' against individual pressures and to lay down the proper moral values. This could be the position of most democratic political parties except those holding the views of classical liberalism.

Dyson also suggested three non-historical conceptions of the state.

1. *The state as legitimacy.* This incorporated 'the state as law' as long as the laws were accepted by the people as right and proper. It rejected the 'state as might' assuming that nothing based on sheer force could be legitimate.

2. *The state as law.* This conception was implied by Weber, but was best stated in the exegesis of Hans Kelsen (1883–1973) whose theory was that legal systems were based on ordered norms. Among positive norms the most general is the constitution, the

Grundnorm which, in political terms, is the framework for other norms. This constituted the formal theory of the *Rechtsstaat*.

3. *The state as might* (Macht). This goes back to Machiavelli and Hobbes, but finds its best expression in the political philosophers of two countries which had achieved late nationhood through armed struggle. In Italy the elitists, Mosca and Pareto (see Chapter 15) perceived the state as an instrument of force manipulated by elites. A united Germany, Bismarck said, would be achieved by 'blood and iron'. This sentiment was reflected in the writings of the historian Heinrich von Treitschke (1834–96) who said war was an element that unites nations,[6] and more recently of Carl Schmitt (1888–1985), who described politics as concerned with the friend-enemy relationship. He began as a protagonist of the state-as-law school, but joined the Nazis in 1933.

   Yet the 'state as might' has not been monopolised by nationalists. In his account of phases of history Karl Marx argued that the state had always been used as an instrument of repression by the class that at that time owned the means of production (see Chapter 13) Under capitalism the state was controlled by the capitalist class who oppressed the industrial workers. When they revolted and overthrew capitalism the means of production would belong to everyone. There could be no class domination and the state would 'wither away'.

3.3.2   Modern perceptions of the state

Since the late nineteenth century perceptions of the state have changed. Marx perceived the state as a mere instrument. Thus it was not a power in itself but a tool to be used by those who controlled it. Although ostensibly under the rubric of state theory, much of modern discussion is about where state power is located and how it is exercised. Three forces have been at work. First, neo-Marxists, aware that Marx's prophecy about the state withering away was not being fulfilled, have devised all sorts of explanations for its resilience and proliferation. Second, the complexities of modern democratic industrialised society, its pluralistic nature, have led to state theories compatible with this situation. The pluralists have argued about the relationship between the state and civil society. Third, the expansion of political science has greatly increased the number of people keen to make a reputation by advancing their own theories.

Neo-Marxist perceptions

Neo-Marxists have been concerned with an advanced capitalism that Marx never knew. They have to explain why the workers' revolution has not happened, why capitalism and 'bourgeois democracy' are still flourishing and why the state has not withered away. Several explanations are advanced, some of them combining the following factors:

1. Marx was wrong in ascribing the role of revolutionary agent to the working class. Marcuse (1898–1979) argued that the impetus for revolution had to be found elsewhere, among students, dropouts and the underclass.

2. The state has developed resources of coordination that Marx had not foreseen. Poulantzas (1936–79) argued that the state maintained the cohesion of democratic regimes by managing to retain the balance of various factions in which monopoly capitalists dominated, at the same time keeping the appearance of state autonomy. This had led to the decline of democratic institutions such as legislatures and the rise of a type of regime he called 'authoritarian statism'.

3. The state exerted moral leadership in civil society through its control of the education system, culture and value-forming organisations like the churches. Hence it manufactured a dominant ideology which shaped people's perceptions so that they thought the status quo was the natural order. Gramsci (1891–1937), who first presented this thesis, argued that, therefore, in democracies the hegemony of the capitalist state was founded on consent rather than force.

4. Habermas (1929–) argues that the modern capitalist state faces a crisis of legitimation in which it is led into many contradictions. Science and technology are no longer liberating and enlightening, but serve as a legitimating ideology. Likewise the affluence of modern society and the welfare state produce values of hedonism and a lack of initiative which are detrimental to capitalism. Not knowing how to deal with these contradictions, the state is consequently faced also with a motivation crisis. For Habermas the capitalist system is in decline, though he does not speculate about how it will end or who will end it.

5. Offe (1940–) and other neo-Marxists depict the state as excluded from capitalist decision-making, especially the most important decision, that of investment. The policies of the democratic state are constrained because of the need for capitalist accumulation. Welfare benefits are largely paid out of taxation revenue and are thus financed by the community: this is a way of socialising employers' labour costs. Thus the major function of the state is that of a legitimating framework for the established system. It has many functions, but relatively little power. The working-class

capacity to mobilise is easily surpassed by that of the capitalist class.

6. Some neo-Marxists, especially those from the developing world, argue that the class division is between the people of the underprivileged countries and the opulent advanced in-dustrialised states. The cleavage is between 'North and South'. This application of the writings of Hobson, Hilferding and Lenin[7] has been much extended by the threat of crises in globalised capitalism in which the developing countries will suffer most.

7. The dual state thesis perceived the main opportunities for work-ing-class assertion and eventual power lying in local govern-ment. This was derived especially from the success of left-wing parties in retaining control for long periods in large cities such as Bologna. Local government was a key part of the capitalist state because it provided the services which helped to reproduce the labour force. Thus the duality consisted of local government being concerned with consumption and central government with production.

Pluralist perceptions

A pluralist society is usually regarded as a natural consequence of democracy (see Chapter 4). Freedom of association is one of its neces-sary conditions. The right of collective organisation allows voluntary associations to form. These can be seen as counterbalancing state power, or balancing one another and so preserving a social equilibrium. In the nineteenth century it was de Tocqueville who extolled the virtues of a system of diverse local pluralism such as he found in the USA. He saw it as an important check on centralised power supported by democratic majorities, the consequence of revolution in his native France. At the beginning of the twentieth century Bentley argued that the study of groups should be the basis of a scientific study of politics.[8] Empirical investigation, for example Dahl's analysis of power in New Haven, confirmed that oligarchy was not present. In democracies power might not be divided equally, but it was not concentrated. Dahl called this system polyarchy.[9] It left open the position of the central power apparatus, but it did appear that the state was merely a player in the game, though perhaps sometimes a 'dirty player'.

Dunleavy and O'Leary in their comprehensive survey depict three models of the democratic state.[10]

1. The 'weathervane' model perceives the state as responding to the direction of the political wind, that is to the balance of pressures

in society. In this model the state has no 'autonomy' because it can be captured by a powerful group. Presumably this may vary with time and place. For example, on agricultural policy the producers, the farmers, win much more often than the agricultural consumers, a very much larger number of people. Executive departments and legislative committees concerned with agricultural policy become 'colonised' by those persuaded by farmers' pressure groups. The same situation will apply in numerous other policy fields. The state is constantly swinging in the wind. Highly responsive, a state of this kind is open to pressures from citizens for programmes of increased public expenditure.

2.   The 'mediator and harmoniser' model envisages the state as neutral between different groups. But neutrality, as Dunleavy and O'Leary point out, can cover three stances – that of the detached bystander, that of the concerned referee and that of promoter of values of 'fairness'. In this third stance the state is not in the business of conciliating powerful interests. In this version, the ideal of liberal pluralists, unorganised interests like consumers and children will have their needs attended to. Unfortunately democracy is not much concerned with objective fairness. Majorities may be very 'unfair' or, to look at it another way, they will have their own ideas about what is fair.

3.   The 'broker' model perceives the state as a middleman with interests of his own. In this model the state has some autonomy. Public servants involved in the processes of bargaining between different pressures may secure the outcome they would prefer. On the other hand, there may be another group of public servants who would prefer another outcome. With the broker model, conflict takes place as much, or more, within the state apparatus as outside it.

The broker model may approximate in certain circumstances to 'liberal corporatism', a term initiated by Schmitter. Under liberal corporatist systems the bargaining groups were 'recognised or licensed . . . by the state'.[11] (This contrasts with 'liberal pluralism' where groups unrecognised by the state compete freely.) But the examples usually quoted by liberal corporatists – Sweden, Norway, Denmark, Finland and Austria – where strategic elites such as business, labour and agriculture are accorded regular and institutionalised bargaining over economic policy with the state, do not diverge greatly from the broker model. Rokkan called this system, mainly operating in Scandinavia, 'corporate pluralism' and contrasted it with 'numerical democracy', the conventional decision-making system, asserting tersely 'votes count: resources decide'[12] (see Chapter 4) The fact is that all the liberal corporatist arrangements suffered great shocks in the 1980s including, most dramatically, the Swedish national lock-out in 1980.[13]

To sum up: the relationships between the democratic state and interest groups are likely to be intermittent and temporary, however permanent they may appear to be in certain periods. Incumbent governments will think more about numerical democracy when elections approach and subsequent events may result in movement between all these models. The assumption that all groups have equal power – never really credible – gave way among later pluralists (neo-pluralists), to the view that corporate capital was the most powerful group. In consequence they formed links with the neo-Marxists. Hence we may conclude that the models are aids to understanding different patterns of modern pluralist society–state relationships, not definitive systems of rule.

The idea at the crux of pluralism was that there are many power centres beyond that of the state, especially in democracies. Yet this is no indication that governments will deal with them. The realisation gradually sank in that constraints on governments are great and are imposed not only by electorates, but also by the economy and, increasingly, by the world economy.

Bringing the state back in

There was also questioning among social scientists about the concentration of group power. The historian Otto Hintze argued that the nature of any state's power was dependent on its history of internal class conflicts and its strategic scope and positioning in the world. To understand how a state developed one has to know its social and military history.[14]

Foremost among such commentators was Theda Skocpol who asserted that states were unique structures with their own histories.[15] The pluralists were in error in thinking of the state as a black box into which inputs went and out of which outputs came, or as an arena in which contests between social and political groups were staged. Each state was an administrative and coercive apparatus extracting resources from society and deploying them as it thought fit. In her analysis of revolutionary changes to states she begins with the Chinese Empire, before 1911 ruled by about 40,000 officials whose overriding attachment was to maintain the irrigation system, and continues with the imperial bureaucracies of France and Russia.

Wallerstein's contribution to state theory was to emphasise how state sovereignty had been compromised by links with other states in the world economy.[16] The globalisation of world markets by the GATT agreements makes this point especially apposite. It is argued that the nation-state is being hollowed out by the growing strength of international organisations and the increasing regulatory power of confederations like the European Union. Is the decline of the nation-state unstoppable?

Notes

1. Quoted in M. G. Schmidt, 'The growth of the tax state' in C. L. Taylor (ed.), *Why Governments Grow* (London: Sage, 1983), p. 262f.
2. S. E. Finer, *A Primer of Public Administration* (London: F. Muller, 1950), p. 35.
3. A. P. D'Entrèves, *The Notion of the State* (Oxford: Oxford University Press, 1967).
4. For example, see J. L. Talmon, *The Origins of Totalitarian Democracy* (London: Secker & Warburg, 1952).
5. K. Dyson, *The State Tradition in Western Europe* (Oxford: Martin Robertson, 1980).
6. H. von Treitschke, *Selections from his Lectures on Politics* trans. A. L. Gowans (London: Gordons & Gray, 1914), p. 23.
7. J. A. Hobson, *Imperialism* (London: Allen & Unwin, 1902); R. Hilferding, *Finance Capital: a Study in the Latest Phase of Capitalist Development* (London: Routledge, 1910); V. I. Lenin, *Imperialism: the Highest Stage of Capitalism* (London: Lawrence & Wishart, 1916).
8. A. F. Bentley, *The Group Theory of Politics* (Cambridge, Mass: Belknap Press of Harvard University Press, 1908).
9. R. A. Dahl, *Polyarchy* (New Haven, Conn.: Yale University Press, 1971).
10. P. Dunleavy and B. O'Leary, *Theories of the State* (London: Macmillan, 1987), p. 43f.
11. P. Schmitter, 'Still the century of corporatism', *Review of Politics*, vol. 36, 1974, p. 93f.
12. S. Rokkan, 'Numberical democracy and corporate pluralism', in R. A. Dahl (ed.), *Political Oppositions in Western Democracies* (New Haven, Conn.: Yale University Press, 1966).
13. W. Korpi, *The Democratic Class Struggle* (London: Routledge, 1983), p. 159. See also F. W. Bealey, *Democracy in the Contemporary State* (Oxford: Oxford University Press, 1988), p. 180f.
14. See F. Gilbert (ed.), *The Historical Essays of Otto Hintze* (New York: Oxford University Press, 1975).
15. T. Skocpol, *States and Social Revolutions* (Cambridge: Cambridge University Press, 1979).
16. I. Wallerstein, *The Modern World System* (New York: Academic Press, 1974).

Questions

1. To what degree is it realistic to study the relationship between the individual and the state?
2. What are the problems of the democratic state in dealing with interest groups?

4

Political regimes

A political regime has a conceptual breadth and complexity beyond that of a political system. Until recent decades (for the more recent and wider conception of 'political system' see Chapter 6) a political system referred to the interaction and relationships of the political institutions of a country. It could be categorised in the manner constitutions are categorised (see Chapter 7). Essentially the criteria for categorisation were legal/constitutional. Thus the Soviet Union could be perceived from inspection of its 1936 constitution as possessing both parliamentary government and a federal structure. This told us little about political arrangements in the Soviet Union.

Political regimes are distinguished by the terms under which individual and collective activity affects, perhaps even determines, authoritative collective decisions. This tends to be something more pervasive than relationships between institutions and their procedures. Between 1870 and the present day, France experienced one change of political system – in 1958 when parliamentary government gave way to a hybrid form of presidential government. But the regime change was between 1940 and 1944 when an authoritarian regime of a clerico-fascist hue prevailed. At other times France has been under the same type of regime – democracy. It needs little understanding to grasp that regime change is far more of a shock to the political system than legal/institutional change.

There are two main types of political regime: authoritarian and democratic. Although these are ideal-types and most states may be in an intermediate position, the ease with which one can allocate the world's 174 states to the two categories is impressive.

4.1 Authoritarian regimes

About 130 of the world's states can be characterised as authoritarian, that is they claim to have the right to impose their values and policies on their subjects who do not have means to respond freely. There are three broad sub-types.

4.1.1 Absolutist regimes

Absolutist or despotic regimes have usually been a feature of dynastic rule. Hereditary rulers are legitimised by tradition (see Chapter 2). A common belief in Europe until the end of the eighteenth century was that kings had a Divine Right to rule. They were appointed by God. Hence absolutist regimes often have a flavour of theocracy. A religious sanction to rule may cause a ruler to behave in an arbitrary fashion. Law may emanate from his personal decrees or even whims. The reign of Tsar Ivan the Terrible (1530–84) illustrates this tendency. In Russia absolutism lingered on until 1917 with only the slightest concession to democracy in the early years of the century.

Absolutist regimes are a feature of economic under-development, primitive countries with poor communications and often semi-literate populations, minimal political culture (see Chapter 6) and a dearth of institutions. In the contemporary world a few survive where conditions are unusual. Bhutan, remote on the southern slopes of the Himalayas between India and Tibet, with a population of 700,000, had a theocratic government until 1907 when it was replaced by the Wanghcuk dynasty. Its monarchs have ruled despotically. Since the 1980s decrees have ordered people to wear only Bhutanese dress and in an effort to assert Buddhist culture Indian labourers have been expelled.

Economic development, the opening up of countries to world trade and outside culture, is likely to threaten absolutism. Prime examples of this type of regime were Bahrain, Qatar and the seven smaller Arab Gulf emirates with their traditional ruling families, but the exploitation of oil wealth modernised their economies and led in Bahrain to trade unions striking in 1974. Later threats have come from Islamic militants. The Gulf states' rulers have so far yielded little but their regimes remain unstable.

"Modernisation" is the term applied to the economic and social changes that affect the developing world. It is a portmanteau concept encapsulating industrialisation, secularisation, urbanisation and institutionalisation. Samuel Huntington regards the latter process as the main distinguishing mark between states.[1] Institutions include legal systems, bureaucracies, police forces and regular armies.

4.1.2   Military regimes

These are states where rule is by the armed forces. The navy and air force are sometimes involved, but because they are a territorially based force the army is almost invariably at the centre of military regimes. When Finer wrote about thirty years ago he estimated that over thirty countries in the world were governed in this way.[2] There were more military regimes than democracies. Probably there are as many now. Government by soldiers was almost endemic in Central and South America from the time of liberation from Spain in the 1820s. Many of these countries have in recent years established democratic institutions: on the other hand, one can note a growth of military rule in Central and West Africa.

As we noted earlier (see Chapter 2), weaponry is an important power resource and where other power resources are slight the military may well be disposed to use their strength. Their disposition to interfere in civil affairs springs from their perception that they are the only institution capable of safeguarding the integrity and sovereignty of their country, and their contempt for civilian politicians whom the generals see as indecisive and incompetent. The army's chain-of-command system with its automatic response to orders seems to them a much more efficient way of taking decisions than by discussion, negotiation and compromise. Opportunities for the military to take over government will obviously arise from war and the threat of war. They are then needed by the politicians. Other opportunities may arise from domestic crises and some countries are racked by almost perpetual crisis. In the Balkans, Latin America and the Middle East military rule is common. Sometimes there is a power vacuum which allows the army to act as it pleases. In primitive states they may be the only institution providing technical training: for example, men can only learn to drive lorries in the army. In countries with highly institutionalised political cultures, such as France and Germany between the wars, the officer class, largely recruited from the aristocracy or *haute bourgeoisie*, did not regard the civilian government as legitimate.

The military often come to power by *coups d'état*. They occupy all government buldings and the broadcasting stations and usually rule repressively, suppressing civic freedoms and often installing generals at the head of civilian institutions such as universities. In Burma the military not only dominate the economy, they take part in administration. In fairly well developed countries such as Brazil, the generals, when they ruled, could not proceed without the help and consent of business and financial interests who feared the threat of working-class power to economic stability. In Turkey, where the constitution makes the army the guardian of the secular, civilian government, General Evren took power in 1980 and guided his country back to civilian rule three years later.

The military have been responsible for about three-fifths of over 60 instances of the downfall of democracy[3] but there have been many more instances where they have overthrown non-democratic governments. Sometimes one lot of soldiers replaces another: there are factions in the armed forces. Consequently a good deal of military rule has been through committees of generals, the famous 'junta' of South America. Where a single soldier is in power, there is a military dictatorship. Private armies may be the weapon of some dictators. In Haiti where the army was weak, Papa Doc Duvalier, and later his son 'Baby Doc', ruled from 1957 until 1986 with a gang of 5,000 thugs known as the Ton ton Macoute who exerted power by protection rackets and assassination.

With the development of more and more lethal weapons armies may become more powerful. Popular insurrection is difficult against tanks. One must conclude that soldiers are not in power everywhere because they do not often want power. Their business is soldiering.

4.1.3 Totalitarian regimes

Totalitarianism is a modern form of authoritarianism. It could not exist without modern systems of mass information, communication and control. The term originated with Mussolini (see Chapter 15) and refers to the totality of state control. A totalitarian regime encompasses all human activity. Hence for the individual a completely private social and cultural life is impossible. Civil society does not exist. The main features of totalitarianism are:

1. a regime with clearly defined ambitious goals such as conquering the world and/or revolutionising society;
2. a mobilised society supervised, energised, exhorted and instructed by a single party and its activists;
3. an official doctrine of admonitory precepts, explanations of the past and prophecies for the future purveyed by the party (see Section Three).

Totalitarianism was perhaps the main political innovation and leitmotif of the twentieth century. At one time there were about twenty such regimes in the world. Today there are only three – China, Cuba and North Korea – though others may be qualifying because the mobilising single party is a useful instrument for elitist rulers modernising their developing countries. To date, however, two main types of totalitarian regime have existed. Their goals and doctrines differed though they both ruled through the single party, an idea Mussolini borrowed from Lenin, and Hitler, who admired Mussolini, followed suit. (see Chapter 15). But the goals and doctrines of the regimes are so different that Communist and Fascist parties can hardly behave in the same way. The primary party unit or cell of the Communist parties was intended to spread its message amongst the workers in agriculture and industry as part of the objective of establishing socialism. The units of the Fascist party were essentially platoons of a private army intended to secure compliance by discipline. Hence Fascist regimes are programmed to go into battle.

Fascist regimes

As the ideology of Fascism is based upon will (as opposed to reason under Communism), the major value is that of active leadership. Fascist leaders are nothing if not charismatic, legitimating their regimes with their personalities, leadership styles and dramatic performances on the world stage. Individual leadership rules over state, people and party. Mussolini called himself 'Il Duce' and Hitler copied him with 'Der Führer'. Everyone else was supposed to follow them in their intention to initiate a new moral order. This was to be implemented by subordinate hierarchies – state bureaucracies composed of the old administrators and the new party cadres with control functions that civil officials had never possessed.

These functions were part repressive, quite often arbitrary and part charismatic. The charisma of the leader in the Nazi Party, for example, was transmitted downwards through forty-three *Gauleiter* (provincial leaders) to *Kreisleiter* (district leaders) and beneath them *Ortsgruppenleiter* (local branch leaders). Charisma was transmitted by symbols such as flags, marching songs and exhibiting the leader's photograph at mass rallies. Fascist rule was by a mixed semi-political, semi-military elite skilled and trained in mass domination. In this context mention should be made of the paramilitary formations whose organised intimidation brought the Fascist dictators to power. Mussolini's *Squadristi* in black shirts were recruited from unemployed ex-servicemen. In the industrial troubles of 1919–22 they broke up strike pickets and set fire to or occupied local socialist committee rooms and newspaper offices. Hitler's Third Reich had two such private armies – the *Sturmabteilung* (SA) or brownshirts, formed in the 1920s, and later the *Schutzstaffel* (SS) or blackshirts, Hitler's own praetorian guard, set up after he quarrelled with the SA leaders. To supplement the functions of these units the state police wielded the weapon of 'state terror'.

All these instruments were used to coordinate the national effort towards the national goal: time was to tell this was victory in war. The economy was guided towards this objective by its structuring in what became known as the 'corporate state' (see Chapter 15).

Communist regimes

These have persisted much longer than Fascist regimes. The Communist model has spread to many countries outside the archetype, the Soviet Union (see Chapter 13 for a brief summary). Lenin designed a new type of party and anchored it on the principle of 'democratic centralism' which envisaged decisions being made at lower levels and proceeding up to the Central Committee and, finally, the Politbureau of the party where collective leadership was practised. Decisions made at the top were binding and were passed down through intermediate levels to the primary party units. Hence dissent within the party was permitted, but party discipline was very important.

Yet Marxism-Leninism, as it became, could only serve as a legitimating ideology for Communist regimes; it was of limited use for building an industrial economy and solving the problems of their society. Lenin died in early 1924 when the revolutionary state was only beginning to deal with them. Stalin, who succeeded to the leadership of the CPSU, by 1936 had collectivised agriculture, vastly increased industrial production in the first Five-Year Plan (1928–1933) and established himself as sole ruler until his death in 1953, using a 'personality cult' to fashion an image of legitimacy. None of the higher institutions of the Party met in this seventeen–year period.

Communist regimes have attempted to improve the material standards of their citizens by giving priority to industrialisation and technological advance. True to the ideology, they have set out to do this without private ownership, entrepreneurial activity or the free forces of the market. Hence the central organisation of the state decides what is to be produced and how it is to be distributed. Communist regimes have central direction of their economy by detailed planning. They have 'command economies'. It is this suspension of market forces and the profit motive which makes the regimes distinctive, not so much public ownership which can be found even in capitalist countries. Production targets are set, often in great detail, for the extent of the Plan (usually about five years), and investment programmes, prices and wages are also fixed. Strikes and normal trade-union activity are forbidden, so wages can be settled at a level low enough to give employment to almost everyone. The temptation is to keep wages stable so that production decisions are simplified and the surplus can be used for investment programmes. Communist regimes build for the distant future. With wages stable the important factor for ordinary citizens is the level of prices. If they are fixed too low goods will sell out quickly as queues form. If they are fixed too high they stay on the shelves. The authorities may in time react to these citizen responses, but they will not do so quickly because everything has been determined by the Plan. So innovatory policy has to wait until the next Plan.

Hence a command economy may seem a rational way of distributing production, but it is rigid and unadaptable to change. It stifles initiative and does not encourage the introduction of new technology. (The Communist regimes often bought their advanced technology from capitalist countries.) Indeed, as criticism of official policies and procedures is not allowed except at very high levels, a compliant citizenry is almost guaranteed. The political system and economy are not open to change unless it comes from the top. Debate in Communist regimes takes place behind closed doors and at the very highest levels, in Central Committees of a few hundred people or even in Politbureaus of twenty or thirty. The state of the economy is the main topic of discussion. Foreign policy is also important which ensures priority for heavy industry because it is essential to arms production.

Although the Soviet bloc disintegrated in 1989–90 and Communism as a ruling ideology and party disappeared in Eastern Europe it remained in power in the world's largest state, the People's Republic of China (PRC) with a fifth of the world's population. Chinese Communism has exhibited some features which are common to Communism and some which are distinctive. A major difference was that while the Communist Revolution in Russia took at the widest calculation twelve years (1905–17) to arrive, the period of gestation in China was thirty-eight years (1911–49). Further, the main revolutionary instrument for the Chinese Communists was not workers' and soldiers' councils but the People's Liberation Army. The PLA, based in the remote North-west, fought against both the invading Japanese and Chiang Kai Shek's Kuomintang, (a party formed to restore China's greatness), before advancing on Peking in 1949. In consequence army commanders had an importance in China that they never acquired in the Soviet Union.

In its early years, however, the PRC pursued a very similar course to the USSR. Land was first distributed to the peasants and then collectivised in the mid-1950s. The First Five-Year Plan in 1953 was based on the Soviet model with an emphasis on heavy industry. A command economy was established, operating on similar lines to other Communist regimes. By 1957 the Plan was showing some success and industrial output had increased 130 per cent. Collectivised agriculture was based on co-operative farms with about 250 families in each.[4] The Chinese

Communist Party, composed of about 5 per cent of the population, supervised these efforts in the prescribed Leninist way.

Furthermore, the party was modelled on the CPSU although during its years on the periphery of China two different types of party existed.[5] In the Communist 'red-base' area the party chairman was Mao Tse-tung (now transliterated as Mao Zedong) who decried bureaucracy and tried to build the party into one in which the main relationship was between him and 'the masses'. In most of China, where either the Japanese or the Kuomintang ruled, a more Leninist type of structure prevailed in the Communist guerrilla bands, among whom the chief leader was Liu Shao-chi (now Liu Shaoqi). Hence in the Chinese Communist Party the Stalinist and Leninist models of the party were in conflict. Robert Tucker called these respectively the 'führerist' and 'Bolshevik' types of Communist Party.[6]

From 1949 until Mao's death in 1976 the regime's failures can all be attributed to Mao's success in establishing a Stalinist-type domination over the Communist Party. He was never satisfied with the pace of revolutionary progress and invested his energies in a struggle to accelerate it. In 1956 in an attempt to spur socialist advance, Mao decreed that 'a hundred flowers shall bloom', an invitation to intellectuals to criticise. When this provided no boost to party activity Mao arrested the critics. In 1958 he decreed the 'Great Leap Forward' to expand production. The communes were merged into giant cooperatives of 5,000–20,000 families and expected to produce steel in rural furnaces. Industrial production did not appreciably increase and famine in the devastated countryside accounted for 20–30 million deaths. Mao was to blame but by 1965, after a return to a form of collective leadership, he accused Liu and his supporter, Deng Xiaoping, of betraying China. Mao then launched the Cultural Revolution. This was a mobilising of youthful activists, waving little red books containing *The Thoughts of Mao*, against the bureaucrats of the party and others in high positions. Liu and Deng were imprisoned. The former died in prison, but in 1977, after Mao's death, Deng was released and straightaway began to argue that conflictual politics should give way to economic modernisation. By 1978 Deng had established himself as leader. He decollectivised agriculture, relaxed central planning, introduced the beginnings of a market economy and opened up China to the world. Outcomes were a high rate of inflation, the growth of a black market, corruption among officials and the rise of youthful dissent culminating in the Tiananmen Square massacre in July 1989. Hence in China we have the oddity of the gerontocratic leadership of a Communist Party presiding over a non-Communist regime. The death of Deng in 1997 does not seem yet to have changed the situation.

The experiences of Stalinism in Russia, Maoism in China and other Communist regimes like North Korea pose the question of whether collective leadership is only a temporary phase in Communist regimes and that reversion to personal dictatorship within them is inevitable. It has been convincingly argued that Lenin is unique among leaders of monolithic ruling parties in that he 'tried to keep the Party organization strong and publicly played down his own role as leader'.[7] He was also unique in only being in power for five troubled years before he died. Otherwise it would seem that Communist regimes must tilt much more towards the 'führerist' pole of organisation and away from the 'Bolshevik'. It is easy to see similarities between the purges of Hitler, Stalin and Mao. The same ruthlessness and treachery were employed against those perceived as potential rivals. Old comrades were not spared. Mao sometimes resembled Mussolini in his comic efforts to exhibit machismo.

The explanation is simple. A totalitarian regime in command of society, the economy and the political system cannot survive for long where there is no one to take responsibility for everything. A chain of command pattern of decision-making requires a commander. In this respect, therefore, Fascist and Communist regimes are similar, if in no other way.

4.4.4   Authoritarian regimes of a mixed kind

Perhaps the largest group of regimes are those that are not absolutist or totalitarian, but which can by no stretch of the imagination be called democratic. Their armed forces are powerful but do not provide the incumbent leadership. There is thus a certain complexity about their social and political arrangements, making them difficult to categorise. There are Asian countries such as Pakistan, South Korea, Indonesia and Taiwan in this bracket, and Latin American countries such as Nicaragua, Colombia, Argentina and Brazil, to name a few.

4.2 Democratic regimes

The intellectual roots of democracy have been attributed especially to Rousseau and the Utilitarians (see Chapter 12). Here we are concerned with the essential features of democratic regimes. These are familiar and easily identifiable. Robert Dahl sums up the distinguishing characteristics of democracy under two rubrics: 'inclusiveness' and 'public contestation'.[8] Both are essential to democracy and both were achieved a good deal later than many commentators assume. It is often believed that democracy in North America and Europe was established by the mid-nineteenth century, but it was not really accomplished until the twentieth.

4.2.1 Distinguishing features of democracy

The principle of inclusiveness implies that all adults should have the equal right to vote in general and local elections and in referendums. They should also have the right to stand as candidates for democratic assemblies and elected office, both at a local and a national level. There should be very few exceptions to inclusiveness. It is usual to exclude certified lunatics and convicted criminals and to have an age limit. There is some variation in the age at which the voting right is reached, though in recent years eighteen has become the norm. It is not uncommon for the age of the right to candidacy to be somewhat higher. In Britain since 1970 one can vote at eighteen, but one cannot stand as a candidate until one is twenty-one. In the USA the 26th Amendment (1971) also extended the franchise to eighteen-year olds, but citizens under thirty are not eligible to be elected to the Senate and those under thirty-five cannot be President.

Thus by the principle of inclusiveness equal participatory rights are given to all democratic citizens. They may not choose to use them. Roughly three-quarters of democratic citizens usually vote in national elections, but the proportion standing as candidates cannot be anything but tiny and perhaps as few as 5 per cent regularly participate in other ways – for example, as activists in pressure groups and political parties.

The principle of public contestation subsumes freedom of self-expression about the political situation in one's country and the right to organise with other citizens. It encapsulates what are often called the 'civic freedoms' or 'civil liberties'.

Freedom of speech allows one to state preferences about policies and to criticise government action. Freedom of the press permits wider dissemination of dissenting views. Freedom of assembly guarantees the right of citizens to gather in groups for all lawful purposes including that of demonstrating and voicing combined opposition to government activities. Freedom of association enlarges freedom of assembly, for it allows temporary combination to become permanent. Hence it safeguards the right to organise, on a nationwide scale if necessary, in order to oppose the government. Thus freedom of association is the basis for pluralism. Of course, organised groups can exist outside a democratic framework – in medieval society there were churches and guilds – but democracy cannot be complete without pluralism. Pressure groups and political parties are manifestations of pluralism. They are necessary accompaniments of representative democracy (see pp. 125–35).

The principle of governmental accountability is also an essential of democracy. This should ensure that governments are responsive. They should be ready to reply to criticism, even if only to rebut it. It is common for there to be a procedure by which executives answer questions, either formally in legislatures or informally as with American Presidents in presidential press conferences. Democratic governments are also supposed to be responsible. They must be held to account for their actions and if their explanations are unsatisfactory in the eyes of the electorate the latter must be given an opportunity to dismiss them. This is ensured by periodic free and fair elections or by votes denoting lack of confidence which can be held in most legislatures where parliamentary government obtains[9] (see Chapters 7 and 8).

4.2.2 Democratic decision-making

Democratic decisions are taken by majorities. If decisions have to be taken – and it is hard to see how a modern state can avoid it – it would be difficult to take them by minority votes. (If they were taken in this latter Alice-in-Wonderland way, people would vote against the option and/or outcome they wanted.) Majority rules may mean that a 50 per cent + 1 majority of those voting carries the day, or that a 50 per cent + 1 of the electorate is needed to be decisive. At other times, or in other places, a two-thirds or even three-quarters majority may be required. Many democracies will use more than one of these methods.

There are two main forms of democracy – direct democracy and representative democracy.[10] Most states have a mixture of them, but representative democracy is the dominant method.

Direct democracy

Direct democracy has three components: the recall allowing constituents to force a representative to face re-election or resign; the initiative allowing a proportion of the electorate to present a petition to be put to a referendum, a ballot of the whole electorate. Referendums are widely used in a few democracies, such as Switzerland, and occasionally in most others. Most commonly the occasion is either constitutional amendment or a national decision of historic importance such as whether or not to join the European Union, but in some contexts less grave decisions, such as whether cinemas should open on Sundays, may be referred to the people.

The alleged advantages of direct democracy are implied criticisms of representative democracy. For example, it is argued that clarity of issue in a referendum is preferable to the welter of different issues the voter has to deal with in a general election. Referendums are specific. Moreover, issues can be dealt with as they arise: the voters do not have to wait for three or four years until the next election takes place. Therefore, direct democracy has a decisiveness that representative democracy can never have, and it also removes the need for political parties and politicians with their capacity for confusing issues in their desire to attribute all sorts of mistakes to their opponents.

Representative democracy

This is an indirect way of popular participation in decision-making. The voters elect representatives to make decisions for them, thus allowing people more time for other activities. Other advantages are that highly technical decisions, such as those concerned with economic management, are handed over to people experienced at dealing with them. They are discussed in a small chamber in which every legislator can be heard by every other. Moreover, the representatives provide a small core of people from whom political executives can be chosen. The latter present policies which, because of the centralised context, can be interrelated. Agendas can be drawn up and priorities accorded. Policy can be rationalised in programmes.

In consequence representative democracy almost inevitably implies political parties. They are needed to inform electorates, articulate issues and aggregate voters (see Chapter 10). They are needed to select candidates for elections and to provide a government, or to coalesce and share governing with other parties. Critics of parties complain of their complex bureaucratic structures and the way they add to the blurring of contemporary issues in the process of compromise. Their leaders are professional politicians who are sometimes corrupted by power and whose wish to hold on to it by offending as few voters as possible drives them into obfuscation, half-truths and even direct deceit. The clarity and specificity of direct democracy are missing from party-dominated representative democracy.

Objections to representative institutions are many. They clearly interpose a layer between government and people. Representatives are not representative in two senses: they are predominantly middle-class males and their way of life and method of selection through the agency of party (except in the USA where in many states they are chosen by party voters in primary elections) makes them remote from their constituents. Electoral systems can distort public opinion (see Chapter 8). It is also contended that legislatures are in decline because of the increased technicality of policy-making and the growth of technocratic intervention by political bureaucrats who cannot be present in legislatures. (see Chapter 9).

Yet there is a further complication to representative democracy: the activities of pressure groups who lobby governments in pursuit of ends which are selfish and often highly specific. They are of diverse kinds. Some are concerned with promoting a cause; others like churches are cultural and only concerned with policy when it occasionally impinges on them; others are functional to the state and often walk in the corridors of power, like large-scale business enterprise, trade union movements and armies. Democratic governments are constrained to have relations with them in certain circumstances. For example, in war senior soldiers will need to be consulted. In times of economic crisis, the social partners, business and labour, may become especially important. Democratic governments may often need the knowledge and even expertise of pressure group leaders. Consequently they will be drawn into bargaining with them, an activity outside the framework in which policies are hammered out in executive and legislative committees.

Stein Rokkan stressed that there were two types of decision-making in every modern democratic state.[11] 'Numerical democracy' was the term he applied to the traditional system in which elections determine the balance of party competition, and debate and discussion lead to final decisions being taken in legislatures. Most voters still see this as the decision-making system of their country. For governments making policy by bargaining with pressure groups he coined the term 'corporate pluralism'. (This did not necessarily involve 'corporatism' – see pp. 36–7). In this process technocratic civil servants usually participated. Final decisions might be rubber-stamped by legislatures, but there is no access for most legislators, let alone voters, into the process. Consequently democratic accountability is lacking. Moreover, the two systems operate at the same time rendering the decision-making procedures of the modern democratic state highly complex.[12]

4.3 Summary

Clearly these differing regime-types will have very different impacts on their peoples. They produce societies with quite different kinds of social behaviour and political cultures. A visitor does not have to be very observant to note how reluctant citizens of authoritarian states are to say anything about their rulers, while in democracies people can be heard everywhere, and even seen on television, criticising their governments. It is possible to envisage a spectrum of regimes stretching from totalitarianism to democracy. The degree of civil liberty and voluntary political participation would determine positions on the spectrum.

At one time it was commonly envisaged that democracy was the ideal to which all states should strive. Some nineteenth-century liberals with an optimistic view of progress (see Chapter 12) believed humanity was advancing in that direction anyway. This view was dispelled during the 'era of the dictators' (roughly 1919–89). Today it is again a vision seen by liberals. Political scientists are especially interested in 'regime change': studying the circumstances in which a country moves from authoritarianism to democracy, or vice versa, and then generalising from numerous instances. The cultural and socio-economic factors that bring about such changes are the subject of wide academic debate.

Notes

1. S. Huntington, *Political Order in Changing Societies* (New Haven, Conn.: Yale University Press, 1968).
2. S. E. Finer, *The Man on Horseback*. 2nd edn (Harmondsworth: Penguin, 1976).
3. F. W. Bealey, 'Stability and crisis: fears about threats to democracy' *European Journal of Political Research*, vol. 15, 1987, pp. 687–715.
4. See C. Riskin, *China's Political Economy: The Quest for Development since 1949* (Oxford: Oxford University Press, 1987); J. D. Spence, *The Search for Modern China* (New York: W. W. Norton, 1990); Joint Economic Committee, Congress of the United States *China's Economic Dilemmas in the 1990s* (Washington, DC: 1991); G. White (ed.), *From Crisis to Crisis: The Chinese State in the Era of Economic Reform* (Armonk, NY: M. E. Sharpe, 1991).
5. L. Schapiro, and J. W. Lewis. 'The roles of the monolithic party under the totalitarian leader' in J. W. Lewis (ed.), *Party Leadership and Revolutionary Power in China* (Cambridge: Cambridge University Press, 1970), pp. 114–145.
6. R. C. Tucker, 'Towards a comparative politics of movement regimes', *American Political Science Review*, vol. LV, June 1961, pp. 281–9.
7. Schapiro and Lewis, Roles of the monolithic party, p. 143.
8. R. A. Dahl, *Polyarchy* (New Haven, Conn.; Yale University Press, 1971), p. 2f.
9. See A. H. Birch, *Representative and Responsible Government* (London: Allen & Unwin, 1964).
10. F. W. Bealey, *Democracy in the Contemporary State* (Oxford: Oxford University Press, 1988), pp. 28–60.
11. S. Rokkan, (1966) 'Numerical democracy and corporate pluralism', in R. A. Dahl (ed.), *Political Oppositions in Western Democracies* p. 106.
12. Bealey, *Democracy*, p. 194.

Questions

1. How representative are representative institutions?
2. In what circumstance might a democratic country turn to military dictatorship or totalitarian rule?

5

Problems of modern democratic government

The basic problem of all states is to maintain legitimacy and sovereignty in the face of internal and external pressures and constraints. Modern democratic states have an especial problem: they operate within the constraint of general approval. Governments within these states, unlike those where democracy does not exist, are faced with a barrage of public criticism and the ever-present threat of being dismissed from office either by a majority in a dissatisfied legislature or in an election by a discontented public. Thus democratic politicians become very sensitive to public opinion. Representative democracy does not require them to put every specific policy to the electorate, but when election time comes governments will be judged on the outcomes of their whole programme. Hence incumbent democratic governments are greatly disposed to do what is popular and not to do what is unpopular.

This tendency explains a good deal of the development of policy in those states where extended franchises were introduced. To win the votes of the poorer section of the community, then in a majority, nationwide welfare measures were introduced, leading to a great increase in state functions in the first half of the twentieth century (see Chapter 3). At the same time the older functions of law and order and defence did not decline in necessitude: in fact, their urgency was intensified by two world wars followed by the threat of nuclear war. The consequence of all these contingencies was that governing democracies became more difficult. A major problem was making ends meet.

5.1 The fiscal crisis of the democratic state

All states in the not too long run have to balance their revenue and expenditure. To spend more they have to raise more money and the only way to obtain most of it is through taxing citizens. But taxes are inevitably unpopular and increases in taxes, especially large ones, or unexpected new taxes, are bound to be followed by some loss in voting support. The alternative to increasing revenue is to decrease public expenditure which often must involve cuts in public services and/or social benefits. This will also be followed by loss of voting support though among a socially different section of the electorate. Of course, right-wing governments will be more inclined to cut public expenditure and left-wing governments will be more inclined to increase taxation. The balance varies between one democracy and another, but they all face the dilemma of wondering where to strike it in order to maintain, if not extend, their popularity.

The problem became particularly pronounced in the 1970s. In 1973 the increase in the oil prices by the oil-producing states led to higher transport costs and, ultimately, to higher prices and then demands for higher wages which, when implemented, set in motion an inflationary spiral. James O'Connor, a Marxist writer (for Marx see Chapter 13), argued that the democracies could no longer sustain their levels of spending on the welfare state.[1] This would endanger their legitimacy. It would also endanger capitalism because social expenditure financed by taxation reduced employers' potential costs and underpinned industrial peace. The fiscal crisis was a crisis of capitalism as well as a crisis of capitalism's protective facade – democracy. O'Connor's thesis gained some acceptance in the later 1970s. In 1976 the International Monetary Fund would only grant the British government a loan on condition that it cut public expenditure. The crisis spread to local governments, often dependent on subventions from the centre. In 1977 New York City became bankrupt.

Inflationary problems added to a rather apocalyptic mood which was enhanced by certain right-wing authors. Prominent among these was Samuel Brittan who argued that democratic politicians were not disposed to face up to the problem.[2] They promised two irreconcilable policies – not to increase taxation and not to cut public expenditure. Democracy was 'in crisis', a theme among political scientists in the 1970s.[3] The Thatcherite and Reaganite policies of the 1980s, however, dispelled these gloomy prognostications about the future of democracy. It became clear that a majority of the voters would accept somewhat lower benefits. Moreover, many democratic governments not only made inroads into the welfare state, they also considerably contracted state functions and the size of the public sector's labour force. It had been argued that democratic states were overloaded with expensive functions and public employees.[4] The answer was to trim them severely.

Measures going further than stricter financial rectitude were adopted in several instances. One was to tackle spiralling labour costs by creating a pool of unemployment and passing laws severely restricting trade union activity. Another major policy was the contraction of public ownership. Privatisation became the watchword of many democratic governments. In this way overloading became less of a problem. Many democratic governments also withdrew from both formal and informal arrangements of consultation and bargaining they had with business and labour. Thus both 'socialism' and 'corporatism' were in decline. Management of the economy, an important and assumed necessary task of governments since the Second World War, was no longer a prime concern.

Yet, as always, other problems arose from the outcomes of these policies. Perhaps the most important was the greater extremes of wealth and poverty they created. At the top end of the income league lower taxation benefited the rich, while at the bottom, lower public expenditure and increased unemployment swelled the ranks of the very poor. It became common to describe this bottom 10 per cent as the 'underclass'. One consequence of their deprivation was the rise in crime and the areas in which the underclass lived became uncongenial for the great majority among them who remained law-abiding. Homelessness and drug addiction were, for the most part, not effects of social and economic policies though poverty undoubtedly exacerbated them. The existence of this group of socially and economically underprivileged also revived the concept of the 'undeserving poor' which many thought had been banished in the 1940s if not earlier.

5.2 Globalisation

Both managing the economy and dealing with incipient financial pressures became more difficult from the 1980s onwards as states moved more and more in an international framework. The shrinking of the world brought about by a transportation and communication revolution was accompanied by the loosening of international trade as the stages of the General Agreement on Tariffs and Trade gradually unfolded. All these trends have been encapsulated in the term 'globalisation'.

Globalisation takes several forms.[5] Cultural globalisation has been evident for some decades. Early channels were newsprint, broadcasting and the cinema, but their influence was weak compared with satellite television and the Internet. The growth of air travel also brought people into contact with cultures other than their own as well as allowing people to choose where they would live, though this was much restricted by immigration legislation. As far as governments were

concerned, however, their main problems arose from economic globalisation, especially the internationalisation of financial markets.
Rapid electronic communication allowed both information and misinformation to be transmitted almost instantaneously between the
increased number of financial centres. Multinational corporations,
owing no particular loyalty to any country, are able to deploy their
resources easily and their investment and deinvestment decisions can
make a considerable impact on the economy of a state, especially one
which is small or weak. The latter may need to trim its economic
policies to suit the multinationals.

Since the mid-1990s the progressive integration of the world economy has accelerated, one outcome being the economic crisis of the
Asian 'tiger economies'. Industrialised states with quite strong economies now have to subject themselves to the discipline of international
capital which can move freely around the world seeking the highest
returns. Thus national economic policies have to be trimmed to be in
accordance with the dictates of market forces, and governments have to
be prepared to adapt themselves to changes in the world economy.
Hence countries no longer have complete control over their own
decisions and living standards.

5.3 Accountability

A brief account of governmental accountability has been given in
Chapter 4. In practice, however, making governments accountable
to their electorates has always been difficult. This is because attributing
blame is not easy for various reasons. For example, in the case of local
governments many of their shortcomings may really be the result of
constraints imposed upon them by central governments. More basically, comprehension of the origins of policies, the intentions of the
policy-makers and what has been achieved is necessary before blame
can be placed on the correct shoulders. It is not uncommon, however,
for electorates not to possess the information on which judgements of
this kind can be based. To some extent this is doubtless owing to a lack
of interest in political matters, though another factor is the technicality
of much social and economic policy. This in turn gives party politicians
the chance to avoid serious questioning and/or to indicate that their
political opponents were responsible for the policy in question. As
much modern legislation may take years before it produces intended
outcomes – economic policy may require a decade before its success or
failure can be assessed – problems of attributability are highly likely
especially where parties alternate in office. It is often thought that the

prosperity of De Gaulle's first Presidency (1958–69) of the Fifth Republic owed much to the economic policies of those politicians of the
Fourth Republic he so much despised. More recently both Clinton and
Blair, succeeding to power in 1993 and 1997 respectively after governments of a different political complexion, seem to have profited from
the economic policies of their predecessors.

Globalisation, however, provides yet another problem of accountability. Voters tend to blame incumbent governments for most of what
happens during their spell in power and surveys usually show that the
state of the economy is the most important factor in determining the
vote of those whose allegiance to party is weak. It is also known that
strong allegiance to party has declined in recent years. Yet the effect of
economic globalisation is to make governments much more vulnerable
to external events. They have to make unwanted policy changes to
accommodate them and to take responsibility for those policies at the
next election. The same situation arises where democratic states are
members of a confederation such as the European Union. Directives
from the central authority in such organisations will have to be
accepted and implemented even when originally formulated by un-
elected technocrats. Hence states' governments become responsible (in
the sense that they will be blamed or rewarded by voters) for policies
they have only slightly been involved with and which have not been
through the normal democratic processes.

5.4 New decision-making styles and new issues

The drafting of policies has seldom been done in large legislative
bodies. Parliaments are not appropriate places for considering and
discussing details. Hence much legislative detail is debated in committees of legislatures though, where party discipline is strong, it is likely to
be drawn up in the executive or its sub-committees. Much will depend
on the type of political system, but in general legislatures have tended
increasingly to be by-passed, especially in the framing of economic
policy. Economic policy may be too much for many legislators. Even
ministers, who in some systems frequently move about between departments, may have difficulty in grasping its technicalities. Increasingly, therefore, the drafting of medium- and lower-level policies are in
the hands of specialised bureaucrats, now known as technocrats. High-
er-level policy may emanate from a majority party or a coalition of
parties forming a majority in legislatures, but as Lehner and Schubert
argue,[6] the capacity of parties to formulate policy guidelines and
programmes is rather low. So is the capacity of opposition parties to

criticise. The problem of democratic accountability, described above, is thus enhanced.

One can exaggerate the extent of the decline of legislatures (see the end of Chapter 7), but even so it is not implausible to argue that we now live in a different type of democratic system. There has been a certain amount of citizen withdrawal from political participation. In elections it has only slightly declined, but the role of party organisation has diminished. National party leaders perform on television during elections rather than touring countries addressing local meetings. Compared with the decade after the Second World War, political activism in most democracies has greatly diminished. Local organisation is generally weaker and party memberships have shrunk.[7] People seem less concerned with what happens in legislatures whose proceedings have never been widely reported in the press. Today the tabloid press scarcely ever mentions them unless a row has occurred, while their treatment in the 'quality' press has been marginalised.

Indeed, the power of the mass media of communications has never been greater and modern technology has increased their range and extended their markets. Satellite broadcasting is another example of globalisation. Television has both social and political importance: in fact, its social influence has political implications. It is not only that much political information is purveyed by television, but also that its prime function it to entertain.[8] Surveys reveal that many people spend some hours watching it every day. In general, the result is a public with less time for political issues. Television and the newspapers trivialise them. Yet when presenters of current affairs programmes skilfully cross-examine politicians about their positions and statements on policy (though they are not always that skilfull), they often elucidate matters to a degree that questions in legislatures never succeed in doing and they do so before a much larger audience.

The impact of television on politics is therefore somewhat paradoxical. It has made seriousness about politics unpopular and yet is has become indispensable to political parties who need it to convey their declared intentions to the public in order, they hope, to mobilise support. Consequently television has become particularly important at elections. It has made the choice of personable and articulate leaders crucial and has become essential for the kind of public relations and image building that all parties now indulge in. Yet party managers and 'spin doctors' are aware how unpopular too much political broadcasting which upsets viewers' scheduled entertainment can be during elections and they attempt to keep the messages short. The ultimate in brevity is the 'sound bite', a brief snappy statement, often one abusing political opponents.

A very important problem for democracy relates to the ownership of the media and their relationship to political parties and governments. Clearly a free press is a crucial element of democracy, yet whether a medium is privately or publicly owned its freedom may be restricted by pressure from the owners. The chief concern of the latter may be to sell their product, but their own views, or those of their editors, may be disseminated throughout the nation. For example, the Murdoch enterprise, the largest media empire in the world, is an outspoken and irreconcilable opponent of the European Union. This can be attributed to the Australian-turned-American pedigree of its proprietor. Democracy is best served by a plethora of accurate news and a diversity of informed views. It is hardly tendentious to say that the citizens of the democratic world have difficulty in obtaining either of these blessings. On the other hand, it sometimes seems they do not want them very much.

Finally, the political atmosphere has changed, it is argued, because the salient issues have changed during the last quarter of a century. The old issues that dominated politics dated from the French and Industrial Revolutions. What emerged from these events were cleavages over religion and class. Clericals versus secular anti-clericals and supporters of capitalism against socialists were the two contests that proceeded simultaneously in some countries (see Section 3). While it would be premature to claim that these cleavages have disappeared by the end of the twentieth century, it can hardly be denied that their depth and intensity have diminished. To some extent they have been replaced by a new type of issue.

5.5 Single-issue politics

The crux of the case, first asserted in the early 1970s, that we now have a 'new style of politics', single-issue politics, was based on two propositions. One was the argument that the materialism of the 1960s, reflected in the pursuit of economic growth, was yielding to a recognition of its disadvantages.[9] The other was that citizens of the industrialised democracies were becoming more skilled at participating politically.

There was evidence that much of the political energy, and many of the sort of people who would at one time have become party activists, were involved in promoting the causes of certain pressure groups. Many of these groups had non-economic objectives with global implications. They rejected materialist values like physical comfort and affluence and stressed personality development and the quality of life.

Their altruistic motives caused Inglehart[10] to describe their politics as 'post-materialist'. Surveys he undertook in the 1970s in seven countries, later extended in the early 1980s to over two dozen, indicated a divergence between generations brought up during the 1930s and 1940s with experiences of war and depression and later generations who had known more security. Younger people were much more inclined to 'post-materialism' and to support environmental groups, to be more liberal about sexual orientation and to belong to peace movements. These sympathies naturally placed them to the left, though they tended to distrust the materialist values of trade unions and the working class. Ownership of industry they saw as irrelevant. If anything, industrial pollution was worse in countries where industry was publicly owned.

A vague term used to cover these promotional pressure groups, one which nevertheless has become generally accepted, is 'new social movements'. Inglehart found that post-materialism was strong among their memberships. In non-democratic states new social movements sometimes emerge as the only opposition. They are especially strong in the democracies and have all developed international organisations which, when they lobby international gatherings, are known as 'non-governmental organisations'. Their activists tend to be young internationally-minded students who quite often belong to several such groups. Frequently they take up local causes, such as opposition to new bypasses, airports and nuclear power stations, and forge extraordinary coalitions of graduate activists with local farmers, landowners and middle-class housewives. They are sceptical of conventional democracy and party politics and stress participation and direct democracy.

The following are probably the most prominent single issues.

5.5.1 Environmentalism

The environmental movement is the classic example of single-issue politics. Its theoreticians have a clear *Weltanschauung*. (see Chapter 11). They idealise an inter-dependence of Man and Nature in an ecological balance that can be, and has been, upset by man's ravages. People must learn the importance of maintaining this delicate equilibrium. They must see the world as a whole in which the largest and smallest units have their interconnections both physically and politically. One environmentalist slogan of recent years was 'Think locally and act globally', but conversely the environmentalists' local actions were guided by global thinking. Environmentalism has a universal vision.

Problems for governments arise from a basic paradox. Technological advances usually result in ecological retreats. The results of social change and economic development are always uncertain. Hence future generations may suffer from policies that benefit the present generation. It is difficult to make assessments because the outcomes of different policies will not be apparent simultaneously. Some environmental processes, once set in motion may be irreversible, though we cannot determine which ones at the moment. Finally, the impact of environmental change may be very unfair. For instance, global warming may destroy Pacific micro-states (the message can be apocalyptic), while invigorating Siberia and the Yukon.

During the Cold War states became aware of these problems. The agitation against nuclear weaponry and the unknown effect of nuclear power through possible radiation in the atmosphere was complemented by fears about air pollution by industry and the motor car, the spoiling of rural areas by motorway development and the destruction of animal species like the whale. As a result in 1972 a World Environment Conference was held at Stockholm. It led to a UN Environmental Programme and eventually the UN General Assembly setting up institutions to deal with the problems on a world scale. Non-governmental organisations like Greenpeace and Friends of the Earth became very much involved with UN deliberation and in 1987 the Protocol for the Protection of the Ozone Layer was a monument to their pressures. In the same year the Brundtland Report, an offshoot of the World Economic Commission, said sustainable development needed management of change so that the environment would not be eroded.

Governments were not unaffected by these events. By the 1970s environmental pressure groups were active in nearly all democracies. They put up candidates for parliaments with varying fortunes. In the European Parliament a green group emerged. In Britain their only success was when they obtained 15 per cent of the vote at the 1989 European elections. In Sweden they profited from farmers' opposition to nuclear power stations and allied themselves with the Farmers' Party. In Germany a Green Party was founded in 1979. In its early programme it declared support for disarmament, equal rights for women, decentralised and alternative production and the development of an alternative political culture through passive resistance. Entering the Bundestag after the 1983 election, the Greens became divided between the 'realos' who were willing to coalesce with other parties and the 'fundis' who rejected compromise. Devastated at the 1990 election when they only won 3.9 per cent of the vote and so lost all their seats, they re-entered the Bundestag after the 1994 election when they picked up 7.3 per cent of the vote. They coalesced with the Social Democrats after the 1998 general election to form a government with a majority.

Scarcely any politicians reject the ecologists' arguments – it is very difficult to make increased pollution an attractive prospect – but when the costs to industrial development are considered governments give environmental policies low priority. At the Rio de Janeiro UN Conference in 1992, however, a set of agreements on the principles and practices of environmental control were reached. The Kyoto environmental summit at the end of 1997 attempted to achieve international agreement on the need to reduce levels of air pollution, but met with stiff opposition from the USA, the world's worst polluter, and from the developing nations who pollute little but want to pollute more. Eventually an agreement was reached. Japan, the USA and the European Union should reduce emanations of six environmentally damaging gases by 6, 7 and 8 per cent respectively from 1990 levels by the years 2008–12. Thirty-eight other industrial countries agreed to make cuts of 5.2 per cent.

5.5.2   Peace and human rights

These groups both have foreign policy implications. The peace movements have fluctuated in cycles determined by periods of international tension and tranquillity. For example, the British Campaign for Nuclear Disarmament was founded in 1958 when relations between the superpowers were bad and Britain was testing nuclear weapons. It quickly made international contacts and peace movements grew in strength until the Partial Test Ban Treaty in 1963, after which they declined. With the failure of détente and the decision in 1979 to install in Europe Cruise and Pershing missiles directed at the Soviet Union, a new and vigorous phase of campaigning against nuclear strategy opened in Western Europe. Inevitably this lapsed with the disintegration of the Soviet empire and the end of the Cold War. Today the causes of the 'peaceniks' are arms control, peacekeeping and the non-proliferation of nuclear arms.

Human rights are another concern, though their pursuit may sometimes evoke hostility from governments of states accused of abusing them. The concept of absolute rights that should be upheld internationally is enshrined in the UN Charter and the UN Declaration of Human Rights, 1948 adopted by all states except South Africa, Saudi Arabia and the Soviet bloc. From that time states' treatment of their subjects – with respect to freedom from arbitrary imprisonment, degrading punishment and torture – became a potential factor in international relations. Several non-governmental organisations were founded to monitor human rights records. By far the largest was Amnesty International initiated in London in 1961. By 1990 it had

700,000 members and had sent one petition to the UN signed by 300 million people from 130 countries. It lobbied international organisations incessantly, campaigned for the abolition of torture and the death penalty, and drew up reports on violations of human rights, especially wrongful and lengthy imprisonments.

Human rights received stimulus after President Carter acceded in 1977. He made them a matter of international concern and the 1980s was a period of great fulfilment. Canada, Australia, the Netherlands and all the Scandinavian countries made the promotion of human rights part of their foreign policy. Turkey, because of its human rights record, could not persuade the European Union to consider its application to join. Pressure, including economic sanctions, was brought to bear on states like South Africa that did not comply with standards. The suppression of the student demonstration in Tiananmen Square in June 1989 was internationally condemned. The overthrow of Communism in Eastern Europe in 1989 owed something to policies pursued since the Helsinki Agreement in 1975, reaffirming human rights and signed by the USSR. By the 1990s there existed the beginning of an international will to observe the UN Declaration.

5.5.3   Gender rights

Gender politics is largely about the female gender. As yet the male gender, being the politically dominant one, has not organised itself to any great extent. Feminism, however, dates back to the Enlightenment when free-thinking women like Mary Wollstonecraft made demands for female equality. The earliest strategy was to press for votes for women and organisations to this end sprang up in North America and Europe at the end of the nineteenth century. First successes were in Finland (1906) and Norway (1907). By the mid-twentieth century women were enfranchised in many countries, but they had much less success in securing representation in legislatures and they were still under-represented in the professions.

The main political thrust of women has been through pressure group activity. Only in Iceland has a women's party had any great success. When women discovered that possession of the vote did not deliver parity with men they turned to publicity and demonstration. Stimulus came from expanding higher education for women and increased female participation in the labour market. The 'women's liberation' movement of the 1960s raised female consciousness by indicating all forms of gender inequality. Radical feminists argued that the inability of women to secure many top positions in business and public service was the result of collective male prejudice. In many countries the movement achieved considerable success in securing laws to prohibit gender discrimination. Socialist feminists argued that exploitation of women was part of capitalist exploitation and could only be ended by revolutionary action. Lesbian feminists alleged heterosexuality was the root cause of the oppression of women. The pressure of others, influenced by the sociology of linguistics, was to change words such as chairman to 'chairperson'.

In recent years the issue has assumed global proportions. Women persuaded the UN that their cause was just and it declared 1976–85 a Decade for Women. Three women's conferences were organised. Initially there was some disagreement between the women of the developed and the developing countries, but by the time of the third conference at Nairobi in 1985 signs of unity were emerging. The Gulf War (1990–92) drew attention to the very underprivileged position of women in Moslem countries. Military dictatorships in Latin America, like the Pinochet regime in Chile, have also been targeted by international women's groups. In Eastern Europe the end of Communism, which in some ways had reduced the gender gap, brought in regimes seemingly more male-oriented. In Poland, for example, the first post-Communist parliament contained a smaller proportion of women than the last Communist one and its Catholic majority strongly supported the anti-abortion lobby. It seems merely a matter of time, however, before women in the English-speaking world and Western Europe win equality of political power with men. Many democracies had had women leaders by the late twentieth century and in Sweden more than half the legislators were women.

5.5.4 Gay rights

Organisations of homosexual men and women have argued that homosexuality is a biological phenomenon and so sexual relations between people of the same sex is quite natural. A gay sub-culture, tolerated in pre-war Berlin, was eradicated by the Nazis who exterminated many thousands of homosexuals in the death camps. This aroused some sympathy for them and in 1946 the oldest gay organisation, the Cultural Relaxation Centre, was founded in Holland. On 28 June 1968 the Stonewall Riots in New York City took place when gay men battled with the police who were harrassing them. This date became an anniversary at which demonstrations for gay rights are held. In 1978 the International Lesbian and Gay Association was founded. At over thirty international conferences since it has organised various projects which have borne fruit; for example, the World Health Organisation removed homosexuality from its list of diseases, the

Council of Europe passed a resolution to fight discrimination against homosexuals and Amnesty International in 1990 publicised the cases of people imprisoned for their sexual preferences. The AIDS crisis, however, had a profound impact on the movement.

Unlike women, who are at least half the human race, homosexuals are too small a proportion to benefit from the political equality of the franchise, though where they congregate in communities they may acquire some political clout. It was the existence of the gay vote in California, electorally marginal and with a large electoral college vote, that led Clinton to promise that if he were elected President in 1992 he would end discrimination against gays in the American armed forces.

5.5.5   Reproductive rights and duties

This is an international 'single issue' with two single-issue groups. On the one side pro-choice and on the other pro-life groups battle over the unborn child. Controversy arises from the dilemma over whether a mother has more rights over her body than the foetus has the right to be born. The feminist movement in North America and Europe supported access to legalised abortion during the 1970s. In 1973 in the case of *Roe* v. *Wade* the US Supreme Court declared there was a constitutional right to abortion. In 1978 the Women's Global Network on Reproductive Rights was founded at Amsterdam. By the time of the 1985 Nairobi Conference (see p. 64) the movement was asserting the right to safe contraception and legal abortion services for the world's women.

The pro-life group has an international base in the Roman Catholic Church whose teachings reject contraception and abortion. These principles were reasserted under the Papacy of John Paul II from 1978 onwards. A Pole, as Archbishop of Cracow he had opposed the Communist regime which offered abortion more or less on demand. In Western Catholic countries the force of anti-clericalism has produced compromise and abortion policy, even in Italy, is quite liberal. In the USA, however, there is a strong fundamental Protestant element with its core in the South which, allied with Roman Catholics, has formed the Moral Majority, dedicated to reversing *Roe* v. *Wade* by constitutional amendment. On its extreme fringe are people prepared even to bomb abortion clinics.

5.6   A new style of politics?

It is not possible to deny that new issues, espoused by new or revitalised pressure groups, have been prominent in political life in the last two decades. The emergence of new issues, however, is scarcely a novelty. It is bound to happen in a changing world and one in which change takes place at an accelerating pace. In democracies there is always scope for new groups to make themselves heard and television provides a new visibility. The real questions are to what degree the 'new social movements' reflect changing patterns of values and behaviour, and to what degree they have changed, or will change, representative democracy.

In the first place the term 'materialism' needs some consideration. Concern with material issues may not be based on selfish calculations. Much of the support for the welfare state, for example, came from middle-class people who believed that a better quality of life and a more pleasant public environment for all would result from paying higher taxes to help the poor and sick. Yet this issue was undoubtedly materialistic. Secondly, hailing the 1970s as the beginning of 'post-materialism' seemed a hollow claim by the mid-1980s in the age of Thatcher and Reagan and the 'low tax state', when welfare was under attack and public affluence and private squalor characterised the socioeconomic environment. This was an era of selfish materialism with which the altruistic promotional pressure groups offered a striking contrast.

Indeed, it can be argued that the post-material climate has been exaggerated. Of Inglehart's American sample only 12 per cent belonged to that tendency. The significant finding was the generational difference: the largest proportion of post-materialists in all countries was among the young. What had changed most compared with the postwar decades was the channelling of their energies into new social movements. Their exploits provided excitement for the media – sailing the seas to impede cargoes of nuclear waste, tunnelling under the ground to delay new airport extensions and living in trees to forestall the construction of new roads. Again, although their unusual behaviour and its expression throughout the world by international movements captured the headlines, the environmental groups in particular achieved most success, Dalton argues, through conventional pressure-group methods such as campaigns in the media and lobbying executive departments and legislative committees.[11] Even where they have isolated themselves from the established political parties and preferred to found their own parties (usually, as in Germany, where conditions such as the electoral system are favourable), it can be argued that the newsworthiness of their legislators has had the same function of publicising their cause.

Consequently, though new social movements have caused some changes in values and political behaviour, these can be overestimated. Their most important impact on the political parties has been a negative one. For example, in Britain the years between 1945 and 1951 witnessed a phenomenal increase in party membership and party activism.[12] By the 1960s this ideologically motivated enthusiasm had largely been dissipated. The factors responsible for this decline have been discussed above and the new social movements are shown to be in the last three decades merely an additional element in the changing style of politics. In the 1970s they kindled similar enthusiasms, but this time in favour of specific objectives rather than general programmes. In doing so they deprived the parties, already seriously embarrassed organisationally, of their potential reservoir of new blood.

Modern democratic parties, as we have noted, have tended less and less to be concerned with agenda-setting and detailed policy-making which have been left to the media and to the technocrats. Yet they have retained their usual functions of selecting candidates for elections, providing executive leadership and rationalising and prioritising policies. Where pressure groups have easy access to them, as in the USA, it is because the parties have lost these functions save for the choice of executive leaders. The difficulties new social movements have with European parties lies in the latter's problems with aggregation and incorporation of new issues and groups. The basis of this dilemma is the still almost traditional links of the right with business and the left with labour. Neither group is sympathetic to new social movements, especially ones costly to industry. Yet parties cannot be inimical (openly anyway) to the women's movement because women are half the electorate. The likelihood is that as the environmental and human rights causes become more accepted as priority issues parties will adapt more to their policies. To do this they will have to become more aggregative and incorporative. Politicians will need to be flexible and imaginative.

Pressure in many cases, it seems, will come from international organisations in which the new social movements have been very active. Moreover, demands for referendums are likely to become a common tactic. Hence while it is difficult to foresee political party government and representative insitutions in Europe being displaced by direct democracy, it may well be that a more participatory and more pressure-group oriented style of politics will ensue. This will not be entirely owing to the new social movements – party allegiance and organisation were declining anyway. It is doubtful, however, whether this will entail any threat to democracy – in fact, it may reinvigorate it.

Notes

1. J. O'Connor, *The Fiscal Crisis of the State* (New York: St. Martin's Press, 1973).
2. S. Brittan, 'The economic contradictions of democracy' *British Journal of Political Science*, vol. 5, 1975, pp. 129–59.

3. M. J. Crozier, S. P. Huntington and J. Watanuki, *The Crisis of Democracy* (New York: New York University Press, 1975).
4. R. Bacon, and W. Eltis, *Britain's Economic Problem: Too Few Producers* (London: Macmillan, 1978).
5. M. Featherstone, (ed.) *Global Culture, Nationalism, Globalization and Modernity* (London: Sage,1990); R. Robertson, *Globalization, Social Theory and Global Culture* (London: Sage, 1992).
6. F. Lehner, and K. Schubert, 'Party government and the political control of public policy', *European Journal of Political Research*, vol. 12, 1984, p. 133.
7. R. Hague, and M. Harrop. *Comparative Government and Politics*, 2nd edn. (London: Macmillan, 1987). p. 158.
8. N. Postman, *Amusing Ourselves to Death* (London: Heinemann, 1986).
9. See D. Meadows, et al., *Limits to Growth* (Cambridge, Mass.: Ballinger, 1972); D. Bell, *The Coming of Post-Industrial Society* (New York: Basic Books, 1973).
10. R. Inglehart, 'The silent revolution in Europe: inter-generational change in post-industrial societies' *American Political Science Review*, vol. 65, no. 4. December 1971, pp. 991–1017.
11. R. J. Dalton, *Environmental Groups in Western Europe* (New Haven, Conn.: Yale University Press, 1994), p. 187f.
12. See F. W. Bealey, J. Blondel and W. P. McCann, *Constituency Politics* (London: Faber, 1965) p. 405f.

Questions

1. 'The basic problem of modern democratic government lies with the voters. They want more public expenditure, but wish to pay fewer and lower taxes.' Discuss.
2. 'If you want to influence the government don't join a party: join a pressure group.' Discuss.

Section One

Bibliography

Chapter 1 Politics and political science

Blondel, J., *The Discipline of Politics* (London: Butterworth, 1981).

Brown, A., *Modern Political Philosophy* (Harmondsworth: Penguin 1986).

Crick, B., *In Defence of Politics* (Harmondsworth, Penguin, 1962).

Dahl, R. A., *Modern Political Analysis* (New Haven, Conn.: Yale University Press, 1963).

De Crespigny, A. and Minogue, K. (eds), *Contemporary Political Philosophers* (New York: Dodd Mead, 1975).

Dickerson, M. O. and Flanagan, T., *An Introduction to Government and Politics* (Toronto: Methuen, 1982).

Ferns, H. S. and Watkins, K. W., *What Politics is About* (London: Sherwood, 1985).

Heywood, A., *Politics* (London: Macmillan, 1997).

Laski, H. J., *An Introduction to Politics* (London: Allen & Unwin, 1931).

Laver, M., *Invitation to Politics* (Oxford: Martin Robertson, 1983).

Oppenheim, F., *Political Concepts* (Oxford: Blackwell, 1981).

Pickles, D., *Introduction to Politics* (London: Methuen, 1951).

Sedgwick, H., *The Elements of Politics* (London: Macmillan, 1891).

Wiseman, H. V. (ed.), *Political Science* (London: Routledge, 1967).

Chapter 2 Power, legitimacy and authority

Bachrach, P. and Baratz, M. S., *Power and Poverty: Theory and Practice* (Oxford: Oxford University Press, 1970).

Beetham, D., *The Legitimation of Power* (London: Macmillan, 1991).

Boulding, K. E., *Three Faces of Power* (Newbury Park, Calif.: Sage, 1989).

Clegg, S. R., *Frameworks of Power* (London: Sage, 1989).

Connolly, W. (ed.), *Legitimacy and the State* (Oxford: Blackwell, 1984).

Dahl, R. A., 'The concept of power', *Behavioural Science*, vol. 2, 1957, pp. 201–15.

Dowding, K., *Power* (Milton Keynes: Open University Press, 1996).

Eckstein, H. and Gurr, T. R., *Patterns of Authority* (New York: Wiley, 1975).

French, M., *Beyond Power* (New York: Summit Books, 1985).

Friedrich, C. J., *Tradition and Authority* (London: Pall Mall, 1972).

Galbraith, J. K., *The Anatomy of Power* (Boston, Mass.: Corgi Books, 1985).

Gaventa, J., *Power and Powerlessness* (Chicago: University of Illinois Press, 1980).

Habermas, J., *Legitimation Crisis*, (Boston, Mass.: Beacon Press, 1975).

Hay, C., 'Divided by a common language: political theory and the concept of power', *Politics*, vol. 17, no. 2, 1997, pp. 45–52.

Lukes, S., *Power: a Radical View* (London: Macmillan, 1974).

Nagel, J., *The Descriptive Analysis of Power* (New Haven, Conn.: Yale University Press, 1975).

Riker, W., 'Some ambiguities in the notion of power', *American Political Science Review*, vol. 58, 1964, pp. 341–9.

Russell, B., *Power: A New Social Analysis*, 2nd edn (New York: W. W. Norton, 1969).

Watt, E. D., *Authority* (London: Croom Helm, 1982).

Wrong, D. H., *Power: Its Forms, Bases and Uses* (Oxford: Blackwell, 1979).

Chapter 3 **The state**

Aristotle, *Politics* (London: Dent, 1959).

D'Entrèves, A., *The Notion of the State* (Oxford: Oxford University Press, 1967).

Dunleavy, P. and O'Leary, B., *Theories of the State* (London: Macmillan, 1987).

Dunn, J. (ed.), *Contemporary Crisis of the Nation State?* (Oxford: Blackwell, 1995).

Dyson, K., *The State Tradition in Western Europe* (Oxford: Martin Robertson, 1980).

Hall, J. and Ikenberry, J., *The State* (Milton Keynes: Open University Press, 1989).

Hegel, G. W. F., *The Philosophy of Right* (Oxford: Oxford University Press, 1967).

Held, D., *Political Theory and the Modern State* Cambridge: Polity Press, 1984).

Hilferding, R., *Finance Capital: A Study of the Latest Phase in Capitalist Development* (London: Routledge, 1981).

Hobbes, T., *Leviathan* (Harmondsworth, Penguin, 1968).

Hobson, J. A., *Imperialism* (London: Allen & Unwin, 1902).

Lenin, V. I., *Imperialism: The Highest Stage of Capitalism* (London: Lawrence & Wishart, 1916).

Locke, J., *Two Treatises of Government* (Cambridge: Cambridge University Press, 1963).

Machiavelli, N., *The Prince* (New York: Mentor, 1952).

Marx, K. and Engels, F., *Selected Works* (Moscow: Moscow Publishing House, 1950).

Miliband, R., *Marx and the State Socialist Register*, 1965, pp. 278–96.

Plato, *The Republic* (London: Everyman, 1906).

Poggi, G., *The Development of the Modern State* (London: Hutchinson, 1978).

Rousseau, J. J., *The Social Contract* (Harmondsworth: Penguin, 1968).

Skocpol, T., *States and Social Revolutions* (Cambridge: Cambridge University Press, 1979).

Skocpol, T., 'Bringing the state back in', in B. Evans et al. (eds), *Bringing the State Back In* (Cambridge: Cambridge University Press, 1985).

Tilly, C. (ed.), *The Formation of National States in Western Europe* (Princeton, NJ: Princeton University Press, 1975).

Treitschke, H. von, *Selections from Treitschke's Lectures on Politics* (Glasgow: Gowans & Gray, 1914).

Weldon, T. D., *States and Morals* (London: John Murray, 1946).

Chapter 4 **Political regimes**

Barber, B., *Strong Democracy* (Berkeley, Calif.: University of California Press, 1984).

Bealey, F. W., *Democracy in the Contemporary State* (Oxford: Oxford University Press, 1988).

Bobbio, N., *Democracy and Dictatorship* (Cambridge: Polity Press, 1989).

Bracher, K. D., *The German Dictatorship* (Harmondsworth: Penguin, 1973).

Burnheim, J., *Is Democracy Possible?* (Cambridge: Polity Press in association with Blackwell, 1985).

Crozier, M. J., Huntington, S. P. and Watanuki, J., *The Crisis of Democracy* (New York: New York University Press, 1975).

Dahl, R. A., *A Preface to Democratic Theory* (Chicago: University of Chicago Press, 1956).

Dahl, R. A., *Democracy and its Critics* (New Haven, Conn.: Yale University Press, 1989).

Dahl, R. A., *Dilemmas of Pluralist Democracy* (New Haven, Conn.: Yale University Press, 1982).

Daniels, R. V. (ed.), *The Stalin Revolution: Foundations of the Totalitarian Era* (Lexington, Mass.: Lexington Books, 1990).

Duncan, G. (ed.), *Democratic Theory and Practice* (Cambridge: Cambridge University Press, 1983).

Dupuy, A., *Haiti in the World Economy* (Boulder, Colo.: Colorado University Press, 1989).

Finer, S. E., *Man on Horseback* (Harmondsworth: Penguin, 1976).

Finley, M. J., *Democracy, Ancient and Modern* (New Brunswick, NJ: Chatto & Windus, 1973).

Friedrich, C. J. and Brzezinski, Z., *Totalitarian Dictatorship and Autocracy* (New York: Praeger, 1967).

Held, D., *Models of Democracy* (Cambridge: Polity Press, 1987).

Held, D. (ed.), 'Prospects for democracy', *Political Studies*, Special Issue, 1992.

Hill, R. J., *The Soviet Union: Politics, Economics and Society* (London: Pinter, 1985).

Kelleher, C. M., *Political-Military Systems* (Beverly Hills: Sage, 1974).

Lawson, F. H., *Bahrain: the Modernization of Autocracy* (Boulder, Colo.: Colorado University Press, 1989).

Lucas, J. R., *Democracy and Participation* (Harmondsworth: Penguin, 1976).

MacFarquhar, R. and Fairbank, J. K. (eds), *The Cambridge History of China*, Vol. 14: *The Emergence of Revolutionary China 1949–1965*; Vol. 15 *Revolutions within the Chinese Revolution 1966–1982* (Cambridge: Cambridge University Press, 1991).

Macpherson, C. B., *The Life and Times of Liberal Democracy* (Oxford: Oxford University Press, 1977).

Nordlinger, E. A., *Soldiers in Politics* (Englewood Cliffs, NJ: Glencoe Free Press, 1977).

Perlmutter, A., *The Military and Politics in Modern Times* (New Haven, Conn.: Yale University Press, 1977).

Plamenatz, J., *Democracy and Illusion* (London: Longman, 1973).

Rose, L. E., *The Politics of Bhutan* (Ithaca: Cornell University Press, 1977).

Sartori, G., *Democratic Theory* (New York: Praeger, 1965).

Talmon, J. L., *The Origins of Totalitarian Democracy* (London: Secker & Warbury, 1952).

Unger, A. L., *The Totalitarian Party* (Cambridge: Cambridge University Press, 1974).

Wang, J. C. F., *Contemporary Chinese Politics* (Englewood Cliffs, NJ: Pretince Hall, 1991).

Weale, A., *Democracy* (London: Macmillan, 1998).

White, G., *From Crisis to Crisis: the Chinese State in the Era of Economic Reform* (Basingstoke: Macmillan, 1991).

White, S., Pravda, A. and Gitelman, Z. (eds), *Developments in Soviet and Post-Soviet Politics, 3rd edn* (Basingstoke: Macmillan, 1994).

Chapter 5 **Problems of modern democratic government**

Bassnett, S., *Feminist Experiences: the Women's Movement in Four Cultures* (London: Allen & Unwin, 1990).

Choucri, N. (ed.), *Global Accord: Environmental Challenges and International Responses* (Cambridge, Mass.: MIT Press, 1993).

Claude, R. P. and Weston, B. H. (eds), *Human Rights in the World Community* (Philadelphia: University of Pennsylvania Press, 1989).

Dalton, R. J., *The Green Rainbow* (New Haven, Conn.: Yale University Press, 1994).

Dalton, R. J. and Kuechler, M. (eds), *Challenging the Political Order: New Social and Political Movements in Western Democracies* (Cambridge: Cambridge University Press, 1990).

Goodin, R. E., *Green Political Theory* (Cambridge: Polity Press, 1992).

Hooks, B., *Yearning: Race, Gender and Cultural Politics* (Boston, Mass.: South End Press, 1990).

Inglehart, R., *Culture Shift in Advanced Industrial Society* (Princeton, NJ: Princeton University Press, 1990).

Inglehart, R., *The Silent Revolution* (Princeton, NJ: Princeton University Press, 1977).

Kolinsky, E., *The Greens in West Germany* (Oxford: Berg, 1989).

Lovenduski, J. and Randall, V., *Contemporary Feminist Politics* (Oxford: Oxford University Press, 1993).

Muller-Rommel, F. (ed.), *New Politics in Western Europe: The Rise and Fall of Green Parties* (Boulder Colo.: Colorado University Press, 1989).

Petchesky, R. P., *Abortion and Womens Choice: the State, Sexuality and Reproductive Freedom* (London: Longman, 1984).

Rochon, T. R., *Mobilizing for Peace* (Princeton, NJ: Princeton University Press, 1988).

Smith, M. J., *Ecologism* (Milton Keynes: Open University Press, 1998).

Sylvester, C., *Feminist Theory and International Relations in a Postmodern Era* (Cambridge: Cambridge University Press, 1994).

Section Two

Comparative Institutions

Frank Bealey

6

The comparative approach

In what ways does comparison help us to understand things? When we compare (and contrast) we are looking for similarities and differences because in doing so we can better describe and explain what we are studying. Comparison is an essential part of any academic investigation. Moreover, it helps us to define what our purposes are.

Would we want to compare an elephant with a house? The differences are very great. One is alive and moves: the other is inanimate and immobile. Although the elephant is the largest of land animals it is a good deal smaller than most houses. The differences between them are so much greater than the similarities that we can conclude there is little point in comparing them. Indeed, the only value in the comparison is that it makes us think why we compare. It seems ridiculous to compare entities whose differences are extreme and readily apparent.

Consequently we usually compare entities in the same category. It follows that to do this we have to define the category. It would be much more sensible to compare elephants with other mammals, a well-defined category. If one wanted to go into more detail one could compare the African elephant with the Indian elephant. These are sub-categories of the category, 'elephant'.

The main category considered in these chapters is that of the political institutions of democratic states. A political institution is a public body with formally designated structures and is intended to regulate certain defined activities pertaining to the whole population. Governments, politicians and the law courts are political institutions. Their inter-relationships are defined in constitutions discussed in Chapter 7. Legislatures and executives are described in Chapters 8 and 9. Political parties, discussed in Chapter 10, are political associations, as are pressure groups. An association is a voluntary body, a grouping of people who have come together for the same common purpose, or least through their common identity. Associations will usually have rules and some defined form.

Every democratic state (see Chapters 3 and 4) has a political system, the recognised and regularised process by which it makes its decisions.

Numerous commentators have described the properties of a political system as follows:

1. Politics involves 'a persistent pattern of human relationships', [1] as Robert Dahl puts it. There is some continuity.
2. A political system exists within the framework of some sort of collectivity – an organisation, a community, a state.
3. There will be agreed procedures for making decisions binding upon the collectivity.
4. A political system makes binding decisions and promulgates them. Where there is disagreement politicians are indispensable.
5. A political system by no means makes all the decisions in a state. Many decisions are made in markets, courts of law and social institutions of all kinds. The political system has a general supervisory capacity for regulating such decisions and the way they are made. Therefore, as David Easton says, it allocates values in society.[2] Outcomes of the political system's decision-making will profit some, penalise others and not affect yet more.

6.1 Political investigation

There are two approaches to the study of politics, as outlined below.

6.1.1 The historical method

The traditional method, existing before political science, was through history. This could be pure narrative: a chronology of kings and queens and battles long ago. On the other hand, historians may be concerned with causality, an attempt to explain how present situations developed and why change took place, an approach still of value to political scientists. For example, it helps us to understand the present British political system if we examine the causes of its change from the system that existed before 1880. This will involve making a general comparison between one period and a later one, and within that numerous other comparisons between how factors such as political roles and political parties differed in the two periods.

6.6.2 The comparative method

The comparative method is a form of analysis which is the nearest political science comes to the methodology of the natural sciences. As already indicated, it involves examining a category and then making generalisations about it as a result of looking for the similarities and differences between its members. For instance, suppose our chosen category was 'democracies'. We would first need to define the term. About thirty-four of the world's 174 states would, by most definitions, be democracies. In looking for similarities one would need to be careful to avoid tautologies – it would not be enlightening to discover that they all had freedom of speech, because that is contained within the terms of the definition of democracy. If we can make a generalisation about some feature that they all share which is not present within the terms of the definition, then we are able to voice a scientific statement.

One of the major problems in the social sciences is that so many entities in the economy, society and the polity are always changing. It is difficult to find a constant. For example, if we start with the proposition 'all two-party systems result in stable government' we assume that this will be the case regardless of all other variables such as the social and cultural environments and historical period. If we discover that some two-party systems have not resulted in stable governments we will want to investigate the reasons for the differences between those with governmental stability and those without it. If stable government is common in some multi-party systems we might reach the conclusion that there is little or no relationship between the number of parties and whether there is governmental stability.

Of course, a natural scientist would probably be able to isolate a variable in a test-tube in order to examine it. In the social sciences there are so many variables affecting human behaviour, all possibly influencing one another, that it is rare to be able to advance absolutely impregnable explanations. One can only try to account for the phenomenon as precisely as possible. Furthermore, precision is only relative because though some political variables can be measured – people, votes, legislators, guns, money – many cannot. In political science the main basic concept, power, is unquantifiable, as we have noted.

Thus the comparative method is a common resort of political scientists. It has taken three forms, as discussed in the following sections.

6.2 Comparison of institutions

The conventional form of comparing states' political systems is by examining the operation and relationship of the three 'powers' between one country and another. The trinity of executive, legislative and judicial powers was the nineteenth-century framework for comparing political systems and these three terms are still used. The legislature made the laws, the executive implemented them and the judiciary made judgements upon them. An important notion was that the judiciary should be independent of, or separate from, the executive and legislative powers. But when the separation of powers, was used as a description of an institutional situation it always referred to a separation between the executive and the legislature. It meant they were independent of each other.

It is still customary to use these terms but with many reservations. One important feature of the United States' constitution, as explained later, is that the legislature and the executive are separated. Yet even in the USA their separation is only relative. One purpose of the Founding Fathers was to ensure that the 'Powers' were balanced against each other. So the pinnacle of the judiciary is the Supreme Court, but its members are nominated by the President. The upper house of the legislature, the Senate, can endorse or reject the nominations. All three powers check one another. Again, the Supreme Court's judgements often affect the workings of the constitution. It has been called the third legislative chamber. Its rulings have tended to restrict the powers of the legislature and executive and to strengthen its own. For example, by its verdict in *Marbury* v. *Madison* 1803 it claimed for itself the right to declare legislation unconstitutional. This right is certainly not made explicit in the constitution.

A more general objection to the conventional form of comparison is that it lacks reality in the twentieth century. Executives have so much increased their powers to the detriment of legislatures that law-making is virtually a function of governments. As Franz Lehner and Klaus Schubert write:

> Parties and parliaments do not possess to any degree the necessary information, processing and planning with regard to highly complex problems, nor do they have a sufficently professionalized personnel.[3]

Consequently governments draft most important legislation and parliaments merely formalize it. Perhaps only the US Congress is an exception to this generalisation.

The conventional approach is an example of structural functional explanation, that is the political system is analysed in terms of its structures and the functions they possess (see below). The trouble is that the classical structures and functions – the 'conventional trinity' of legislature, executive and judiciary – is not, in the modern world, a good enough explanatory model.

6.3 Comparison of political behaviour

A more recent approach perceives political systems as best studied through the political activities that take place within them. These can be compared across different countries. We can compare the political styles of countries and we can compare their political actors – their voters, activists, leaders, political parties and pressure groups.

6.3.1 Political actors

Political actors, at least those who are people, can be dealt with in terms of political stratification. By this method people are divided into layers depending on their level of political participation.

1. At the bottom are the vast mass of most citizens who take no active part in politics. About a quarter do not vote at all and for the others casting their vote is the only active part they take. They are bound to be an important subject of study, however, and one can compare them in the same country at different elections, or in different countries using the same categories such as age, gender and social class. Such studies have revealed rather similar trends between one country and another. For example, the most well-educated are the most comprehending of the democratic political process. The lower their income the more likely it is that people will vote for radical parties.
2. At the next level are the political activists, those who have functions in the localities selecting candidates and assisting in electoral organisation. They can be compared as between different parties as well as between different countries.
3. Political leaders, those with full-time engagement in politics, are likely to differ most. Yet it is possible to compare them and make generalisations about them in terms of their psychologies and leadership qualities.

Turning from individual political actors to groups, we can also have comparative studies of political parties and pressure groups.

1. With parties the study can take several forms. A system with two major parties compared with one with numerous parties will reveal contrasting electoral strategies. Where a party knows that its limited voting support is bound to prevent it ruling by itself it will probably confine itself to preserving its assured support

rather than attempting to win new voters with new policies. In a two-party system the party out of office expects to govern on its own. To become the government it must strive to win over people who have not previously supported it. A comparison of party systems in Britain and Holland reveals such differences. (see Chapter 10).

2. It is possible also to compare attitudes of parties to governing. In the multi-party situation parties are likely to be less enthusiastic about governing because it will involve bargaining with other parties to form a coalition, compromising about policies and so betraying their election promises. It will lead to a difficult relationship between the leaders who receive posts in the government and other members in the legislature who do not. In the two-party situation there is one-party government, while the other party is the alternative government able to frame policies in the expectation of putting them into practice if it wins the next election. (This is more an account of an ideal rather than of what actually happens.)

3. Comparative studies of pressure groups examine their general behaviour in different countries, or the different behaviours of the same type of pressure group in two or more countries. Because the goals of pressure groups tend to be specific, and because they do not aspire to participate in government, they differ less than the same types of political parties. Churches, trade unions, business organisations, groups dealing with children or animals, civil liberty associations, farmers, unions and ecological groups, all will have agendas like their counterparts in other countries. Much of their contrasting behaviour will depend on their different conditions of access to the political process. For example, French and British pressure-group leaders will not usually find it profitable to lobby ordinary parliamentarians because the latter are constitutionally prevented from introducing any legislation involving the spending of money. Only governments can do this. By contrast, in the USA any member of the House of Representatives can introduce a bill enabling money to be spent. Therefore an American pressure group may try to persuade a majority (218) of Representatives to vote for its policies.

6.3.2   Political styles

'Style' is not a very precise word. The dictionary defines it as 'a distinctive or characteristic manner; a manner of behaving'. Political style refers to the manner in which political matters are conducted. It differs greatly from one country to another.

Political style is significant for both citizens and politicians. How politicians speak and act and relate to others may well depend on whether they expect support and how much they expect. A politician who depends greatly on the support of other politicians – a very common situation – will be involved in balancing or brokerage. He or she will proceed very carefully, often not expressing views explicitly. Indeed, obscurity may be an important subterfuge for the broker-politician. Conversely a political leader who is secure in the expectation of continuing in power, or one who has no expectation of power, may speak and act forthrightly and decisively.

Political style, however, may well be matter of a country's culture. The rhetoric of the politicians, their modes of appeal and the symbols they use may be a reflection of their expectations of the public's response. A country's political style is portrayed in the relationships between the politicians and the voters. For example, the American style of politics is said to be populistic. An American appealing to the voters in order to be successful needs to be a 'regular guy'. Intellectuals are at a disadvantage. American politicians should be folksy, hail-fellow-well-met, not visibly interested in the arts. Thus in the 1992 election campaign President Bush who was a Connecticut Yankee, a patrician who traced his family back to the seventeenth century and a graduate of Yale, an Ivy League university, masqueraded as a Texan and attacked his opponent, Governor Clinton of Arkansas, a hill-billy state, for having spent a year at Oxford University. The need to appear unsophisticated and guileless reflects the low status that politics has as an activity in the USA. In Europe, where it has a rather higher status, the voters often like to feel that their politicians are a little superior, especially better educated, than themselves.

Political style is also reflected in the relationships between political leaders, particularly between opponents. Their dialogue may vary considerably from one democracy to another. Civility may characterise some and rude abuse others. British political opponents treat each other with polite hostility in the House of Commons. Outside the chamber they are often on friendly terms and Christian names are commonly used.

To sum up: the behavioural approach covers the larger part of political life. One can argue that the political parties and pressure groups – and political behaviour generally – is the real stuff of politics and much more important than political institutions. Yet the institutions, the framework within which individuals and collectivities act, facilitating them and restricting them, may be crucial in defining the politics of a country. Suppose that the British decided to replace their collective executive by a popularly elected individual executive as in the USA. There is no doubt this would profoundly change British politics. We know this because it happened in France in 1962 and it changed the nature of French politics and French political behaviour.

6.4 Functional comparison

The functional approach seems to make two claims. First, it claims to be more realistic in its analysis because it has moved away from a rigidly political science treatment of politics. Second, it perceives politics in a universalistic way, taking account of elements which are outside the formal political system, looking at societal and cultural factors and asking, 'What roles do they have in the political regime?' 'Regime', as here defined, has a wider connotation than 'system'.[4] It implies a consideration of attitudes and values.

By no means all models that claim to be functional, however, demonstrate this second approach. A functional scheme can be devised to encompass the activities of political parties and pressure groups as follows:

1. Articulation of issues
2. Recruitment of political leaders
3. Combination of issues and leaders
4. Formulation of policies
5. Allocation of priorities
6. Ordering of agendas
7. Conversion process
8. Implementation
9. Adjudication of laws

Here 1 to 6 are the functions of the opinion-forming and policy-shaping forces in society and 7 to 9 are the functions of the formal political system.

Such models, however, omit the question of how to maintain the system. The development of new states, especially in Africa and Asia from the 1960s onwards, and the collapse of the Congo into anarchy, widened the comparative efforts of political scientists. Gabriel Almond approached the problem of finding a framework to use for the comparison of all states by asking the question: 'What are the basic functions?' His answer was that they were integration and adaptation.[5] Such basic functions could only be supported by structures outside the formal political system – indeed, outside political life as it is generally conceived. Hence such an approach looks at the society and culture of a country and asks: 'What roles do social agents and their values have in supporting a political regime?'

Almond considered that integration and adaptation were pursued more specifically through four input functions and three output functions. These were:

Input functions:
1. Political socialisation and recruitment
2. Interest articulation
3. Interest aggregation
4. Political communication

Output functions:
5. Rule-making
6. Rule application
7. Rule adjudication

In considering function 1, he developed with Sidney Verba the concept of 'political culture'.[6] He took structures rather for granted, but functions 2, 3 and 4 are clearly the realm of social and political groups and political parties. Functions 5, 6 and 7, as Almond acknowledged, will rely on structures very much like the conventional trinity.

David Easton in *The Political System* and later works[7] was much concerned with the survival and maintenance of political systems. An early version of his model (later ones were more sophisticated) is as follows:

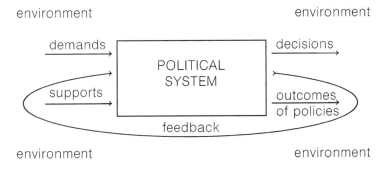

The model obviously owes a great deal to computer systems. It could almost be used to depict the legislative process, but if this were the case the box would be Parliament. Instead it is something much more general. The model does, however, bear some resemblance to the policy-making process because at the output end decisions and policies will often be embodied in laws. 'Feedback' describes responses to the implementation of policies, responses which may, in turn, become inputs. They may add to demands or they may increase support.

At the input end Easton's model is more ambitious than earlier models. The demands or pressures on the system and the supports for it can be both specific and highly abstract. For example, the methods of political socialisation and recruiting leaders can be seen as supports. The desire for more wealth might be a demand and so might the yearning for more national glory. Some demands and supports, moreover, may be external. The balance between demands and supports is crucial for the equilibrium of the system. Too much pressure from demands that the supports cannot manage will lead to 'demand overload': a weakening of supports may result in 'support failure'. Clearly it is also important that the conversion process taking place in the box works effectively.

These later structural-functional approaches are intended for comparing the survival and adaptation potentialities of very different countries. Primitive countries will have primitive conversion processes and their supports may be weak though demands upon them, especially for modernisation, may be exceptional. For example, soldiers may be such a regime's best support. Fail to pay them and they revolt bringing the whole system crashing down. By contrast highly institutionalised countries will have strong civilian control over the armed forces. Here political socialisation may be an important support with the family as the main agent in socialising new citizens in the values that uphold the political system. Extensive family breakdown may then be very destabilising for the system because it may change the political culture, the set of beliefs, attitudes and values that people hold towards the political regime in their country.

Political culture is not a model of a method of approach. It is a concept. It is not an explanation of a country's politics, though it may be a useful beginning to say 'country A's problems are the result of its unevenly developed political culture'. Scholars who find that an insufficient and unsatisfactory explanation (as all political scientists should), will want to examine why its political culture is so. The comparative method will again be relevant to such an investigation.

Comparison by the structural-functional approach is all-encompassing, involving very many variables. It is much absorbed with fundamental questions of regime survival, enquiring why some regimes have collapsed while others have endured. In consequence it is of little help for many of the other comparisons political scientists want to make between regimes of great stability. Hence its universal application may vitiate its usefulness. One could use it, for instance, to compare the USA and Monaco: they are both states with political systems. This would not quite be like comparing an elephant with a house, but it might be rather like comparing an elephant with a flea. In what follows all the approaches to comparative politics are used except David Easton's which is inappropriate to our purposes.

Notes

1. R. A. Dahl, *Modern Political Analysis* (Englewood Cliffs, NJ: Prentice Hall, 1963) p. 6.
2. D. Easton, *The Political System* (New York: Knopf, 1953), p. 146.
3. F. Lehner and K. Schubert, 'Party government and the political control of public policy', *European Journal of Political Research*, vol. 12, 1984, p. 133.
4. Especially since Easton published his 1953 work some have used 'system' as a wider embracing term than 'regime'. But I have preferred to use the term 'model' to describe it and similar models.
5. G. A. Almond and J. Coleman, *The Politics of the Developing Areas* (Princeton, NJ: Princeton University Press, 1960).
6. G. A. Almond and S. Verba, *The Civic Culture* (Princeton, NJ: Princeton Unversity Press, 1963).
7. *A Framework for Political Analysis* (Englewood Cliffs, NJ, 1965) and *A Systems Analysis of Political Life* (New York: Wiley, 1965). The diagram is from the latter, p. 112.

Questions

1. What are the advantages and disadvantages of the comparative method?
2. Why are political institutions easier to compare than political ideologies?

7

Constitutions

Constitutions provide a framework within which political activity takes place. I shall assume that, as we are dealing with democratic politics and the acceptance of the rule of law, political forces operate without attempting to break out of their framework. The study of a constitution will by no means tell us everything about the political life of a country; on the other hand, it is indispensable to such a purpose.

No one has ever provided a better typology for comparing constitutions than the late political scientist and constitutional lawyer, K. C. Wheare. He perceived six variables which help us to classify constitutions, as discussed in the sections which follow.[1]

7.1 Written or unwritten

This distinction really hangs on the definition of the word constitution. It is commonly used to describe a set of rules embodied in a document. So a constitution must be written.

The whole matter is bedevilled, however, by the British constitution. It is difficult to deny that there is such a thing, because it has been discussed at length for two centuries. Montesquieu set the fashion among continental Europeans of expressing great admiration for the British constitution. Numerous books have been written with that title. But there is no document. So the term is used to include a set of rules, conventions and laws which regulate political behaviour in Britain. If one had to make a list of them they would comprise the Act of Settlement 1701 regulating succession to the throne, the Act of Union 1707 by which Britain was founded with Scotland being joined to England and Wales, the Parliament Acts of 1911 and 1949 which restrict the powers of the House of Lords, and successive Representation of the People Acts defining the voting rights and regulating electoral matters. Important conventions would include the Monarch being obliged to sign a bill passed by Parliament and the Prime Minister resigning office when defeated at an election.

Almost all other countries have written constitutions – indeed, it is difficult to envisage initiating a new state without a written constitution. Since the US Constitution of 1787, with the exception of Israel, this has been the usual practice.

It is argued that it is a great advantage for a democracy to have a written constitution because it proclaims to all citizens the rules under which they are governed. Many constitutions like the Indian or the American embody a statement of principles, a Bill of Rights, enunciating certain civic freedoms and giving the constitution a sanctity. It is said every American schoolchild can repeat a few hallowed phrases. Hence where civil rights such as freedom of speech or of the press are vulnerable to the actions of authority, a Bill of Rights may be a valuable protection. Fundamental guarantees in Bills of Rights, however, are supposed to be absolutes. If they become relative their purpose is subverted. It may then become demoralising when citizens desire protection for their rights but they are denied it because some special reason, such as a national emergency, is advanced.

For example, Clause 1 of the American Bill of Rights (the first ten amendments to the Constitution dating from 1791) reads 'Congress shall make no law abridging freedom of speech or of the Press'. This is a very clear statement on which, one might think, no gloss could possibly be put. Yet twice in this century Congress has passed laws which led to these freedoms being abridged. Convictions under the Smith Act 1917 and the Macarran Acts 1950 and 1951 should have resulted in the Supreme Court, to which appeals were made, ruling them unconstitutional. Instead, the Supreme Court, in an atmosphere during the First World War of 'spy scares', evolved the 'clear and present danger' theory by which at moments of national peril the absolute can become relative. But it is in times of stress and crisis that people with unpopular minority opinions may most require protection against what Mill called 'the tyranny of the majority'.[2] Then what appears to be a constitutional guarantee is not guaranteed.

From the above one may induce, first, that constitutions may not always mean what their wording appears to state; second, that there may be good arguments for Bills of Rights, but one should not expect too much from them; and third, that how written constitutions are interpreted is very important and therefore the law and lawyers are likely to have important roles. Constitutional law thus becomes separated from ordinary law.

7.2   Monarchist or republican

At first sight this may appear to be an important category, but today it is of little significance. It is true that monarchist democracies seem to be more stable than republican democracies, though this is not always the case. Greece could hardly have been called stable when it was a monarchy and it is not very stable now as a republic. Stability really stems from other factors. Many monarchies owe their preservation to a stable economy and political system. The monarchy is an indicator of stability, not a cause.

Furthermore, the distinction tells us little about the respective political systems of two countries. Britain is a monarchy and Italy a republic, but the Italian President's constitutional function is very similar to that of the British monarch. In this context it is important to note that while Italy's Head of State is a President, Italy does *not* have a presidential form of government.

7.3   Presidential or Parliamentary

A presidential form of government has a President, but he is not only head of state, a largely honorific role. He is also the chief executive and popularly elected. In classic presidential government, of which the USA is the archetype, the executive and legislature are completely separated. The US Constitution is quite explicit about this. Article 2, Section 6, Clause 2 says: 'No senator or representative shall . . . be appointed to any civil office under the authority of the United States', and goes on: 'No person holding any office under the United States shall be a member of either House . . .'. The so-called 'separation of powers' is twice affirmed.

The consequences for US government are vast. The President may find himself enforcing new laws with which he disagrees. It is true that he can veto legislation, but the legislature, Congress, can then over-rule his veto by a two-thirds vote of both Houses (Article 1, Section 7, Clause 3). Moreover, the separation of powers deprives the President of ministers who can defend him in Congress – they cannot speak there let alone attend sittings. The President may be commander-in-chief of the armed forces, but Congress declares war. Presidential appointments are subject to endorsement by the Senate.

There is no separation of powers in parliamentary government of which Britain is the classic example. It is only a convention that Cabinet ministers should sit in Parliament, but invariably they do, providing the closest possible link between executive and legislature. Most ministers sit in the House of Commons and a few in the House of Lords, taking part in debates and supervising the passage of government legislation. As British governments can usually depend on a parliamentary majority government bills invariably become acts, though with a few amendments. The ministers, who usually belong to the same party, are 'collectively responsible', meaning that they all support government policy and must not oppose it while they are in office. A statement from one of them can be taken as a government statement. They are also dismissible by a majority vote of the House of Commons on an important issue and defeat in a vote on even an unimportant issue will probably lead to a vote of confidence. Such responsibility to the legislature is usually taken as the touchstone of parliamentary government. A British government presents a solid front to the world. It has little to fear from Parliament and usually can only be dismissed by the voters at the next election.

There are few countries, however, where parliamentary government functions as it does in Britain. It is said that imitation is the sincerest form of flattery. Admiration for the British constitution was at one time common throughout the world. It was seen as the most stable and strong democratic government. Consequently new constitution drafters sought to ensure the same sure foundation for their own government by writing the responsibility of the executive to the legislature into their constitutions. For example, Article 54 of the Weimar Constitution (in Germany 1918–33) stipulated: 'The Chancellor of the Reich and the Ministers of the Reich must enjoy the confidence of the Reichstag. If the Reichstag expresses its lack of confidence in either the Chancellor or the Ministers by an explicit vote, he or they must resign.' The Finnish Constitution, which owed much to Weimar, laid down that the Cabinet was responsible to Parliament (the Eduskunta) by Articles 36 and 43. The French Fourth Republic's constitution attempted to ensure greater governmental stability than the Third by similarly embodying government responsibility in Articles 48, 49, 50 and 51.

None of these attempts resulted in governmental stability of the British kind which is not derived from any constitutional characteristic. No law, no inflexible rule can bring it about. It is a feature of the politics of a country. Generally speaking parliamentary government does not ensure stability where there are many parties. A multi-party system implies coalition government which is inherently, though not inevitably, unstable (see Chapter 10). Those thinking that government responsibility to parliament, written into their constitutions, would give them strong and stable executives misunderstood the nature of the

British system whose stable executive is a result of the two-party situation. The misconception has been called 'rationalised parliamentarianism'. But governmental stability is not a matter of translating reason into law. It is a matter of politics.

7.4   Flexible or rigid

Constitutions may also be classified according to the method by which they can be amended. Those that are amended easily are called flexible: those that are amended with difficulty are called rigid. Extreme flexibility characterises those which may be amended in the same way as any other law.

From what has been said it is clear that the British constitution is flexible. So is the constitution of New Zealand which can be amended by passing a resolution in the New Zealand parliament. On the other hand, Australia has a rigid constitution for it is amended by a referendum of the whole country in which there must be not only a majority of citizens approving, but also a majority in four of the six states. The USA has a similar provision. A constitutional amendment must be passed not only by a two-thirds vote of both Houses of Congress, but also by majority votes in three-quarters (38) of the states who may use either legislative votes or special conventions to consider an amendment. If they do not want to, however, they do not need to consider it. Switzerland has a similar process.

These last three countries are federations, but not only federal constitutions are rigid. To amend the constitution of the Fifth French Republic a resolution must be put forward by the President, though on a proposal by the Prime Minister. After the amending bill is prepared and debated by the National Assembly and the Senate it can become part of the constitution in two ways:

1. If passed by both chambers and then passed by a national referendum;
2. If passed by a three-fifths vote of both chambers meeting together it then needs no referendum.

This classification may help us to compare constitutional structures, but the comparison does not tell us much about the propensity to revise constitutions. The Swiss often have referendums and alter their constitutions frequently. In Australia thirty-two amendments were submitted to the nation in the first seventy-four years of the constitution but only five were passed. In 207 years of the US constitution twenty-six amendments have been passed. All three countries have rigid constitutions, but readiness to change in Switzerland is considerable compared with reluctance in the USA and downright obduracy in Australia.

7.5 Supreme or not supreme

A supreme constitution is one which cannot be amended within the sole competence of the legislature. Part of the amending process is outside the ambit of the parliament. Hence the British and New Zealand constitutions are clearly not supreme. Most rigid constitutions will involve other than legislative processes. This applies to the USA, Australia, Switzerland, Ireland and Denmark whose constitutions all stipulate referendums. Therefore they are all supreme.

Sometimes it may be difficult to decide whether a constitution is supreme or not. Belgium is particularly interesting. The Belgian Parliament designates which part of the constitution (1970) should be revised. Both Houses are then dissolved and an election takes place. If after that at least two-thirds of both houses meet and pass the amendment by a two-thirds majority it becomes part of the constitution. Clearly Belgium has a rigid constitution but is it supreme? As the legislature only votes on the actual document it could be argued that the Belgian constitution is not supreme, but because of the provision for an election, in which the amendment is bound to be a major issue, the opposite could be argued.

7.6 Federal or unitary

Finally constitutions may be classified according to the way in which power is territorially divided. With a federal constitution numerous powers are given up by the central government to sub-units of the country called states, provinces or cantons. With classical federalism, as in the USA, there is coordinate authority: in their separate spheres of control the sub-units are paramount. They cannot be over-ruled in some areas. The governor of each state has the right to reprieve death sentences on murderers and the President has no jurisdiction over the matter. Each of the fifty American states has its own constitution with which the federal government and Congress cannot interfere.

Federal states have several common characteristics.

1. Their births usually have been through integration by negotia-

tion. They have thus been marked by something like a contractual agreement. Different territories who wished to retain some of their sovereignty came together and set up a federal union. In consequence there is usually equality in some respect between the sub-units. Frequently, while the lower chamber of the legislature is elected on a basis of population, the upper chamber consists of an equal number of representatives from each sub-unit. This equality is a price that has been paid to persuade the sub-units to relinquish some of their sovereignty. The American, Australian and Swiss constitutions all have this feature. The German does not, but the smaller German *Länder* are considerably over-represented in the Bundesrat, the upper chamber.

2. All federal countries have written constitutions. Many intergovernmental relationships are inevitable in federal countries and need to be defined. This can only be done in a written document specifying how functions and powers are divided. The American Founding Fathers were quite meticulous in doing this, but the states rights people were not satisfied and their leader, Thomas Jefferson, in 1791 secured the passage of the first ten amendments known as the Bill of Rights. The 10th reads: 'The powers not delegated to the United States by the Constitution, nor prohibited to it by the states, are reserved to the states respectively or to the people'. This was intended to ensure that anything that had been forgotten in respect of powers by the drafters of the Constitution should never revert to the federal government in Washington.

3. The effect of this complexity is that in all federations law and lawyers are important. Federalism means legalism, it is often said. Someone has to rule on the disputes arising from all the documentation and all the relationships. This can only be a higher constitutional court. All federal systems have supreme courts which rule on constitutional conflicts. Their rulings may be concerned with individuals rights, as with cases arising from the US Bill of Rights, or they may be in connection with disputes between the sub-units or, more probably, between the governments of the sub-units and the central government.

All constitutions which are not federal are unitary. There will be sub-units in unitary countries, though frequently they will not be mentioned in the constitution. Sometimes local governments in unitary countries will have considerable powers, but these are subject to erosion by the central government. All laws of any importance will usually emanate from the centre. Very often local governments will act as delivery agents for central government services, implementing central decisions.

A recent trend in the larger Western European unitary countries has been towards regional government. France has twenty-two regions which, since 1982, have democratically elected councils. The regions of Italy and Spain have a good deal more autonomy than the French regions. This has received some encouragement from European Community policy which has obliged countries to divide themselves into regions for some aid purposes. In Britain much administration is devolved to Scotland (which also had regions from 1975 to 1996), Wales and Northern Ireland. Edinburgh, Cardiff and Belfast have government departments for this purpose and by the beginning of the new millennium they will have parliaments. Britain then will not necessarily be a federal country, but it will be less highly centralised.

7.7 Value of classifying constitutions

To what extent is there value in classifying constitutions in this way? There is, I believe, considerable value. It conveys a great deal to be able to say of a country, like the USA, that its constitution is written, republican, presidential, rigid, supreme and federal. On the other hand, as you will have gathered by now, the classification has its limitations.

In the first place, like all typologies, it is only an aid to learning and explaining. The categories must not be taken to be iron boxes. Constitutional/legal formulations can have different interpretations and, more importantly, they do not tell us everything about the workings of the political system. The political forces operating within the framework will alter the outlines of the framework.

Second, there were forces which took part in the making of all constitutions. This is not surprising because, after all, constitutions are not found under gooseberry bushes. They derive from the pressures of various groups and ideas at a particular time. Two examples may illustrate this point – the US Constitution and that of the Fifth French Republic.

7.7.1   The American Constitution

The American Constitution was shaped by three sets of factors: economic, historical and ideological.

Economic factors

Different economic interests were in conflict when representatives of the thirteen British ex-colonies met at the Philadelphia convention which drew up the constitution. Some of them had grievances against the Articles of Confederation 1777, a sort of alliance. The ex-colonies with a more commercial interest in the North clashed with those with an agricultural basis in the South. Moreover, the South was anxious to preserve slavery as an institution. The small ex-colonies were afraid that the large ones would overrule them. All of them wished to protect the rights of property.

The constitution is a product of all these pressures. It assured free trade between the states and not only accepted slavery, but allowed the more sparsely populated Southern states to count their slaves as three-fifths of a person for purposes of representation. Each state was allowed to decide the terms of its suffrage. The whole tenor of the document was adverse to popular government: only the House of Representatives was to be popularly elected. In this way property-owners were able to feel more secure.

Historical factors

The constitution was a product of a century of experience. Many of the states had practised viable forms of representative institutions inherited from Britain. Local government had become much more democratic than in the home country, but there were British features persisting after independence, for example the Elizabethan Poor Law. There were also British features retained in the constitution, such as two chambers and a head of state (though elected). Early presidents were not seen as active executives except in case of war. Moreover, the Bill of Rights was an echo of the English Bill of Rights 1688, also a statement of certain civic freedoms. Furthermore, executive power was separated from legislative in the way described. This was regarded as the true British position which the British had deserted. They had ruled in an arbitrary fashion and the colonists' rights as Englishmen had been infringed. The Founding Fathers intended to ensure this would not happen again and separated and balanced the powers accordingly.

Ideological factors

The ideological factors were closely linked to the historical factors. The notion of the separation of powers was derived from Montesquieu who believed that Britain was much freer than France because its parliament and government were separate.[3] Montesquieu's analysis was quite incorrect but was widely accepted in the eighteenth century and was certainly the belief of the Founding Fathers. Moreover, the influence of John Locke, the prophet of the English Revolution of 1688, was very much apparent. Locke's insistence on rights, including the rights of property, were enshrined in many phrases in the Declaration of Independence. The American revolutionaries were concerned to assert their traditional rights. They wanted to exclude any arbitrary element from ruling and institute a 'government of laws and not of men'. Respect for law permeated the whole proceedings at Philadelphia. It was a very conservative revolution. Unlike the French Revolution, the American Revolution was not inspired by the notion of popular sovereignty.

7.7.2   The Constitution of the Fifth French Republic

This constitution represented a compromise between different traditions represented by different groups of people. Between the defeat of France with the collapse of the Third Republic in 1940 and the inauguration of the Fifth in 1958 a debate took place from which a hybrid constitution emerged.

The predominant political tradition in France springs from the Revolution of 1789 and its early institutions. It embodies the Jacobin notion that the people are sovereign. Consequently elected representatives of the people reflect this popular sovereignty, and therefore government must express the will of parliament. The phrase that conveys this ideal is 'government by parliament'. In practice it makes the exercise of governmental authority very difficult. It needs little experience of politics to see that five or six hundred individuals with divided aims will find making national decisions almost impossible.

Opposed to this basic ideology of the French Left there was a right-wing opposition which can be divided into two general tendencies: Monarchist and Bonapartist. The former had never accepted the Revolution, but was of little account by 1945 because of association with the collaborationist Vichy regime. The Bonapartist tradition accepted the achievements of the post-revolutionary settlement many of which were the product of Napoleon I (Emperor 1809–15). This tradition was semi-authoritarian, meritocratic, attached to centralised government, under Napoleon III (Emperor 1852–70) known as the 'administrative state', and sceptical of popular sovereignty and representative democracy.

It was generally agreed, however, by informed students of politics that the weakness of the French executive and the strength of the French legislature had been responsible for governmental indecision and instability since 1870. What was needed, therefore, was to strengthen the executive and, correspondingly, to weaken the legislature.

Most Frenchmen looked to the British example for their guidance.

Britain had not crumbled in 1940, they considered, because it had a strong and stable executive. Already in 1941 a group of senior lawyers of vaguely left-wing persuasion began an underground seminar to consider what should follow the war. It was generally accepted that there could be no return to the Third Republic and its lower house with a fixed term of four years so that every deputy knew he could not lose his seat until a stipulated date. Party discipline had scarcely existed and votes of censure could easily be moved. Consequently there were often successful attempts by ambitious deputies who wished to be ministers to bring the inevitable coalition governments down. This made it very difficult to make decisions.

The underground group, known as the Comité Général d'Experts, entrusted the task of drafting proposals to Michel Debré, a young Jewish lawyer who had escaped from a prisoner-of-war camp. He joined De Gaulle who sent him in 1942 back to France as his agent.[4] The draft that emerged was an approximation to the British system. There was to be a legislature with narrow powers. It would have no specialist committees (each of which would monitor the activities of one government department.) The opportunities to move votes of censure on the government would be restricted. The Prime Minister would have the right to dissolve parliament. A stronger President, elected for twelve years, would arbitrate between government and parliament.

Most of these features were incorporated into the constitution of the Fourth Republic which, in Articles 48 and 51, stipulated government responsibility to parliament and a restricted prime ministerial right to dissolution. Yet it was less stable than the Third which at least had flexibility. After 1945 the highly disciplined mass parties, two of which – the Communists and the Gaullists – did not accept the regime, made decision-making even more precarious. In desperation in 1958, having come to an impasse, the National Assembly elected De Gaulle as the last prime minister of the Fourth Republic. His task was to replace it.

Three groups were especially involved in the deliberations of the Constituent Assembly set up in 1958 to draft the new constitution. (The Communists, neither Left nor Right but East, as people said, were in complete opposition.)

1.   One group was composed of the old politicians of the Third Republic. De Gaulle despised them. He thought their political habits, if not they themselves, had been responsible for national humiliation in 1940–44. In order to conciliate them the Preamble of the constitution of the Fourth Republic and its Articles 1–3, largely of symbolic significance, were incorporated into the new constitution, as well as the form of the upper house the Senate –

unchanged except in name. (In the Fourth Republic it had been called the Council of the Republic.) It was to be elected in the same way, that is indirectly by local government councillors. For this reason it had always been a chamber representing *les notables*, small-town political worthies, often mayors. Consequently it remained a fortress for the old political parties and subsequently was the main source of opposition to De Gaulle. Otherwise what was retained from the former constitution was unimportant for the process of government.

2. The Left and Left-Centre politicians who had led the Fourth Republic were disappointed by its failure to provide the strong government they wanted and devastated by its ignominious collapse after only twelve years. They distrusted the presidential regime advocated by De Gaulle and were dubious of his allegiance to the Republican tradition.

3. The Gaullists were a mixed group. Their leader never made public statements about constitutional details, but he did condemn the irresponsibility of the political parties and advocated strong authority as the remedy for France. In spite of his anti-Americanism the General may have been impressed by President Roosevelt making decisive moves during the war. (Roosevelt could do this as Commander-in-Chief.) Moreover, De Gaulle perceived that an American-style presidency would give him the chance to operate on the world scene in a decisive way. Hence he dedicated himself to advocating presidential government as the institution needed to rejuvenate France. He was probably unaware how powerful Congress was, but a strong legislature was precisely what he did not want. The main task of drafting the constitution De Gaulle entrusted to Michel Debré and it is remarkable how much of his 1943 draft can be identified in it.

Hence the constitution of the Fifth Republic provided for a strong President, largely at first by restricting the powers of the legislature. Later in 1962, as a result of a referendum, the first President, De Gaulle, secured an amendment to allow the president to be elected by popular vote. Thus both the National Assembly and the President owed their democratic legitimacy to the verdict of the people, though in elections at different times. In many ways, therefore, the constitution now seems to have an American provenance. There were some concessions to the old regime – the Senate remained as before – but otherwise British characteristics were also evident.

The constitution is a curious hybrid between presidential and parliamentary government. Article 20 says that the government is responsible to Parliament and that the Prime Minister 'shall direct the opera-tion of the Government'. This might be regarded as ensuring parlia-mentary government if Articles 7 and 8 did not say that the president appoints the prime minister who is responsible to the president. France has a strange two-headed executive. But there is certainly executive power and legislative weakness. The latter is ensured by Articles 38–47 which provide all sorts of restrictions preventing parliament from interfering too much with government proposals. Over 80 per cent of the voters accepted it in a referendum. Presidential power was incorporated into the Fifth French Republic's constitution, but Con-gressional strength which balances it in the USA was excluded. An executive was therefore produced which is usually even more powerful than the British.

To sum up: constitutions can never escape the circumstances of their foundation in which conflicting groups play their part.

Notes

1. K. C. Wheare, *Modern Constitutions*, 2nd edn (Oxford: Oxford University Press, 1966). These six categories are his.
2. J. S. Mill, *On Liberty* (London: Thinkers' Library, 1945; first published, 1859), p. 5.
3. C. de S. Montesquieu, *The Spirit of the Laws* (English trans. New York: Hafner, 1949; first published, 1748).
4. G. Wright, *The Reshaping of French Democracy* (London: Methuen, 1950). Other works on the drafting of the Fifth republic's constitution are M. Duverger, *La Cinquième République* (Paris: Presses Universitaires de France, 1959); P. M. Williams and M. Harrison, *De Gaulle's Republic* (Harlow: Longman, 1960); J. A. Laponce, *The Govern-ment of the Fifth Republic* (Berkeley, Calif.: University of California Press, 1961).

Questions

1. 'Federalism means legalism.' Discuss.
2. What are the differences between parliamentary and presidential government? In which category would you place the French Fifth Republic?

8

Parliaments

The derivation of the word 'parliament' is from the verb 'to speak'. Sometimes they have been pejoratively described as 'talking shops'. John Stuart Mill's term was a 'congress of opinions'.[1] At other times the term used is 'legislatures' though law-making is by no means their only function or, today, their main function. Yet again history suggests their original function was to relay grievances to the ruler. Combining all these functions they often developed as places where a few selected men discussed the main issues of the day and recommended certain laws to deal with them.

It would be true to say that these three primary functions have survived to present times. Legislatures are buildings where representatives meet and discuss the main affairs of the nation; they pass legislation; and they exercise control, or try to exercise it, over governments. It is possible, however, to distinguish other functions which might be regarded as derived from these three. In examining the role of parliaments in modern democratic political systems I will attempt to make comparative judgements. As already indicated, differences between legislatures will often reflect different constitutional frameworks.

8.1 Representation

Parliaments represent people. Having said that, all kinds of questions follow. Which people? What do they represent? In what ways and in what manners do they represent? What does represent mean?

To answer the last question first: 'represent' has two meanings.

1. *To make representations on behalf of the people represented*. The initial war-cry of the American Revolutionaries was 'No taxation without representation'. No one should be subject to laws without having some indirect access to the discussion about their passage. Therefore proxies are needed to relay individual hopes,

fears, expectations, criticisms and disappointments to the forum of the nation. The representatives should pass these on in parliament to government. In order to do this effectively work in one's constituency is essential. In some countries representatives may be able to procure material advantages for their constituents. In all they are likely to spend some of their time answering constituents' letters. Quite often they will return to their constituencies at weekends to hold 'surgeries', regular hours in which individuals can make appointments to meet them.

2. *To resemble.* The inference is that a parliament should, ideally, be composed of a gathering of people representing a cross-section of the nation. The legislature should be a mirror image of society. This ideal has never anywhere been approximated to, let alone realised. Representatives are overwhelmingly highly educated, middle-class males. Manual workers are especially under-represented in this sense; so are women. The average proportion of women in Western European parliaments is about 25 per cent. In the US Congress it is below 5 per cent. Only in Scandinavia have women made much impact – 65 per cent of Swedish legislators were, at the last count, women. In Britain the equivalent figure is 18 per cent.

Both the capacity of a parliament to represent people's grievances and to reflect a cross-section of the nation may be affected by the franchise, the unit of representation and its size, the electoral system, and whether there are one or two chambers.

1. *The franchise* In modern democracies this is commonly given to all sane adults. Frequently one now becomes an adult for this purpose at the age of eighteen.

2. *The unit of representation.* Conventionally this is a territorial one with defined boundaries. Constituencies vary greatly in size. Even those with only one member may, as in the US House of Representatives, average half a million voters, but British MPs are elected from constituencies with, on average, 65,000 voters. Of course, multi-member constituencies will be much larger.

3. *The electoral system.* Multi-member constituencies will be one feature of proportional representation (PR). Where there is PR the way voters' opinions are represented will be affected. Multi-party systems will be the result and usually, though not inevitably, coalition governments (see Chapter 10). Electoral systems really merit a section on their own.

4. *The number of chambers.* The Scandinavian countries and New

Zealand have only one chamber. In all other democracies where there are two the same electorate is, with one or two exceptions, represented twice though in different ways. Yves Mény says bicameral countries may be divided into two groups – federal countries and those where the upper house is 'a survival from the past'.[2]

In federal countries the upper chamber is necessary to represent the states (Australia and the USA), provinces (Canada) and cantons (Switzerland). In all these cases except Canada the sub-units are accorded equality of representation irrespective of size or population. In Canada all 102 members of the Senate are appointed for life by the governor-general on the advice of the prime minister. In Germany the upper house, the Bundesrat, represents the governments of the *Länder*, though not on terms of strict equality: the smaller *Länder* have disproportionate representation. Thus Hamburg has three seats in the Bundesrat and Bavaria only six, though its population is six times as large.

In unitary countries the upper house may be elected in more or less the same way as the lower house. This is so in Italy (except for five members appointed by the President). In France, as we have noted, the Senate is indirectly elected, and in Britain the House of Lords is part appointed for life and part hereditary.

There are several arguments in favour of maintaining upper houses or 'second chambers'. The most convincing is that it is necessary to have another body which can scrutinise legislation passed by the first chamber. Frequently today, especially in the larger countries, the vast volume of legislation being processed may result in not all of it being considered properly. It may be carelessly drafted and some of its clauses may not be consistent. So it is necessary for it to be reconsidered. The strength of this argument is reflected in the fact that in unicameral countries, such as those in Scandinavia, a grand committee of the chamber is chosen to review all legislation. In effect, this has the function of a second chamber.

Other arguments are less respectable. It has often been asserted that an upper house is needed to moderate radical legislation passed by the lower house. This is the 'second thoughts' argument often advanced by conservative parties. It is not clear why third thoughts or even further thoughts might not be necessary. Sometimes this argument has been expressed as the appeal 'from Philip drunk to Philip sober', implying that the lower house is inevitably the intoxicated one. Normally the lower house has a more popular basis and has been most recently elected. Upper houses often are continuing bodies: their memberships are elected in stages and their members have longer terms. One third of both the French and American Senates retires periodically – after three years in the French case and after two in the American. Their equivalent lower houses are chosen *in toto* for five and two years respectively.

It is usual for the lower house to be more powerful than the upper house. In the USA, however, the Founding Fathers intended the Senate to be more powerful than the House of Representatives. They gave the Senate foreign policy powers and it was always imbued with higher status. To this day Senators have more prestige than Representatives, but in the last forty years the House has become more powerful. This has happened because it alone has the power of financial initiative, money has become even more important as the federal government has collected much more to disburse and with the USA emerging as a world power the dollar has become central to American diplomacy. Today the House has probably more foreign policy influence than the Senate. In Italy the Italian Senate is as representative as, and possesses powers similar to, the Chamber of Deputies. Consequently it has as good a claim to represent the true state of public opinion as the Chamber. It probably equals the Chamber in power.

Furthermore, even where upper houses are clearly weaker they may pose problems. The French Senate, as we have noted, became the only prominent obstacle to De Gaulle's policies during the early years of the Fifth Republic. The House of Lords, in spite of its nominal and permanent Conservative majority, became a real impediment to Mrs Thatcher's legislative programme during the 1980s. The German Bundesrat, because of its composition on a *Länder* basis, has interests of its own that the Bundestag and the government has always to bear in mind.

Structures of representation are therefore manifestly complex. This explains why it is often difficult to reconcile their outputs with public opinion as we believe we know it. Representative institutions can distort popular demands, but it is often difficult to discern what these are in any detail.

This raises the question of how people should be represented by their representatives. Here there are two basic concepts: that of the delegate and that of the trustee or parliamentarian.

1. The delegate obeys mandates received from the voters at election times. Having made promises, or having had promises extracted from her or him, the delegate proceeds to fulfil them if elected. A person in this position will obviously have no options or room for manoeuvre. If all in a legislature were delegates there would be much less point in debates. Indeed, it would not be very

different from government by referendum.
2. The trustee is elected on trust, that is the voters elect someone
    whom they trust to participate in the nation's decision-making.
    They do not bind their representative in any way because they
    respect her or his integrity and judgement on matters which they
    are remote from and do not understand. The classic exposition is
    Edmund Burke's address to the electors of Bristol after he was
    elected in 1774. Parliament, he said, was not 'a congress of
    ambassadors . . . but a deliberative assembly of one nation where
    not local prejudices ought to guide . . . but the general good,
    resulting from the general reason of the whole'.[3] Of course, Burke
    was speaking long before the era of mass party politics and,
    anyway, the concept of the general good is a matter of some
    dispute.

Both of these positions are 'ideal-types'. Their equivalents will be few in
modern democratic legislatures. In practice, representatives will be
between these two positions though perhaps approximating more to
one or the other. As nearly all legislators are members of a political party
they would find it very difficult to adhere to either position.

8.2 Legislation

Legislation might reasonably be regarded as the most important function of democratic legislatures. In one sense it is: democratic parliaments still spend the bulk of their time debating and passing,
amending or rejecting proposals for laws. In another sense it is not.
Today the larger proportion of proposals have been drafted by the
executive and the legislature is, to a greater or lesser extent, a mere
formalising agent. For example, in Britain it has been calculated that 82
per cent of all bills begin in the the executive and about 95 per cent of
these are adopted. France in the Fifth Republic has come very close to
this position – deliberately so. In contrast the us Congress frequently
proposes and passes proposals which it has initiated. Yet even in the
usa national legislation often emanates from the President and his
advisers, but getting it passed is a different matter. The Constitution, as
we have seen, sets the executive and legislature in opposition to each
other. Congress has a power over its own activities possessed by no
other democratic legislature.

Indeed, the power of legislatures is a reflection of the amount of
autonomy they have succeeded in maintaining. Their autonomy can be
ascertained by examining their relative control over their own agendas

and their facilities for legislative initiative. They vary greatly in these features. This can be illustrated by comparing Italy and the USA on one side and Britain and France on the other.

As no member of the executive can sit in Congress it is completely in control of its own agenda. (The Vice-President presides over the Senate though without any influence over its proceedings.) Any member of the House of Representatives can propose legislation, including that involving the spending of public funds. Hence every Representative, unsurprisingly, is concerned to introduce proposals that will confer financial benefit on his or her own Congressional District. The constitutional concept of the Italian parliament is *centralità del parlamento*. The Chambers draw up their own agendas which differ from what the government would like. Unlike the USA the executive sits in parliament and can introduce there its own legislation, but it finds the passage of it difficult. Those members who are not ministers, even when they are members of the governing parties, like to emphasise their own power and executive business is frequently roughly handled. The government then may fall back on issuing decrees in order to make parliament deal with the matter *post hoc*. In consequence there is constant friction between Italian governments and the Italian parliament. There is a resemblance between the two countries' legislative strength but its causes lie in disparate origins. In the USA it is the Constitution while in Italy it is the multi-party system and the notion that popular sovereignty is represented by parliament that so weakens the executive to the benefit of the legislature. The Italian situation is most reminiscent of the Third French Republic.

Britain is in direct contrast. The agenda of Parliament is drawn up by negotiation between government and opposition front benches. It is strictly organised so that while the rights of the opposition are guaranteed – it is allowed thirty-five days of the 180 approximately that the House of Commons is in session – British governments at other times are able to act without much hindrance. No one except a minister can introduce any legislation which involves the spending of money and non-ministers can only introduce legislation on Fridays, when about 10 per cent of 'private member's bills', as they are called, are actually passed. None of them are about matters that would affect government policy – any such proposals would be defeated by the imposition of party discipline. The situation in the French National Assembly is very similar. Article 48 of the constitution rules that the government has priority in determining parliament's business. Laws which have originated with individual deputies are scarcely 10 per cent of the total and they are not of prime importance.

Germany stands in between these two groups. The agenda of the

Bundestag is drafted by a committee composed of the president and Vice-Presidents of the Bundestag together with representatives from the parties in proportion to their strength in the chamber. Even so most bills emanate from the government. Between 1972 and 1987 1,218 originated with the government, 488 from Bundestag members and 222 from the Bundesrat.[4] Thus the Bundestag has a certain measure of autonomy but the government controls much of the business.

It is truly said that the strength of a legislature is reflected by the strength of its committee system. The strongest legislature in the democratic world, the US Congress, has the strongest legislative committees. They are 'specialised', that is each one relates to a government department such as Agriculture or Foreign Affairs. The legislators on the committee will specialise in its subject matter and so will be well briefed on the issues, including legislation, that come before it from the House or Senate. (Each chamber has its own set of committees.) Moreover, US Congressional committees are quite capable of initiating their own legislation as well as monitoring executive policies in their field. In fulfilling these functions they are assisted by their own specialised staffs.

France, on the other hand, has a weak legislative committee system. Because under the Third and Fourth Republics the legislature had had strong specialised committees the drafters of the Fifth Republic's constitution set out to weaken them. Their number is restricted to six which means that they are very large, about 120 members each. It is impossible for such large bodies to specialise in, or indeed to examine, anything in detail. Similarly the British legislative committees are unspecialised – in fact, they have no permanence as a different committee membership is appointed for every piece of legislation. They scrutinise details of legislation after broad general discussion in the House, but party discipline operates in legislative committees and helps to facilitate the passage of government business. Since 1979 specialised committees of the US type have also existed and have made reports on government policy in several fields. It is perhaps too early yet to assess their influence, but there is little evidence that they have affected government policy to any great degree. It remains true that in France and Britain weak committees reflect weak legislatures.

Germany and Italy have strong specialised committees, but in Europe only in Scandinavia can one find strong legislative committees that are not specialised. For example, in Sweden ministers are forbidden from taking part in committee discussions which take place, Gordon Smith says, in a 'spirit of informed objectivity'.[5] Hence parties that are not in government may have a real say in legislation. Consequently Swedish legislation can be as much a creation of the legislature as of the executive.

Hague and Harrop sum up the strength of democratic parliaments in four categories.[6] The 'dominant parliament' is exemplified by the French Fourth Republic – 'government by assembly' – where twenty-five governments came and went in twelve years. 'Autonomous parliaments' have substantial independence from the executive but do not dominate it. For example, the US Congress has strong influence over policy and the executive, but it cannot dismiss the latter which is elected independently of it. In 'adversary parliaments' ritualised confrontation takes place between government and opposition. The British system illustrates this category. Finally 'inhibited parliaments' are much weaker than governments, though the latter may not completely dominate. France under the Fifth Republic obviously comes to mind.

8.3 Controlling the executive

One of the most important functions of legislatures is supposed to be exercising control over the executive. From what has been said so far it might appear that they do not exert much control and, perhaps, control is too strong a word. Yet they all exercise some kind of supervision of government activity. There are three main methods by which they can try to do this.

8.3.1   Dismissal of governments

First, it is almost inevitable that in democratic countries with parliamentary systems the parliaments can make, and unmake, governments. In this sense the legislature can be regarded as a sort of electoral college. British governments are formed from the majority party. Where there is no majority party coalition-building will ensue. In both situations there will be an early vote to ensure that the government is accepted by the parliament. Conversely, if the government loses its majority it will be powerless and must resign. Hence parliaments can control governments by hanging the threat of dismissal over them. Much will depend on the strength of party discipline, but ultimately, even where it is strong as in Britain, the government cannot forget that its survival rests on the support of its followers. 'Responsibility' in this sense means 'dismissability'.

In some parliaments occasions arise when snap votes may be taken on government policy. In Britain any MP can table a motion about a specific matter which justifies urgent consideration. If the Speaker can be persuaded that it is urgent, and if the signatures of forty other MPs can be obtained, a debate can be arranged for the following day. These 'motions on the adjournment', however, may influence the government but are scarcely likely to lead to its overthrow. In France similar motions are called *interpellations*. An oral question is immediately followed by a debate. This device brought down many governments in the past, but it cannot operate in the Fifth Republic. In Italy, however, the interpellation is flourishing, and it has become popular in Germany where debate follows a written question posed by at least twenty-six members of the Bundestag. About 500 uses of this procedure now take place annually in Germany though they do not lead to government defeat.

These instances all apply to parliamentary government. They could scarcely be appropriate for presidential government. In the US Congress the future of the executive is not at stake in any vote. The President is elected separately. He and his ministers can play no part in the proceedings of Congress. There is no alternative government or leader of the opposition in Congress and no one planning an opposition programme, except possibly some aspiring presidential candidate. The American executive remains there, unless he dies, until January in the year after leap year. The only way the Congress can dismiss the President is for the House to impeach him and the Senate to find him guilty. This has never happened, though in 1974 Richard Nixon resigned when faced with almost certain dismissal.

8.3.2 Questions in Parliament

Much less dramatic and much more humdrum control can be exerted, it is claimed, by parliamentary questions to ministers. Britain is regarded as the doyen of this procedure. Question time – about three-quarters of an hour – takes place on four days a week before other business begins. MPs can ask two questions per day after giving forty-eight hours notice. Most of them, however, are not asked orally because time does not allow and questioners have to be content with written answers. Germany has a similar system, so has Italy, and they were introduced into France with the Fifth Republic. The questions tend to have two purposes. The practical one is to obtain information and will probably arise as a last resort after the questioner has failed to obtain it by informal enquiry. The second purpose is to embarrass the government. The minister may be confronted with information that is derogatory and asked to comment on it. Supplementary questions can be asked in an attempt to catch the minister off balance. But it is not unknown for supporters of the government to put down questions that they know will allow the minister to present government policy in a self-congratulatory manner. Moreover, with the help of officials it is not difficult for ministers to construct disingenuous or evasive replies. Hence, though parliamentary questions are often praised they are not an effective way of keeping a watch on governments. Question time in the House of Commons is gladiatorial fun, but it is not a way of controlling the government.

8.3.3   Committees of inquiry

Easily the most satisfactory method of legislative supervision over governments is through committees of inquiry or investigation. Specialist committees may undertake these tasks. American Congressional committees have the power of subpoena: they can compel witnesses to appear before them. They frequently cross-examine heads of federal agencies. They have the power of investigation including calling for official documents though, since the Supreme Court judgement, *Watkins* v. *USA* 1956, they have been restricted to matters relating to legislative activity. French deputies have inaugurated committees of investigation, though their duration is limited to six months. As they are composed proportionately according to the parliamentary strengths of the parties the government has usually had a majority upon them and they have been very reluctant to be critical. In Italy such committees can only be initiated by special laws. Since 1970 they have been very much involved in the scandals which have beset Italy, but they have not always yielded results. For example, the committee on the P2 affair, a sort of freemason/Mafia conspiracy, was discreetly wound up without clear conclusions. Perhaps their findings were so damaging for the whole system that they were afraid to publish reports. In Britain, too, as observed, specialist committees have existed since 1979, but when action might be demanded party loyalties have ensured the government is unharmed.

It is easy, given the above evidence, to identify the circumstances in which a legislature will be able to exert control over an executive. There are four main features of the situation:

1. The legislature is separated from the executive by the constitution. No one is simultaneously a member of both and they are separately, though popularly, elected.
2. There is no clear majority support for one party so coalition governments have to be formed.
3. Cleavages between parties are considerable so coalitions are unstable.
4. Party discipline is weak.

These circumstances produce weak executives and strong legislatures. It is noticeable how the pattern of a country's parties affects the situation (see Chapter 10).

8.4   Recruitment and socialisation of leaders

Legislatures are also places where the nation's leaders are selected and trained. The new member meets representatives from other parts of the country, other social backgrounds and other political parties. For the first time he or she may realise how difficult decision-making is when such a variety of opinions and attitudes is present in the country. Common first reactions to life in the legislature are feelings of disappointment, ineffectiveness, frustration and even cynicism. Members who learn to accept the situation and to participate in dialogue with other groups in order to arrive at a viable policy are likely to be those who will emerge as political leaders. In parliamentary systems it is usual to choose members of the executive from among members of the legislature, and even in the USA Presidents have often earlier sat in Congress.

8.5   Acting as a forum

Finally parliaments function as forums for nations. This function may have become more important since the advent of television, allowing everyone to get a glimpse of their legislature and, in some countries, very much more than a glimpse. In parliaments a sort of permanent debate about national circumstances and objectives continues. Even when the outcome of debate is known, as in Britain, where the main performers are 'going through the motions' when they engage in verbal conflict, the public, it may be argued, will benefit from hearing, seeing and reading about it. Nineteenth-century liberals saw one purpose of parliament as that of educating the public about the chief issues of the day. It would be incorrect to believe that this ideal has ever been fulfilled. Yet a parliament is the main centre of political life of a democracy. It is there that the legitimation of decision-making takes place; it is there that national issues will be discussed; and it is in the proximity of parliament, if not in the chamber itself, that much political bargaining and compromise will be completed.

It has become common in recent years to lament the 'decline of parliaments'. This may be partly nostalgia, but there is a clear basis for the sentiment. Everywhere executives are much more the source of policy-making, the details of which are often drawn up by technocratic officials. The complex and specialised nature of much public policy does not make it suitable for debate in large assemblies. Moreover, much policy emanates from outside parliament, or even from outside the political parties, as a result of bargaining with corporate groups, business and organised labour being the most important. Public meetings are not good places for working out detailed policy.

Even so parliaments have not declined in every respect. They have become more representative in the sense of being better cross-sections of their electorates though they are still far from being very representative in this respect. They are probably better reservoirs of political leadership than they were, although the prestige of politicians has declined, it seems, in most democracies. But their decline as policy-making bodies and controllers of governments is most clear. The former is inevitable because they are not appropriate bodies for policy-making. It is their decline as supervisors of governments that is serious because it is generally agreed that modern democratic governments need more and more vigilant supervision.

Notes

1. J. S. Mill, *Considerations on Representative Government* (People's edn. 1886. first published, 1861), p. 42.
2. Y. Mény, *Government and Politics in Western Europe*, 2nd edn (Oxford: Oxford University Press, 1993), pp. 188ff. The book is invaluable for all students of the subject.
3. E. Burke, Speech to the electors of Bristol, in B. W. Hill (ed.), *Edmund Burke on Government, Politics and Society* (London: Harvester Press, 1975), pp. 157ff.
4. W. E. Paterson and D. Southern, *Governing Germany* (Oxford: Blackwell, 1991), p. 309.
5. G. Smith, *Politics in Western Europe* 2nd edn (London: Heinemann, 1976), pp. 173ff.
6. R. Hague and M. Harrop, *Comparative Government* (London: Macmillan, 1982), pp. 135ff. Actually they have a fifth type, submissive parliaments, not relevant here because it applies to undemocratic systems.

Questions

1. 'Legislatures everywhere are very much under the control of executives.' Discuss.
2. If second chambers are necessary, how should they be elected, what should be their length of term and how should their powers relate to those of the first chamber?

9

Governments

Executives in the modern democratic state are today concerned with much more than the traditional function, that is to execute the laws. Governments are now a centre of power and leadership. Their many roles often far exceed those envisaged by those who drafted their constitutions. To govern today means more than to implement, or even to control. It consists of supervising, guiding, planning, coordinating, stabilising and many other activities.

In most states all these roles are divided into two groups: the dignified and honorific roles of receiving ambassadors, having one's head on the coinage, pardoning murderers, presiding over national ceremonies, conferring medals, sending telegrams to centenarians and nominally appointing ministers, etc., and the other more substantive roles mentioned above.

9.1 Dignified roles

It is usual for the dignified roles to be carried out by heads of state who are of two kinds – monarchs and presidents. Monarchs succeed to the position by inheritance and there is seldom trouble over their accession. Presidents are elected, some by popular vote as those of France, Ireland, Finland and Iceland. Others are chosen by parliament as is the Greek president, or by electoral colleges. In Italy the president is chosen by both chambers meeting together plus three delegates from each region. The German president is chosen by the *Bundesversammlung*, half of whose members are Bundestag deputies and half representatives of the *Länder* parliaments chosen in proportion to party strengths within them. The US President is chosen by an electoral college composed of people chosen by popular vote in each state – a form of indirect popular election.

Although the French and American presidents are heads of state they are also the chief executives. Except for these latter two, Heads of State often have three functions.

9.1.1 Symbolic function

This might be regarded as a shadowy function, but it is probably the most important. The most successful heads of state are those who have been able to give the impression that they personify the country's chief characteristics and that they identify with its fundamental values and interests. The head of state is supposed to represent something above partisan conflict. (This has been recognised by presidents usually being given a longer spell of incumbency than the legislature.) Of course, it is not always easy for an elected president to possess these qualities, so it is hardly surprising that monarchs tend to exercise the symbolic function with more ease and with less opposition. King Haakon of Norway, called upon to abdicate by Quisling after the German invasion of his country, not only refused but left for Britain and broadcast regularly to his occupied countrymen and women from London. Thus he personified the spirit of national resistance. War may be the circumstance when kingly virtues are most needed. George VI and Queen Elizabeth walking amid the ruins of bombed-out London marked the high peak of the British monarchy's popularity in the twentieth century.

9.1.2 Guardianship function

Heads of state are often perceived as guarantors of their countries' institutions. Some presidents, like those of France, Finland and Iceland, are entrusted with this duty by the constitution. The King of Spain is credited with saving democracy in 1981 when he successfully called upon the army not to support those officers who stormed the Cortes and told its members they were under arrest. One could, however, overestimate this capability. Neither the Italian king nor the German president were able, in 1925 and 1933 respectively, to halt the rise of Mussolini and Hitler. Indeed, they did not try.

9.1.3 Arbitration function

This is perhaps the most important of the functions of heads of state. Sometimes where there is civil strife a head of state can act as a pacifier and neutral go-between. George V of Britain fulfilled this role twice. He persuaded the Lloyd George government to sit down with the leaders of the Irish rebellion and negotiate the settlement in 1920 by which Ireland became an independent state. In 1926 he did much to prevent oppressive measures being used against the strikers in the General Strike. The head of state as 'father', or indeed, 'mother', of all the people fulfils a parental role in such a situation. Again monarchs may have less difficulty with this role because presidents have often been party politicians and are therefore identified with some sectional interest. Yet presidents are not incapable of maintaining a balance between feuding groups. In particular the first president of a new regime may set the tone for subsequent national political life. Vincent Auriol, first president of the French Fourth Republic, Theodore Heuss, first president of democratic Germany, and Luigi Einaudi, first president of the Italian Republic, were much respected for their fairness and ability to influence political conduct without becoming personally involved.

The most awkward test of a head of state occurs when a prime minister has to be chosen and it is not clear who it should be. This is not unlikely in a multi-party legislature where no party has a much larger number of seats than any other and coalition-building has apparently reached an impasse. Skilful diplomacy by the head of state may then bring results. Some Italian presidents, notably Einaudi (1948–55) and Pertini (1978–85) were so exceptionally popular and so visibly above party strife that they were able to act in this way.

9.2 Executive structures

9.2.1 Executives in presidential systems

The substantive activities of governments in parliamentary systems are carried out by leading politicians with bureaucratic apparatuses to assist them. But the USA and France are presidential systems and their heads of government departments are different. In the USA the only party-based politician in the executive may well be the President. (Even he, as was the case with Eisenhower, may have had little to do with politics until nominated.) In France there is both an executive president and a government led by a prime minister. Although the prime minister and his heads of ministries are usually elected deputies, they must resign their seats on taking up office. Unlike the American heads of ministries, however, members of the French Cabinet sit in parliament, take part in its debates and help to steer through legislation which concerns them.

Government action, as we have noted, may be limited by constitutional and other factors. For example, French governments (to be distinguished from 'French executives', a term which would include the president) only face hostile votes under Articles 49 and 50. Such a vote can only be carried by a majority of the whole membership of the National Assembly (289 votes). Only one such vote, a motion of no confidence, has been passed – in 1962. The constitution makes the government responsible to parliament (Article 20) and the prime minister responsible to the president (Article 8). The president is also given the power to hold referendums (Article 11), to dissolve the Assembly (Article 12) and to assume emergency powers (Article 16).

Factors other than constitutional have increased the power of the French president as against that of the government. Presidents have usually not only decided who holds ministerial posts but have also drawn up national policies. Presidential power over the government is the result of the popular election of the president and his support from the party of which he is the head controlling the majority in the Assembly. When he is not in this position the whole situation changes and the government and prime minister are then in the driving seat. This was the situation between 1986 and 1988 and after 1993 and 1995. In those years a Socialist president, Mitterrand, faced after legislative elections with a right-wing majority, was left only with the powers to refuse to sign a decree and those of commander-in-chief, allowing him to claim foreign policy functions. (He insisted on attending international summits.) The fact is that most of the power of the president over the government in the Fifth Republic has been owed to the parliamentary majority being composed of the president's party and its allies. For thirty-three out of forty years this has been the case.

The American President, in spite of being unambiguously vested with executive powers by the Constitution, is in a much weaker position than the French. His agency heads (they are never called ministers) may be people who are non-party or even hold allegiance to the opposing party. People who have been in Congress are seldom appointed. They are primarily administrators and so the Presidential cabinet has no coherence. Initially they may consider themselves 'president's men' but experience may teach them otherwise. All of their appointments have to be confirmed by the Senate (Article 2, Section 2) and from the House of Representatives they will need to obtain their funds to implement their programmes. Hence relations with the appropriate House of Representatives committee may become more important than those with the President. In these circumstances it is impossible for the President to use his cabinet as a policy-making body. It meets fairly infrequently and its proceedings often take the form of a report from each agency. Agency heads have as little to do with one another as possible. Each one is responsible as an individual to both President and Congress.

9.2.2   Executives in parliamentary systems

Governments in parliamentary systems are responsible to parliament, though this does not mean that legislative power is dominant. Where there is no party in a majority governments will inevitably be coalitions which may be unstable. The relative power of executive and legislature, therefore, depends much on the pattern of the party system (see Chapter 10).

Legislatures are weak and governments strong where a two-party system exists as in Britain. This is a situation where there are two parties holding a large preponderance of the seats in the House of Commons. One party will invariably hold a majority of seats and consequently British governments are able to be composed of ministers who all belong to one party, though this is not constitutionally necessary. (The convention is that the government needs to command a majority support.) The most important ministers sit in the Cabinet, chaired by the Prime Minister, who can 'hire and fire' ministers. He or she is thus in a powerful position to guide policies in the direction favoured. Ministers must not step out of line once government policy has been decided. If they wish to speak publicly against such policy they must resign first. This is the doctrine of collective responsibility. Combined with prime ministerial power it explains the dominance of the British executive which has great coherence.

In many parliamentary systems, where a multi-party system leads to coalition government, governments will be weaker. The Italian premier, known as the President of the Council, has to allocate posts in his government in arithmetic proportion to the strengths of his coalition partners, though smaller parties, like the Liberals and Republicans, may manage to obtain a disproportionate allocation sometimes by threatening to withdraw vital support. Italian governments are thus very weak *vis-à-vis* the legislature, though a skilful Premier can become surprisingly strong if he can balance his fragmented government. He needs to be a power-broker as Craxi was. Peremptory behaviour will not help.

The German situation is not unlike that in Britain. Each party in election campaigns is headed by a leader who is, in effect, a candidate for Chancellor. The Basic Law insists that the Chancellor must be voted into office by the Bundestag. It is difficult for him to be removed. It needs a 'constructive vote' of censure by which the person to replace him must be nominated and receive the votes of more than half the Bundestag membership, that is 249. There have only been two of these votes and only one has been successful, that in 1982 which unseated Chancellor Schmidt by 256 votes and installed Helmut Kohl. The German Chancellor is thus a strong figure. He chooses his ministers though he is somewhat restricted because German governments are usually two-party coalitions.

In all executives, parliamentary or presidential, certain imperatives are bound to apply irrespective of the power of the prime minister or president. Allocation of posts must bear in mind geographical distribution. American Secretaries for Agriculture usually come from the 'hog and corn' farming states of Illinois, Indiana and Iowa. Bavaria must be represented in German cabinets. The Italian minister for trade and industry is chosen from the North. Even in one-party cabinets there may be factions to be conciliated. Mrs Thatcher announced she wanted a 'conviction Cabinet', but she found it necessary in her first Cabinet to include some 'Heath-men', those who had had favour with her defeated predecessor as Conservative leader. Faction-fighting is a feature of all governments.

9.3   Policy making

For the ordinary purposes of administration modern cabinets usually consist of some fifteen to twenty-five members. Most offices relate to functional requirements. There always has to be a foreign minister, a finance minister and one responsible for domestic law and order. More modern requirements have necessitated ministries for social welfare, health, education, transport, and trade and industry. These will all be high-spending ministries. Funds are bound to be restricted however prosperous a country is because of the demands of these functions. Hence ministers are likely to expend much of their energy 'fighting their corners' for a share of the money for their departments. All modern democratic governments have evolved some procedure for dealing with this internecine conflict. It inevitably enhances the power of the finance minister and, over him, the Prime Minister. They will be the arbiters in this struggle.

Over a century ago the governments of the industrialised states began to be concerned with much more than dealing with events as they cropped up and ensuring internal and external security. Today the volume and complexity of policy is such that no government can operate without advice, consultation and the delegation of sub-areas of policy. A great deal of governmental policy-making needs the assistance of specialised expertise and a network of committee systems.

9.3.1   United States of America

In the USA, as we have seen, the Presidential Cabinet is of little use as a policy-making body. One vice-president described it as the president's 'natural enemy'. American presidents, therefore, have to appoint their own advisers to assist them. They are part of a White House bureaucracy, not concerned with routine administration but with broader policy in the longer term. Presidents have had foreign policy advisers of this kind, 'roving ambassadors' as they have been called, for most of the twentieth century – Woodrow Wilson's Colonel House is a famous example. But the large-scale proliferation of the 'Executive Office of the President', its official name from 1939, began with Franklin Roosevelt (1933–45). Today it numbers about 2000 people. The Executive Office is directly under the control of the President and contains (at the last count) nine agencies, including Councils on Environmental Quality, and Science and Technology. The White House Office manages public relations and the President's timetable and agenda. The three most important are the National Security Council (NSC), the Office of Management and Budget (OMB) and the Council of Economic Advisers (CEA). How these operate may depend on Presidential preference. The NSC was set up by Truman (1945–53) as a major foreign policy forum. The President may take the chair but if he is not there it will be occupied by the National Security Adviser who may be far more important than the Secretary of State. Other members are the Defense Secretary, the Secretary of State, the Vice-President and the Director of the CIA. The NSC should coordinate all these agencies which are inclined to run their own foreign policies.

The OMB became crucial with the vast growth of federal spending caused by social welfare expenditure in the 1930s and defence spending from the 1940s onwards. The OMB always finds itself in conflict with the spending departments – Defense, Agriculture, Health and Human Services, Education, Housing and Urban Development. They use the specialist committees of Congress which are supported by the interested pressure groups. Hence the OMB may be frustrated in its attempts to restrict, coordinate and rationalise federal spending. The House makes great demands on the public purse. Directors of the OMB have often reflected the outlook of the President who has appointed them. For example, David Stockman, a young right-wing economist was appointed by Reagan (1981–89) as a radical 'budget-cutter'. But the OMB only recommends the White House Budget to Congress which has its own research and expertise in the Congressional Budget Office, founded in 1974 to introduce some rationality into Congressional demands for money. In the economic depression of the early 1980s it became especially difficult for Congressmen to vote for cuts in social spending or for increased taxes. Moreover, Reagan embarked on a policy of escalating defence spending. Hence, after a few months Stockman resigned. The episode reflects the ambivalent nature of the US voter – indeed, all voters want to receive higher benefits but to pay less tax. The tactics of a Presidential candidate therefore are to promise either to cut taxes or not to put them up. Once elected the taxes can be increased in the first year of office, in the hope of bringing them down again before the next election.

9.3.2 France

The equivalent situation in France, with its dual executive, is one of conflict, though not as open as in the USA. Both President and Prime Minister have their own staffs and, unsurprisingly, they are often at loggerheads. At the Elysée Palace is the Presidential secretariat – 15–30 officials at the head of it – dating from 1958, De Gaulle's first year as President. At the Matignon Palace is the General Secretariat of the Premier, a long-standing apparatus of career officials, entrusted with the framework of administration and the details of legislation and working through inter-departmental committees. It has a coordinating and monitoring function and its members tend to stay in their positions whoever the Premier. At the Elysée the top bureaucrats are all personal appointments of the President, engaged in longer-term policy-making. But the work of the two bureaucracies is bound to overlap and clashes are common. One prime minister, Chaban-Delmas, was dismissed by President Pompidou partly as a result of conflict between his staff and that of the President. On the whole, the presidential bureaucracy, as one might expect, tends to dominate over the prime ministerial bureaucracy. De Gaulle set the precedent. He divided his secretariat into 'Task Forces', each based on a French problem. By the constitution the President chairs the Council of Ministers, but this has become a formal body merely rubber-stamping decisions already taken in the inter-departmental committees which finalise policy. During 'co-habitation', however, in 1986–88 when Mitterrand was forced to appoint the Gaullist, Chirac, as Premier, the position was reversed. The government committees became all-powerful and, except for the Defence Committee, where Mitterrand insisted on taking the chair, the Premier's committees and his policies were paramount.

It is small wonder, then, that in the Fifth Republic relations between the President and the Prime Minister have been difficult. Presidents have expected loyalty from their prime ministers (except when 'co-habitation' has obtained). They have not always received it, nor have presidents reciprocated. De Gaulle sacked Pompidou because the latter organised an alternative right-wing group separate from the Gaullists which was brilliantly successful in the legislative elections of June 1968. As we have noted, Pompidou removed Chaban-Delmas, a rather recalcitrant Gaullist, who went to the National Assembly and made a speech criticising the 'rigidities' of French society, a theme raised by the rioting students in 1968! Giscard fired Chirac for disagreeing with him on numerous issues, though Chirac said it was merely because he had asked for more freedom of action. Mitterrand dismissed Mauroy partly over a disagreement about subsidies for schools. There is much evidence to suggest that French presidents see their prime ministers as rivals. They are bound to have different supporters within the govermental coalition. Prime ministers are almost certain to consider themselves as possible candidates for the presidency.

9.3.3   Germany

Within systems of parliamentary government, policy-making may be simpler, but that is not to say that it is uncomplicated. Problems of co-ordination may be severe. For example, the German Chancellor's Office, which organises and coordinates the federal government's activities, is divided into six functional divisions and has a total staff of about 500. The Office provides the Chancellor with information and researched advice on all major aspects of policy. The SDP–FDP coalition under Brandt set up a planning system which penetrated and attempted to coordinate all departments. The large number of inter-departmental committees composed of civil servants clashed with the planning activities of the Chancellor's Office and eventually in 1972, as a result of this conflict, the Office reverted to a more traditional system of advice, information and organisation of agenda. Chancellor Schmidt used his cabinet more for coordinating policies and since that time the Office has had crisis functions, especially important during the period of unification 1989–90. Yet it must always be remembered that Germany has a federal system with *Länder* governments being responsible for virtually all administration.

9.3.4   Britain

British government, too, has developed on similar lines. Since 1918 there has been a Cabinet secretariat which has developed into the Cabinet Office. It grew out of the circumstances of the War Cabinet formed by Lloyd George in 1916. Until then Cabinets had proceeded without minutes and without a secretary. The Cabinet Secretary takes note of all decisions and issues agendas, not only for the weekly meetings of the Cabinet, but for Cabinet committees. These latter, numbering eighteen, whose purposes were until recently secret, consist of ministers of appropriate departments and also civil service advisers. Present also are, usually, a representative from the Treasury and, always, a civil servant from the Cabinet Office, which is thus in a position to keep track of decisions and coordinate as far as possible. Hence the structure of British policy-making has become very complex. Most decisions are made in Cabinet committees and the weekly Cabinet meeting rubber-stamps them. Any important decisions actually made in Cabinet are likely to be either a crucial dispute between departments that has been referred upwards or an event that has suddenly emerged as critical.

Prime ministers who feel the civil service may be unsympathetic to policy innovation have recently begun to bring in their own personal advisers from outside the service. Harold Wilson in 1974 set up the No. 10 Policy Unit at his house in Downing Street and Mrs Thatcher, who had a very low opinion of the civil service, continued this practice. Disliking the Treasury and distrusting the Chancellor of the Exchequer, she appointed her own economic adviser, Sir Alan Walters, to what is now called the Prime Minister's Office. Disagreement between Walters and the Chancellor, Nigel Lawson, led to the latter's resignation from the government. She also appointed a foreign policy adviser for the same reason. Thus the British premiership has gradually evolved a department of its own in spite of being a non-departmental post. This may have increased the potentiality for conflict within British governments as well as adding to the complexity of policy-making.

9.3.5 'Prime ministerial government'

During the later twentieth century the gap between premiers and other ministers has tended to widen. As the volume of business has increased ministers have had little choice but to become immersed in their own department's affairs. Only non-departmental ministers can think about future general policy and only one of these can act with any authority on it. This is the prime minister, traditionally only 'first among equals'. Moreover, the need for a referee in the battle between spending departments over funding, which inevitably has policy implications, enhances the role of the prime minister. Resources determine capacity, so the act of dividing up public expenditure is really a determination of priorities. Two other factors have accentuated this trend. One is international summitry. The totalitarian regimes would not finalise agreements unless the top man was present. This denigrated foreign ministers and gave more kudos to prime ministers. The second is television, offering 'photo-opportunities' which any politician would find difficult to neglect. Failure to take advantage of them presents rivals with a bonus.

In Britain the operation of all these factors has given rise to the view that cabinet government is giving way to 'Prime ministerial government'. (The term is put in inverted commas because it is a trend rather than a recognised category.) There is some evidence that similar forces are at work in other countries with parliamentary government. The Spanish premier, called the President of the Council, dominated Spanish politics under the leadership of Felipe Gonzalez. The German Chancellor stands out from among the other ministers for reasons similar to those of the British Prime Minister, though Gordon Smith believes unification will make his prominence less sustainable.[1] The Dutch Prime Minister, however, because he lacks the resources of strong party and coalition backing can never, Rudy Andeweg says, assert himself in the same way over his ministerial colleagues.[2] It is perhaps fair to conclude that the factors of allocative conflict, television publicity and international summitry, though important, can be outweighed in certain circumstances by constitutional restraints and party pressures.

9.3.6   Bureaucrats and politicians

Another development in modern democratic government is the blurring of the line between administration and politics. The classic situation where they were two quite different activities is less attainable than ever. The simple fact is that governments have far too many complex decisions to make and politicians cannot make them all. Moreover, because bureaucrats have longer and more secure tenure they will have more familiarity with, and possibly more understanding of, the problems. Even in the USA, where politicians have much mistrusted bureaucrats their function in providing information makes them indispensable. But career federal administrators are not greatly respected. The original American concept of administration was that anyone could do it and that it is dangerous to develop a sense of security in the minds of bureaucrats. Presidents have frequently been neither politicians nor bureaucrats.

The European concept is a complete opposite. Bureaucrats are given careers for life with pensions to follow retirement. They are highly trained people who have advanced to their positions by careful selection after passing examinations. Often they are committed to certain policies and in Germany senior bureaucrats are visibly involved. Senior civil servants are chosen by ministers because of their sympathetic attitude to governmental policy. Some of them attend cabinet meetings as a proxy for their minister; other civil servants from *Länder* governments may attend meetings of the Bundesrat as representatives of their *Land*. This provides an easy passage into politics. It was estimated in 1978 that 12.3 per cent of the CDU's legislators, 10 per cent of the SPD's and 14 per cent of the FDP's were former civil servants. Encouragement for the transition is provided by the rule that they can have five years in politics and then return to public service without losing pension rights.

In France the distinction between the civil servant and the politician is probably least and growing less. French administrators have been selected as an intellectual elite and trained in specialised schools. This tradition received its most extreme recognition in the foundation in 1946 of the École Nationale d'Administration which produces what are now known as 'technocrats'. Its graduates, who are largely qualified in the social sciences, not only dominate the senior levels of administration in the public sector but also in the private. A further practice, going back to 1815, is for ministers to form their own ministerial *cabinets* – a small coterie of advisers known to be sympathetic to ministerial ideas. The *cabinet* is a sort of buffer between the minister and the administration. These trends have been greatly enhanced in the Fifth Republic. Often described as a return to the Bonapartist 'administrative state', the present regime reflects Gaullist views that many French problems can be solved much better by rational examination and technical application than by discussion between competing politicians. Moreover, the habit of presidents appointing as ministers senior figures in public sector administration has made administration a common avenue into politics. French technocrats have become even more involved with party policy-making while French politicians have become more technocratic.

British civil servants remain most generalist and least specialised, and Britain still retains the separation between a career in the civil service and a career in politics. There are no civil servants in the House of Commons and very few ex-civil servants. Increasingly civil servants are involved in policy-making behind the scenes, and they are now named when they appear before the new select commitees. Ministers still make policy statements and are supposed to take all responsibility.

To sum up: the governments of the democracies resemble one another more than do their legislatures and a good deal more than their constitutions. This is because the problems that their governments face in the modern world are not very different. On the other hand, their constitutions are legal and institutional frameworks, usually derived from an earlier era when economic and political circumstances were quite different. Political institutions frequently are partial legacies from the past which have to be adapted to confront the pressures and problems of the present.

Notes

1. G. Smith, 'The resources of a German Chancellor', in G. W. Jones (ed.) *West European Prime Ministers* (London: Frank Cass, 1991), p. 59.
2. R. B. Andeweg, 'The Dutch Prime Minister: not just chairman, not yet chief?', in G. W. Jones, *West European Prime Ministers,* p. 116.

Questions

1. Has power increasingly become centralised, not in cabinets, but in the hands of prime ministers and Presidents?
2. Compare and contrast the German executive with the British.

10

Political parties

When we turn to political parties we move away from comparative institutions and enter the area of comparative political behaviour. Studies of political behaviour involve examining the behaviour of political actors. There are many of these: individuals, the media and associations, pre-eminently parties and pressure groups. It is possible to learn much about them from transnational comparisons, or even by comparing different parties in the same country. Of course, when we undertake transnational comparisons we have to take account of numerous variables, the most important being the constitutional framework. Different institutions can produce differing patterns of political behaviour.

Political parties in democracies have some clear similarities and many differences.

10.1 Identifying political parties

A political party may be defined as an association with the following four features:

1. It has considerable continuity, that is its life must be independent of the life of one leader and it should, if it is in a democracy, exist for more than one election.
2. It operates at both national and local levels: there is at least an elementary form of communication between centre and periphery.

These two features, however, could apply to any continuing organisation.

3. It endeavours to participate in and to influence the decision-making of the country.

This third feature could also apply to a pressure group.

4. It wishes to be either the government, or to coalesce with others in forming a government, or to change the whole framework within which the parties operate.

This fourth feature can only apply to parties.

10.2 Functions of political parties

The above descriptive definition of parties raises the question of what parties do. We are here only concerned with democratic political systems. What are the functions of parties within them? (see Chapter 6.)

1. Parties are necessary to representative institutions. They are the intermediaries between the voters and the government. A party is a channel of opinion, protest, dissent and criticism. The parties' representatives in the parliament should be communicating these citizen concerns to the leaders who may select from among different feedbacks to construct their electoral programme.
2. Parties, therefore, provide a choice of policy options at election times. They may rationalise and collate these in policy programmes with a statement of priorities. If they are very responsible they may relate it all to the practical question of resources. Where and how are they going to find the money?
3. Parties, therefore, need an apparatus to inform the voters at election times about their policies and their personalities. They will need electoral organisations if they want to be successful. These provide the parties with the following functions: (a) selecting candidates, (b) helping to get the candidates elected, (c) informing and educating the voters and trying to recruit some of them as party members and activists, (d) assisting in policy formation; and (e) providing and raising funds for the parties.
4. Parties, therefore, as a function of maintaining the democratic regime (unless they are anti-democratic), are involved in recruiting a country's leaders in at least two stages: (a) selecting legislators, (b) choosing ministers from among the legislators.
5. Parties provide a focus for different social groups. They have symbols and traditions which convey a feeling of continuity for their followers. The history of a party contains within itself part of the history of the country.

10.3 Classification of parties

There are at least five ways of categorising political parties.

1. According to the extent of their goals. Very generally these types
    are: (a) parties which merely want to take over power from the
    incumbent governing party, (b) parties which want to change
    society, though they accept the political framework; and (c)
    parties which want to change the political framework.
2. Parties which accept democratic procedures and those which do
    not. Those which do not are one variant of (c) above. We are not
    concerned with such parties here.
3. Parties which accept the legitimacy of their nation-state and
    those, such as ethnic minority parties, which do not.
4. Parties may be classified according to their type of organisation.
    Maurice Duverger used this classification in two ways:[1] First,
    according to local organisation; and second, according to na-
    tional organisation or its absence. He described the four basic
    party units as the caucus, the branch, the cell and the militia.
    Parties with caucuses – small local informal groups as the elec-
    toral organisation – he called 'cadre' parties. These were parties of
    the old-fashioned type. The other types with numerous rules,
    founded on individual membership in local branches and with
    nationwide bureaucratic structures, he called 'mass' parties.
    These were modern organisations.
5. Parties may also be divided functionally into either articulative
    parties or aggregative parties. Articulative parties disseminate and
    pursue issues. They may sacrifice the opportunity of power in
    order to be true to their aims. Aggregative parties prefer power for
    its own sake. They attempt to win it by collecting together
    diverse opinion groups and socio-political forces. They are some-
    times called 'catch-all' parties.

Parties can be classified according to these five categorisations,
though all are 'ideal-types'. None of these categories excludes any
other. For example, the French Gaullist party wants to govern – by
itself if possible; accepts the legitimacy of both democracy and the
French nation; is a party of branch units and a mass party; and
aggregates more than it articulates.

10.4 Origins of parties

How a party begins has much to do with how it behaves. This can be regarded as another method of categorisation. As Dahl enquires, 'Does the party evolve from traditional competition, or has it acquired its ethos from post-revolutionary populism?'[2] Most parties in the world today belong to the latter grouping.

10.4.1 Traditional parties

Parties which evolved from traditional circumstances, pre-dating the French Revolution, are exemplified by the British Conservative and Liberal parties. They developed when the franchise was very limited and Parliament was the arena in which their competition took place. They reflect a respect for the parliamentary system and their necessary adaptation to universal suffrage has not entirely eradicated their hierarchical values. The British Labour Party, conversely, began outside Parliament and still retains something of the structure and values of an extra-parliamentary party, but it long ago accepted the civilities of parliamentary life in spite of its egalitarian origins.

10.4.2 Post-French Revolution parties

Many European parties arose after the overthrow of their countries' *anciens régimes*, beginning with the French Revolution. Even today the rhetoric of French parties has echoes of the slogans of 1789. A section of the French right has never accepted the Revolution and refuses to sing the *Marseillaise*. They resent the lay state, the secular state system of education and the position the Catholic church was relegated to by a series of measures ending in 1904. The Vichy regime of 1940–44 was in some degree the victory of these forces. Throughout Catholic Europe the parties took up positions on either side of this division. It was not until after the Second World War that the Catholic church became reconciled to democracy. The new Italian democracy from 1870 onwards suffered because voters who participated in it risked excommunication. Only when the Vatican realised democracy could be used as an instrument of opposition to Communism did Christian Democratic parties emerge strongly in Italy, Germany, Austria and France. With the end of the Cold War, and growing secularisation, Christian Democratic parties have weakened and may disintegrate. They have always been uneasy alliances between right-wing clericals, progressive semi-socialist Catholics and representatives of Catholic trade unions. The Italian

Christian Democratic party, long in power, now seems on the verge of extinction.

10.4.3 Post-Industrial Revolution parties

As opposed to French Revolutionary provenance, the birth of many European parties may be attributed to the Industrial Revolution. A historical breaking point is when an industrialised working class begins to organise. If the suffrage has been extended before the working-class party becomes successful, as in Britain, Sweden, Norway and Denmark, the language of party conflict will be less intense. Moderate democratic socialist parties characterised these four countries where Communist parties remained weak. On the other hand where, as in Finland, the working class received the vote as a direct result of the 1905 Revolution (the country was a Grand Duchy within the Russian Empire) and a General Strike, the dialogue of class conflict was more harsh. The strength of Communism in Finland, relative to the other Scandinavian countries, was very much the result of working-class experience in the period 1905–17. The Russian Revolution is certainly a historical breaking point and most of the world's Communist parties date from the early 1920s. Although scorning democracy many of them have operated in democratic contexts. By some strange paradox, however, they seem to have been most successful in countries without a great deal of industrialisation.

10.4.4 Post-colonial parties

Even more dramatic circumstances attend the birth of parties in a post-colonial situation. Usually, to begin with, the only important party is the one which has led the independence struggle. The takeover of power may be traumatic. Samuel Huntington writes that a nationalist party 'faces a major crisis when it achieves its goal and has to adapt itself to the somewhat different function of governing a country'.[3] Its difficulties all spring from the fact that it represents an intellectual elite trained in foreign universities (usually in Britain, France or America) with modernising aspirations and unprepared for criticism and opposition. Universal suffrage provides it with a tribalised electorate of illiterate, conservative people. They naturally oppose attempts to organise and mobilise them for the purposes of a nation with which they are not especially identified. A post-colonial democracy may therefore be one of tribal parties in conflict, as in Zimbabwe or Kenya. It may lapse into civil war. A party of independence, like the Congress Party in India, may find it difficult not to fragment. One outcome may be an authoritarian one-party state.

A striking exception to this portrayal of post-colonial parties is obviously the situation in the USA after independence. The language of its politics may be, to repeat what Dahl says, one of 'post-revolutionary populism', but party relationships have never been conducted in terms which prevent compromise. The Civil War was not principally a breakdown of party relationships, but a breakdown of relations between one part of the country and another.

10.5 Comparative party systems

10.5.1 The nature of party competition

From the above it is clear that the character and style of a country's politics very much depend on the relations between its parties. It will also depend on their number and the depth of the cleavages that divide them. They are competing for power and in pursuit of conflicting goals. The nature of the democratic debate will be affected by the trust they have in one another. This will depend on past experiences, as well as the current situation, and also on their expectations of one another's behaviour in the future. For example, if a party has cheated at election time, there may be an incentive for other parties to cheat. Certainly it will be a long time before such a party will be able to reassure its competitors that it will not cheat again. Of course, all competitive situations are capable of breeding mistrust, and where the prize for success is a share of political power distrust may easily arise.

One extremity of political behaviour would be where one party, having achieved power, eliminated all the others. The other extremity would be an absence of political competition. Democratic situations will lie between these two poles. Political parties reflect different groups, demonstrating the differences over policy issues which may exist within a country. They may be based, as we have noted, on different cultural, socio-demographic and ethnic features. These cleavages and the intensity with which their disagreements are held are the basis of the party systems of countries. Most countries will have parties of more than one type. Hence party systems vary considerably.

10.5.2 Structural/functional analysis of party systems

The sort of configuration of parties that a country possesses will reflect not only the number of cleavages within that country, but also its constitutional and electoral systems.

A non-party system

This only exists in a democratic situation with a classic presidential system of government like the USA. Instead of a collectivity governing an individual does. Of course, the President is the nominee of a party, though in the USA this is hardly the whole story because many of the delegates at the parties' nominating conventions which choose presidential candidates are chosen by the voters at what are called 'primaries', not by party meetings. (Indeed, one can argue that the Republican and Democratic parties are not parties in that they do not fulfil the basic functions of parties. They scarcely have any individual membership, they have no nationwide organisation in the European sense, the bulk of campaign funding for party candidates comes from sources other than party funds, the candidates for office construct their own personal electoral machines and they are selected at primaries and not by party organisation.) Candidates rather than parties, therefore, win or lose elections. Once elected the policies pursued are those of the successful candidate and not of the party. The policies of the President are his own and his party's programme is relatively unimportant.

Non-party government implies non-party opposition. The US Congress, which may or may not have a majority from the same party as the President, is the centre of opposition and presidential policies may be opposed by Congressmen of his own party and supported by Representatives from the other party. The minority in Congress does not spend its time drawing up a programme: there is no opposition party to be returned to office and there is no leader of the opposition with which voters can identify. Many suggestions for alternative policies come from pressure groups. Numerous other decision-making centres exist within the states. Thus beyond securing the nomination of a presidential candidate the American political party has no strong function within the political system.

A question of interest to political scientists is whether France with a popularly elected President since 1962 will eventually approximate to the American position.

Two-party systems

This term is applied to where two major parties dominate political life. The situation is not common and can only be found in Britain, Australia and New Zealand. Britain has classic 'adversarial politics'. Two parties usually dominate the legislature and, though there are minor parties, they seldom hold the balance. The leader of the majority party becomes Prime Minister. Thus the voters have not only chosen the party to govern and the Prime Minister, they have also chosen a party programme. Consequently the larger part of the electorate will be responsible for the policies the country is introducing. In the other major party there is an alternative government, waiting in the wings, criticising the government and drawing up an alternative programme for the next election. It is led by the Leader of the Opposition (paid a salary), an alternative Prime Minister. This is opposition with a 'capital O' as Allen Potter says.[4] The Opposition does not expect to persuade the government to deviate from its policies by argument. The criticisms are directed at the voters, enough of whom it hopes to win over in order to win the next election.

At one time it was thought that adversarial politics was the type of politics that every country would want to emulate. Governments were responsive to public opinion because the 'pendulum' could swing back to the opposition and put them in power. The alternation of parties in power would take place fairly regularly. In reality Britain does not always even approximate to this 'classical' model. Out of twenty-two elections since and including 1918, an opposition with a clear majority has supplanted an incumbent government on only eight occasions. In the eighty years since then Conservative governments or Conservative-dominated coalitions have ruled for forty-nine years, coalitions for nine and the Labour Party for twenty-two. In fact, incumbent governments have the advantage of choosing a suitably tactical moment for an election during the statutory five-year session of Parliament. It is also a dysfunctional system for managing economic policy which normally needs more than five years to bear fruit.

Multi-party systems

Where there are numerous parties in the legislature and none has a majority, majority governments will be formed from coalitions. There are several theories of coalition-building. A formal theory, however, is unlikely to provide an explanation, let alone a prediction, because it assumes rational behaviour and takes no account of widely differing and differently valued goals. For example, the best known theory is Riker's concept of a 'minimal winning coalition',[5] that is all those not essential to a winning coalition will be excluded. It is not borne out by the facts.

Decades ago British and US political scientists used to write as though all multi-party systems were similar, but they are clearly not. Several positions can be identified.

The grand coalition

This happens where the two major parties, neither of whom has quite a majority by itself, join together and completely dominate the situation in the legislature. It is not a very common situation. In Austria until 1966 the second Republic experienced rule by a Socialist/People's Party coalition. After independence the fraught foreign policy situation of Austria demanded that national unity should be stressed. Both parties discarded an ill-fated 'lager' tradition inherited from the disastrous First Republic of 1918–38. The People's Party claimed it had shed its alliance with the Catholic church and in 1958 the Socialists renounced 'Austro-Marxism'. They bargained and produced a sort of contract embodied in the *Proporz*, an agreement to share all posts. At elections they campaigned against each other but renewed the contract afterwards. In between, opposition was only provided by legislators who were not government members introducing motions to displace appointees of the other party. It was a strange system of commingling government and opposition.

Another grand coalition was in Germany from 1966 to 1969 when the Christian Democrats and the Social Democrats ruled together. Normally Germany has what has been called a 'two and a half party system'. A majority government until recently was formed from either the Christian Democrats plus Free Democrats, or Social Democrats plus Free Democrats. Thus the small FDP tended always to be a member of the government. The Grand Coalition was formed while the Federal Republic was still in the process of forming a stable party system and it may not occur again.

Multi-party instability

The classic examples of this situation may now be extinct. Italy (until very recently) and France under the Third and Fourth Republics found it difficult to maintain stable government. The two examples, however, are not absolutely identical.

Italy's largest party, the Christian Democrats, though never quite a majority dominated the government until 1976. Yet there have been fifty governments in the last forty-seven years. This can be explained by rampant factionalism within the Christian Democrats, almost a coalition in itself. Much of their support was owed to their strong anti-Communism. The Communists were the largest opposition party, but all the other parties agreed the Communists could never be in the governing coalition. From 1947 the Socialists were divided between the Social Democrats, who favoured the NATO alliance, and the 'Nenni Socialists' who did not. Otherwise there were the Liberals, the Republicans and the MSI, a right-wing party with monarchist and Fascist leanings. After 1976 with the growth of Communist strength the Christian Democrats needed support from other parties and in 1982 and 1983 they found themselves a major partner in a coalition under

Prime Ministers of smaller parties – Spadolini of the Republicans and Craxi of the now united Socialists. Since 1989 the Communists have become democratic socialists, the Christian Democrats have disintegrated as a result of the exposure of widespread corruption, and new parties have arisen and declined – Umberto Bossi and his regional party, the Northern League, and Silvio Berlusconi with his National Alliance, a right-wing appeal to all voters. The result has been more governmental instability.

The French Fourth Republic was likewise faced with a large Communist Party which collected about a quarter of the votes. After 1947 it was assumed it could never be part of a coalition. It was 'neither Right nor Left but East'. There were four disciplined parties in the parliament – Communists, the Socialists, the Radicals and the MRP, this last a Christian Democratic party. The last three formed most of the coalitions which, on average, lasted ten months. In all these four parties there was strong rank-and-file control over the leadership. Governmental crises usually persisted for 2–3 weeks because external control made negotiation between the leaders very difficult. In both these cases indiscipline existed within parties in parliament in spite of strict party discipline, imposed from outside more than within the chamber. Revolt against the leadership, in fact, was pursued in the name of discipline, the argument being that it was the leaders in the coalition who were breaking the rules.

Multi-party stability

That the presence of many parties does not necessarily result in political instability can be illustrated by the case of Holland. In fifty-three years since the war Holland has had only twelve governments, though within governments reshuffles have sometimes taken place. The country has a system of proportional representation (PR) favouring small parties. As a result at the 1982 election, for example, twelve parties successfully won seats in parliament. But three parties accounted for 93 per cent of the vote at that election. These three, Labour, the Christian Democrats and Liberals, are frequently partners in the same government.

Early democracy in Holland faced the the issue of public lay education and Catholic disagreement with secular education. The country's cultural history is Protestant, but Catholicism gathered strength in the nineteenth century and with the rise of the labour movement a strong secular element appeared. Thus the country had three cultures. In 1919 they finally agreed to live with one another in harmony, each with its own associational life. Hence in Holland each of three 'pillars' of Dutch society has its own organisations, schools newspapers, broadcasting and TV stations and, until 1977, political parties. (In 1977 the two largest Protestant parties and the Christian Democrats amalgamated in the Christian Democratic Appeal). This is Dutch 'consociationalism', a procedure of bargaining, compromise and power-sharing resulting in remarkable stability and tolerance in society.

Single-party government in multi-party systems

This type of situation can be found where there are several parties, but there is one large party dominating political life which does not suffer from factionalism like the Italian Christian Democrats. In Norway and Sweden, the Social Democrats (called Labour in Norway) have been paramount. In Norway Labour, sometimes supported by the Liberals, was in power from 1933 to 1965, except for the war and a short four–week period.

In Sweden the Social Democrats came to power in 1934 and ruled almost unaided until 1976. The opposition parties are divided and small. The Communists have had a small representation. Opposition is therefore heterogeneous and coalescing against the Social Democrats on an agreed programme is very difficult. The opposition has consisted of three small parties, the Conservatives, Liberals and Farmers (known as the Centre Party since 1959). These three with diverse agendas have always had the difficult task of deciding how to oppose. Should they put themselves forward jointly as an alternative government? This would need compromising on a programme. What do they do in the Riksdag about the Social Democratic government's legislation? Some of it is acceptable to one or two, but not all of them. Should they each bargain individually for entry into a coalition with the SPD? The Farmers have tended to favour this last strategy. It is easy for them, being little more than a pressure group with sectionalised goals, and their support is easily bought with subsidies for farming.

What the three parties have done represents a compromise between these strategies. At elections they put forward their several policies, but all campaign against the Social Democrats. In between elections in the Riksdag they collaborate and bargain separately with the governments, only occasionally all opposing together. Conferences between all party leaders in the Riksdag is common – there is much searching for consensus in Sweden. The Farmers, especially have desired a coalition with the Social Democrats and they have sometimes protested at being omitted when the Social Democrats have won an overall majority at an election.

In 1976 the Conservatives, Liberals and Farmers all fought the election on opposition to the Social Democrats' nuclear policy. They won and formed a coalition under a Conservative prime minister. But by 1978 a new nuclear policy, devised by the Liberals, was opposed by the other two parties who left the coalition. The coalition was renegotiated in 1979 after working out a compromise. Then the Farmers disagreed with the economic policy of the two more market-oriented parties and left the coalition. Consequently the Social Democrats returned to power at the 1982 election.

10.6 Factors affecting party systems

It is impossible to study these varied types of party system without becoming aware of the importance of (a) constitutional structures and conventions; and (b) social and political culture. But another factor emerges from the above survey: (c) there is a clear connection between the configuration of the party system and electoral mechanisms. In this way it might be argued that electoral systems are vital to the whole working – and even survival – of the political system. For example, it is often said that the Weimar Republic collapsed because of the impossibility of making decisions when there was never any clear majority in the Reichstag. This instability was partly the result of a system of PR favouring small parties.

The argument has even been taken as far as an assertion that electoral systems are the main determinants of party systems. Yet it must be remembered that electoral systems are the product of someone somewhere – usually the majority in the legislature. Thus the parties in a majority are likely to want a system that favours their endeavours to win seats. Where the majority varies the electoral system may frequently change. This occurred in the French Third and Fourth Republics and has happened twice in the Fifth. With the British 'first past the post' system the minor parties, who are grossly under-represented, naturally favour PR but the only likelihood of change is if neither major party gains a majority in the House of Commons. In this unlikely, though not impossible, event the Liberal Democrats, the largest minor party, will make electoral reform the price of their cooperation in a coalition. The recent Italian move away from PR was the result of popular revulsion against the corruption of political leaders. The power of the latter can be almost unchallengeable under PR because the need to draw up a list of candidates for each party, carried out under central or regional control, results in high list placings for party leaders. Their seats become impregnable. Electoral systems tend to reflect the values of a political system with regard to the balance between the need to provide stable government and fairness in reflecting the different strands of public opinion. Where they provide both, as in Holland, it says much for the political skills of the politicians and the political maturity of the electorate.

Notes

1. M. Duverger, *Political Parties* (London: Methuen, 1954).
2. R. A. Dahl, *A Preface to Democratic Theory* (Chicago: University of Chicago Press, 1956), pp. 34f. *passim.*
3. S. Huntington, *Political Order in Changing Societies* (New Haven, Conn.: Yale University Press, 1968), p. 17.
4. A. Potter, 'Great Britain: opposition with a capital 0', in R. A. Dahl (ed.), *Political Oppositions in Western Democracies* (New Haven, Conn.: Yale University Press, 1966), p. 3.
5. W. Riker, *The Theory of Political Coalitions* (New Haven, Conn.: Yale University Press, 1966).

Questions

1. 'The configuration of parties and their relationships with each other is the most important and distinctive feature in a country's political life.' Discuss.
2. Discuss the view that the most important role of parties is their linkage of formal governmental power with civil society and individual citizens.

Section Two

Bibliography

Chapter 6 **The comparative approach**

Almond, G. A. and Powell, G. B., *Comparative Politics: A Theoretical Framework* (New York: Harper Collins, 1993).

Axtmann, R., 'Society, globalization and comparative method', *History of the Human Sciences*, 6, 1993, pp. 53–7.

Ball, A., *Modern Politics and Government* (London: Macmillan, 1977).

Barbrook, A., *Patterns of Political Behaviour* (London: Robertson, 1975).

Blondel, J., *An Introduction to Comparative Government* (London: Weidenfeld, 1969).

Blondel, J., 'Theory, Meta-theory and comparative politics', *Comparative Politics*, 4, 1971.

Cantori, L. and Ziegler, A. H., *Comparative Politics in the Post-Behavioral Era* (Boulder, Colo.: Rienner, 1988).

Dahl, R. A., *Modern Political Analysis* (London: Prentice Hall, 1976).

Davies, M. R., and Lewis, V. A., *Models of Political Systems*, (London: Macmillan, 1971).

Finer, S. E., *Comparative Government* (London: Penguin, 1974).

Hague, R. and Harrop, M., *Comparative Government and Politics* (London: Macmillan, 1982).

Holt, R. T. and Turner, J. E., *The Methodology of Comparative Research* (New York: Free Press, 1970).

Kronenberg, A. L., 'The logic of comparison', *World Politics*, vol. 19, 1966.

Lichbach, M. I. and Zuckerman, A. S., *Comparative Politics* (Cambridge: Cambridge University Press, 1997).

Lijphart, A., 'Comparative politics and comparative methods', *American Political Science Review*, 65, 1971.

Mahler, G. S., *Comparative Politics: An Institutional and Cross-National Approach* (Englewood Cliffs, NJ: Prentice Hall, 1992).

Marsh, D. and Stoker, G., *Theory and Methods in Political Science* (London: Macmillan, 1995).

Mayer, L. C., *Comparative Political Inquiry* (Homewood, Ill.: Dorsey, 1972).

Mayer, L. C., 'Practising what we preach: comparative politics in the 1980s', *Comparative Political Studies*, 16, 1983.

Mayer, L. C., *Redefining Comparative Politics* (London: Sage, 1989).

Mayer, L. C., *Comparative Politics* (London: Prentice Hall, 1993).

Meckstroth, T. W., 'Most different system and most similar system: a study in the logic of comparative inquiry', *Comparative Political Studies*, 8, 1975.

Meehan, E. J., *Theory and Method of Political Analysis* (Homewood, Ill.: Dorsey, 1965).

Mény, Y., *Government and Politics in Western Europe* (Oxford: Oxford University Press, 1990).

Peters, B. G., *Comparative Politics* (London: Macmillan, 1998).

Przeworski, A., and Teune, H., *The Logic of Comparative Social Inquiry* (New York: Wiley, 1970).

Ricci, D. M., *The Tragedy of Political Science* (New Haven, Conn.: Yale University Press, 1984).

Roberts, G. K., *An Introduction to Comparative Politics* (London: Arnold, 1986).

Sartori, G., 'Concept misinformation in comparative politics', *American Political Science Review*, 64, 1970.

Sigelman, L. and Gadbois, G., 'Contemporary comparative politics: an inventory and assessment', *Comparative Political Studies*, 16, 1983.

Simon, H. A., *Models of Man* (New York: Wiley, 1957).

Somit, A. and Tannenhaus, J., *The Development of Political Science from Burgess to behavioralism.* (Boston, Mass.: Alleyn & Bacon, Inc., 1967).

Teune, H., 'Comparative research, experimental design and the comparative method', *Comparative Political Studies* 8, 1975.

Vedung, E., 'The comparative method and its neighbours', in B. Barry (ed.), *Power and Political Theory* (London: Wiley, 1976).

Verba, S., 'Some dilemmas in comparative research', *World Politics*, 20, 1967.

Chapter 7 **Constitutions**

Andrews, W. G., *Constitutions and Constitutionalism* (New York: Van Nostrand, 1961).

Beard, C. A., *An Economic Interpretation of the Constitution of the United States* (London: Macmillan, 1961).

Birch, A. H., *Federalism, Finance and Social Legislation in Canada* (Oxford: Oxford University Press, 1955).

Bogdanor, V., *Multi-party Politics and the Constitution* (Cambridge: Cambridge University Press, 1983).

Brown, R. E., *Charles Beard and the Constitution* (Princeton, NJ: Princeton University Press, 1956).

Chubb, B., *The Constitution of Ireland* (Dublin: Institute of Public Administration, 1963).

Corwin, E. S., *Presidential Power and the Constitution* (Ithaca: Cornell University Press, 1976).

Dash, S. C., *The Constitution of India* (Allahabad: Chaitanya, 1968).

Dearlove, J., *The Constitution in Crisis* (Cambridge: Polity, 1984).

Duverger, M., *Les Régimes Politiques* (Paris: Presses Universitaires de France, 1961).

Fesler, J. W., 'Approaches to the study of decentralization', *Journal of Politics*, 27, 1965, pp. 536–66.

Finer, S. E., *Five Constitutions* (Brighton: Harvester Press, 1979).

Fournier, P., *Canada's Quest for a New Constitution*, Canada House Lectures, 1991.

Gillett, N., *The Swiss Constitution: Can it be Exported?* (Bristol: YES Publications, 1989).

Lane, P. H., *An Introduction to Australian Constitutional Law* (Sydney: Sydney Law Books, 1967).

Livingston, W. S., *Federalism and Constitutional Change* (Oxford: Oxford University Press, 1956).

MacMahon, A. W., *Federalism, Mature and Emergent* (New York: Columbia University Press, 1955).

Marshall, G., *Constitutional Theory* (Oxford: Oxford University Press, 1971).

Merkl, P. H., 'Executive-legislative federalism in West Germany', *American Political Science Review* 53, 1959).

Scott, K. J., *The New Zealand Constitution* (Oxford: Oxford University Press, 1962).

Senelle, R., *The Belgian Constitution* (Brussels: Ministry of Foreign Affairs, 1974).

Strong, C. F., *Modern Political Institutions* (London: Sidgwick & Jackson, 1963).

Tarlton, C. D., 'Symmetry and asymmetry as elements of federalism', *Journal of Politics*, 27, 1965.

Vile, M., *Constitutionalism and the Separation of Powers* (Oxford: Oxford University Press, 1967).

Wheare, K. C., *Federal Government* (Oxford: Oxford University Press, 1963).

Wheare, K. C., *Modern Constitutions* (Oxford: Oxford University Press, 1966).

Chapter 8   **Parliaments**

Blondel, J., *Comparative Legislatures* (Englewood Cliffs, NJ: Prentice Hall, 1973).

Bogdanor, V. (ed.), *Representatives of the People? Parliamentarians and Constituents in Western Democracies* (Aldershot: Gower, 1985).

Boynton, G., *Legislative Systems in Developing Countries* (Durham, NC: Duke University Press, 1975).

Colliard, J. C., *Les Régimes Parlementaires Contemporains* (Paris: FNSP, 1978).

Dale, S. W., *Legislative Drafting: a Comparative Study of Methods in France, Germany, Sweden and the United Kingdom* (London: Butterworths, 1977).

Di Palma, G., *Surviving Without Governing: the Italian Parties in Parliament* (Berkeley, Calif.: University of California Press, 1977).

Eldridge, A., *Legislatures in Plural Societies* (Durham, NC: Duke University Press, 1977).

Green, M., *Who Runs Congress?* (New York: Viking, 1984).

Hale, D. (ed.), *The United States Congress* (New Brunswick, NJ: Transaction Books, 1983).

Hirsch, H. and Hancock, M. D., *Comparative Legislative Systems* (New York: Free Press, 1979).

Judge, D. (ed.), *The Politics of Parliamentary Reform* (London: Heinemann, 1983).

Kolinsky, E. (ed.), *Opposition in Western Europe* (London: Croom Helm, 1987).

Loewenburg, G. and Patterson, S. C., *Comparing Legislatures* (Boston, Mass.: Little, Brown 1979).

Mezey, M. L., *Comparative Legislatures* (Durham, NC: Duke University Press, 1979).

Norton, P., *The Commons in Perspective* (Oxford: Robertson, 1981).

Norton, P., *Parliaments in Western Europe* (London: Frank Cass, 1990).

Olson, D. M., *The Legislative Process: A Comparative Approach* (New York: Harper & Row, 1980).

Patterson, S. C., *Towards a Theory of Legislative Behaviour* (Madison, Wisc: University of Wisconsin Press, 1962).

Suleiman, E., (ed.), *Parliaments and Parliamentarians in Democratic Politics* (New York: Holmes & Meier, 1986).

Sundquist, J. L., *The Decline and Resurgence of Congress* (Washington, DC: Brookings, 1981).

Wahlke, J., *The Legislative System* (New York: Wiley, 1962).

Walkland, S., *The Legislative Process in Great Britain* (London: Allen & Unwin, 1968).

Chapter 9 **Governments**

Albrow, M., *Bureaucracy* (London: Macmillan, 1970).

Allum, P. A., *Italy, Republic Without Government?* (London: Weidenfeld, 1973).

Barber, J. D., *The Presidential Character. Predicting Performance in the White House* (Englewood Cliffs, NJ: Free Press, 1972).

Bogdanor, V. (ed.), *Coalition Governments in Western Europe* (London: Heinemann, 1983).

Brown, R. G. S. and Steel, D. R., *The Administrative Process in Britain* (London: Methuen, 1979).

Butler, D., *Governing Without a Majority* (London: Macmillan, 1983).

Fry, G., *The Changing Civil Service* (London: Croom Helm, 1985).

Greenwood, J. and Wilson, D., *Public Administration in Britain* (London: Allen & Unwin, 1984).

Hennessy, P., *Cabinet* (Oxford: Blackwell, 1986).

Hennessy, P. and Seldon, A., *Ruling Performance: British Governments from Attlee to Thatcher* (Oxford: Blackwell, 1987).

Howorth, J. and Cerny, P. (eds.), *Elites in France: Origins, Reproduction and Power* (London: Frances Pinter, 1981).

Johnson, N., *State and Government in the Federal Republic of Germany: the Executive at Work* (Oxford: Pergamon, 1982).

Jones, G. W., *West European Prime Ministers* (London: Frank Cass, 1991).

Kellner, P. and Crowther-Hunt, Lord, *The Civil Servants* (London: Raven Books, 1980).

King, A., *The British Prime Minister* (London: Macmillan, 1985).

Koenig, L., *The Chief Executive* (New York: Harcourt Brace, 1981).

Laver, M. and Schonfield, N., *Multiparty Government: The Politics of Coalition in Europe* (Oxford: Oxford University Press, 1990).

Lijphart, A., *Democracies: Patterns of Majoritarian and Consensus Government in 21 Countries* (New Haven, Conn.: Yale University Press, 1984).

Lowi, T. J., *The Personal President* (Ithaca: Cornell University Press, 1985).

Mackintosh, J., *The British Cabinet* (London: Stevens, 1977).

Marshall, G. (ed.), *Ministerial Responsibility* (Oxford: Oxford University Press, 1989).

Neustadt, R. E., *Presidential Power* (New York: Wiley, 1980).

Page, E. C., *Political Authority and Bureaucratic Power* (Brighton: Harvester, 1985).

Paterson, W. and Southern, D., *Governing Germany* (Oxford: Blackwell, 1991).

Richardson, J. J., *Policy Style in Western Europe* (London: Allen & Unwin, 1982).

Rose, R., *The Postmodern President: The White House Meets the World* (London: Chatham House, 1988).

Rose, R. and Suleiman, E. N., *Presidents and Prime Ministers* (Washington, DC,: American Enterprise Institute, 1980).

Seidman, H., *Politics, Position and Power* (Oxford: Oxford University Press, 1980).

Spotts, F. and Wieser, T. (eds), *Italy: A Difficult Democracy* (Cambridge: Cambridge University Press, 1986).

Suleiman, E. N. (ed.), *Bureaucrats and Policy Making* New York: Holmes & Meier, 1980).

Von Beyme, K., *Policy and Politics in the Federal Republic of Germany* (Aldershot: Gower, 1985).

Von Beyme, K., *The Political System of the Federal Republic of Germany* (Aldershot: Gower, 1985).

Chapter 10 **Political parties**

Ball, A. R., *British Political Parties, (London: Macmillan, 1987)*.

Bartolini, S. and Mair, P. (eds), *Party Politics in Contemporary Western Europe* (London: Frank Cass, 1984).

Bell, D., *Contemporary French Political Parties* (London: Croom Helm, 1982).

Bell, D. and Criddle, B., *The French Socialist Party: the Emergence of a Party of Government* (Oxford: Oxford University Press, 1988).

Blackmer, D. L. M. and Tarrow, S. (eds), *Communism in Italy and France* (Princeton, NJ: Princeton University Press, 1975).

Blake, R., *The Conservative Party from Peel to Thatcher* (London: Fontana, 1985).

Bogdanor, V. (ed.), *Liberal Party Politics* (Oxford: Oxford University Press, 1983).

Braunthal, J., *The West German Social Democrats 1969–1982* (Boulder, Colo.: Westview Press, 1982).

Budge, I. and Farlie, D., *Voting and Party Competition* (New York: Wiley, 1977).

Castles, F. (ed.), *The Impact of Parties* (London: Sage, 1982).

Chambers, W. N. and Burnham, W. D. (eds), *The American Party System: Stages of Political Development* (New York: Oxford University Press, 1975).

Cole, A. (ed.), *French Political Parties in Transition* (Aldershot: Dartmouth, 1990).

Daalder, H. and Mair, P., *Western European Party Systems* (London: Sage, 1983).

Duverger, M., *Les Partis Politiques* (Paris: Colin, 1951).

Finer, S. E., *The Changing British Party System 1945–1979* (Washington, DC: American Enterprise Institute, 1980).

Frears, J. R., *Political Parties and Elections in the Fifth French Republic* (London: Hurst, 1977).

Frears, J. R., *Parties and Voters in France* (London: Hurst, 1991).

Hall, P., Hayward, J. and Machin, H., *Developments in French Politics* (London: Macmillan, 1990).

Irving, R., *The Christian Democratic Parties of Western Europe* (London: Allen & Unwin, 1979).

Lange, P. and Maurizio, V. (eds), *The Communist Parties of Italy, France and Spain* (London: Allen & Unwin, 1981).

Lawson, K., *The Comparative Study of Political Parties* (New York: St. Martins Press, 1976).

Layton-Henry, Z. (ed.), *Conservative Politics in Western Europe* (London: Macmillan, 1982).

Mair, P. (ed.), *The Western European Party System* (Oxford: Oxford University Press, 1990).

Mair, P. and Smith G. (eds), *Understanding Party System Change in Western Europe* (London: Frank Cass, 1990).

Merkl, P. H. (ed.), *West European Party Systems: Trends and Prospects* (New York: Free Press, 1980).

Muller-Rommel, F. (ed.), *New Politics in Western Europe: The Rise and Success of Green Parties and Alternative Lists* (Boulder, Colo.: Westview Press, 1989).

Nugent, N., *The Left in France* (London: Macmillan, 1982).

Padgett, S. and Burkett T., *Political Parties and Elections in West Germany* (London: Hurst, 1986).

Paterson, W. E. and Thomas, A. H., *The Future of Social Democracy* (Oxford: Oxford University Press, 1986).

Polsby, N. W., *The Consequences of Party Reform* (Oxford: Oxford University Press, 1983).

Pridham, G., *Christian Democracy in West Germany* (London: Croom Helm, 1977).

Pridham, G., *The Nature of the Italian Party System* (London: Croom Helm, 1981).

Rokkan, S. and Urwin, D. W. (eds), *The Politics of Territorial Identity: Studies in European Regionalism* (London: Sage, 1982).

Rose, R., *Do Parties Make a Difference?* (London: Macmillan, 1981).

Sartori, G., *Parties and Party Systems* (Cambridge: Cambridge University Press, 1976).

Smith, G., *Democracy in Western Germany: Parties and Politics in the Federal Republic* (Aldershot: Gower, 1986).

Sorauf, F. J., *Party Politics in America* (Boston, Mass.: Little, Brown, 1984).

Tannahill, R., *The Communist Parties of Western Europe* (Westport, Conn.: Greenwood Press, 1978).

Von Beyme, K., *Political Parties in Western Democracies* (Aldershot: Gower, 1985).

Von Beyme, K., *Right-Wing Extremism in Western Europe* (London: Frank Cass, 1988).

Waller, M. and Fennema, M. (eds), *Communist Parties in Western Europe: Decline or Adaptation?* (Oxford: Blackwell, 1988).

Wattenberg, M. P., *The Decline of American Political Parties, 1958–1980* (Ambridge, Mass.: Harvard University Press, 1984).

Section Three

Political Ideologies

Frank Bealey

11

The concept of ideology

Many of the terms one finds in political science need careful exposition because they have been used differently by different commentators, devalued by the media and exploited by politicians for their own convenience. It is in the nature of the subject that this is so. 'Ideology' is a prime example of this abuse.

Because of this uncertainty the term is often considered in a pejorative light. John Adams, an early US President, described it as 'the science of idiocy . . . taught in the school of folly'. Ernest Barker said in the 1930s it was 'a barbarous term, a boundless, formless, horrendous monster without any light'. Charles Beard admitted that for our own time with its anti-intellectual tendencies, the concept is very convenient.

11.1 History of the concept

The word 'ideology' is a product of the French Enlightenment and is an Anglicisation of *idéologie*. A school of ideologues flourished after the French Revolution, propounding what they claimed to be a science of ideas. The leader of the group, Destutt de Tracy (1754–1836), produced his volume *Elements of Ideology* between 1801 and 1815. De Tracy paid particular attention to those philosophers who had been concerned with the study of the formation of opinion and the workings of the human mind, for example Francis Bacon, who had put forward his theory of the *idola*, or 'idols' – preconceptions and prejudices which gripped men. Bacon referred to the idols of the cave, the market and the theatre, the influences of family, commerce and taste. They were all souces of error, obstacles in the path to true knowledge. Thomas Hobbes, de Tracy thought, should be regarded as the founder of ideology, for he believed that political principles were derived from a knowledge of how the human mind reacts to sensations and ideas. John Locke was also praised because he first treated the study of the human intelligence as a science.

Imprisoned during the Terror, de Tracy on release created with his friends the *Institut National*, an Academy including a School of Moral Sciences. This was at first well regarded by Napoleon, but later, when the ideologues criticised his decision to assume the title of Emperor, he denounced them and blamed France's defeats upon them.

The history and origins of the ideologues bears out all the later comment about the term ideology Their ideas, springing from the pre-revolutionary *philosophes*, portended the later development of the term. They were concerned with universal explanations.

11.2 Contemporary usage

Modern usage of the term can be categorised, I believe, under four headings.

11.2.1 Totalitarian ideology

This is, perhaps, the most familiar usage. During the 1930s and 1940s 'ideology', one might say without much exaggeration, was on every journalist's lips. It became very popular and was applied to Communism and Fascism. Although the philosophic foundations of these two types of regime were quite diverse their ideologies could together be characterised by the following features:

1. Each offered a set of propositions, both normative and empirical, intended to explain the human condition. They claimed to be universal systems of thought.
2. Each was concerned with the historical process. The present was explained in terms of the past and there was vision of a better future. According to Ed Shils they were 'obsessed with futurity'.[1]
3. Each depicted a 'new order', a society which was their goal. It would supplant the old order reflecting dominance by some discredited group – Jews, capitalists, socialists, liberals – which had brought ruin. Reconstruction, resurgence and rejuvenation were needed.
4. Each put an emphasis, therefore, on revolutionary action, needed to overthrow the old order and to put their ideology into practice.

It is often said that this sort of ideology is a 'secular religion' and, as we have noted, ideology arose when older religions began to be questioned. Disoriented, alienated people were offered hope by these ideologies. Communism and Fascism promised their adherents the opportunity to fulfil their emotional and psychological needs in a better ordering of things. They encouraged participation in an effort to attain salvation. The certainty they offered was akin to a faith – indeed, they were faiths to many.

Could a world religion be categorised as an ideology under the above typology? Religions offer a system of beliefs, a set of a moral principles and a claim to be universal explanations. On the other hand, by no means all world religions call on their followers to prepare for a new order. Only proselytising, aggressive creeds do that. Any form of militaristic religious fundamentalism, therefore, is very much like an ideology.

11.2.2   Mind-sets

'Ideology' is sometimes used to indicate a system of beliefs held not among a large group of people, but on the part of some particular individual. Nearly all individuals will have some conception of the world, even if it is only a fragmentary one. Of course, such a perspective may not be related to politics, though even a lack of interest in politics is to some extent a political attitude. These mental constructs of beliefs, attitudes and values are often called 'mind-sets'.

Philip Converse refers to a configuration of ideas and attitudes in which the elements are bound together by some form of constraint and functional inter-dependence. He calls these 'belief systems'.[2] His concern is with political belief systems which he attempts to analyse.

The first stage of the formation of such systems is the acquisition of necessary information and for many people this is not simple. Few people obtain much political information. They are only aware of political happenings through reports in the media. But then the interpretation of the information may present almost insuperable difficulties. Without the necesary contextual information reports may be difficult to comprehend with any degree of sophistication. For example, the announcement by a finance minister that the bank rate is to be changed can mean little unless one understands the workings of the economy. Contextual knowledge is, therefore, very important, but contextual knowledge diminishes greatly below the level of higher education.

Converse says belief systems have three elements: the logical, the social and the psychological. Again education is important with respect to the logical element. One needs to be aware of one's own belief system before one can reject ideas inconsistent with it. Only people with higher education tend to be intellectually self-conscious in this respect. They will usually be aware, for instance, that it is illogical to want more public expenditure without more taxation.

The social element of belief systems is obviously likely to be influenced according to one's level in the structure. Subordinates will probably have different belief systems from superordinates, workers from bosses, men from women, and Catholics from Protestants. When Converse turns to the psychological element, however, his analysis is unsatisfactory. One would expect one's psyche to affect one's belief system, but the influences he quotes appear to be cultural rather than psychological.

The most detailed and thorough study of mind-sets was probably that undertaken by Robert Lane. He spent many hours studying the political ideas of fifteen men in Westport, Connecticut.[3] The results, as one might expect, were diffuse and indeterminate.

Lane hypothesises that, though some Americans might have some experience of the operation of democracy through membership of associations, most will have political beliefs and values – such as they are – based on a brief acquaintance with the Declaration of Independence and the Constitution in their school days. He suggests these are:

1. A belief that most people are more or less the same: 'We hold these truths to be self-evident, that all men are created equal.'
2. A belief that people should be allowed, and are allowed in the USA, to aspire to self-fulfilment. This is equality of opportunity. The self-evident truths include an endowment with 'unalienable rights' among which are 'life, liberty and the pursuit of happiness'.
3. A belief that American rulers depend ultimately for their power upon the people. As the Declaration continues, 'to secure these rights governments are initiated among men, deriving their just powers from the consent of the governed'.

Lane found that most men did not see themselves as deprived of opportunity, though most of them could be described as 'working class' and some of them were socially deprived. Yet among manual workers and businessmen he found little affection for either equality or liberty. Only the professional classes strongly defended redistributive social policies and only among them were there strong defenders of the right of free speech. A high proportion of the sample – 80 per cent – thought Communists should not be given the right to express their opinions. There was, in fact, a small group of men Lane calls the 'undemocrats' who had little faith in popular democracy and who had developed conspiratorial theories about politics. They had found it difficult to cope with their careers. Disappointed in themselves, they tended to be alienated. They were second-generation immigrants who lived in two cultures – Italian or Polish, and American. (Westport has a large 'ethnic' population.) They saw their low status as a result of behind-the-scenes manipulation by bankers/Jews/foreigners.

Several of the others were aware their lives had scarcely been a success, but they felt it was their own fault. A strong belief in individualism prevented them from explaining it in terms of social and economic forces. The same individualism prevented them from taking collective action. They did not see themselves as part of a class – indeed, they were unsure as to whether they were middle or working class. This, Lane says, explains their uncertainty about their political position. They were deprived of 'the moral justification that comes from a rationalised group position' so their conflictual urges were individual and, therefore, ineffective. They lacked the motivation to participate and found relating themselves to politics difficult. What political parties stood for seemed obscure and policies were often seen in personal terms. In common with many without higher education they looked to personal leadership and explained politics as the reflection of emotions and the goodwill or illwill of leaders.

It is the diffuse nature of this political ideology, Lane argues, that helps to preserve American democracy, together with high and increasing affluence. It could hardly provide fertile ground for potential totalitarian leaders. Anything more different from a totalitarian ideology would be difficult to imagine. Indeed, it is hardly an ideology at all – it can scarcely be called a 'system'. There is nothing systemic about it. Moreover, the people in question do not really have the necessary information, or habit of reasoning, to construct a system for themselves.

Perhaps, then, the term mind-set is more appropriate.

11.2.3   *Weltanschauung*

The third use of ideology describes what we might call a collective mind-set. It refers to the beliefs, attitudes and values of a group of people, or perhaps a historical era. Ideas are systematised enough to have a semblance of universality or 'world outlook' – a *Weltanschauung*.

Hegel first used this term to mean an image of the world, but it became common in academic discourse through the work of Karl Mannheim and his book, *Ideology and Utopia*, published in German in 1929 and in English in 1931.

Mannheim was aware that in real life there could be no completely systematised mind-set. He wrote that individual workers could not hold all the elements of their proletarian *Weltanschauung*. 'Every individual participates only in certain fragments of their thought system'.[4] In general, however, Mannheim thinks that the individual speaks the language of his group or class.

With Mannheim, as with Marx, 'ideology' connotes error. He argues that the opinions of any individual or group cannot be wholly 'scientific' or detached. People will be biased by their social and cultural environment and their own interests. Hence political argument will not be characterised by rationality. It will not usually be well-informed, logical, unemotional, objective or based on a realistic view of the context of the issue under discussion. Individuals and groups may labour under illusions – they may come to believe their own propaganda. (It must be remembered that he wrote during the Weimar Republic (1918–33) with its conflicting political currents and ideological feverishness.) Although he rejects Marxism he accepts Marx's interpretation of why people's attitudes are what they are. He says:

> The concept ideology reflects the one discovery that emerged from political conflict, namely, that ruling groups can in their thinking become so intensively interest-bound to a situation that they are simply no longer able to see certain facts which would undermine their sense of domination'.[5]

Thus Mannheim perceives people as much more aware of belonging to a social class (doubtless a European perspective) than did Lane in Westport.

When Mannheim recounts the illusions under which most people labour and the capacity of politicians to mislead he reflects his reading of Pareto who argued that the political elite are more concerned with the persuasive power of their speeches than with any attachment to objectivity. They sought not the most rational argument, but the one most likely to convince, which probably would be one to set in motion the irrational impulses that spring from our congenital predispositions. Pareto called these latter 'residues' and the manipulative arguments he called 'derivations' (see Chapter 15).

These notions are remote from what is usually seen as rationality. Yet the connection is that the statements of politicians are attempts to convince by apparent reasoning. They are 'rationalisations', attempts to give rationality and objectivity to what is irrational and subjective.

The view that politicians' ideas are merely distorted reflections of their situations in life reflects the influence of Freud upon Mannheim. Freud's discoveries had resulted in the unmasking of the unconscious part of the human mind. People's opinions could be seen as the expression of their 'unconscious interests'. From Pareto and Freud, Mannheim concluded that it is inevitable 'that increasingly people will take flight into scepticism or irrationalism'.[6]

From this angle of approach Mannheim analysed the history of our times in which the decisive factor was the breaking of the monopoly of the 'priestly' caste and the 'rise of a free intelligentsia'. The ideas of the Enlightenment destroyed the alliance of Church and dynastic state, based on a structure of illusions, for example that Christian brotherhood could be reconciled with a society based on serfdom.[7] In pointing this out the philosophers of the Enlightenment destroyed what had been a unitary order with fixed values and norms. The outcome was a society in which conflicting groups espoused conflicting sets of ideas. 'Ideology' for Mannheim is a general term for the illusory ideas ruling groups propound; 'Utopia' is a general term for the ideas of dissident groups who are so absorbed with the destruction of the society in which they live that they only perceive the factors favouring its overthrow. Utopia is the ideology of insurgent groups.

It is interesting to list the most important ideologies Mannheim thought (in about 1930) had emerged.

1. Bureaucratic conservatism associated with German officialdom and its illusion that legal order could not be irrational.
2. Conservative historicism based in universities and parties preaching tradition and romanticism.
3. Liberal-democratic bourgeois thought with its claim to be 'scientific' though its arguments were far from being a search for the truth.
4. Socialism-Communism which attacked (3) and its ideology of 'freedom' as 'false consciousness'. Their thinking was a mixture of the rational and irrational.
5. Fascism was the ideology of outsiders hoping to seize power by exploiting the crises of a society under transformation.

Hence for Mannheim the distinctive feature of political/intellectual life during the last two centuries had been the power of ideologies. Their purveyors have not been, *pace* Marx, rigidly defined classes but people recruited from an extensive area of social life and unattached to any class. Their common characteristic is education. Political expression and activity in our time is dominated by the intellectuals.

Ed Shils writes similarly of the creation of a 'class of intellectuals'[8] as a a result of the wider diffusion of ideas caused by the invention of printing and the Reformation, encouraging people to read the Bible. Literacy was no longer the privilege of a priesthood 'dependent exclusively on patronage or inheritance'. The *Weltanschauung* of modern intellectuals Shils ascribes to three traditions: *scientism*, an almost millenarial vision of a world governed by rationality; *Romanticism*, placing great emphasis on creativity, spontaneity and 'naturalness', and on the idea of community expressed in 'the people' or 'the folk', and *Bohemianism*, repudiating sophisticated manners and stressing the figure of the lonely artist.[9]

The *Weltanschauung* of the modern intellectual is thus concerned with denying the values of the present and depicting a vision of the future.

11.2.4   Family of concepts

The fourth usage of 'ideology' is as a bundle of ideas. Plamenatz, accepting that the term has several meanings, describes an ideology as a 'family of concepts'.[10] Such words as 'Socialism', 'Liberalism' and 'Conservatism' are mental portmanteaus holding assorted heavy intellectual baggage. Yet academic commentators such as Eccleshall et al.[11], describe them as 'ideologies' and so we have to come to terms with this usage.

The usage probably gained strength from the postwar attempt to present various democratic values as antidotes to Communist subversion during the Cold War. It was argued that the West must promote its own ideology, 'Democracy'. Some Americans even thought, (improbable as it may seem) that Americans might be seduced by Marxist–Leninist ideology and Communism would then take over. Thus 'our way of life' adumbrated a feeling about culture, economies, societies and politics that was akin to an ideology, at least in the loose sense in which the word has come to be used.

11.3   The end of ideology?

Daniel Bell and other writers like Shils and Aron from about 1960 onwards tried to soften the impact of the postwar debate with the thesis that we had reached the 'end of ideology'. It must be noted, however, that Bell's seminal essay is entitled *The End of Ideology in the West*.[12] While Bell thought that 'the old nineteenth century ideologies and debates' had become exhausted, he acknowledged that there were new ideologies being fashioned in the ex-colonies and newly independent states in Africa and Asia. Such ideologies were a faith in technology and nationalism (including Pan-Arabism). But while the Western ideologies were 'universalistic, humanistic and fashioned by intellectuals', those of Asia and Africa were the creation of political leaders and specific to a country and a set of circumstances.

In his contention that ideology has come to an end in the West, he is referring to the lack of passion which gradually permeated political argument in the 1950s. A 'rough consensus' was the result, amounting to the acceptance of the Welfare State, Keynesian economics, the mixed economy, industrial relations based on tradeunion rights and 'piecemeal engineering' rather than 'social engineering' (large-scale, detailed planning on the Soviet model). In democratic parliaments both Right and Left (with the exception of the Communists who were weak outside France and Italy) accepted these propositions while disagreeing about the precise degree of application.

As a result of this trend politics had become dull and 'intellectually devitalized'.[13] Young intellectuals, therefore, had no 'cause' to pursue with fervour though they yearned for one. A promising instance appeared to be the condition of popular culture, especially the influence of television on taste and behaviour. But this was difficult to deal with politically. Moreover, it was much patronised by the working class who, in a sense, had been the main beneficiaries of the postwar changes ('in a sense' because their expectations had been so much less than those of the intellectuals). Deserted by those it saw as its natural allies, the new revolutionary Left, Bell feared, would translate its revolutionary rhetoric into violence.

In this respect Bell's apprehensions were realised. The Vietnam War gave young American intellectuals a cause and this had its echoes in Western Europe. An adaptation of Marxist thought by Herbert Marcuse presented student radicals with an ideology. He asserted that the working class had failed to fulfil Marx's prophecy that it would be the vehicle of revolutionary change. The revolution must now be carried out by an underclass of revolutionary students, Marcuse maintained.[14] The adoption of radical lifestyles and the tendency to indulge in revolutionary theatre was exemplified by the events of May 1968 in Paris which had all the outward manifestations of a nineteenth century revolution, though the working class refused to have much to do with the revolt whose origins lay in unpopular university reforms. It showed that the young were bored. The widespread strikes occurring at the same time arose from industrial workers' determination to gain higher wages by taking advantage of governments' weakness. The events perhaps showed that Mannheim was nearer the truth than Marx.

11.4 Conclusion

Obviously, although they are connected, there are wide discrepancies between the four different usages of 'ideology' set out earlier. The widest divergence is between totalitarian ideology and the mind-set of the individual. The former is a prescription handed down from authority to a population probably seen as 'the masses'. Above all it translates theory into action. The mind-set may well stem from early socialisation in the family and the school. It has little consistency about it. Yet a totalitarian ideology to be successful must obviously be based on a mind-set held by a large part of the population, what Juan Linz prefers to call a 'mentality' rather than an ideology.[15] Latent, diffuse ideas may be sharpened and simplified and then mobilised by political leaders, perhaps the ideological leaders of ideological parties.

The Fascists were aware that people's consciousness of their national identity, however slight, might be aroused by action in the form of demonstrations and riots against internal enemies. This needed a semi-military organisation. Marx's idea was that the working class had a revolutionary potential which they would understand better if they were persuaded of the repressive nature of capitalism. Organised revolutionary activity would be necessary to accomplish this task. It was Lenin's contribution to realise that only a tightly disciplined, ideological party could achieve Communism.

Ideology as a 'family of concepts' includes the other three usages. It denotes any set of beliefs held by an individual or by groups, though it is more commonly used of groups. The looseness of the term can be attributed to the sloppiness of the media and to the exploitation of language by politicians. This makes it all the more important to analyse it.

Notes

1. E. Shils, 'Ideology and civility: on the politics of the intellectual', *Sowanee Review*, 1958, reprinted in R. H. Cox (ed.), *Ideology, Politics and Political Theory* (Belmont, Calif.: Wadworth, 1969), p. 218.
2. P. E. Converse, 'The nature of belief systems in mass publics', in D. E. Apter, *Ideology and Discontent* (New York: Glencoe Free Press, 1964), p. 207f.
3. R. E. Lane, *Political Ideology* (New York: Glencoe Free Press, 1962).
4. K. Mannheim, *Ideology and Utopia* (London: routledge, 1936), p. 52.
5. Ibid., p. 36.
6. Ibid., p. 279.
7. Ibid., p. 175.
8. Shils, 'Ideology and civility', p. 225.
9. Ibid., p. 23lf.
10. J. Plamenatz, *Key Concepts in Political Science: Ideology* (London: Macmillan, 1979), p. 27.
11. R. Eccleshall, V. Geoghegan, R. Jay and R. Wilford, *Political Ideologies* (London: Unwin Hyman, 1984).

12. D. Bell, *The End of Ideology* (New York: Collier Books, 1962), p. 393f.
13. Ibid., p. 399.
14. See especially his *Eros and Civilization* (London: Routledge, 1956) and *An Essay in Liberalism* (London: Allan Lane, 1969).
15. J. J. Linz, 'An authoritarian regime: Spain', in E. Allardt and S. Rokkan, *Mass Politics* (New York: Free Press, 1970), p. 257.

Questions

1. Can there ever be an 'end to ideology'?
2. Are ideologies rational or irrational?

12

Liberalism

Liberalism cannot be classified as anything but a 'family of concepts'. Some would argue that it cannot be described as an ideology at all. Clinton Rossiter would like to place it, with Conservatism, 'on the scrap heap'.[1] Yet it tends to be represented in collections of essays about ideologies, for example Eccleshall, Geoghegan, Jay and Wilford.[2] On the other hand, it must be said that the term has been used to characterise all kinds of disparate currents of thought. To indicate this point John Gray entitled his book, *Liberalisms*.[3] Yet there are very basic values which underlie all versions of liberalism.

Liberalism is perhaps best seen as the affirmation of the right of the individual to protest and ultimately to rebel against the established order. Seventeenth-century liberalism owed its stimulus to the Reformation and the revolt of Protestants in Britain and Holland against the Catholic Church. Eighteenth-century liberalism attacked the alliance between Catholic Church and State known as the *ancien régime*. The American Revolution was a spur to its overthrow. The French Enlightenment provided the intellectual ammunition for the French Revolutionaries. The two revolutions, beginning in 1776 and 1789 respectively, popularised liberal ideas which had earlier been propagated by philosophers.

12.1 Values

Although it is not easy to be definitive about the meaning of liberalism, certain core values can be identified in all its manifestations.

12.1.1 Individual freedom

Every person is an autonomous agent, that is, has a right to make decisions for him or herself. This contention has a philosophic basis in the writings of John Locke (1632–1704). Locke asserted that we all have a 'natural right' to freedom. He wrote two *Treatises on Government*. In the former in 1689 he criticised the doctrine of hereditary power; in the second in 1690 he presents his theory of how and when we have an obligation to obey political authority. He does this with a parable in which he depicts man, before there is a State, living in a state of nature. It is 'a state of liberty, yet . . . not a state of licence'. Most people obey an accepted code of conduct, but a few do not. Thus property becomes endangered, and in Locke's view the preservation of property was the 'great and chief end' for instituting civil government. Governments are set up as a result of a contract with the people by which those in power have contracted to defend the citizens by upholding the law. If the government breaks its side of the agreement, for example by failing to defend property, the people have the right to revolt. Historically Locke's ideas were a defence of the English revolutionaries who had first deposed Charles I for flouting the wishes of Parliament and then, in the Glorious Revolution of 1688, his son James II for similar reasons.

The implication was that if governments exist to carry out the wishes of autonomous individuals, and if they can be overthrown when they do not do so, the authority of hereditary rulers from God was no longer viable. The American Revolution was a practical expression of Locke's theories. The colonists had revolted because they were being taxed without representation in Parliament. Their rhetoric echoed many of Locke's phrases. The Declaration of Independence 1776 pronounced:

> We hold these truths to be self-evident, that all men are created equal, that they are endowed by their creator with certain unalienable rights, that among these are Life, Liberty and the pursuit of happiness. That to secure these rights, governments are instituted among men, deriving their just powers from the consent of the governed. That whenever any form of government becomes destructive of these ends, it is the right of the people to alter or abolish it, and to establish new government.

The American Revolutionaries inspired the French Revolutionaries whose philosophic impetus came from two intellectual sources: first, the rational philosophers of the Enlightenment (see below); and second, the Swiss philosopher Jean Jacques Rousseau (1712–78). The opening sentence of his Social Contract, 'man is born free yet everywhere he is in chains', was a virtual declaration of war on the *ancien régime*. Rousseau argued that in a primitive state people were free and happy. It was institutions which had enslaved humanity. Hence the existing social and political order should be overthrown and government of the people, based on a contract, should replace it. Unlike

Locke, Rousseau did not think individuals relinquished their sovereignty once the contract was sealed. The sovereignty of the people was inviolable, nor could it be represented. This implied direct rather than representative democracy.

The French Declaration of the Rights of Man 1789 echoed both the *philosophes* and Rousseau. It was rather lengthier and less abstract than its American counterpart. (The generalities of the US declaration were given practical expression in the Constitution and its first ten amendments, the Bill of Rights 1791.)

Article 1 of the French document was declaratory: 'Men are born and live free and equal as regards their rights.' Articles 2 and 3 were political:

> The end of every political association is the conservation of the natural and imprescriptible rights of man. These rights are liberty, property, security and resistance to oppression.

> The principle of all sovereignty resides essentially in the nation. No office and no individual can exercise an authority not expressly emanating from it.

Article 11 proclaimed that every citizen had the right to speak, write and publish freely. Article 15 enshrined the right to demand from every public official an account of his administration. The other twelve articles related to the free and fair administration of justice.

Thus in the late eighteenth century the rights of the individual were asserted against the dynastic and despotic State. But it is worth noting what the Declarations did not say. There was no guarantee of what has come to be called 'pluralism' and, indeed, the French Revolutionaries in 1793 passed a law banning trade unions. Moreover, although freedom and equality vibrate throughout the Declarations, there is no explicit affirmation of the right to vote. Popular sovereignty did not imply representative democracy as we understand it today.

12.1.2   Rationalism

Rationalism is an assertion of the imperative necessity of Reason. This had its roots in Descartes and Locke. By declaring 'I think therefore I am' Descartes emphasised the claim of the individual to make rational personal choices. Locke saw the mind at birth as a *tabula rasa*, a blank sheet on which experience and cultural environment would leave their marks. Yet individuals could develop their minds, or they could be shaped by others. Helvetius (1715–71) accepted Locke's idea and strongly asserted the value of education as against influences from custom and religion. (His books were burnt.) Condorcet believed philosophers were beginning to apply the methods of the natural sciences to their reflections. The power of Reason was growing. Yet the philosophers of the Enlightenment who proclaimed the need for rationality were largely intuitive in their proclamations of Natural Rights. These were discarded by the Utilitarians (see p. 162) who were otherwise much influenced by the Enlightenment.

Rationalism as a liberal tendency took several forms. It was expressed in attempts to remove the arbitrary element from government. Governments should explain themselves and behave predictably. Liberal rationalists therefore emphasised the need to have a fair, undiscriminating system of justice with standardised rules. The Code Napoléon, which spread from France to other parts of Europe and even Louisiana, was the epitome of this principle. The preamble to the constitution of the Commonwealth of Massachusetts declared the intention to inaugurate 'a government of laws and not of men'. A written constitution was a definitive framework outside which governmental activity should not stray. Within the limits of a constitution the roles of other entities should be defined. Thus the us Constitution defined and balanced the powers of executive, legislature and judiciary against each other.

Rationality also implied that relationships of all kinds should be conducted through discussion and compromise, and fuelled the belief that physical conflict should be avoided wherever possible. Indeed, liberal pacifists argued that fighting was never justified. Nineteenth-century liberals presented the case for industrial and international arbitration and conciliation and the provision of legal framworks for industrial and international relations. The League of Nations and the United Nations were outcomes of this tendency. The 'Brotherhood of Man' may be an emotional term, but it is also a liberal rationalist notion.

12.1.3   Equality

Berlin writes that equality 'is one of the oldest and deepest elements in liberal thought',[4] but although early liberals proclaimed the equality of men (not women!) at birth, none of them went as far as advocating absolute equality. In fact what they were campaigning against was inequality in its various forms – social, economic and political – embodied in the old order. Feudalism was a social structure in which great status inequalities were upheld by law and custom. The ownership of land which conferred political power on the aristocracy and gentry also resulted in great inequalities of wealth.

The propagation of the notion that individuals had natural rights strengthened the feeling that equality of consideration was important, a view already present in Christian doctrine. This ought to be recognised, liberals contended, in laws and institutions. Hence the need for constitutions not only guaranteeing law and order, but also defining governmental powers so that no office or institution should have too much power. Constitutionalism of this kind certainly diminished political inequality, but the real gauge of a form of political equality was the willingness to grant the franchise to all adults. The first French Revolutionary assembly was elected on the basis of manhood suffrage, but there were numerous retrogressions in France from this before it was finally assured by the Third Republic in 1870. There was slow progress to universal suffrage, not realised until the twentieth century.

Equality of opportunity was another facet of egalitarian promise. For example, equality of access to education implied a uniform system with the eventual outcome being a meritocratic society. Furthermore, it might imply a minimum standard of living below which no one should sink. Otherwise there would be children unable to set foot on the bottom rung of the ladder which could only be attained by a measure of redistributive justice (see Chapter 13).

The pursuit of equality of opportunity would inevitably change economic and social relationships. Feudal society, bound by status relationships, gave way to one in which contractual obligations, protected by law, existed between individuals in a market economy. The classical economists argued that sovereignty for the consumer implied that sellers in the market must not be protected by the State. Economic individualism would allow the self-fulfilment of economic man.

12.1.4   Optimism

Late eighteenth-century thinkers believed that once humanity was released from its chains it would be capable of indefinite improvement. This followed from Locke's thesis that all our minds at birth were blank sheets. Education was all that was needed to nourish our potential. This precept was propagated by the French Encyclopaedists. They were nothing if not optimists. Condorcet (1743–94), for example, wrote a history of civilisation in terms of increasing human enlightenment and equality brought about by the spread of education. This optimistic belief in inevitable progress characterised liberals for two centuries. It explains their internationalism. They expected that technological advance, the emancipation of mankind from oppression, greater rationality and the advent of democratic institutions would produce more harmonious societies and more harmonious relations between states.

12.2 Liberal currents of thought

From the above values quite different versions of liberalism may be derived. These tendencies or traditions may be expressed in philosophic, political or socioeconomic terms. Frequently these currents of thought may merge with one another producing various permutations.

12.2.1 Democracy

Although in contemporary usage democratic regimes are described as 'liberal democracies', eighteenth- and nineteenth-century liberals conceived liberalism and democracy as two separate concepts. 'Democracy' was conceived, after Aristotle's *polis*, as a situation where the general body of citizens was involved in decision making. In the nineteenth century this implied a great extension of the suffrage. 'Liberalism' was perceived as implying (a) freedom from oppression by Church and throne, and (b) its replacement by a constitution guaranteeing civil rights under the law (sometimes called 'guaranteeism'). Those supporting this outcome were often concerned to limit the suffrage to householders and the middle classes who owned property. The fear was that if the propertyless were given the vote there would be a majority for confiscation.

C. B. Macpherson argues that a liberal, not a democratic, regime was needed for the development of capitalism.[5] The liberal state operated through competition between political parties responsible to a limited middle-class electorate. Macpherson believes the franchise was only extended when 'the working class had become strong enough to demand that it should have some weight in the competitive process'. Certainly hesitation in giving the vote to the lower social orders was a reflection of the belief that they could not be trusted with it. The first French Revolutionary assembly was chosen by manhood suffrage and the Terror followed. The middle classes therefore believed that rational and moderate policies and constitutional guarantees might be swept away by participatory democracy. Intellectuals like Benjamin Constant (1767–1830) perceived that enfranchised people might not only be a danger to property, but also likely to disregard inalienable rights like that of free speech. There were American and British politicians with similar views and in France, François Guizot (1787–1874), the leading politician under the Orleanist Monarchy, used similar arguments to restrict the electorate to a quarter of a million.

The main early proponents of participatory democracy were Rousseau and the British Utilitarians. Rousseau was the first theorist of populism. In order to ascertain the General Will of society it was necessary to take a vote of all citizens. Rousseau disliked legislatures which reflected sectional wills. (He was probably thinking of the feudal system of estates.) Therefore he foresaw decisions made by referendums, a device he was familiar with in his native Geneva. He was a democrat, though he could hardly be considered a liberal for he had little time for constitutions and he regarded property as an evil.

The Utilitarians were anxious to reform British government according to their principle of utility. This defined the good society as one in which there was the greatest happiness for the greatest number. But how could this be discovered? Jeremy Bentham (1748–1832) concluded that everyone had to be allowed to express their preferences and the only practical way do this was by allowing free speech and a universal franchise. He was very reluctant about the latter and so was his disciple, James Mill (1773–1836) who at one time wanted the vote restricted to men over forty. James's son, John Stuart Mill (1806–73), was similarly worried, believing that only the educated classes could make national policy, especially economic policy. He feared that an enfranchised working class would demand 'class legislation', but living through the Chartist troubles of the nineteenth century, he knew the growing organisation of the working class. Like the earlier Utilitarians he feared the 'tyranny of the majority' (his phrase), though he was more aware than his father of the inequalities of British society, and he differed from him in that he saw democracy as an educative process in which citizens, by participating, could realise their full potential. Worrying about the extension of the suffrage, he came up with the 'fancy franchise': every adult should have a vote but some, like university graduates, should have more than one vote.

Participation has remained a democratic ideal even when it has become clear that the majority do not often want to participate. There are also still echoes of the nineteenth-century fear that many people participating may destabilise the democratic process. This emphasises the democratic dilemma: people must be treated as though they are informed and responsible even when they are not. Yet in putting trust in them civil liberties and national security may be endangered. For the democrat, however, there is no option but to take the risk.

12.2.2   Secularism

The Age of Reason also queried the existence of God. The Reformation had produced a Protestant individual with freedom to approach his God without the intercession of a priest and with a free conscience to make up his own mind. In countries where Protestantism had made little headway, the French Revolution provided the impetus for the introduction of a lay state. The revolutionaries confiscated church lands and introduced civil marriage and secular state education. Anti-clerical liberals demanded a separation of church and state as foreshadowed in Article 1 of the US Bill of Rights (1791): 'Congress shall make no law respecting the establishment of religion.' With the disestablishment of churches minority religions received freedom and religious toleration emerged as an important liberal principle.

12.2.3 Romanticism

The romantic disposition is not obviously connected with rationalism. Yet the idea of Reason can inspire emotions. Romanticism is associated with Rousseau rather than the Enlightenment. It reflected the mood of the young, the dispossessed and the artistic. Rousseau idealised the 'noble savage', undefiled by institutions. The primitive was to be preferred to the sophisticated. Rousseau had also declared that the people were sovereign and this had been embodied in the Declaration of the Rights of Man, where it was first worded as sovereignty residing in 'the nation'. In fact, there are two streams of liberal romanticism, one with its roots in 'the people' and the other in 'the nation'.

'The people' was more likely to apply where a country had a well-established ethnic identity and the struggle was against hierarchy and class. The British romantic poets claimed to be getting their inspiration from ordinary people. Robert Burns wrote poetry in the Scots dialect. William Wordsworth in his preface to the Lyrical Ballads in 1800 spoke of his choice of 'low and rustic life as a source of inspiration because in that situation the essential passions of the heart . . . are less under restraint and speak a plainer and more emphatic language'. The Romantic movement, much influenced by Rousseau and the emotions of the French Revolution, discovered the 'common man'.

'The nation' was a concept more likely to be involved with emancipatory emotions where common men were unable to express themselves and develop their potential because their ethnic identity was stifled and they had no legitimate organisation. The French Revolutionary and Napoleonic armies carried their ideas into the rest of Europe where many subject peoples lived under three empires – Russian, Austro-Hungarian and Turkish. Hence the subject nations began to strive for statehood. Moreover, Italy and Germany were still in the nineteenth century mere geographical expressions. They were divided into many states under the rule of many dynasties. Three dates – 1848, 1870 and 1918 – mark milestones in the nationalist struggle.

Nationalism conceives of the nation as a cultural expression and as an instrument of power. The nation as cultural entity is clearly linked with liberalism: individual potential cannot be developed where one's national culture is restricted by a more powerful culture and where one cannot advance socially without renouncing one's native ethnicity. Hence the emancipation of the individual and the repressed nation are as one. In the nineteenth century the terms liberalism and nationalism were often intertwined.

The Romantic movement naturally was in sympathy with the aspirations of repressed peoples and numerous literary figures championed their cause. For example, the poet Byron, proclaimed in the 'Isles of Greece':

> The mountains look on Marathon
> And Marathon looks on the sea;
> And musing there an hour alone,
> I dream'd that Greece might still be free.

He became a strong supporter of the Greek revolt against the Turkish empire and when in 1823 he died in the course of the struggle he was sanctified by European liberals as their romantic hero.

Two nations which had no legal identity, even after 1815, were the Germans and the Italians. It is significant that the inspiration for early liberal nationalism came from a German, Johann Herder (1744–1803) and an Italian, Giuseppe Mazzini (1805–72). Herder was a Lutheran pastor and a Mecklenburger whose hobby was collecting the folk songs of the peasantry and studying the German language. In his *Thoughts on the Philosophy of Mankind* he argued that the natural basis of a state was the distinctive culture and character of its people reflected in a common language. Each *Volk* should have its own state. This had revolutionary implications for Germans were living in over 300 states at this time. Yet Herder believed every *Volk* should respect the aspirations for statehood of every other *Volk*. Mazzini at an early age was a member of the Carbonari, a secret society working to rid North Italy of Austrian rule and unite its various parts in 'one nation from the Alps to the sea'. He was imprisoned, went into exile and returned in 1848 to set up, with Garibaldi, a Constituent Assembly for an Italian Republic. His writings are polemical and shallow intellectually, but they express a passionate rationalist belief in Progress and the common interests of humanity. In the *Duties of Man* he told Italians their duty was to humanity. Mazzini spoke for oppressed nationalities throughout Europe and sincerely believed that when they were emancipated they would embrace democracy and live in peace with each other.

Romantic nationalism and popular sovereignty reached their

apotheosis in 1918 when President Wilson enunciated the doctrine of the self-determination of peoples and the map was changed. The logical conclusion was a Europe of nation-states. A state, however, is an instrument of power and the use of power is often unromantic and quite illiberal. Furthermore, new states are not always democratic. Nationalists are often quite illiberal.

12.2.4 Capitalism

Capitalism certainly reflects the values of individualism and freedom from restriction. It is often associated with the Protestant belief that we are the best judge of our own interests. If this idea is transferred to the marketplace there emerges 'economic man', who rationally assesses his preferences when he buys and sells so that the outcome is the one most favourable to him. It only happens, however, when there is no interference in the economy by political authority. This was hardly so under the *ancien régime* when the system of mercantilism ensured that trade should be controlled. The main assault on mercantilism was delivered by the Scots economist Adam Smith, (1723–90) in his book *The Wealth of Nations* (1776). Smith argued that unrestricted competition should be maintained between sellers by allowing free access to markets. The buyers would compete on their side and the eventual price would be reached as if by an invisible hand. Cheaper goods, a much greater volume of trade and a more prosperous economy would follow. Businessmen might not like this outcome: they want high profits not competition. Smith's doctrine, however, was a charter for the consumer.

Not all states would accept this attack on protectionism. The 'state as an economic actor' school rejected liberal economic theory which implied an international market and international free trade. It was argued that the promotion of national prosperity was a matter for governments, most thoroughly by Friedrich List (1789–1846), a German economist. In *The National System of Political Economy* (1841) he rejected the 'shopkeeper's theory' of Smith and stressed that developing a country's productivity took preference over consumer sovereignty. Individuals are not merely economic men but citizens with obligations to the nation. The polity should control the economy and even war may be necessary if it advances prosperity.[6]

The concept of a free market remained something of a liberal ideal to which some countries approximated and which was more strongly realised at some times than others. Perfect competition, however, was only one aspect of capitalism – there was a strong attachment to the idea of private property which became more complex with the advent of industrial and finance capital. When early small-scale entrepreneurial capitalism gave way to corporate capitalism there arose great inequalities of wealth and power. Monopoly capitalism could scarcely be consistent with classical liberalism's championship of the consumer.

12.2.5 Social reform

Liberals perceived themselves as the emancipators of the individual. Yet as industrial capitalism developed the lot of all individuals by no means improved. Social problems such as the spread of slum housing, the recurrence of depressions leading to large-scale unemployment and the very visible differences between the wealthy and the impoverished restricted the potential of some individuals. Liberals, therefore, began to consider whether their commitment to *laissez-faire* was any longer appropriate.

As Britain was the first country to industrialise it is not surprising that the first 'social liberals' were British. T. H. Green (1836–82) in his *Principles of Political Obligation* (1882) asserted that will not force was the basis of the state, which had a duty to remove impediments to a good life. He thus imbued the State with a moral purpose, the development of the human personality. Public and private institutions should be guided to this end. The state should provide universal education, greatly improved housing, work for the unemployed and a better standard of health. Green did not blame capitalism for the condition of the British working classes, but rather the relics of feudalism. His ideas influenced the reforming Liberal government before 1914. Another social liberal, Leonard Hobhouse (1864–1929), believed the state could be much more active in its social policy. In *Liberalism* (1911) he argued that state intervention would develop the 'self-directing power of personality'.[7] To do this capitalism would have to be modified. Later in the 1940s the legacy of Green and Hobhouse was taken up by two other liberals, Keynes and Beveridge, whose policies underpinned the British welfare state.

12.2 Conclusion

The ideas of two revolutions and the theories of liberal philosophers provided some basis for early liberalism which, even then, was quite wide-ranging. As the franchise was established and extended, political parties and pressure groups emerged. The first use of the term as a political party label was by the group sponsoring the Spanish constitution of 1812. Liberal leaders' pronouncements and their parties' policies shaped the perception of what 'liberalism' was. Often the distinction was made between the Liberalism of Liberal parties, with a capital 'L', and the liberalism of the critical intellectuals with a small 'l'.

A survey of how liberalism has developed in different countries reveals how different political cultures and circumstances can affect a family of concepts. For example, in the USA 'liberalism' in the nineteenth century applied to the anti-slavery movement, mostly Republicans. By the 1930s it applied to Democratic New Dealers and their interventionist economic policies in favour of labour. Today it is used to describe the 'free marketeers', largely found on the Republican Right, standing for everything the New Dealers opposed. In Germany the nineteenth-century national liberals would be considered conservatives by other countries' standards. They supported the constitution of the new Empire after 1870 which included manhood suffrage, but also unresponsible government. Their heir in the Weimar Republic, and the party of big business, was the People's Party, but the anti-clerical Democrats represented the small shopkeepers. Both tendencies since 1949 have been combined in the Free Democrats who are often described as the 'German Liberal Party' though they sit to the Right of the Christian Democrats in the Bundestag. Initially they opposed entry to the European Community. After some secession to the Christian Democrats the more liberal Free Democrats were more disposed to reform, though they remained strict about public expenditure.

Like the British Liberals the Free Democrats became a classic centre party. Unlike the British Liberals, however, the Free Democrats, by virtue of proportional representation, had a balancing and bargaining position in the legislature. The British Liberals, when the Labour Party became a major party after 1918, saw most of its commercial support desert to the Conservatives. They were decimated by the 'first past the post' electoral system and became a small centre party with reformist policies and little political power in a Parliament dominated by a majority party. Their *Yellow Book* in the 1920s, much inspired by Keynesian ideas, rejected *laissez-faire* and socialist planning. Since then they have remained between Labour and the Conservatives on most issues, though they are the strongest advocates of devolution and of becoming more integrated into Europe.

Early Liberals in France and Italy resembled the German National Liberals in that they stood for constitutional government. In both countries they were anti-clerical. The Italian Liberals supported the monarchy, but the Republicans were the heirs of Mazzini. Today both are tiny parties. French liberalism might, therefore, be found in the Radical Party supporting orthodox republicanism, but many might consider the Radicals a conservative party. Since 1945, however, with the clerical issue losing much of its bitterness and with the decline of the peasantry, the Radicals have ceased to be a major force.

To sum up: since the Second World War Liberal parties have been in decline. On the other hand liberal values have been preserved and, some would say, extended. Other groups than Liberal parties have accepted many liberal ideas. The general effect has been that 'liberalism' has become a vague term, shifting in meaning according to speaker, circumstance and audience.

Notes

1. C. Rossiter, *Conservatism in America* (London: Heinemann, 1955), p. 5.
2. R. Eccleshall, V. Geoghan, R. Jay, and R. Wilford, *Political Ideologies* (London: Unwin Hyman, 1984).
3. J. Gray, *Liberalisms* (London: Routledge 1989).
4. I. Berlin, 'Equality', *Proceedings of the Aristotelian Society 1955–6*, p. 326, quoted in J. Rees, *Equality* (London: Pall Mall, 1971), p. 122.
5. C. B. Macpherson, *The Real World of Democracy* (Toronto: Canadian Broadcasting Corporation, 1981), p. 35.
6. A. Gray, *The Development of Economic Doctrine* (London: Longman, 1931), p. 238f.
7. Eccleshall et al., *Political Ideologies*, p. 65.

Questions

1. Some say liberalism is based on freedom of the individual, others on the notion of emancipation. To what degree are these two views irreconcilable?
2. How is liberalism related to democracy? Could liberals ever be undemocratic?

13

Socialism

Socialism is often described as an ideology because it is a set of principles for action, but in the terms of Chapter 11 it belongs to the category of 'family of concepts'. It has come to be used very loosely, sometimes by right-wing politicians who want to denigrate opponents, sometimes by left-wing politicians who need to assert that almost everything they say and do is 'socialist'. Socialism comprises a variety of principles and policies. D. B. Rappoport in his *Dictionary of Socialism* (1924) gives thirty-nine definitions. Some so-called socialists are totalitarian ideologues: many are moderate democratic people of a rather conservative disposition.

The values underlying socialism are partly derived from the French Revolution and partly a reaction against the results of the Industrial Revolution. As regards the former, when they assert the same values as liberals, the socialists often add a twist of their own. Their reactions against the Industrial Revolution were against its inequity and inequality, its waste and inefficiency, and its squalor and ugliness.

13.1 Values

13.1.1 Liberty

Like liberals, socialists would claim to represent 'freedom'. They proclaim the need to emancipate. Like liberals, they are motivated by the metaphor of Humanity's need to break its bonds. Rousseau wrote that man should cast off the chains of the old order. Marx and Engels in the *Communist Manifesto* attacked of the new capitalist order. 'The proletarians have nothing to lose but their chains. They have a world to gain. Working men of all countries unite!' The argument in both cases was that repression could only be overthrown by vigorous action.

13.1.2 Reason

The eighteenth century is often described the Age of Reason because the French *philosophes*, as we have noted, then questioned the dominance of

Church and Throne, asking 'Why?' 'Is it susceptible to Reason?' In the nineteenth century this questioning began to be applied to the industrial order and the type of economy we now call 'capitalism' (though this term was not commonly used until the mid-century). The industrial order was seen to be wasteful and inefficient and, therefore, inimical to rationality which postulated a purposive and efficient approach to life and to the economy and society. Capitalism was believed to be chaotic, while socialists put a premium on administration and organisation. Socialism would be a more rational order.

13.1.3 Moralism

Socialism has often been moralistic. Early socialists were either Christians or non-Christian humanists who still retained the Christian ethic which militated against greed and selfishness, features they identified in the capitalist system. The Catholic Church had always condemned usury, and the Christian teaching that everyone had worth and that we were all brothers and sisters might imply that we should not exploit or attack one another. Christian socialists deprecated profiteering and believed industrial and international conflict should, as far as possible, be avoided. Like liberals, socialists tend to be pacifist and internationalist. Even when, as in the case of Marx, socialism is identified with atheism, one is aware of a strong distinction being drawn between what is good and what is evil.

13.1.4 Equality

Berki says egalitarianism is the 'classical principle of socialism'.[1] This is correct because, though liberals would assert the principle of equality in a legal and civic sense, many liberals would not support social equality. It has been said that 'socialism is about equality', but the difficulty here is that equal treatment cannot sensibly be applied to everyone. It does not make sense to treat the sick like the healthy, or grandmothers like babes in arms. We cannot behave as though there is uniformity of humankind.

Therefore most socialists argue for much less inequality of wealth. They are egalitarians, believing that the gap between rich and poor should be mitigated by redistribution of wealth. They condemn the concentration of wealth in a few hands. Two basic policies emerge from socialist egalitarianism:

1. higher taxation to be used for spending on the alleviation of poverty, the promotion of public health and the development of national education;

2. common or cooperative ownership to replace, to a greater or
    lesser extent, individual, competitive enterprise.

13.1.5 Fraternity

Like liberals, socialists believe in the Brotherhood of Man. This reinforces their internationalism and weakens nationalism. Practically,
comradeship has been expressed in the various Socialist Internationals
(confederations of socialist parties).

Finally, these underlying values have not always been evident. There
has been much disagreement and even hatred at times between different socialist factions and parties. Such rancour and cleavage can be
better understood from an examination of how the different socialisms
have developed.

13.2 Socialist theorists

Both words, 'socialism' and 'sociology', appeared at about the same
time. The former seems to have been first used by St Simon and the
latter by Auguste Comte (1798–1857). That they are contemporanous is
no coincidence because, as the Industrial Revolution gathered strength,
la question sociale became an issue. The conditions in society were the
starting point for all early nineteenth-century socialists, and unlike
liberals, they advanced prescriptions for a good society. Nearly all their
writings were theoretical. Without consideration of practical policies
they had no sense of reality.

13.2.1   Early Utopian thinkers

Henri St Simon (1760–1825)

St Simon wanted so to organise industrial production that it would be
for individual well-being. His eighteenth-century rationalism persuaded him that only publicly owned and directed industry would
not be wasteful. Later in life he evolved a 'new Christianity' with a new
universal morality, the Cult of Humanity by which he thought artists,
scientists and business leaders should guide the world. Thus he was an
elitist and not an egalitarian.

Charles Fourier (1772–1837)

Like St Simon he is often regarded as a founding father of socialism.
Fourier was a Utopian socialist who attacked parasitism – the armed

forces, bureaucrats and most of the merchants and manufacturers. He deplored the wastage of much agricultural land and believed it could be avoided by organising cooperatives, largely rural, which would be self-sufficient. They would be called *phalanstères*, communes in which free love would be the practice. Conflict and poverty would no longer exist, neither would the distinction between producer and consumer. This anarchist, visionary society he called Harmony.

Robert Owen (1771–1858)

The Utopian socialists were often French, a legacy of the rationalism of the French Revolution. The Industrial Revolution came much earlier in Britain and socialist thinkers were more aware of the problems of the urban working class. Owen was a succesful capitalist, a textile manu-facturer, who came to believe that cooperation was superior to com-petition. He was appalled by the contrast between rich and poor in Britain and became convinced that some sort of collective organisation of society was necessary in order to improve living standards and prevent class conflict. To this end he was involved with both the early British cooperative movement and the first large trade union. (It failed.) Owen was really an early, rather elitist, utilitarian.

13.2.2   The social question

The emergence of *la question sociale* in the mid-century was the result of people observing the plight of the industrial workers. Prominent among these was Louis Blanc (1813–82), an intellectual who, in his *Travail* (1839), proposed the establishment of industrial cooperatives as a first step towards the socialisation of capital and the abolition of the wage system. The revolutionary government of 1848 set up national workshops which failed, but they were a travesty of his scheme and were probably intended to discredit him. Blanc was much more prac-tical than the Utopian socialists. He did not believe in class war, but was moved by the condition of the workers and tried to help them. For his pains he was exiled by Louis Napoleon.

13.2.3   Karl Marx (1813–83)

Marx claimed to transcend the ideas of the Utopian socialists and to present a theory of 'scientific socialism'. His analysis is much more profound and wide-ranging than anything previously produced. Both a scholar and a thinker, undoubtedly a revolutionary socialist in the theoretical sense, he probably never heard a shot fired in anger.

Marx's immense volume of writing can perhaps be discussed under four headings: an explanation of the economy based on the labour theory of value; a theory of history with philosophic underpinnings; a body of prophecy; and a general strategy and programme.

Labour theory of value

Marx adapted this theory from the classical economists, notably Ricardo. Briefly, it alleges that the value of a product depends on the amount of labour which has gone into its production. The worker sells his labour to the entrepreneur for a wage, but it does not reflect the whole value of what he produces. The entrepreneur takes a share for himself, a 'surplus' of something which is not his and which he does not merit. His profit is at the expense of his workers. Moreover, besides being exploited, the workers have lost status as craftsmen because their tools have been taken away from them – they work on the employers' machines and do not even know, owing to the division of labour, what they are producing. Consequently they are alienated from their work and their product which is sold by someone else. They are wage-slaves. This situation can only be changed by an expropriation of the means of production and their transformation into public property.

Theory of historical development

Marx's theory of history was much influenced by the German philosopher Hegel (1770–1831) from whom he took the following four features: history is divided into epochs; each epoch is distinguished by a different type of society based upon a change of the essential basic motivating force; changes take place as the result of a dialectic; and eventually the historical force will triumph, ushering in a final phase in which the destiny of humanity will be realised.

Hegel, in his *Philosophy of History* (lectures delivered 1830–31), had written:

> The history of the world is the discipline of the uncontrolled natural will, bringing it into obedience to a universal principle and conferring objective freedom. The East knew . . . that One is free; the Greek and Roman world that some are free; the German world that All are free.

In the German epoch the Spirit is at 'perfect maturity and strength'. 'The German nation', Hegel says, was the 'first to attain the consciousness that man is free.'

Marx believed mankind, or rather the proletariat, was moving towards a final realisation of a higher and better destiny, though for him ultimate consciousness would be attained not through the Spirit but by the realisation of class solidarity and the need to emancipate by revolutionary action. Marx's division into epochs was dependent on the changing type of property relationship. Asiatic society was based on property ownership by the state; the ancient world was based on slavery; feudal society depended on landed property and serfdom, a form of status slavery; capitalist society was based on capitalist ownership and exploited wage labour. The nature of each epoch was thus determined by the economic system and the dominant class in each period. In the capitalist era the capitalist class used the state as its instrument of hegemony.

Marx also took from Hegel the concept of a dialectic. In each epoch there were conflicting forces, thesis and antithesis, a contradiction eventually leading to breakdown. Each succeeding social order disintegrates similarly because of inner contradictions. Capitalism will likewise disintegrate giving way to the final epoch, socialism. Socialism will be the last stage of human history, the final synthesis. The dominant contradictions in Marx's changes are economic. Hence his theory is called dialectical materialism.

A body of prophecies

From his analysis of capitalism and his theory of history Marx felt he could predict the future. Capital would become more concentrated and economic competition between large enterprises would become fiercer. So workers' wages would be cut and unemployment would increase.

Consequently in the later stages of capitalism the class struggle would become more intense. Intermediate classes would be ground down, leaving only the employers and the workers fighting each other. The end would be imperialist conflict caused by international economic competition.

The workers would have nothing to gain from these wars. Eventually they would realise their common interests and identity, become organised and overthrow capitalism. In the course of doing this they would set up a dictatorship of the proletariat, a transition strategy while private capital was being expropriated and common ownership installed. Then a classless society with a socialist form of production would ensue in which the free development of each would be a condition for the free development of all. There would be no need for repression so there would be no state. It would 'wither away'.

Suggested programme

It is often said that Marx was vague about socialist policies. Yet in the *Communist Manifesto*, published with Engels in 1848, the following measures which workers' governments might be expected to implement are listed.

1. abolition of property in land: all rents to be used for public purposes;
2. a heavy progressive or graduated income tax;
3. abolition of the right of inheritance;
4. confiscation of property belonging to traitors;
5. centralisation of credit in the hands of the state through a national bank;
6. centralisation and nationalisation of communication and transport;
7. extension of state ownership of factories and instruments of production, the cultivation of waste lands and the improvement of the soil in accordance with a common plan;
8. all equally obliged to work – industrial armies to be established, especially for agriculture;
9. gradual abolition of the distinction between town and country by distributing the population equally;
10. free state education, child labour to be abolished, education to be combined with industrial production.

13.3 Socialism after Marx: options for working-class action

When Marx died, thirty-five years after the *Communist Manifesto*, the world was a very different place. Industrialisation had spread greatly and was accelerating. The urban working class had become much larger. Improved communications had facilitated nationwide organisations of all kinds, including trade unions and socialist political parties. In Western Europe and North America the male section of the working class had, either wholly or partially, been enfranchised and was beginning to make its weight felt in legislatures.

Socialists were divided about how they should deal with these developments. What strategy should they pursue? For serious adherents of Marx's views, still few in number, the strategy was clear. Workers' organisations should be used to advance the revolutionary consciousness of the working class. Marxists should permeate and infiltrate them. To begin with they might be concerned to win workers' support only by making economic gains, but in confrontational situations with employers grievances could be exploited. In a later stage of consciousness workers' organisations would become aware of political objectives. The proletariat would realise its common identity and purposes. As Marx said it would be 'a class for itself'. The final stage of consciousness would be when the working class grasped it had a historic role, that of a sort of collective hero destined to inaugurate socialism throughout the world.

These ideas were difficult to understand and did not seem realistic to many. Various options for working-class action were put forward between 1880 and 1914.

13.3.1   Socialist internationalism

By the 1880s enough camaraderie existed between socialist parties for them to inaugurate an international organisation at Paris in 1889. It was called the Second International. (Marx had founded the abortive First International in 1864.) The body was dominated by the German Social Democrats who professed Marxist views. Significantly Marx had seen Germany as the home of the revolution in his later years. In 1907 at its Stuttgart conference the Second International discussed a resolution supporting a General Strike to avert war. It was argued that the workers had no interest in fighting other workers – their common enemy was the capitalist class. The plan was, if war broke out and workers were mobilised in their national armies, for them all to mutiny. War would then be impossible and an international alliance between the different proletariats would have been forged. It would then be easy to overthrow capitalism everywhere. But the resolution finally adopted said it was the duty of working classes to do everything to prevent war, but it did not specify a strike though it did not exclude one. Unfortunately for Marxists in 1914 national consciousness proved much stronger than class consciousness.

By 1914 it had become clear that the Socialist movements were very much divided: between non-Marxists and Marxists, and within the latter over interpretation and tactics. Different answers to the question, 'What is to be done?' were being proffered.

13.3.2   Syndicalism

Marx had condemned anarchism. If he had been alive he would have condemned syndicalism, a collective anarchism of the trade-union movement. The syndicalists often used Marxist terminology and they believed they were engaged in the class war. Their strategy was to turn the workplace into a battlefield by direct, if necessary violent, industrial action. They had no faith in parliamentary activity and prescribed a General Strike to end capitalism. Georges Sorel (1847–1922), the philosopher of syndicalism, pictured the Parisian workers going for a weekday picnic in the Bois de Boulogne instead of to work. Capitalism would then collapse and the workers would take over and run the factories. Even if these tactics were unsuccessful it would remain as a 'myth', a vision to give the workers hope. A more practical French trade union leader, Fernand Pelloutier (1867–1901), supported the local Bowses du Travail and, in 1892, helped them to unite in a national federation, becoming its secretary in 1895. In Britain Tom Mann of the engineers' union was a declared syndicalist. In the USA the Industrial Workers of the World, organised among workers in extractive industries, made inroads with its syndicalist preachings.

13.3.3   Libertarianism

Libertarianism with its roots in liberty, equality and fraternity is the romantic stream of socialist thought. It has tended to be espoused by artists and writers and often has come to be a protest against conventional ('bourgeois') forms of behaviour. At its beginning it was a reaction against the ugliness and commercialism of taste in the Industrial Revolution. Again Britain as the home of industrialism probably saw its strongest expression. William Morris (1834–96) idealised the days before the factory arrived, when all men were craftsmen and artists. Now they were alienated, with their aesthetic feelings suppressed. Other libertarians were concerned with sexual emancipation. Early 'gay rights' activists in Britain were the artist Edward Carpenter, who in *Towards Democracy* (1905) argued that sexual repression was part of the capitalist ethos, and Oscar Wilde, who in *The Soul of Man* (1907) reconciled socialism with extreme individualism. Rupert Brooke, the poet, in the Fabian Tract, *The Arts Under Socialism* (1913) forecast government support for the arts when socialists came to power.

13.3.4   Parliamentary socialism

Marx had usually scorned democracy which he regarded as a bourgeois sham to keep the capitalists in power. Yet as socialist and labour representation grew in European parliaments, relations with the class enemy were unavoidable. This was a particular problem for Marxist representatives.

Marxist parties

The German Social Democratic Party was the doyen of socialist parties and its ideas and rhetoric were Marxist. After manhood suffrage was introduced in the German Empire (founded in 1871) it became the largest party in the Reichstag, although it could never govern because the government was not responsible to the legislature. Moreover, Bismarck was hostile and banned the party from 1878 to 1890.

During the First World War the Social Democrats were split. The leader of the anti-war group, Eduard Bernstein (1850–1932), claimed to be a Marxist all his life. Yet he is regarded as the most prominent revisionist and in his later years came under attack from the Communists. He believed that enterprises should not be publicly owned when they operated efficiently. He did not think the state would wither away: in fact, he thought it had great possibilities for the purpose of redistributing income and running the social services. Like many socialists Bernstein abhorred violence and he considered the idea of class dictatorship 'belonged to a lower order of civilisation'. Socialism would come because the industrial proletariat had the vote and was easily the largest class in Germany.

Bernstein's position, presented in *Evaluating Socialism* (1899), was based on a reappraisal of capitalism's development. From an analysis of the trade cycle in the last quarter of the nineteenth century he detected no evidence that the crisis of capitalism was becoming more acute. Trade unions and cooperative societies, he pointed out, provided a countervailing power to the employers. Consequently, though Bernstein was a Marxist, his views became rather different from those of his mentor.

Non-Marxist parties

British labour developed differently from the European socialist parties. Its origins were largely the result of the trade unions wanting representation in Parliament. (A confederation of trade unions, the Trades Union Congress, had existed since 1868.) In 1900 trade union delegates and those of three socialist bodies – the Fabian Society dating from 1884, the Social Democratic Federation founded in 1881 and the Independent Labour Party founded in 1893 – met and inaugurated the Labour Representation Committee which became the Labour Party with thirty MPs after the 1906 General Election. Its socialism was largely ethical and its programme pragmatic. It had little time for 'class war' notions and its only Marxist component, the tiny Social Democratic Federation, withdrew in 1901 after failing to obtain the passage of a class war resolution.

The Labour Party's policies at this stage often stemmed from the Fabian Society, a study group of professional people who tried to influence leading politicians with Fabian ideas. The two most prominent Fabians were Sidney and Beatrice Webb whose lifelong researches were directed towards national social policy. Sidney served in two Labour governments. Unlike Marx they saw the state as the principle instrument for the attainment of socialism. Their two basic policies were a considerable extension of public ownership with the mines and the railways being organised on the lines of the Post Office (adjudged a great success), and the establishment of a National Minimum, a standard of living below which no one should be allowed to slip. This latter measure involved a reformed poor law with larger social benefits and a minimum wage enforced by wage boards.

The French socialist party was divided into Marxists and the majority non-Marxists led by Jean Jaurès (1859–1914). It had an internationalist tradition as its name, the French Section of the Workers International (SFIO), suggests. It was too small to come to power and Jaurès was willing to ally himself for some purposes with the 'bourgeois' parties. He was anti-clerical and a defender of the Republic, but he was too pacific to advocate revolution and he opposed the romanticism of Sorel. The French working class, he believed, could come to power through the ballot box rather than the bullet, and he condemned revolutionary notions as leading to chaos and only playing into the hands of counter-revolutionaries.

Hence two main factors, which were to become very important in the twentieth century, modified the stance of the socialists. Capitalism failed to expire and the proletariat, far from becoming increasingly impoverished, enjoyed an increasingly high standard of living. At the same time the franchise widened and political organisation and parliamentary representation provided an alternative to revolutionary action.

13.4 Socialism since 1914

By the First World War socialist ideology was clearly a 'family of concepts'. Numerous intellectual currents were in circulation, and even the Marxist current was dividing as economic and political changes caused Marx's theories to be questioned. Some of the measures mentioned in the *Communist Manifesto*, such as the prohibition of child labour and a progressive income tax, had been implemented in several industrial countries. Furthermore, socialist ideas were being blurred by radical politicians, who used them as electoral propaganda rather than as principles to be adhered to and implemented.

In 1917, however, an explicit assertion of Marxist ideas somewhat changed this picture.

13.4.1 Communism

In March 1917 the Czar was dethroned and in October the Bolsheviks seized power. The Bolsheviks had been the dominant faction in the

Russian Social Democratic Party since 1903 under the leadership of Lenin who attacked the parent body's imitation of Social Democrats further West and, in *What is To Be Done* (1902), advocated a small party of revolutionary intellectuals. The Bolsheviks interpreted their 1917 coup as the proletariat assuming its dictatorship as prophesied. Lenin constructed his edifice of power around his Communist Party which, throughout the country, acted as the chief monitoring and mobilising agent. It implemented policies which were designed to be on Marxist lines. A new type of economic, social and political order was thus inaugurated.

The main features of this regime (see Chapter 4) were as follows:

1. A command economy was instituted. Wages and prices were fixed by the government, i.e. the Communist Party, which operated a system of centralised planning.
2. Public ownership was effected within two–three years and later agriculture was collectivised in large holdings.
3. The Communist secret police made critical opposition impossible. Only one candidate could stand in each constituency at elections, so the candidates of the Communist and non-party bloc were the only ones elected.
4. The Communist Party and its satellite bodies in youth organisations, cooperatives, cultural societies, etc. were the only organisations allowed to exist.
5. The official Marxist doctrine was taught in schools and disseminated in simple slogans among the masses.

Hence Communism is, or was, a totalitarian ideology, fulfilling all the criteria mentioned in Chapter 11.

13.4.2   Social democracy

Parliamentary socialist parties were thrown into confusion by the Bolshevik Revolution and by the foundation, in 1920, of the Third International, a confederation of Communist Parties throughout the world. Where they had been little influenced by Marxism, as in Britain, democratic socialist parties condemned Communism and rejected Communist advances. In France, however, the Socialist Party lost many of its activists and voters to the newly formed Communist Party. In Germany the Social Democratic Party remained Marxist in rhetoric and still attached to class-war politics, though competing with the growing Communist Party. There is no doubt that the rise of Soviet Communism delayed the progress to power of Social Democrats everywhere.

Democratic socialist parties came to power gradually: in Australia and New Zealand before 1914, in Sweden in 1934, in France in 1936, in Britain in 1945, in Germany in 1969, and in Spain in 1982. Although there were considerable cultural differences between these countries their socialist governments pursued not dissimilar policies.

1. Public ownership was applied to a relatively small sector of the economy. The market for most commodities remained the method of distribution. Economies were mixed.
2. A welfare state was set up, based on fairly high taxation. Economies were managed on Keynesian principles to maintain a high rate of employment.
3. Socialist parties could only govern with the consent of a large proportion of the voters. They could be dismissed from office – in fact, it has been their common experience. Their ideas and policies were constantly under challenge. In no way, therefore, could social democracy become an official state doctrine.

It was common in Eastern Europe to describe Communism as 'socialism', and social democratic government as 'capitalist' and certainly social democracy has more in common with liberalism or democratic conservatism than with Communism. In fact, whether a country has a democratic system or not is a more appropriate criterion for assessing the type of society and the sort of polity it possesses than the absence or presence of public ownership. Democracy is inimical to ideology.

Note

1. R. N. Berki, *Socialism* (London: Dent, 1975), p. 25.

Questions

1. To what degree is socialism compatible with democracy? At what point, if any, could a democratic socialist government become undemocratic?
2. Compare and contrast socialism with liberalism.

14

Conservatism

Conservatism is clearly a 'family of concepts', if it is an ideology at all. It is often included in works about various ideologies, but many conservatives would argue that it is the reverse of an ideology. Conservatives do not believe in doctrines or programmes of long-term objectives. They are pragmatic. Conservatism is not a creed but a 'disposition', says Oakeshott. Some would contend it is merely a matter of temperament. Nevertheless, adopting such an attitude to politics implies certain values, to a greater or lesser extent found in all conservatives.

14.1 Values

14.1.1 Stability

A core value of conservatives is the desire to conserve things as they are, or as near to what they are as possible. Hence conservatives with a small 'c' have no necessarily ideological leaning. They may want to conserve a piece of waste ground, a derelict factory or a meaningless ritual. Moreover, one status quo may differ very much ideologically from another and yet any defence of the established order will be described as 'conservative'. A good example of this confusing practice is the Western media's description of those in post-Communist Europe wanting to retain as much of the Communist heritage as possible as 'conservative'. In this Chapter the term is used to indicate politicians, political parties and ideas familiarly called 'right wing'.

The conservative is predisposed against change. This does not imply that all conservatives think the status quo is desirable: it is merely that many think that change will result in a worse situation and need to be persuaded that even slight change will bring improvement. Thus the conservative disposition tends to be rather pessimistic. Conservatives are sceptical about programmes promising social justice and even more about a new order for the progress of humanity. They believe human beings are capable of folly. With some fear of change can border on timidity, with a few, hysteria.

14.1.2 Security of property

It follows from their attachment to stability that conservatives are concerned with the maintenance of property. Liberals may argue that property is important for the development of the individual. While agreeing with this, conservatives would add that if property is not secure no one can have any safe expectations about the future. Hence anarchy might follow. Furthermore, they see property as the basis of the economic welfare of the state. Originally conservatives perceived land as the basis of national prosperity. Later they came to defend industrial and financial property – property in business investments and enterprises.

14.1.3 Authority

The necessity of authority is another core value of conservatives. Because human nature is fallible and capable of rapacity, instability will occur if authority is not asserted. As there can be no freedom where anarchy rules, freedom of individuals must be limited in the interests of the community by legitimate rulers. The supposition is that those few in authority are in a better position to judge the public good than the many who are not. (Conservatives would differ about why those in authority have this superior judgement.) Consequently authority should be respected and, some conservatives would say, deferred to. Thus conservatism puts a premium on leadership in society.

14.1.4 Law and order

Authority cannot be maintained without rules and and an apparatus to enforce them – the state. Furthermore, in order to conserve what is familiar and desirable there must be consistency about the activities of the state. It must obey the rules like everyone else if it is to be respected. Once promulgated, the rules become laws rather than mere customs. The forces of order are then needed to interpret and implement them. Coercion may sometimes be needed. The conservative philosopher, Thomas Hobbes, said 'covenants without swords are but words'. As we have noted, a state that can defend itself against external aggression and preserve its laws against internal law-breaking is said to be 'sovereign'. The sovereignty of the state remains for many conservatives their main rallying point.

14.1.5　Patriotism

Love of country is an important element of every conservative anthology. It is bound up with love of what is desirable and familiar: what one is used to and remembers from childhood. To conservatives such emotions are an acceptable part of political life. They believe too much value can be attached to cold reasoning. The family is a natural facet of human existence and we identify with our family in a way that has nothing to do with logic. Beyond the family is civil society in which a host of other associations may claim loyalty from their members. These are the 'little platoons' of which Burke spoke with approval. It is easier for people to feel at ease at this level than within the greater concourse of the nation. Yet conservatives believe that this feeling of loyalty should eventually extend to the whole country. We should possess a sense of responsibility towards our country as we do towards our community or our family. So we pay our taxes and are prepared to take up arms to defend our country's territory.

It is difficult to dissociate the value of patriotism from the concept of culture. Our language, upbringing, social behaviour, symbols and experiences we may hold in common with many of our countrymen and women and not with the men and women of other countries. Culture is something transmitted from generation to generation and so is linked to the national memory. Indeed, such a heritage is bound up with what Oakeshott calls 'the voice of poetry in the conversation of mankind'.[1] Patriotic conservatism can be linked with romanticism. The poetic voices of other nations will speak in other languages.

14.1.6　Tradition

Conservative caution about change and conservative preference for the tried and familiar, when linked with patriotism, produce a respect, sometimes a reverence, for tradition. This may be demonstrated in a determination to proceed with ancient rituals and to preserve national symbols. Politically it may be expressed in support for traditional institutions. Ancient families, hereditary titles, established churches and dynastic monarchies may be the recipients of this respect. Arguments to abolish such institutions may be met with the objection that whatever is put in their place is hardly likely to be any better and may well be worse.

The conservative feeling for tradition brings continuity and reverence together. We revere what has stood the test of time. Moreover, this emotion is often tinged with mysticism. What is so precious does not need to be explained or rationally defended. Conservatives, perhaps, are more likely to be religious than adherents of other political creeds. National symbols and institutions can become almost God-given. Our traditions are a precious trust, bequeathed by earlier generations and must not be betrayed. It follows logically, therefore, that conservatives do not value rationality as much as liberals or socialists.

14.2 Orientations

To a greater or lesser extent all conservatives would accept the above values, but the order of priorities they accord would vary with time and place. Conservatives want to preserve the status quo, but the status quo varies with circumstances. Even in a single country there may be disagreement about what composes the status quo. Furthermore, it is impossible for a social and political order to remain static. Technology advances, economies ebb and flow and social issues arise which governments must deal with. Even politicians and political parties disliking changes may be forced to adapt to them. Perhaps the most important adaptation that conservative parties have had to make in the last century was towards the extension of the franchise. On the whole they were successful in adapting to, and eventually accepting, universal suffrage.

Conservative attitudes can be categorised according to their stances towards change in several ways. Clinton Rossiter's classification from left to right is 'Conservatism', 'Standpattism', 'Reaction' and 'Revolutionary Reaction'.[2] The last category describes those who are willing to use violence to overthrow the existing order as a way to return to an earlier order. This can be considered, however, as a form of Fascism (separately dealt with in Chapter 15). Reaction, a wish to return to the past, has not been a common feature of the English-speaking world, though in European Catholic countries it was a characteristic of political life before 1914. Standpattism, the belief that society can be static, is probably a temperamental disposition, without clear mental focus, that can be found among ordinary non-political conservatives, but it is doubtful whether a national politician would adopt this as a policy position, though he might find it useful as an electoral stance.

Here I wish to examine the historical background of three categories of conservatism based on different reponses to change: 'reactionaries' recoil from change and wish to revert to an earlier order; 'moderates' believe one must slowly adapt to change, but ensure that it does not happen until society is properly prepared for it; and 'radicals' want to change society drastically, though not by revolutionary methods. Some people would call these latter, confusingly, 'liberal conservatives'.

14.2.1   Reactionary conservatives

These conservatives react against the social and political order in which they find themselves and want to return to one which they regard as fulfilling properly conservative values, an attitude depending upon a belief in a 'golden past' from which one's country has strayed. It is more likely to be found where the old order, or *ancien régime*, was overthrown by revolutionary forces. Reaction can flourish where the restoration of the old order has taken place. The classic example is Europe after the defeat of Napoleon in 1815. The monarchs returned to their thrones and the doctrine of *légitimité* – the Divine Right of Kings – was reasserted. The dynastic alliance intended to prevent the return of revolution was led by Metternich, the Chancellor of the Austro-Hungarian empire, who imposed a repressive regime for more than three decades.

The principle philosopher of this counter-revolution was Joseph de Maistre (1753–1821). For him the perfect governance was the Papacy's control over the Church. In fact, he championed the Catholic Church to the extent of attacking French Gallicanism, the claim that French Catholicism had some independence from the Vatican. He was an Ultramontane *par excellence*: for him true authority was over the mountains in Rome. De Maistre attacked Protestantism, 'politically inferior to Islam and paganism', and also condemned the 'revolt of individual reason' against the 'general reason' of the Catholic church. Rationalism and liberalism he considered eithteenth-century aberrations. A nation should be 'surrounded by dogmas from the cradle', he contended. According to de Maistre a nation was the sovereign joined to the aristocracy. The ultimate instrument of the ruler was the gallows. The executioner, a mysterious figure, is the cornerstone of society. Remove him and 'order is superseded by chaos, thrones fall and states disappear.'

Although the French Bourbons were overthrown in 1830, Ultramontane conservatism remained a force in French politics and Royalism persisted until the twentieth century. The policies of the Papacy were bound to affect its impact. In 1864 Pope Pius IX published the *Syllabus of Current Errors* which repudiated freedom of worship and of the Press, condemned popular sovereignty and universal suffrage, and claimed complete freedom for the Church to revoke any legislation of which it disapproved. In 1870 he proclaimed the doctrine of Papal Infallibility, dismaying liberal Catholics and infuriating anti-clericals. In Imperial Germany it divided the conservatives between the ultra-nationalist Prussian Protestantism of Bismarck and the Ultramontane Catholics against whom he waged a *Kulturkampf*. It reflected the Protestant acceptance of state power against the Catholic view of the spiritual dominance of the Church.

The French conflict, unlike that in Germany where Protestants and Catholics were about equal in numbers, was between Catholics and secularists. It was accentuated by the condemnation in 1894 for treasonable espionage of Captain Alfred Dreyfus, the first Jew to have served on the General Staff. The Ultramontane journals, read by army officers, had always been anti-semitic and they exploited the affair. Evidence that Dreyfus was innocent was ignored by the Army and Emile Zola, a journalist who criticised their court-martial procedure, was condemned. The anti-Dreyfusards argued that if Dreyfus were declared innocent (which he was), the honour of the Army would be impugned, the Army Chiefs revealed as conspiring in a travesty of justice and national safety thereby endangered. They identified Jews, socialists and republicans as enemies of France, tacitly asserting that national honour and security outweigh justice to the individual. The Dreyfusards were those conservatives and others who argued that national honour and safety cannot be served by the commission of such an injustice.

The rift remained in French politics for at least half a century. In 1905 Charles Maurras (1868–1952) founded his *Action Française*, a reactionary, royalist journal which poured out invective against foreigners, foreign immigrants, Jews and freemasons. He argued France had declined since the Revolution and could only regain her greatness if the monarchy were restored and the laic state of the Republic abolished. In 1927 the *Croix de Feu* was founded, an ex-servicemen's organisation with semi-military features. Inevitably, the rise of Communism in the 1920s strengthened the paranoia of the reactionaries, contributing to the demoralisation of the French Army and the collapse of the Third Republic in 1940. The Vichy regime of 1940–44, has been described as 'the revenge of the anti-Dreyfusards'.

In Britain and the USA there have been occasional traces of these tendencies, but in neither country was there a golden past to be reclaimed. Few Americans or Britons have wanted to return to the days of George III. Yet there were earlier societies for which nostalgia might be engendered. In the USA this could be found in the South since slavery was abolished after the Civil War, or the reforms of 1964 and 1965 guaranteed the franchise to blacks. George Fitzhugh of Virginia, writing in the 1850s, championed feudalism and regretted that the USA had neither monarchy nor established church.[3] A more recent form of reaction with political significance and considerable support is the fundamentalist Right, combining anti-Communism, revivalist religion and opposition to abortion and homosexuality. They want to revert to a simple, moral, Christian past that can only have existed in a limited way.

In Britain such views have much less support and there is no 'moral

Right' of any size, though a few voices deplore 'the contagion of democracy'.[4] The most prominent intellectual to take up this position is Roger Scruton who called the journal he founded the *Salisbury Review* because the Marquis of Salisbury was the last British Prime Minister to sit in the House of Lords and, therefore, is a symbol of the pre-democratic age. Scruton defends the hereditary principle and is very sceptical about the worth of the franchise. Democracy, he says, 'can be discarded without detriment to the civil well-being as the conservative conceives it'.[5] Of course, these views have little support.

The comparative weakness and gentleness of the Anglo-Saxon re-actionaries can be explained by the absence of a religious issue. Else-where in Europe where Protestantism dominated, as in Scandinavia, there was also a lack of serious reactionary conservatism inveighing against democratic institutions. Until the Catholic Church came to terms with democracy, Ultramontanism was likely to be prevalent. After the Second World War it lost its importance because of Catholic need for democratic allies against the threat of Soviet Communism.

14.2.2 Moderate conservatives

Most conservatives are supporters of continuity and concerned to pre-serve the present order. This presupposes that they are in stable situa-tions which is often the case. They may not always entirely approve of the status quo, but the prospect of an unknown different social and political order, with all its uncertainty, is a deterrent to wanting change. Moderate conservatives reflect all the conservative values.

Edmund Burke

The most important early moderate conservative is undoubtedly Ed-mund Burke (1729–1807). In Burke we see an almost religious reverence for contemporary British institutions, an attitude inspired by their success over a long period. Burke argued that membership of a society in which custom and tradition were respected was what had imbued the British with morality far more than reason. In Britain individuals were free because they were subject to law and order guaranteeing their traditional rights.

This made Burke a vigorous opponent of arbitrary rule. For example, he attacked the behaviour of the East India Company and complained about their treatment of their Indian subjects. He defended the Amer-ican colonists in a famous speech in March 1775, declaring that 'the people of the colonies are the descendants of Englishmen,' who wanted not abstract liberty but their liberty, 'according to English ideas and on English principles'. They studied law closely and were aware of British constitutional principles and knew that taxation without representation was entirely against those principles. Burke, therefore, defended the stand of the colonists and supported their Declaration of Independence.

In his thoughts about the American question Burke never stated abstract principles: he was concerned with asserting legal and traditional rights. It was his opposition to the French Revolution which led him to declarations about rights. He was affronted by the militancy of the revolutionaries and horrified when they executed the Royal family. Anarchy, he believed, had been brought about by the abstract assertion of equality. A pyramid of social rankings facilitated control in society and the extermination of the French aristocracy boded ill for the future. He held a semi-feudal view of the lower orders who should 'obey the natural aristocracy' even though their lot was miserable. Any discontinuity was harmful.

Hence Burke emphasised the need for a network of relationships nurtured by mannered rules. Ultimately this could only be maintained by law which he saw as the basis of authority. In a famous passage he argued that the state was much more than a business contract – it was:

> a partnership . . . not only between those who are living, but between those who are living, those who are dead, and those who are to be born. Each contract of each particular state is but a clause in the great primeval contract of eternal society.

Thus though Burke emphasised the need for authority to keep civilisation intact, he drew no clear distinction between the State and society, perceiving culture and rules of civilised behaviour as part of the necessary control function.

Burke is typical of much moderate conservative thinking with its emphasis on continuity and tradition, its belief that reason is not as important as wisdom, its distrust of sudden and comprehensive change, its perception that human beings are imperfect and that their worst instincts must be controlled and its regard for law and constitutional convention. Conservatism owes little to eighteenth-century rationalism. 'Rights' to a conservative are not natural rights, but legal and constitutional rights.

The Federalist

Although the Founding Fathers of the American Revolution reacted against the hereditary and aristocratic principles and the deference associated with them, the revolution they accomplished resulted in a very conservative settlement. The Constitution (1787) had little time for the

French Revolutionary concept of popular sovereignty. The lower chamber, the House of Representatives, was to be elected by popular vote, but the Senate and the President were to be elected indirectly and to interpret the Constitution a Supreme Court was set up. (It was soon ruling legislation unconstitutional.) The Constitution balanced the executive, legislative and judicial powers against each other in order to prevent any one of them from becoming too powerful. This was largely a reaction against British centralised rule which had denied them constitutional rights. Most of the leaders of the Revolution, such as George Washington and John Adams, were conservatives opposed to the rule of the 'vulgar mob'. Furthermore the system was federal. The separate ex-colonies with their different interests were given a great deal of autonomy.

Early American conservatism is best expressed in *The Federalist* written largely by Alexander Hamilton and James Madison. The former attacked the excesses of the French Revolution, 'the great monster'. 'The tyranny of Jacobinism', he said, 'confounds and levels everything.' In issue no. 6 of *The Federalist* he wrote of 'the fallacy and extravagance of those idle theories which have amused us with promises of an exemption from the imperfections, weaknesses and evils incident to society in every shape'. Madison likewise spoke of the need to control government abuses. Governments were composed of men sharing the imperfections of all men. Constitutions must check the arbitrary power of governments. Thus the American Revolutionaries from the start were consolidating a new set of institutions whose continuity they hoped to assure. Their successors continued the process and the Constitution became an object of sanctity to generations of Americans. It was essentially a Burkean achievement.

Hence by the first part of the nineteenth century the philosophic foundations of moderate conservatism had been laid. Its roots were in societies with an aristocratic ethos. Although no formal ranks or aristocratic titles existed in the USA, the Founding Fathers were a largely patrician, land-owning class with many of the suspicions of the lower orders that could be found in England. Early conservatism could be described as Anglo-American conservatism. Its belief in limited representative government and individual rights could elsewhere only be found in other English-speaking countries and Scandinavia. It was clearly linked with Protestantism.

Conservatism in Catholic countries

Moderate conservatives in predominantly Catholic countries were placed in a difficult position by the rise of even limited democracy. Not only French revolutionary ideas, but also the threat of the *Risorgimento*, (the movement to unify Italy) to the Papal States horrified the

Papacy. Moderate Catholic conservatives, preaching reconciliation between the Church and republicanism and democracy, received short shrift from the Vatican. In France, where they were tainted with support for Dreyfus, they founded *Le Sillon*, opposed to the excesses of *Action Française*. The young Catholics who supported it were clerical democrats, though the anti-clericals claimed you could only support the Republic if you were opposed to Catholicism. Eventually *Le Sillon* was suppressed by the Church. Its main figure, Charles Peguy, on mobilisation described himself as a soldier of the Republic in favour of general disarmament and the end of war. He was killed in 1914 at the First Battle of the Marne. Reconciliation between the Papacy and democracy did not occur until after 1945 when experiences under Fascism and the need to oppose Communism gave rise to the movement known as Christian Democracy. This might be described as 'moderate conservatism' though others might call it, with its highly developed welfare programme, 'mildly socialist'.

The philosophic foundations of moderate conservatism were laid before two profound changes in the later nineteenth century: the advent of industrial society and the rise of mass democracy. Reactionary conservatives, as we have noted, could not adapt to these new phenomena, but moderate conservatives with characteristic pragmatism were able to come to terms with capitalism and democracy.

Conservative adaptation to industrialism and democracy

Industrialisation produced a society unforeseen by Burke and the Federalists. First the new entrepreneurial class began to clamour for political rights and favours; then the urban proletariat they employed began to demand the suffrage. Governing conservatives who had largely catered for the needs of the land-owning classes were faced with pressures from quite different interests. In the USA, for example, a tariff on imported goods in order to protect domestic industry was an early response. In addition, the spread of urban poverty, consequent on technological change and economic depression, forced conservatives to reconsider their social policies. The social question and the working-class reaction to it, noted in Chapter 13, led to socialist demands for a welfare state. Conservatives responded variously, depending on temperament, circumstances and values.

With many conservatives the need for stability and authority in order to safeguard property was the predominant value. The fear that the workers who congregated in the large cities might revolt influenced many. with others the tradition of *noblesse oblige*, the old feudal obligations, suggested assistance for the poor. Consequently paternalistic intervention was a common conservative response. With others expediency was the motive.

Thus the very conservative Bismarck supported a welfare state in the new German Empire as a means of conciliating the newly enfranchised proletariat and 'dishing' the Social Democrats. Indeed, the expansion of the suffrage, reluctantly accepted by many conservatives, made it necessary to appeal to a wider section of the electorate. Moreover, the state as an instrument of welfare policy could be justified on patriotic grounds because a contented and healthy working class was needed for service in the armed forces. In Britain, Disraeli (1804–81) conceived the supra-class appeal of 'one Nation', arguing that the wealthy had neglected the poor and the nation was divided. The Conservative Party must ensure that the newly enfranchised workers had a decent life. Joseph Chamberlain (1836–1914) and his son Neville (1869–1940) were social reformers and supporters of a protective tariff. Birmingham businessmen, they symbolised the transformation of the party from one run by country gentry to one run by commercial and industrial employers. Harold Macmillan (1894–1986) and R. A. Butler (1902–82) were typical of British mid-twentieth century Conservatism. The former in *The Middle Way* (1938) advocated Keynesian management for the economy: the latter steered through a radical reform of the educational system in 1944 and, as Chancellor of the Exchequer, accepted many of the policies of the postwar Labour Government. None of these men espoused free-market economics. Paternalistic concern for everyone involved intervention in the economy.

British conservatism is often identified as the set of ideas and policies presented by the Conservative Party. Elsewhere the absence of the label exemplifies the problem of definition. For instance the largest grouping (hardly a party) in the Third French Republic – that of the Radicals and Radical Socialists – represented the interests of many small businessmen, shopkeepers and peasant proprietors. They often saw themselves as the heirs of the Jacobins and were separated from the reactionary conservatives by their anti-clericalism. The status quo they upheld was the Revolutionary settlement. Claiming they were on 'the Left', they were staunchly conservative in social and economic policy. In the Fifth Republic the Radicals are much reduced in power and many people would consider the Gaullists as the party of French conservatism. Yet they accepted, under De Gaulle's leadership, many aspects of left-wing policy such as public ownership and the welfare state.

The advent of mass democracy was bound to make conservatism more variegated and even less definitive. Like liberalism, conservatism in the twentieth century passed from the hands of philosopher/politicians like Burke and Hamilton into those of politicians who were anxious to win votes rather than enunciate principles. Moreover industrialisation involved attempting to maintain stability, if not continuity, in an ever-changing world. At the same time the increasing preponderance of business interests led to demands for the maintenance of commercial property rights and prosperity. Businessmen want governmental policies which assist their desire for steady profits, but this does not necessarily imply they desire competition. As Adam Smith well knew, it is easier for businessmen to come to profitable agreements between themselves than to compete. Moderate conservatives have stood for private enterprise against public ownership as advocated by socialists, but they have usually accepted that much is not best dealt with in the marketplace.

14.2.3   Radical conservatism

There is a new conservatism which is variously called that of the 'new right' or of the 'radical right', or 'neo-conservatism'. Many people, however, would consider it to be neo-liberalism because the backward glance seems to be directed at the classical economists and the simple non-interventionist state of early nineteenth-century industrialism.

Radical conservatives distinguish themselves from moderate conservatives by their attitude to the relationship between the state and the economy and by the consequent conflictual stance this implies towards people and parties with other views. Their contention is that conservatives in the period 1930–70, had come to terms too much with socialism in accepting (a) the welfare state, (b) a high rate of taxation to pay for it, (c) corporatism, i.e. economic policy being made by negotiations between business, labour and civil servants imbued with Keynesianism, and (d) the public ownership of utilities which was stultifying to entrepreneurial enterprise. The industrialised countries were suffering from the compromises made by moderate conservatives with leftist governments. A reassertion of principles was needed.

One effect of this reaction against the postwar consensus was that theorists became important and influenced Conservative politicians. Those who are perhaps the best known are discussed in subsequent paragraphs.

Frederick von Hayek (1898–1992) was an economist who argued in *The Road to Serfdom* (1945) that a Labour government would take Britain along the road to serfdom. In many ways he was an old-fashioned liberal, rather suspicious of democracy because it involved the uneducated in decision-making, and anxious to limit the role of the state, by law if necessary. Law was only needed to protect private property. Historians, he argued, had represented 'the achievement of a powerful state as the culmination of cultural evolution whereas it had often marked its end'.[6] Commerce, not government, had spread culture and civilisation. Economic decision-making was too complex for governments and should be left to the market. Interference with its delicate mechanism would result in inefficiency and consumers losing their proper benefits. Hence in spite of his disavowal of British conservatism, Hayek was admired by Mrs Thatcher and hailed as the prophet of the 'new right'.

Milton Friedman (1912–), an American economist, had been a student of Hayek. Famous for his adage 'there is no such thing as a free lunch', his theoretical attack was on Keynesian economics to which he attributed the chief blame for contemporary inflation. Keynes was responsible for lavish expenditure and high taxation, a feature of all developed democracies. More practically, the only instrument of economic management should be the control of the money supply. 'Monetarism', as it was called, was a return to orthodox economics. Friedman asserted that the welfare state must be drastically pruned and free-market principles established. That the free market and democracy were mutually dependent he argued in *Capitalism and Freedom* (1962).

Michael Novak (1933–), in his *Spirit of Democratic Capitalism* (1982), strongly supported free market economics but added a moral dimension, arguing that individual economic choice and initiative followed logically from Christian teaching.

Robert Nozick (1938–), in his book *Anarchy, State and Utopia* (1974), advocated a 'minimal state' which should do nothing but keep order to defend individual rights, including rights to property. He does, however, believe voluntary organisations may enforce obligations not open to the state to assert. Nozick supports a free-market economy, but says little about either capitalism or democracy. Nevertheless he is espoused by the 'libertarian conservatives'.

Palle Svensson detects four claims in neo-conservatism:

1. A crisis of authority has overtaken the democracies. Governments and other institutions have lost their legitimacy, so that stability and even liberal civilisation are threatened.
2. The crisis is primarily moral and has little or nothing to do with economic recession.
3. Governments have responded too much to electoral pressures for increased expenditure and are overloaded with too many functions.
4. A new class of professional people – scientists, journalists, teachers, social workers and higher administrators – are enemies of the new right's values and policies. They represent an 'adversary culture' which must be confronted. Authority must be reasserted.[7]

14.3 Conclusion

It is not easy to see anything very much in common between these different strands of conservatism. The radicals are, unsurprisingly, unpopular with the reactionaries. Scruton says authority and traditions are incompatible with 'minimal statism'.[8] Oakeshott condemns the infection of conservatism by rationalism expressed, for example, in the 'ideology' of Hayek.[9]

Reagan and Thatcher in their statements and policies expounded a form of radical conservatism, but their actions were inevitably a good deal more pragmatic than their ideological rhetoric which was, anyway, only occasionally evident. 'Common sense' and electoral expediency were more often their guides. One can also discern that all three orientations of conservatism have associations with other ideologies. Radical conservatism is close to classical liberalism and some reactionary conservatives share values with Fascism. The moderate conservatives, with their paternalistic belief in state action and their acceptance of democratic procedures, are closer to social liberals and democratic socialists than they are to their radical and reactionary wings.

Notes

1. M. Oakeshott, *Rationalism in Politics and Other Essays* (London: Methuen, 1962), p. 197f.
2. C. Rossiter, *Conservatism in America* (London: Heinemann, 1955), p. 12.
3. Ibid., p. 124.
4. R. Scruton, *The Meaning of Conservatism* (Harmondsworth: Penguin, 1980), p. 53.
5. Ibid., p. 16.
6. F. von Hayek, *The Fatal Conceit: The Errors of Socialism* (London: Routledge, 1983), p. 33.
7. P. Svensson, *Democratic Theory* (Aarhus: University of Aarhus Press, 1994), p. 329f.
8. Scruton, *Meaning of Conservatism*, p. 31.
9. Oakeshott, *Rationalism in Politics*, p. 21.

Questions

1. 'Conservatism can only be understood in terms of its history.' Discuss.
2. 'Conservatism and capitalism are quite distinct concepts.' Discuss.

15

Fascism

Fascism is a totalitarian ideology. In power it exhibited all four criteria mentioned in Chapter 11. Fascist regimes claimed to embody universal systems of thought. These were official doctrines and no other could be propagated. They were intended to inaugurate a new social, economic and political order proclaimed by Fascists while out of power. This would replace the old order which, they argued, had brought the nation to disaster. Fascist regimes were thus promoting a historical process to end in the fulfilment of the nation's destiny. There would be much conflict on the way. Thus Fascism is best understood as a form of militaristic nationalism. The Third Reich of Adolf Hitler (1933–45) and Fascist Italy under Benito Mussolini are the best examples.

15.1 Values

15.1.1 Unreason

Much of Fascism is a rejection of values, especially those of the Enlightenment. Fascists assert that feeling and instinct and will are more important than thinking and knowledge and logic. Fascism rests on irrationality.

The intellectual milieu in which Fascism gestated is known as the 'Revolt against Reason'. It was revulsion, taking place at the end of the nineteenth century, against such outcomes of rationalism as liberalism and democracy. In many ways it was a turning back. Prominent in this movement was the German writer, Frederick Nietzsche (1844–1900). He hated the common man and condemned the masses for their 'slave mentality'. Nietzsche repudiated conventional behaviour and believed Christianity and democratic ideas reflected mediocrity. In their place he praised assertive strength and egotistical pride though these could only be possessed by a few heroic, creative individuals who could rise above vulgarity and philistinism. The Superman had the will to power.

Yet Nietzsche condemned nationalism and anti-semitism as vulgar. He criticised Bismarck. Nevertheless his attitudes influenced the Nazis. Rosenberg, the Nazi Director of *Weltanschaaung*, regarded him as one of the movement's intellectual godparents, while the hero of Goebbels's autobiographical novel carried a copy of Nietzsche's *Thus Spake Zarathustra* wherever he went.[1] But there is no evidence that Hitler was directly influenced. Nietzsche is not mentioned in *Mein Kampf*. He was not a Fascist, but he did much to nurture an intellectual ethos in which Fascist values could flourish.

Politically, the Revolt against Reason was reflected in the disillusionment with democracy and representative institutions felt by many intellectuals. This was strongest in Italy and Germany, two countries dating as political entities only from the 1870s. By the turn of the century they were disenchanted. In Italy this was evident in the work of Vilfredo Pareto (1848–1923), an economist who interpreted politics in psychological terms. Rejecting Locke, he asserted that at birth we are programmed with a congenital set of dispositions which explain much of our behaviour. He called these 'residues'. Political life he saw as irrational discourse: politicians trim their arguments according to their audiences. They manipulate, obfuscate and prevaricate in attempting to obtain acceptance of their policies. He called such utterances 'derivations'. Mussolini was much impressed by this analysis and also by the arguments of another theorist who decried rationality, Georges Sorel (see Chapter 13), who in *Reflections on Violence* (1908) rejected the ballot box as a means for the working class to attain its ends and advocated the General Strike. Sorel believed this should be asserted even if it was not practicable because all important movements needed a myth. Mussolini had been a syndicalist before 1914 and he incorporated the idea of the myth into his action-oriented philosophy, proclaiming in 1922: 'We have created our myth. It is not necessary that it should be reality. Our myth is the nation; our myth is the greatness of the nation.'[2]

15.1.2 Inequality

The Age of Reason had advanced the idea of equality. The Superman as a role model refuted it. Nietzsche said 'I am no man: I am dynamite.' Much of the public stance of the Fascist dictators and their followers reflected this value. Fascist conviction of the inequality of humanity is derived from elitist theory and racial theory.

Elitist theory

Elitist theory, holding that a few people are superior to the mass of humanity by virtue of special characteristics, was one of the intellectual bases of Italian Fascism. Pareto believed rule by elites was inevitable and Gaetano Mosca (1858–1941) argued that throughout history one elite or another had dominated. Roberto Michels (1876–1936), a German who taught at the University of Pavia and like Mussolini, a disillusioned socialist, asserted that oligarchy was inevitable in every organisation. Leaders naturally led the masses by virtue of superior knowledge, closeness to decision-making and charismatic personality. Ultimately Michels joined the Fascist Party.

Racial theory

Racial theory was pre-eminently German – indeed, Fascist Italy did not adopt racial laws until 1937. In *Mein Kampf* Hitler made numerous references to the misfortunes the Jews had brought on Germany. He described seeing on a Vienna street in his twenties, 'a phenomenon in a long caftan and wearing black side locks'. His first thought was 'Is this a Jew?' Yet the longer he gazed at this strange countenance the more the question became 'Is this a German?'. He bought some anti-semitic pamphlets for the first time in his life.[3] From these he learnt that Jews controlled prostitution, cultural and artistic life, banks and industry, the Social Democratic Party and, in the Protocols of the Elders of Zion (a forgery dating from 1905), had expressed the aim of controlling the world. It was difficult to oppose Jews because they were slippery and cunning and had permeated German society and culture. They had seduced German women and so corrupted pure German blood.[4] From these circumstances in his early years in cosmopolitan Vienna he developed his hatred of the multi-ethnic Habsburg Empire and his conviction of the superiority of the German race.

The arch-priest of Nazi racism was Hitler's chief theorist Alfred Rosenberg, who, in his *Myth of the Twentieth Century* (1930), poured out in a torrent of clever nonsense the Nazi biological doctrine. Born in Estonia, Rosenberg was the most anti-Russian Nazi leader, claiming that Jews had financed the Russian Revolution because they were behind both Wall Street and Communism. His inspiration went back to Wagner whose anti-semitism had led to a break with Nietzsche; but his principal influence was Houston Stewart Chamberlain, an Englishman married to Wagner's daughter. Chamberlain told Hitler in 1923 that he was his 'John the Baptist'.[5] Rosenberg's myth was that people's characteristics are determined at birth partly by physical inheritance and partly by 'race soul'. Indeed, individuals did not have souls – only races did. God had created races and miscegenation, destroying racial personality, was an affront to God's will. The Aryan race, blonde and blue-eyed, to which Germans belonged was the highest form of humanity: all other races were incapable of realising the Aryan potential. Jews were at the bottom of the human ladder and in between were the *Untermenschen*, blacks who ought to be enslaved, and Slavs incapable of higher thought.

The inegalitarianism of Fascist regimes can be seen in the contempt the leaders felt towards their people. Hitler, who believed Germany had been defeated in 1918 by the spreading of Allied and Bolshevik propaganda, devised the strategy of 'the big lie': if one had to lie the bigger the lie the better. The masses could easily be manipulated by oratory and propaganda.

15.1.3   The need for national solidarity

National unity is a major consideration with all Fascist movements. Surrounded by enemies the nation has always to be on the alert. In Germany since the nineteenth century the unity of the 'Volk' had special significance because they were scattered from the Vosges to the Urals, in the Ukraine, the Baltic states and all the provinces of the Habsburg Empire. The Nazi aim was to unite them all and claim more German land – *lebensraum* – in which a Greater Germany could realise itself. 'Unredeemed Italy' also existed, the Fascists said, in Savoy, Nice, Corsica, the Tyrol and Istria. United Italy could only be finalised by their annexation.

There were also internal enemies the regime must guard itself against. The enemy within included Jews and other ethnic minorities, Communists, socialists, liberals, trade unionists and the Christian churches. (Mussolini came to terms with the Vatican in the Lateran Treaty of 1929, but, like Hitler, had little respect for religion.) Stern measures were needed to deal with all dissent.

The type of nationalism which emerged from these values was not the internationally oriented kind of Herder or Mazzini. It was romantic, but it did not envisage Europe as a happy family of nations living in peace with each other. Singling out foreign and internal enemies produced a nationalism of hatred. It was espressed in an emotional appeal for national solidarity foreseeing the battlefield as the testing arena.

15.1.4   Discipline

Thus a Fascist regime requires discipline. Indeed, the need for a movement with military structure is the logical consequence, Fascists argue, of living in a society in a state of decay and disorder. In Germany and Italy the years after the First World War were troubled times. People felt threatened by this instability. But the Fascist parties with their semi-military organisation and discipline – private armies in effect – contributed to the disorder by attacking the committee rooms and newspaper offices of their political opponents. In this way they were preparing for their Fascist version of order, their 'new order' to be imposed when they came to power. They would legitimate their claim to power by establishing harmony where there there had been conflict, for example between capital and labour. Those advancing dissenting views had to be eliminated. One way of regarding Fascist regimes is as hooligans in power asserting hooligan values. The hooligans become the disciplinarians.

15.1.5   National rejuvenation

Fascists perceive their nation as fallen from its former eminence. Their belief in a historical process teaches them that to recapture its glorious past it must renew its national spirit and so enjoy a glorious future. To march forward to greatness the nation needs drastic prescriptions. Discipline is important; weaknesses must be purged and a programme of renewal begun. New elites are also required with the old values which made the nation great, but recast in modern technological and meritocratic terms. Hence the emphasis on youth and the need to inspire it with the national mission. The Fascist view of their nation's history is greatness in the past, decline and decay in the present, and glorious rejuvenation as a result of vigorous Fascist policies.

15.1.6   Emphasis on will and action

In a time of indiscipline and internal conflict national decision-making will be difficult. In democracies protracted discussion is likely before decisions are taken. They will be unsatisfactory compromises. Fascists regard all this as time-wasting: they favour a military chain-of-command method of making decisions. Speculative thinking, therefore, is adjudged as almost emasculating. Indeed, the people who indulge in it, the professional classes, liberals, socialists, artists, intellectuals, etc., are condemned as ineffective and almost effeminate. To this Fascists oppose the value of action, the assertion of the aggressive male. It might have sexual undertones as when the Futurist, Marinetti, an admirer of Mussolini, alleged Italian diet explained national decadence. 'Spaghetti is no food for fighters,' he affirmed. 'A weighty and encumbered stomach cannot be favourable to physical enthusiasm for women'.[6] Mussolini stressed the virility of his young Fascists by sending them on commando courses where they jumped through blazing hoops.

Thus Fascism is anti-intellectual. It is against the 'chattering classes' (to coin a phrase). Conversely it applauds those (those few) with the will to act. Thinking leads to uncovering complexity and reasons for delay: in action lies the virtue of simplicity. Hence action can become an art form. There is beauty in battle. The son of Ciano, Mussolini's foreign minister, dropped bombs on undefended villages in Ethiopia, setting them on fire. He described the aerial vision of the burning as 'like a rose blooming'. The glorification of war and the romantic hero was exemplified by the Nazi poet, Stefan George, and Fascist beatification of the poet D'Annunzio. In 1919 D'Annunzio with a troop of adventurers seized the Yugoslav port of Fiume, part of 'unredeemed Italy'. This restless adventurism in foreign policy became a feature of Fascist governments. In the 1930s almost any weekend might be the occasion for another swoop.

15.2 Explanations of the success of Fascist ideology

Many of the above values are found in many countries. In fact, Fascism exists almost everywhere. All the long-standing democracies, for example, have had tiny Fascist parties. Countries with liberal political cultures like Britain, the USA and the Scandinavian countries have all had some manifestation of Fascism. The important fact is that it did not flourish. Other factors must explain the Fascist rise to power. Let us deal, in the first place, with some of the unsatisfactory explanations.

15.2.1   Unsatisfactory explanations

Fascism as the last stage of capitalism

Marx prophesied that the capitalist system would become more and more oppressive as it developed. Its apparatus of repression would be the armed forces of the state which would become more brutal when the capitalist class in its dying throes attacked the organisations of the increasingly impoverished working class. Hence, when in the 1920s and 1930s Fascist regimes broke up left-wing parties and abolished trade unions, it heralded the last stage of capitalism. Some Socialist and Communist parties adopted the tactic of 'revolutionary defeatism'. Fascism was a short-term phenomenon. Encouraging it would hasten the end of capitalism. Communist and Fascist pickets cooperated in the Berlin transport strike in 1932.

This interpretation may be one reason why labour movements

offered so little opposition to Fascist parties in the interwar years. Yet it is quite wrong to regard Fascism as a variant of capitalism. Much Fascist vituperation was directed at capitalism, especially finance capitalism. (The banks have always been a target for populists.) In Germany it was the Nazi attack on usurers and war profiteers which won it great electoral success. Hitler castigated what he called 'pluto-democracy', the conspiracy of high finance (the Jews) to favour democratic parties in order to maintain capitalism intact. Rosenberg argued that the overthrow of the *Kaiserreich* in 1918 was secretly intended to deliver German industry and agriculture into the power of 'the super-state of finance capital'. Robert Ley, director of the Labour Front, the Nazi labour organisation, said in 1940, 'workers of all lands unite to smash English capitalism'. Mussolini emphasised the Fascist state was a new political and economic order, 'the antithesis of democracy, plutocracy, freemasonry and the immortal principles of 1789'.

There is no denying that Fascist regimes used capitalists. They needed industry for rearmament. The bankers and industrialists for their part, unless they had been expropriated, collaborated. They certainly preferred Fascism to Bolshevism, and like other elements of the nation the price of survival was obedience. The Fascists controlled capital, not vice versa.

Fascism as an extreme reactionary conservatism

It is usual to describe Fascism as a right-wing notion and it is true that some conservative values, such as patriotism and the need for authority, might be found among Fascist values. Yet it is most misleading to regard Fascism as an extreme version of conservatism. Fascism is a revolutionary creed. Its methods of achieving power are disorderly, and its vision of a new world order such as a 'thousand-year Reich' are repellent to those of conservative disposition. Fascists have no time for traditions and conventional institutions, or for aristocratic values of honour and *noblesse oblige*. On their side the old-fashioned nationalists regarded it as vulgar. In Italy and to a less extent in Germany the aristocracy may have collaborated because they feared Bolshevism and wanted to revise the postwar peace settlement. Fascism generally, however, is too populist and insurrectionary to appeal to patrician taste.

Fascism as an activist style of politics

This explanation, advanced by Noel O'Sullivan with considerable erudition, might seem irrefutable at first sight. Fascism was undeniably activist – indeed, it was quintessentially dynamic. 'Style', however, refers to how people behave, not to why they behave in that way, nor to the results of their actions. It is misleading to argue that Fascism was merely a more extreme form of the activities of European liberal movements since 1789, after which date good government was to be identified with democratic or republican government.[7] Like Fascism, nineteenth-century European liberal/nationalist politics was concerned with the overthrow of a certain type of regime. This involved an activist style, emotional language and the identification of an enemy. But the enemy was the *ancien régime*, an antiquated socio-political system which liberals hoped to replace with democracy. Fascist activists sought to overthrow democracy and set up a highly mobilised regime. What Fascists did, and why they did it would seem to be more important than the style in which they did it. Furthermore, democratic activism is in no sense compulsory; in fact, most democratic citizens are not politically active. Fascist regimes mobilise people for compulsory activity: in participatory democracies participation is seen as the ideal, but it is voluntary. The popular sovereignty of the French Revolution ended in repression and terror, but the French Revolutionaries were not democrats. Twentieth-century democracy offers no example of mobilising a united people except in wartime. It recognises that the people are divided.

Fascism as the extremism of the centre

This is the analysis of Seymour Lipset in *Political Man* (1959).[8] It is based on the clear indication that between 1928 and 1932 a high proportion of the support of the liberal centre parties deserted to the Nazis and that their representatives in the Reichstag also helped Hitler to power. Yet the research of R. F. Hamilton and T. Childers, *Who Voted for Hitler?* (1982),[9] shows that a much higher proportion of both Protestants and small-town and rural dwellers than city people or Catholics voted for the Nazis. Moreover, as the working class was a large section of German society inevitably, as Childers shows, the Nazis had a significant following among the manual workers.[10] By 1932 they had become a 'catch-all party of protest'. This may not tell us much about their ideology, however, except that it appealed to those who, despising the democratic status quo, felt that drastic measures were necessary. It is true that the social centre of gravity of Fascist voting support, and especially of their leaderships, was in the lower-middle class, but their appeal was above class divisions and to the nation.

Fascism is invalid as a concept

This non-explanation advances the thesis that extremist, militaristic and nationalist regimes, especially in Europe, are sufficiently different for any treatment of them as a universalistic phenomenon to be invalid. It was the opinion of the philosopher T. D. Weldon that it was a confusion to call states 'Fascist' whose 'alleged intellectual foundations are Hegelian idealism'. He continued that it was 'largely accidental that this nebulous ideology has been so closely associated in recent experience' with Italy and Germany. Fascism was 'only a vague word of abuse'.[11]

There were certainly differences between Italian and German Fascism and, surprisingly in view of Weldon's comment, one lay in their different philosophic influences, such as they were. German Hegelians often criticised the Nazis, while a component of Italian Fascism doctrine derived from the Hegelian philosopher Giovanni Gentile, who is supposed to have ghosted Mussolini's article *La Dottrina del Fascismo* (1932), maintaining that 'it is not the nation which generates the State' but 'the State which generates the nation'.

Yet Mussolini was also influenced by Sorel and it is doubtful whether he was a genuine Hegelian, though he believed a strong Italian state was needed to justify his rule. The engine of this state, however, was to be a strong disciplined party, a concept he had learnt from Lenin. Hitler, on the other hand, was more concerned with the *Volk* because Germany already had a strong state (in the judicial and bureaucratic senses). His racialist theories did not appeal to Italians. One could very much exaggerate, in fact, any philosophic foundation in Nazism. The only intellectuals mentioned in *Mein Kampf* are Schopenhauer (to quote his view that the Jew was 'the great master of lies'), Marx (by way of condemnation), Goethe (for his anti-semitism and criticism of bad German art); Clausewitz (on the shame of military defeat), and Houston Stewart Chamberlain for his racialist theories. Only the latter really influenced the Nazis. Moreover, the Italian Fascists never succeeded in establishing the total state though the term *totalitarismo* was Mussolini's. Church and Monarchy were never completely encompassed – indeed, both were involved in the overthrow of Italian Fascism in 1943.

15.2.2   Historical and political circumstances

Yet the similarities between the German and Italian Fascist regimes, in spite of disparate national cultures, far outweighed the differences. The situations of both countries in 1918 were similar. Both had been humiliated in war. The Versailles Treaty not only pushed back the German frontiers, but also imposed reparations and stipulated that the Rhineland was to be occupied by British and French troops. Italy had been a victor nation but its armies had been routed in the war and peace did not give them 'unredeemed Italy'. After the war both countries experienced social instability and economic depression. Large-scale unemployment and inflation followed and democratic governments seemed powerless to provide remedies. In these circumstances the foundation in 1920 of the Italian and German Communist Parties and the Third International in Moscow caused great alarm. Internal revolution supported by external support from the Red Army seemed a distinct possibility for many people and politicians.

Similar Fascist parties arose in both countries soon after the war. The Italian Fascist Party, founded in March 1919, went into action the following winter when ex-servicemen at the Milan Polytechnic sacked the offices of *Avanti*, the Socialist daily. After workers occupied factories in North Italy in 1920 the Fascists recruited 200,000 members in 2,000 organisations. The collapse of the Habsburg Empire inspired the foundation of the German National Socialist Worker's Party in Vienna. A similar party, initiated at Munich in 1920, was the one Adolf Hitler joined shortly after his discharge from the army.

Both parties had leaders with similar experiences. Benito Mussolini had edited *Avanti*, but he had been expelled from the Italian Socialist Party in 1914 for suggesting Italy should enter the war on the side of Britain and France. When this happened in 1915 he was called up and served as an infantry sergeant until he was wounded and discharged. He ended the war a nationalist. Hitler, an Austrian citizen who joined the Bavarian infantry in 1914, ended the war as a corporal. He had less education than Mussolini whom he admired and copied. Both men felt deeply about the humiliation of their countries, preached and prophesied their resurgence, and recruited thousands of ex-servicemen, many of them rootless and unemployed, for their private street armies.

Both leaders came to power by similar methods in similar circumstances. In October 1922 the Italian Fascists, having become the largest party in Parliament as a result of the recent elections, everywhere occupied public buildings and Mussolini, declaring that his party was to become the state, led a march on Rome, though he arrived there by train. He was then asked to form a coalition government. Hitler, emulating him, decided to take over Munich in 1923 and, with the help of General Ludendorff, led his followers to occupy municipal buildings. The police opened fire, and Hitler was arrested and imprisoned. Released on parole in 1924 he began years of organisation, profiting especially from heavy unemployment which reached over six million in 1932. In the elections of July 1932 the Nazis received 13,750,000 votes and became the largest party in the Reichstag with 230 seats. In elections in the following November, however, their votes and seats declined and the left-wing parties made gains. The centre parties then supported the Nazis and Hitler became Chancellor as head of a coalition government in January 1933.

Thus both parties and leaders came to power by constitutional processes, though to a background of civil disorder, national demoralisation and the menace of revolution. Once in power they moved quickly to ensure that they could not be deposed by putting an end to opposition. In 1925 all parties except the Fascists were suppressed in Italy and the press became government controlled. Hitler acted with more speed, in March 1933 obtaining consent from the Reichstag to act as he wished without consultation. Democracy was ended.

In both countries representative institutions had never become completely legitimate. Inaugurated with national unification in the 1870s their democracies had never functioned satisfactorily and post-1918 events accentuated the feeling among many that national disaster resulted from betrayal by democratic politicians. Thus the time was auspicious for the rise of insurrectionary ideologies. The Fascist parties sought to reassert the heroic values of the past. In Italy this allowed the Fascists to claim they were the heirs of the Roman Empire. In Germany there was no past empire and the German myth had to be derived from legends provided by Rosenberg adapting Wagner. The Nazi mythology evoked the Teutonic hero, a reborn Siegfried who would arise to restore Germany to its former greatness. In both countries the betrayal had been by the same people – foreign statesmen, liberals with their endless parliamentary discussion, high finance with its international connections and the left-wing parties who divided the nation on class lines.

Hence Fascism was an insurrectionary ideology which looked both backward and forward. Its vision of the future perceived the nation made glorious again in a modernised version of original greatness. The old regime had an elite of inherited status. The Fascist regime would have a meritocratic elite with technological skills. Hence youth was mobilised in organisations from which potential leaders were chosen. There was a hierarchy of leaders under the charismatic authority of 'the Leader' – Il Duce or Der Führer. Fascist leaders acted without impediment. Flair was more important than cogitation. The nation followed.

Apparatuses of mobilisation and control dispensed the official ideology and controlled information to prevent contrary ideas entering the country. Travel abroad became more difficult. Opposition was stifled by the range and scope of the Fascist state. Disharmony and conflict must not deflect the nation from its unquestioned goals. Hence private life was intruded into and civil society was very restricted. Totalitarianism eclipsed pluralism. All associations were required to register with the police and all aspects of the heroic national effort were co-ordinated. Within the Italian economy Mussolini instituted 'the corporate state' by the Vidoni Palace Pact in October 1925. Trade unions were controlled by the state and the right to strike was abolished. By the Pact a sort of tripartite system between the unions, the employers' organisations and the state, was inaugurated, ostensibly for consultation and bargaining. In practice it allowed domination by the Fascists of industries and services throughout Italy. Profits and wages were fixed independently of market forces. It was a guided economy.

A very similar, though less formal, structure existed in the Third Reich where the Nazis inaugurated what was called a *Gleichschaltung*, a system of coordination and rationalisation in which the state exercised authority over all economic activity. As in Italy trade unions were abolished, former trade union leaders imprisoned, wages controlled and the unemployed organised on public works. Labour was organised in the National Labour Front under Robert Ley. A general national plan was supervised by two agencies, the Commission for Economics under Walther Funk and the Four-Year Plan Office under Goering, the *generalissimo* of the war economy. Capital was not expropriated (except for Jewish capital), but priority was given to those capitalists who accepted the national economic purpose.

15.3 Conclusion

Italy and Germany remain the only examples of large Fascist states. In neither case did they survive for more than two decades. Some may consider therefore that Fascism is a thing of the past – a brief aberration. Yet others may argue that the sort of values it represented will always be present and, given certain historical circumstances, will find expression in Fascist movements.

During the 1930s some European states experienced strong Fascist parties. Austria, populated by ethnic Germans, had a large party which paved the way for Austria's accession to the Reich in 1938. In many countries the Fascists allied themselves with reactionary conservatives. For example, the *Falange* in Spain, after assisting the victory of General Franco in the Civil War was the only party allowed to operate. Yet it had little power. The Franco regime of 1939–75 was repressive and authoritarian, but Spain was not a mobilised, forward-looking Fascist state. It was a return to the past, the alliance of Church and Throne the Republic had overthrown in 1934. Franco, a regent for the monarchy restored after his death, was never a member of the *Falange*[12]. Where in such alliances Fascists were in a stronger position, as in Vichy France or Croatia between 1941 and 1944, regimes were sometimes called 'clerico-Fascist'.

A plethora of Fascist parties, however, does present a problem if each one, emulating the Nazis, wants to establish a new world order. History tells us militaristic nationalisms are likely to clash. The Fascist states we have known have been mobilised for battle as an ultimate objective. They have an inevitable tendency to destroy themselves as well as others. Nations embarking on a Fascist adventure have a suicidal urge.

Since the deaths of Hitler and Mussolini among the ruins of their regimes Fascism has been discredited. Yet it has survived almost everywhere, though often in insignificant proportions. It could possibly revive where a combination of certain intellectual, cultural and social factors coincide with certain historical circumstances. Indicators of a disposition towards Fascism would be (a) an intellectual malaise in which the feeling was engendered that modern society could best be dealt with by will and instinctive response rather than reason; (b) national humiliation and disaster as a result of war/economic depression/social conflict; (c) the feeling that there is an enemy within; (d) threats either real or imaginary from outside. In contemporary Russia Zhirinovsky and his party exhibit many of the features of a Fascist Party and his speeches and writings are reminiscent of those of Hitler and Mussolini. The condition of Russia, suffering from dislocation, economic upheaval, political instability and, in some quarters, grievance at the loss of empire, provides the historical circumstance for Fascism to thrive.

Notes

1. P. Viereck, *Metapolitics: The Roots of the Nazi Mind* (New York: Capricorn, 1965), p. 183. I am indebted to this work for much of the background to the Nazis.
2. G. H. Sabine, *A History of Political Theory* (London: Harrap, 1937), p. 724.
3. *Mein Kampf,* unexpurgated edn (London: Hurst & Blackett, 1939), pp. 58–9.
4. Ibid., p. 460.
5. Viereck, *Metrapolitics*, p.148.
6. N. O'Sullivan, *Fascism* (London: Dent, 1983).
7. Ibid., p. 46.
8. S. M. Lipset, *Political Man* (London: Heinemann, 1959).
9. R. F. Hamilton and T. Childers (eds) *Who Voted for Hitler?* (Princeton, NJ: Princeton University Press, 1982).
10. T. Childers, *The Nazi Voter* (Chapel Hill NC: University of North Carolina Press, 1983), p. 268.
11. T. D. Weldon, *A Vocabulary of Politics* (London: John Murray, 1953), p. 87.
12. In 1937 Franco peremptorily united the Falangists with the Carlists and assumed leadership of the amalgamation. See H. Thomas, *The Spanish Civil War* (Harmondsworth: Penguin, 1965), p. 639.

Questions

1. 'A mixture of hooliganism and Hegelianism'. Discuss this veridct of Fascism.
2. Are totalitarian regimes inevitably dictatorships?

Section Three

Bibliography

Chapter 11 **The concept of ideology**

Aiken, H. D., *The Age of Ideology* (New York: New American Library, 1956).

Allardt, E. and Littunen, Y. (eds), *Cleavages, Ideologies and Party Systems* (Helsinki: Academic Book Store, 1968),

Arendt, H., *The Origins of Totalitarianism* (New York: Harcourt, 1973).

Benewick, R., Berki, R. N. and Parekh, B. (eds), *Knowledge and Belief in Politics: the Problem of Ideology* (London: Allen & Unwin, 1973).

Blackburn, R., *Ideology in Social Science* (Glasgow: Fontana, 1972).

Christensen, K. M. (ed.), *Ideologies and Modern Politics* (New York: Dodd Mead, 1972).

Connolly, W. E., *Political Science and Ideology* (London: Atherton Press, 1967).

Corbett, P., *Ideologies* (New York: Harcourt, 1966).

Drucker, H. M., *The Political Use of Ideology* London: London School of Economics, 1974).

Germino, D. L., *Beyond Ideology* (New York: Harper & Row, 1967).

Gyorgy, A. and Blackwood, G. D., *Ideologies in World Affairs* (London: Blaisdell, 1967).

Halpern, B., ' "Myth" and "ideology" in modern usage', *History and Theory*, vol. 1, no. 2, 1961.

Harris, N., *Beliefs in Society: The Problem of Ideology* (Harmondsworth: Penguin, 1971).

Hersch, J., *Idéologies et Réalité: Essai d'orientation Politique* (Paris: Plon, 1956).

Heywood, A., *Political Ideologies* 2nd edn (London: Macmillan, 1998).

Jordan, Z. A., *Philosophy and Ideology* (Dordrecht: D. Reidel, 1963).

Lane, R. E., 'The decline of politics and ideology in a knowledgeable society', *American Sociological Review*, vol. 31, 1966.

Lenk, K., *Ideologie* (Neuwied: Hermann Luchterhand Verlag, 1961).

Lichtheim, G., *The Concept of Ideology and Other Essays* (New York: Random House, 1967).

McClosky, H., 'Consensus and ideology in American politics', *American Political Science Review*, vol. 58, no. 2, 1964.

McLellan, D., *Ideology* 2nd edn (Milton Keynes: Open University Press, 1995).

MacRae, D. G., *Ideology and Society* (London: Heinemann, 1961).

Naess, A., *Democracy, Ideology and Objectivity* (Oxford: Blackwell, 1956).

Picavet, P. J., *Les Ideologues* (Paris: Alcan, 1891).

Rejai, M. (ed.), *Decline of Ideology?* (Chicago Aldine-Atherton, 1971).

Ricoeur, P., *Lectures on Ideology and Utopia* (New York: Columbia University Press, 1986).

Roucek, J. S., 'A history of the concept of ideology', *Journal of the History of Ideas*, vol. 5, 1944.

Sartori, G., 'Politics, ideology and belief systems', *American Political Science Review*, vol. 63, 1969.

Schwarzmantel, J., *The Age of Ideology* (London: Macmillan, 1998).

Seliger, M., *Ideology and Politics* (London: Allen & Unwin, l976).

Shklar, J. (ed.), *Political Theory and Ideology* (New York: Macmillan, 1966).

Thompson, J. B., *Studies in the Theory of Ideology* (Cambridge: Polity Press, 1984).

Thompson, J. B., *Ideology and Modern Culture* (Cambridge: Polity Press, 1990).

Vincent, A., *Modern Political Ideologies* (Oxford: Blackwell, 1995).

Waxman, C. I. (ed.), *The End of Ideology Debate* (New York: Simon & Schuster, 1968).

Zeitlin, I. M., *Ideology and the Development of Sociological Theory* (Englewood Cliffs, NJ: Prentice Hall, 1968).

Chapter 12 **Liberalism**

Ackerman, B., *Social Justice in the Liberal State* (New Haven: Yale University Press, 1980).

Aron, R., *An Essay on Freedom* (New York: World Press, 1970).

Aron, R., *Democracy and Totalitarianism* (Ann Arbor, Mich.: University of Michigan Press, 1990).

Barry, B., *The Liberal Theory of Justice* (Oxford: Clarendon Press, 1973).

Beeker, C. L., *The Heavenly City of the Eighteenth Century Philosophers* (New Haven, Conn.: Yale University Press, 1932).

Bellamy, R., *Victorian Liberalism* (London: Routledge, 1990).

Berlin, I., 'Two concepts of liberty', in *Four Essays on Liberty* (Oxford: Oxford University Press, 1969).

Bury, J. B., *The Idea of Progress* (London: Macmillan, 1920).

Cacoullos, A. R., *Thomas Hill Green: Philosopher of Rights* (New York: Twayne, 1974).

Carter, H., *The Social Theories of L. T. Hobhouse* (Port Washington, Wisc.: Kennikat, 1927).

Cassirer, E., *The Philosophy of the Enlightenment* (Princeton, NJ: University Press, 1951).

Cobban, A., *The Nation State and National Self-Determination* (London: Collins, 1969).

Constant, B., *Political Writings*, ed. B. Fontana (New York: Cambridge University Press, 1986).

Dewey, J., *Liberalism and Social Action* (New York: Putnam, 1935).

Freeden, M., *The New Liberalism: An Ideology of Social Reform* (Oxford: Clarendon Press, 1978).

Gaus, G. F., *The Modern Liberal Theory of Man* (London: Croom Helm, 1983).

Gellner, E., *Nations and Nationalism* (Oxford: Blackwell, 1983).

Gray, J., *Liberalism* 2nd edn (Milton Keynes: Open University Press, 1995).

Halevy, E., *The Growth of Philosophic Radicalism* (London: Faber, 1935).

Jardin, A., *Histoire du Libéralisme Politique* (Paris: Hachette, 1985).

Kassem, B., *Décadence et Absolutisme dans l'oeuvre de Montesquieu* (Geneva: Droz, 1962).

Kirchner, E. J., *Liberal Parties in Western Europe* (Cambridge: Cambridge University Press, 1987).

Kymlicka, W., *Liberalism, Community and Culture* (Oxford: Clarendon Press, 1989).

Laski, H. J., *The Rise of European Liberalism* (London: Allen & Unwin, 1936).

Leroy, M., *Histoire des Idées Sociales en France de Montesquieu à Robespierre*, vol. I (Paris: Gallimard, 1946).

Lough, J., *The Encyclopédie of Diderot and D'Alembert* (Cambridge: Cambridge University Press, 1954).

Macedo, S., *Liberal Virtues: Citizenship, Virtue and Community in Liberal Constitutionalism* (Oxford: Clarendon Press, 1990).

Macpherson, C. B., *Democratic Theory: Essays in Retrieval* (Oxford: Clarendon Press, 1973).

Macpherson, C. B., *The Life and Times of Liberal Democracy* (Oxford: Oxford University Press, 1977).

Manent, P. (ed.) *Les Libérales* (Paris: Hachette, 1986).

Manning, D. J., *Liberalism* (London: Dent, 1976).

Martin, K., *The Rise of French Liberal Thought: a Study of Political Ideas from Bayle to Condorcet* (New York: New York University Press, 1954).

Milhaud, A., *Histoire du Radicalisme* (Paris: Société d'edition françaises et internationales, 1951).

Moore, M., *Foundations of Liberalism* (Oxford: Oxford University Press, 1993).

Moreau, P. F., *Les Racines du libéralisme* (Paris: Editions du Seuil, 1978).

Neill, T. P., *The Rise and Decline of Liberalism* (Milwaukee, Wis.: Bruce, 1953).

Pennock, J. R., *Democratic Political Theory* (Princeton, NJ: Princeton University Press, 1979).

Popper, K., *The Open Society and its Enemies* (London: Routledge, 1962).

Rawls, J., *A Theory of Justice* (Oxford: Oxford University Press, 1972).

Raz, J., *The Morality of Freedom* (Oxford: Clarendon Press, 1986).

Ruggiero, G., *The History of European Liberalism* (Oxford: Oxford University Press, 1927).

Sandel, M., *Liberalism and its Critics* (Oxford: Blackwell, 1984).

Sartori, G., *Democratic Theory* (Detroit, Mich.: Wayne State University Press, 1962).

Schapiro, I., *The Evolution of Rights in Liberal Theory* (Cambridge: Cambridge University Press, 1986).

Scott, J. A., *Republican Ideas and the Liberal Tradition in France, 1870–1914* (New York: Columbia University Press, 1951).

Seliger, M., *The Liberal Politics of John Locke* (London: Allen & Unwin, 1968).

Simon, W. (ed.) *French Liberalism 1789–1848* (New York: Wiley, 1972).

Tamir, Y., *Liberal Nationalism* (Princeton, NJ: Princeton University Press, 1993).

Thompson, D. F., *The Democratic Citizen: Social Science and Democratic Theory in the Twentieth Century* (Cambridge: Cambridge University Press, 1970).

Vachet, A., *L'Idéologie libérale* (Paris: Anthropos, 1970).

Wade, I. O., *Voltaire and Candide* (Princeton, NJ: Princeton University Press, 1959).

Walzer, M., *Spheres of Justice: A Defense of Pluralism and Equality* (New York: Basic Books, 1983).

Weiler, P., 'The new liberalism of L. T. Hobhouse', *Victorian Studies*, vol. XVI, December 1972, pp. 141–61.

Willey, B., *The Eighteenth Century Background* (London: Chatto & Windus, 1940).

Wintrop, N., *Liberal Democracy, Theory and Critics* (London: Croom Helm, 1983).

Wolff, R. P., *The Poverty of Liberalism* (Boston, Mass.: Beacon Press, 1968).

Chapter 13 **Socialism**

Bealey, F., *The Social and Political Thought of the British Labour Party* (London: Weidenfeld & Nicholson 1970).

Becker, H. and Hombach, B., *Die SPD von Innen* (Bonn: SPD, 1983).

Bell, D. S. and Criddle, B., *The French Socialist Party: Resurgence and Victory* (Oxford: Oxford University Press, 1984).

Bell, D. S. and Criddle, B., *The French Socialist Party : the Emergence of a Party of Government* (Oxford: Oxford University Press, 1988).

Bell, D. S. and Criddle, B., *The French Communist Party in the Fifth Republic* (Oxford: Oxford University Press, 1994).

Bell, D. S. and Shaw, E., *The Left in France* (Nottingham: Spokesman, 1983).

Bell, D. S. and Shaw, E., *Conflict and Cohesion in Western European Social Democratic Parties* (London: Pinter, 1994).

Benn, T., *Arguments for Socialism* (Harmondsworth: Penguin, 1980).

Braunthal, G., *The West German Social Democrats, 1969–82: Profile of a Party in Power* (Boulder, Colo.: Westview Press, 1983).

Braunthal, J., *History of the International 1864–1914* (London: Nelson, 1966).

Cerny, P. and Schain, M. (eds), *Socialism, the State and Public Policy in France* (London: Methuen, 1985).

Cohen, G. A., *Karl Marx's Theory of History: A Defence* (Oxford: Oxford University Press, 1978).

Crick, B., *Socialism* (Milton Keynes: Open University Press, 1987).

Criddle, B., *Socialists and European Integration: A Study of the French Socialist Party* (London: Routledge, 1969).

Crosland, C. A. R., *The Future of Socialism* (London: Jonathan Cape, 1956).

Derfler, L., *Socialism since Marx: A Century of the European Left* (London: Macmillan, 1973).

Desanti, D., *Les Socialistes de l'Utopie* (Paris: Payot, 1970).

Einaudi, M., Domenach J.-M. and Garosci, A., *Communism in Western Europe* (Ithaca, NJ: Cornell University Press, 1951).

Elster, J., *Making Sense of Marx* (Cambridge: Cambridge University Press, 1985).

Forester, T., *The Labour Party and the Working Class* (London: Heinemann, 1976).

Fourier, C., *Design for Utopia* (New York: Schocken, 1971).

Gray, A., *The Socialist Tradition: Moses to Lenin* (Harlow: Longmans, 1946).

Harrington, M., *Socialism* (New York: Saturday Review Press, 1970).

Howell, D., *British Social Democracy: A Study in Development and Decay* (London: Croom Helm, 1979).

Hyams, E., *The Millennium Postponed: Socialism from Sir Thomas More to Mao Tse-tung* (New York: Taplinger, 1974).

Kavanagh, D. (ed.), *The Politics of the Labour Party* (London: Allen & Unwin, 1982).

Knapp, V., *Austrian Social Democracy 1889–1914* (Washington, DC: University Press of America, 1980).

Korpi, W., *The Democratic Class Struggle* (London: Routledge, 1983).

Lefranc, G., *Le Mouvement Sydical sous la troisième République 1875–1940* (Paris: Payot, 1976).

Lichtheim, G., *Marxism* (London: Weidenfeld & Nicholson, 1961).

Lichtheim, G., *The Origins of Socialism* (London: Weidenfeld & Nicholson, 1969).

Lichtheim, G., *A Short History of Socialism* (London: Weidenfeld & Nicholson, 1970).

McLellan, D., *Karl Marx : His Life and Thought* (London: Macmillan, 1973).

McLellan, D. (ed.), *Karl Marx: Selected Writings* (Oxford: Oxford University Press, 1977).

Miliband, R., *Parliamentary Socialism* (London: Allen & Unwin, 1961).

Nash, E., 'The Spanish Socialist Party since Franco', in D. Bell (ed.), *Democratic Politics in Spain* (London: Pinter, 1983).

Paterson, W. E. and Thomas, A. H. (eds), *Social Democratic Parties in Western Europe* (London: Croom Helm, 1977).

Paterson, W. E. and Thomas, A. H. (eds), *The Future of Social Democracy* (Oxford: Clarendon Press, 1986).

Rabinbach, A., *The Crisis of Austrian Socialism 1927–34* (Chicago: University of Chicago Press, 1983).

Rocard, M., *Qu'est-ce que la Social-démocratie?* (Paris: Seuil, 1979).

Saint-Simon, H., *Social organisation, the Science of Man and Other Writings* (New York: Harper, 1964).

Scase, R., *Social Democracy in Capitalist Society* (London: Croom Helm, 1977).

Schumpeter, J., *Capitalism, Socialism and Democracy* (London: Allen & Unwin, 1943).

Shell, K. L., *The Transformation of Austrian Socialism* (New York: New York University Press, 1962).

Sully, M. A., *Continuity and Change in Austrian Socialism* (New York: Columbia University Press, 1982).

Whiteley, P., *The Labour Party in Crisis* (London: Methuen, 1983).
Williams, S. (ed.), *Socialism in France* (London: Pinter, 1983).
Woodcock, G., *Anarchism* (Harmondsworth: Penguin, 1962).

Chapter 14 **Conservatism**

Aron, R., *The Vichy Regime 1940–44* (London: Putnam, 1958).
Benda, I., *Le Trahison des Clercs* (Paris: Gallimard, 1927).
Blake, R., *The Conservative Party from Peel to Thatcher* (London: Methuen, 1985).
Bloch-Morhange, J., *Le Gaullisme* (Paris: Plon, 1963).
Bosanquet, N., *After the New Right* (Aldershot: Dartmouth, 1983).
Brittan, S., *The Economic Consequences of Democracy* (London: Temple Smith, 1977).
Butler, E., *Hayek* (London: Temple Smith, 1983).
Butler, R., *The Conservatives* (London: Allen & Unwin, 1977).
Chapman, G., *The Dreyfus Case: A Reassessment* (London: Hart Davis, 1955).
Dreyer, F., *Burke's Politics* (Ontario: Wilfred Laurier University Press, 1979).
Evans, R. and Novak R., *The Reagan Revolution* (New York: E. P. Smith, 1981).
Friedman, M. and Friedman, R., *The Tyranny of the Status Quo* (London: Secker & Warburg, 1985).
Gamble, A., *The Conservative Nation* (London: Routledge, 1974).
Gilmour, I., *Inside Right: A Study of Conservatism* (London: Hutchinson, 1977).
Hoover, K. and Plant, R., *Conservative in Britain and the United States: A Critical Appraisal* (London: Routledge, 1989).
Jenkins, P., *Mrs. Thatcher's Revolution* (London: Jonathan Cape, 1981).
Jordan, G. and Ashford, N., *Public Policy and the Impact of the New Right* (London: Pinter, 1993).
King, D., *The New Right: Politics, Markets and Citizenship* (London: Macmillan, 1987).
Layton-Henry, Z., *Conservative Parties in Western Europe* (London: Macmillan, 1983).
Letwin, O., *Privatising the World* (London: Cassell, 1988).
Letwin, S., *The Anatomy of Thatcherism* (London: Fontana, 1992).
Maurras, C., *Enquête sur la Monarchie 1900–09* (Paris: Nouvelle Librairie Nationale, 1911).
Micaud, C. A., *The French Right and Nazi Germany* (Durham, NC: Duke University Press, 1943).
Minogue, K. and Biddiss, M (eds), *Thatcherism Personality and Politics* (London: Macmillan, 1987).
Nisbet, R., *Conservatism* (Milton Keynes: Open University Press, 1986).
Niskanen, W., *Reaganomics* (Oxford: Oxford University Press, 1988).
Norton, P. and Aughey, A., *Conservatives and Conservatism* (London: Temple Smith, 1981).
Pangle, T., *The Spirit of Modern Republicanism* (Chicago: University of Chicago Press, 1988).
Peguy, C., *Notre Jeunesse* (Paris: Gallimard, 1933).

Peguy, C., *La France* (Paris: Gallimard, 1943).

Pinto-Duschinsky, M., *The Political Thought of Lord Salisbury 1854–68* (London: Constable, 1967).

Remond, R., *The Right Wing in France from 1815 to de Gaulle* (Philadelphia: University of Pennsylvania Press, 1968).

Schenk, H. G., *The Mind of the European Romantics* (London: Constable, 1966).

Schwab, L. M., *The Illusion of a Conservative Reagan Revolution* (New Brunswick, NJ: Transaction Books, 1991).

Skidelsky, R., *Thatcherism* (London: Chatto & Windus, 1988).

Smith. D., *The Rise and Fall of Monetarism* (Harmondsworth: Penguin, 1987).

Smith, G., *Reagan and Thatcher* (New York: W. W. Norton, 1991).

Spencer, P., *Politics of Belief in Nineteenth Century France* (London: Faber, 1954).

Stockman, D., *The Triumph of Politics* (Sevenoaks: Coronet, 1986).

Tarr, F. de, *The French Radical Party from Herriot to Mendès-France* (Oxford: Oxford University Press, 1961).

Tournoux, J. R., *L'Histoire Secrète* (Paris: Plon, 1962).

Viereck, P., *Conservatism Revisited* (London: Lehmann, 1950).

Weiss, J., *Conservatism in Europe 1770–1945* (London: Thames, Hudson, 1977).

Willetts, D., *Modern Conservatism* (Harmondworth: Penguin, 1992).

Young, H., *One of Us* (London: Pan Books, 1989).

Chapter 15   **Fascism**

Benewick, R., *A Study of British Fascism* (London: Allen Lane, 1969).

Brady, R. A., *The Spirit and Structure of German Fascism* (London: Gollancz, 1937)

Bullock, A., *Hitler – a Study in Tyranny* (London: Odham's Press, 1959).

Carsten, F. L., *The Rise of Fascism* (London: Methuen, 1967).

Chabod, F., *A History of Italian Fascism* (London: Weidenfeld & Nicholson, 1963).

Chamberlain, H. S., *The Foundations of the Nineteenth Century* (1911).

Cross, C., *The Fascists in Britain* (London: Barnie & Rickliff, 1961).

Daye, P., *Leon Degrelle et le Rexisme* (Bruges: Brouwer, 1937).

Duverger, M., *De la Dictature* (Paris: Julliard, 1961).

Ercole, F., *Dal nazionalismo al fascismo* (Florence: De Alberti, 1928).

Fermi, L., *Mussolini* (Chicago: Chicago University Press, 1961).

Gentile, G., *Origini e dottrina del Fascismo* (Rome: Liberia del Littorio, 1929).

Goad, H. E., *The Making of the Corporate State* (London: Christophers, 1932).

Haider, C., *Capital and Labour under Fascism* (New York: John Day, 1930).

Heiden, K., *Der Fuehrer* (London: Gollancz, 1944).

Kitchen, M., *Fascism* (London: Macmillan, 1976).

Kitchen, M., *The Coming of Austrian Fascism* (London: Croom Helm, 1980).

Mussolini, B., *La Dottrina del Fascismo* (Milan and Rome: Tuminelli, 1932).

Neoclous, M., *Fascism* (Milton Keynes: Open University Press, 1997).

Neumann, F., *Behemoth* (London: Gollancz, 1942).

Nolte, E., *Three Faces of Fascism* (New York: New American Library, 1965).

Payne, S. G., *Falange – a History of Spanish Fascism* (Stanford, Calif.: Stanford University Press, 1961).

Payne, S. G., *A History of Fascism 1914–1945* (London: UCL Press, 1996).

Pulzer, P. J., *The Rise of Political Anti-semitism in Germany and Austria* (New York: Halban, 1988).

Rocco, A., *La trasformazione dello stato. Dalla stato liberate allo stato fascista* (Rome: La Voce, 1927).

Rossi, A., *The Rise of Italian Fascism* (New York: Fertig, 1966).

Salazar, O., *Principes d'action* (Paris: Fayard, 1956).

Salvemini, G., *Under the Axe of Fascism* (London: Gollancz, 1936).

Serant, P., *Salazar et son Temps* (Paris: Les Sept Couleurs, 1961).

Skidelsky, R., *Oswald Mosley* (London: Macmillan, 1975).

Stahremberg, E. R., *Between Hitler and Mussolini* (London: Hodder & Stoughton, 1942).

Tannenbaum, E. R., *The Action Française* (New York: New York University Press, 1962).

Tannenbaum, E. R., *Fascism in Italy* (London: Allen Lane, 1973).

Thurlow, R., *Fascism in Britain* (Oxford: Blackwell, 1987).

Weber, E., *Action Française* (Stanford, Calif.: Stanford University Press, 1962).

Section Four

Public Administration

Richard A. Chapman

16

Public administration and public sector management

16.1 Definitions

The term 'public administration' has many uses and definitions. Practitioners of public administration emphasise different elements reflecting their experience and the variety of work they do in different countries and in different sorts of institutions within the public sector. In practice, some practitioners are greatly affected by the political environment within which their activities proceed; for others, their work is hardly affected by government or politicians. As a field of study, there are almost as many definitions as there are academic specialists in the subject, and there is no definition to which they would all agree without reservations. In their textbook *Public Administration in Britain Today*, John Greenwood and David Wilson begin with the warning that 'Any attempt to produce a simple definition of public administration is doomed to failure'.[1]

As with politics, however, it is important to be clear about some of the meanings and uses of the term 'public administration'. Sometimes it is used to refer to groups of people whose daily work is practising an activity in a particular public sector context or contexts. Sometimes it is used about the knowledge studied by some officials during training when it can become no more than a term for selected social sciences regarded as a useful basic education for relatively low-level officials. (The examination in the UK for the Ordinary National Certificate in Public Administration includes papers in economics, economic history and statistics, but no paper called public administration.) Sometimes within the study of politics or management it is a specialised field, where scholars study policy-making, its implementation and examination.

These are only introductory examples to indicate the need for care when using terminology that can have a variety of meanings. The purpose of this first essay is therefore to indicate different ways in which 'public administration' and similar terms are used, to draw attention to its distinctive characteristics and to outline its development in practice and as a field of study.

16.2 Public administration and public sector management: differences and similarities

At the level of minimal or basic agreement in an academic context, public administration is the study of management in the public services. Whether or not it is a new discipline developing its own techniques and methods of analysis, and with prescriptive possibilities, is still frequently debated, and has been the basis of the 'identity crisis' contributing much to the literature in the past two or three decades. As a subject for undergraduate study, however, it usually concentrates on management at all levels from major policy-making down to relatively routine techniques of management, and it differs from business management because it emphasises the political environment within which the management functions take place and which conditions the nature of the management processes. Consequently, it may be argued that studies in public administration are but one strand in a management studies spectrum containing other strands. Students of public administration, therefore, have among their special interests the political constraints on management in the public services involving, on the one hand, politicians and political processes and, on the other, management and management processes. There is no established and distinct discipline, technique of reasoning or single mode of approach, however, and specialists in public administration may therefore find themselves sometimes using philosophy or history or economics or survey methods of investigation in order to analyse and appreciate particular public administration problems.

In order to present as comprehensive and as widely acceptable a definition as possible, R. A. W. Rhodes has said the study of public administration is 'the multi-disciplinary study of the political-management system (structures and processes) of public bureaucracies'.[2] Less recent definitions may be noted in comparison. Leonard D. White, the author of the first modern textbook on public administration (published in 1926) defined it as 'the management of men and materials in the accomplishment of the purposes of the state'.[3] He also reflected his own attitude to government and that of his period when he added: 'government and its administrative organs exist to achieve great human objectives in terms of the health, safety and convenience of the population.' Pfiffner and Presthus define it as 'the co-ordination of individual and group efforts to carry out public policy',[4] and an adaptation of the definition presented by Simon, Smithburg and Thompson would be 'the activities of the executive branches of governments and their agencies'.[5] Other writers have concentrated on analysing the functions involved in the practice of public administration. Probably the most famous example is the mnemonic POSDCORB invented by Luther Gulick, standing for Planning, Organising, Staffing, Directing (i.e. controlling), Coordinating, Reporting (i.e. communication) and Budgeting.[6]

Because there is no general agreement and because circumstances change from time to time and from place to place, all these and other definitions may be analysed and debated. For example, it might be questioned whether 'public bureaucracies' makes Rhodes's definition too narrow – much depends on what is meant by bureaucracy – or it might be questioned whether White's definition assumes a division of powers, like that seen in the United States or the United Kingdom, and concentrates too much on means to the exclusion of ends, so that the definition does not comfortably fit the experience of other countries with different political systems.

The study of public administration, therefore, encounters a number of difficulties, some of which occur elsewhere in the social sciences, though not necessarily to the same degree. Nevertheless, the scope of the study in modern, advanced countries is enormous and continually growing, reflecting such factors as population growth and, at certain stages of development, demands for the state to provide more and more services. The study also encompasses not only the activities of agencies in central and local governments, but also nationalised industries, public boards and statutory commissions, and a large variety of partly official and partly independent bodies (sometimes called 'quangos': quasi-autonomous non-governmental organisations). In addition, the subject is continually changing both in broad general terms because of the differing conceptions of the role of the state held by various governments at different times, and because there are so many and so frequent changes in the structures and functions of particular government agencies.

In the chapters of this Section public administration will refer to management in the public services. This means that background questions, on which light may be shed, may include the following: Where and how are policy decisions really made? Who are the persons with power and influence in public organisations and how have they achieved their positions of authority and responsibility? What standards of responsibility and accountability can citizens expect of their rulers and/or officials, and how can their responsibility and accountability be made more effective? How should public officials be selected and trained? How can the civil service be made more efficient? Why does the implementation of public policies sometimes not achieve intended goals?

16.3 Public sector management and management in other contexts

At an elementary level it is sometimes suggested that key differences between public administration and private, or business, management can be seen when the extremes of both types of activity are compared in terms of selected variables. Six are considered below from both points of view for illustration.

16.3.1 Private sector management

1. In business the motivating force is profit and the purpose of management is to maximise profits for owners. Good management, it is argued, leads to healthy profits and, as an encouragement, staff are sometimes paid incentives for high performance.
2. In most spheres businesses operate in a competitive environment and competition is thought to stimulate the best value for purchasers. The more efficient and effective a business is and the better the quality of its products, the more likely it will be to increase its share of the market. One of the consequences of this is the development of marketing and advertising specialities in business management.
3. In business there is a clear line of authority and accountability to the owners of the business. The owners may, in practice, be the most senior managers, as often applies in, say, small building businesses or retail shops, or they may be non-managing owners or shareholders in larger types of business.
4. In business, sales form a large part of the operations, whether they are sales of goods or sales of services. Consequently, the emphasis throughout the organisation is to give customers' requirements the primary focus. Therefore it is sometimes said that the customer is always right – no matter what the customer wants and however inconvenient the customer's requirements may be. This is because the customer is paying for whatever goods or services are being provided.
5. In business, revenue comes from production and payments are made in relation to identifiable goods and services. If no goods or services are being produced there is no revenue and consequently sooner or later there is no business to manage.

6. A good business gives priority to public relations in all its forms. This may involve advertising, ensuring that employees individually have good relations with customers or clients, paying attention to the appearance of workers (some may be given uniforms or dress allowances, or receive training to improve the way they behave). Similarly, attention may be given to the attractiveness of offices or shops, the promulgation of customer service codes, easy to identify colour schemes and symbols, and the design of note-paper and advertising with distinctive images.

16.3.2 Public sector management

By comparison, the extreme examples of public sector management have different characteristics.

1. Instead of profit being the motivating force, in the public sector emphasis may be given to the ideals of public service. This may be seen in the ethos of a traditional civil service, involving high standards for dealing with the needs of citizens, and ensuring that the public interest is given priority over the interests of particular groups or individuals. Long service provided at high standards in the public sector may be rewarded by incremental pay scales, non-contributory pensions and the award of non-monetary tokens of recognition such as medals, honours or titles of distinction.
2. Instead of competition with other businesses, in large parts of the public sector particular organisations act as monopolies. For example, there is only one national treasury, one police force or fire brigade service, and there is a specialist skill for lawyers whose work is to draft legislation.
3. Instead of accountability to owners there is public accountability. In many democratic countries this accountability may in the first instance be to elected representatives, but it is ultimately to the people. There may also be a sense of accountability to individual citizens, or groups, or to standards required by professional associations which test and sometimes monitor standards in areas of professional expertise.
4. A large proportion – indeed, often the majority – of managers in the public sector are concerned not with sales of goods or services but with the processes of government. This is particularly evident in raising national revenue, managing the judicial system, managing the armed services, or representing one's country both at

home and in embassies or consulates abroad. For these services, aspects of governing become a distinctive skill. There is only one legitimate form of government in any country, and while standards between countries or the scope of governmental activities may differ from place to place or from time to time, the profession of government can be quite different from other professions or skills.

5. The main source of revenue for the public sector as a whole is not the production of goods or services but taxation, a source necessitating special procedures, not only of accountability, but also of uniformity within the jurisdiction of a particular area of government. Whereas price mechanisms in business operations may vary in different parts of a country according to what the market demands or will bear, in the public sector it is usually expected that known rules will be administered fairly and uniformly throughout the jurisdiction of a government or unit of government. This is quite different from obtaining revenue from production. It may have ideological implications. For example, in liberal democracies there tends to be an emphasis on justice, fairness and impartiality in the treatment of citizens.

6. There is a different approach to public relations. In the private sector, chief executives or senior managers at the top of their business hierarchy can be public figures. By contrast, in the public sector, particularly in democratic systems, officials are generally anonymous, or if not anonymous, do not consciously attract personal publicity for their achievements. Instead, credit is taken by ministers or governors in whose name a particular service is provided, and who are ultimately answerable to the people.

By emphasising these differences it is easy to draw attention to the variations between extreme types of management in business and in the public sector, but drawing attention to these differences has only a limited value. Often similarities between the two sectors of management are more significant than differences. Both public sector management and business management may experience problems associated with bureaucracy (the term is being used here to signify a particular type of organisation); there may also be similar processes or techniques in specialist areas like financial or personnel management; certain management techniques may be applicable in both contexts and there may be times when good communication with citizens is very similar to good public relations in business. Indeed, often there are more significant differences between big and small organisations, whatever the management context, than there are between public sector and business organisations. The skills required of managers are sometimes more related to organisation size than to the sectors within which the management processes operate.

Nevertheless, public administration specialists are likely to emphasise the essential differences in one way or another associated with accountability. This is clearly seen in areas where public sector officials are not well known to people generally because public accountability is channelled through governors, ministers and/or representatives; it is seen where citizens have to be treated uniformly and according to known rules within jurisdictional areas (even when the rules embody discretionary features); and it is seen when there are ethical issues distinctively related to conceptions of public service.

Two examples from the United Kingdom illustrate how this applies in practice. To illustrate how motivation to public service worked in the British civil service one Conservative minister told the journalist Anthony Sampson over thirty years ago: 'I remember when we took office in 1951, the same civil servant who had been looking after nationalisation had already got out a plan for de-nationalisation. He went about it with just the same enthusiasm'[7]. To illustrate the distinctiveness of the contemporary civil service the UK's Parliamentary Treasury and Civil Service Select Committee recently said the unifying features of the British civil service were 'impartiality, integrity, objectivity, selection and promotion on merit and accountability'.[8] Of course, most of these features may be found in any good management structure: many organisations may be able to claim impartiality, integrity, objectivity, and selection and promotion on merit, but it is only the civil service that is thought always to have the distinctive feature of accountability through ministers to Parliament. It is from the basis of public accountability that other distinctive features may develop. Thus, one UK senior official, writing to the Civil Service Commissioners in 1855, explained: 'The Foreign Office requires of Clerks great sacrifices of time, of comfort, and of amusement,' and they 'should take such an interest in the office as to consider its credit and reputation as their own'[9].

16.4 New public management

All spheres of management are susceptible to the fashions of new techniques or new approaches. Indeed, renewal and change may be a characteristic of modern approaches to management. New approaches require rethinking of objectives and means and this in turn stimulates and facilitates the reconsideration of all aspects of management. Some new techniques or approaches may originate in one sector of management and are later applied elsewhere. To some extent the development or transfer of techniques or procedures may be the result of management consultants working in different management contexts and taking their techniques with them. Sometimes an impetus is supplied by ideologies – as, for example, with the assertion that business management is best and that the public sector should be made more 'business-like'. Sometimes new techniques or approaches receive so much publicity that they are widely applied without much attention being given to different contexts and environments. This seems to have been the case with what is increasingly known as 'new public management'.

The thrust of new public management is now widely known, though there is not one single basic text which sets out its main features. The term relates to management emphases so well regarded and thought to be worth imitation that they are sometimes global in application. While the management emphases may have a somewhat different mix in different countries and the motivating forces encouraging their introduction may vary, the broad trends are very similar. Six examples, mainly from UK experience – where the features taken together are more advanced and/or more extreme than in many other countries – are considered here. Some of the most important reasons for UK uniqueness will be considered later.

16.4.1   Separation of policy-making from operational matters

First, there is the separation of policy-making from operational matters. It was previously attempted in the United Kingdom and was one of the most important features of the nationalised industries and public corporations from, say, the inauguration of the Port of London Authority in 1908 to the heyday of the creation of the nationalised industries in the period immediately following the Second World War. The original impetus behind the nationalised industries was, as William Robson explained in his monumental work on the subject:

> A twofold desire to secure freedom from parliamentary supervision over management on the one hand and Treasury control over personnel and finance on the other. Both these normal features of British government were regarded, rightly or wrongly, as likely to hamper efficiency and restrict initiative in undertakings of an industrialised or commercial character.[10]

In more recent times this has resulted in the creation of agencies in which nearly 65 per cent of civil servants now work. From time to time the outcome has been controversy among politicians about the dividing line between matters of an operational nature and policy matters, but the publicly stated advantages of the new arrangements are thought to greatly outweigh the difficulties associated with demarcating responsibilities. The disaggregated service organisations – there are now well over one hundred agencies providing specific services where in the past the tasks were generally provided by departments of government – are smaller and recognisable as distinct bodies emphasising their distinctive identities in various ways. Associated with this disaggregation, the new structures have flatter hierarchies, involving what is sometimes called 'delayering', and the promotion of a fundamental reconsideration and clearer identification of tasks, sometimes called 'process engineering'.

16.4.2   Formula funding

Second, there is an emphasis on formula funding to facilitate new approaches to 'best practice'. A good example is the introduction of formula funding into UK universities in the 1980s. The intention was to ensure that universities provided the best possible value for money. At the time it was argued that there was no reason why so much variation existed between the cost of educating students to first degree level at different universities. The implication was that the cost of studying at the more expensive universities indicated they were less business-like and efficient than less costly universities. For example, questions were asked about why it cost much more to run universities at Hull, Durham or Aberdeen, all in the north east of England or Scotland, than at Sussex or Exeter in the south. It was thought that by imposing formula funding, economies would be introduced leading to reductions in public expenditure and more efficient institutions. The formula still applies, and has the advantage of showing that costs always vary because of factors like geographical location. Buildings cost more to heat in the north than in the south, fares to London are more expensive in relation to distances to be travelled, and universities providing residential accommodation cost more than those that do not.

16.4.3   Value of markets for resource allocation

Third, because it is sometimes thought, for ideological as well as operational reasons, that businesses are more efficient than government, new public management has emphasised the value of markets to determine resource allocation. The advantage here is thought to be that by emphasising the advantages of markets, resources are not wasted on providing services or facilities where there is no demand or insufficient demand, and competition stimulates lower prices. Durham University provides good examples of how this works in practice. Having received most of its resources from government through formula funding, the university developed its own allocation systems by modelling its arrangements on the principles in the formula funding allocation it received from the government. Consequently it initially produced ECHO, an allocation model intended to echo the national formula; later it produced DRAM, DRAMA and DREAM. DRAM, the Durham Resource Allocation Model, embodies the principles laid down by the government, but not so slavishly as its predecessor ECHO; however, resources are still devolved right down to individual departments using the same sort of criteria. This has the benefit of allocating resources for the purposes intended by the government. It means, however, that non-funded services are not resourced, and if such services are to continue costs have to be covered in other ways. Also, while a market approach to efficiency works reasonably well for big and expensive departments, because of economies of scale and possible flexibilities in staffing and other resources, it can lead to major problems in very small departments where there is no scope for such flexibilities. Similar formula funding principles have been incorporated in DREAM, the Durham Resource Equipment Allocation Model, and DRAMA, the Durham Resource Allocation Model for Accommodation. In relation to all these models, the ideas have been to ensure that resources are allocated for intended purposes, to get the best value for money, and to introduce market approaches to maximise the benefits from limited resources. With DRAMA, for example, departments receive allocations of space (e.g. the use of teaching rooms) and charge other departments when their allocated space is hired out. Secretaries therefore become specialists in issuing invoices between departments to charge for the use of space, raising invoices becomes a priority and, consequently, secretaries have less time for other secretarial duties. The use of teaching space is a measurable activity, however, where it is easy and arguably beneficial to introduce the features of a market.

16.4.4 Private funding

Fourth, there is an emphasis on private funding wherever it can be obtained, with the management of public services often provided on the basis of contracts. The fundamental ideas associated with new public management, therefore, involve privatising services where it is not absolutely essential for them to be continued by government provision. Where services are 'contracted out' a new sphere of activity is developed for monitoring or regulating systems or services provided through these new arrangements. In the United Kingdom, instead of one Civil Service Commission for recruiting staff for government departments and agencies there are now over 3,000 separate recruitment units, with Civil Service Commissioners charged with the duty of ensuring the recruitment is on the basis of selection on merit, involving fair and open competition, and that there are equal opportunities for all applicants.

16.4.5   Emphasis on cost reduction and value for money

Fifth, techniques of management favour the new arrangements encouraged by new public management. The more important characteristics are cost reduction and improved value for money. These, in turn, have led to an emphasis on accruals accounting. This records revenues and costs as they are earned and incurred, not as money is received or paid, and charges the value of fixed assets against income as depreciation. It has also led to locally determined regimes for recruiting staff, for determining and evolving agency-specific pay arrangements, and for developing agency-specific conditions of service. As with the other characteristics, these have easily identifiable advantages and disadvantages. They may result in lower staff costs, especially where, in regions distant from a capital city, pay can be negotiated at less than a national rate, but they also involve less staff flexibility because agencies develop individual approaches to their work with fewer features in common.

16.4.6   Importance of customers

Sixth, new public management emphasises the importance of customers, with particular stress on customer relations and customer accountability, even where the relationship may be of doubtful relevance. Associated with the emphasis on customer accountability there is an emphasis on quality of service assessed by measurable criteria, generally involving pre-set targets. These targets are reported in annual publications, with special attention to the percentage achievement of targets. In the UK there are also charters, published by departments and agencies, emphasising the rights of customers. They bring the advantage that customers may know more clearly what services they can expect and what their rights are, but they may introduce confusion where the concept of a customer is not as clearly relevant as it may be in a more extreme example of a business management organisation. It is important that performance targets are set with care and sensitivity, because if an organisation is to be judged against the achievement of its measurable targets, it will concentrate on those targets and give minimal attention to other criteria.

Perhaps the overriding feature of the new public management is the associated trend to reconsider the scope of government activities. Whereas, in the years immediately after the Second World War, democratic regimes were involved in increasing the scope of government by giving it a more positive role, by the 1990s there was motivation to reduce the percentage of Gross National Product (GNP) taken by the public sector and anxieties for the future in countries where populations were ageing and the proportion in paid employment was diminishing. The popular catchphrase was to promote the independence of individuals and to reduce the functions of the 'nanny state'. For the purposes of this chapter, however, the details of new public management are less important than the general features of public sector management to which the details draw attention. Those features are especially highlighted by the global trend towards new public management.

Consequently this globalisation process will be considered next.

16.5 Globalisation of approaches

Many countries throughout the world are now favouring new public management approaches for providing public services, a trend so widespread that it has implications for what is meant by the term public administration, and draws attention to some of its already mentioned features. It also leads to new queries about the nature of the subject for study and its practice. Five illustrations of this follow.

16.5.1   New public management and the political environment

First, it should be noted that while many countries, particularly in Western Europe and in liberal democracies elsewhere, wish to economise on the cost of their public services, and in particular wish to reduce the proportion of GNP taken by the public sector, the ease of introducing these measures varies according to the nature of the constitution and the constraints of the political system. Countries with written constitutions and codified legal systems, and where the tasks of senior officials are mainly concerned with administering the law, have more difficulties with introducing these measures than countries with less rigid constitutions, parliamentary sovereignty and common law systems. For example, the new arrangements involving the creation of agencies in the UK required no statutes, nor did the abolition of the Civil Service Commission (the creation of agencies has been by administrative arrangement, and changes to the Civil Service Commission were effected by Orders in Council). However, this general experience has much more significance than the creation of particular new agencies. By contrast, in continental European countries individual officials have accountabilities in law (sometimes through personnel codes or public finance requirements) which simply do not exist in the United Kingdom. It is no accident that the lead countries, as far as new public management is concerned, are the UK and countries with similar constitutional and political systems, including parliamentary government, such as Australia and New Zealand. This in turn re-emphasises the importance of the political environment which affects so many aspects of public sector management.

16.5.2   Public administration in the private sector

Second, the use of the term public administration is also changing. Whereas in the past it was possible to consider and compare the extremes of management in different sectors, this is now by no means so easy. Often public sector management is delivered on a contract basis, so public administration may relate to a type of activity rather than to management in the public sector. Such activity may be only part of a firm's work – for example, personnel selection for a government department may be bought on a contract basis and administered by a firm of personnel consultants mainly engaged in other contracts for many private or business organisations. This in turn means that staff engaged in management may have no public service ethos or traditions, may be less sensitive to the political implications of their daily work, and may have somewhat different conceptions of accountability.

16.5.3   Customer accountability compared with public interest

Third, there is less likely to be an understanding of the public interest, and the use of the concept of customer accountability may be quite different from what is meant by customer accountability in a business context. In a business context a customer may be defined as a person who pays for a good or service benefiting him or her only and not for any other person, but in the context of a public administration the concept of customer accountability may be much less useful. In some instances, of course, there may be no problems. People applying to the

Foreign Office for passports to visit other countries may be like the customers of a business organisation. The concept is much less clear when heads of agencies refer to ministers as their customers, and it has much less relevance for a childless citizen who believes that it is in the national interest to educate children.

16.5.4 Possible conflicts between different features of new public management

Fourth, the adoption of new public management cannot be relied upon to resolve all current difficulties, especially when some of its features are in conflict with others. For example, a university like Durham is not resourced from public funds to build car parks or run a creche for children of its employees or students. If it obtains funds from other sources it may do both. Problems arise, however, when the creche is not covering its expenses and opens its doors to outsiders to become economically viable. Outside parents have to be given car parking facilities, already inadequate for staff doing essential university work. Then the creche increases parking problems, academic staff find there is nowhere to park and, if they come and go during the day, their work is affected. Consequently the primary objectives of the university are affected by accountancy rigidities.

16.5.5 The distinction between policy and operational issues

Fifth, and perhaps most important of all, new public management draws attention again to the means/ends dichotomy with which this chapter began. While at the most elementary level it is possible to argue that politicians and ministers determine the ends or purposes of public sector organisations, in practice many details of those ends have to be planned and refined by officials who understand the problems associated with their fields of operations. The difference between ends or policies and means or operations may be clear in the most extreme examples, especially when presented in the form of ideal-types. In everyday practice, however, there is rarely such a clear distinction. In the potential conflict between a university's objectives, its need to make some activities self-financing and the requirements to introduce the characteristics of a market where no market actually exists, someone or some group has to exercise judgements. These judgements have to resolve immediate difficulties in the context of managerial responsibilities within a particular environment, but in good public administration they also have to bear in mind less immediate considerations. The really testing challenges of public administration may be more frequently found in these grey areas where there is scope for conflicts of interests and where management decisions may be made on the basis of non-management criteria than at the extreme ends of a management typology or spectrum. At the present time there is a great deal of emphasis on improving management efficiency, but there is often a lack of clarity about what management efficiency is. There is also considerable and continuing debate about such issues as motivation, ethics and standards in public life.

It is impossible to resolve all these issues simply, however, without considering the essential and distinctive qualities of public administration, including some of the features mentioned in this chapter. Good judgement is necessary at senior levels in all management contexts, but in public administration the issues can be both more sensitive and more complex than in management elsewhere.

Notes

1. John Greenwood and David Wilson, *Public Administration in Britain Today* (London: Unwin Hyman, 1989), p. 1.
2. R. A. W. Rhodes, *Current Developments in the Study of Public Administration in the United States*, Inlogov Discussion Paper, New Series No. 1, University of Birmingham, 1976.
3. Leonard D. White, *Introduction to the Study of Public Administration* (New York: Macmillan, 1926), 1955 edition, p. 201.
4. John M. Pfiffner and Robert V. Presthus, *Public Administration* (New York: Ronald, 1960), p.5.
5. Herbert A. Simon, Donald W. Smithburg and Victor A. Thompson, *Public Administration (New York: Knopf, 1950; New Brunswick, NJ: Transaction Publishers, 1991).*
6. L. Gulick and L. Urwick (eds), *Papers on the Science of Administration* (New York: Institute of Public Administration 1937).
7. Anthony Sampson, *Anatomy of Britain* (London: Hodder & Stoughton, 1962), p. 235.
8. Treasury and Civil Service Committee, Session 1993–94, Fifth Report, *The Role of the Civil Service*, Vol. I, HC 27–I, HMSO, 1994.
9. E. Hammond to Horace Mann, 25 June 1855: PRO/CSC2/5.
10. William A. Robson, *Nationalized Industry and Public Ownership* (London: George Allen &and Unwin, 1960), p. 59.

Questions

1. Explain the similarities and differences of tasks facing top managers in public and business organisations.
2. What are the possible dangers and benefits in introducing new public management into public sector organisations?

Organisation theory and bureaucracy

The goals or purposes set for public administration organisations are normally decided by rulers. It is the task of such organisations to achieve their given purposes by cooperative action. This requires both formal organisation, which is the pattern of behaviour and relationships deliberately planned for the participants, and informal organisation, which encompasses patterns of human behaviour not deliberately planned for the participants, but which contribute to understanding how participants actually behave. Informal organisation may also include aspects of organisation and facilities, such as social or sports amenities, that may legitimately contribute to the development of cooperative behaviour in ways not directly related to the organisation goals or purposes.

This chapter will concentrate on what formal organisation is and explain basic types of organisation, consider some of the principles on which organisations may be designed, and explain in particular what is meant by bureaucracy and what its advantages and disadvantages are. It will also consider the implications of certain formal organisation structures and the formal relationships of people within an organisation for achieving purposes intended by government.

17.1 Formal organisation theory

Simon, Smithburg and Thompson begin their textbook on public administration by saying that when two men co operate to roll a stone that neither could have moved alone, the rudiments of administration have appeared. There is *purpose* – moving the stone – and there is *cooperative action* – persons using combined strength to accomplish something that could not have been done without such combination. They then explain that, in its broadest sense, *administration* can be defined as the activities of groups cooperating to accomplish common goals. Of course, modern public administration is much more complex

and on a much larger scale, so that the elementary illustration presented by Simon, Smithburg and Thompson of the need for cooperative
action in any organisation is, as they themselves accept, of only
marginal relevance even for teaching purposes. Moreover, public administration tasks must proceed within a particular political system and
with due regard to its values and culture. Therefore arrangements that
may be workable in one place or at one time may differ from the
arrangements for a different place or at a different time. Nevertheless,
there are certain basic features of any formal organisation structure
which are generally applicable and important, not only when formal
organisations are developed, but also continuously as their work proceeds.

At the most elementary level the initial stages in the development of
a formal organisation structure require an appreciation of the work to
be done. This is always necessary when any new service is to be
introduced (such as the provision of a national health service where
none previously existed) or when radical changes involving organisation restructuring are subsequently considered. In some cases this
appreciation of the work may be mainly quantitative and therefore
easy to measure, even if some of the details may at the outset be little
more than estimates. It may also involve an assessment of qualitative
factors – and this is particularly important where personal services are
to be provided for individual citizens or groups. When more qualitative
care is needed for the provision of a service more staff time may be
necessary, and some of it may require specialist skills. Good examples
are the labour-intensive nature of educating handicapped children, and
campaigns to combat adult illiteracy in advanced societies where
illiteracy is thought to be shameful.

Once the total workload has been properly considered, it then has to
be divided and allocated to officials occupying individual positions.
This enables work to be effectively planned, controlled and coordi-
nated, facilitates staff recruitment and training, and allows costings to
be calculated so that adequate financing can be provided. As these basic
features of management are receiving attention, it is essential to consider how the individual positions should relate to each other and also,
in relation to organisations in the public sector, how they should relate
– and be publicly known to relate – to other parts of the political system.
In particular, this requires an understanding of authority and accountability, both within organisations and to governors (and, in democracies, to elected representatives). Once these details are agreed a
statement is usually made on how the organisation's components
are intended to work together and how work is to be allocated to
various positions.

This, in outline, is how a formal organisation is developed from first principles. Specialists in organisation theory have, however, been industrious in producing typologies intended to be useful in developing new organisations or for analysing how organisations work or should work. In some cases these typologies may be more elaborate than is necessary for their immediate purposes. Some scholars (e.g. in the field of advisory bodies for environmental pollution control) have focused on relevant criteria to produce more typologies than are found to exist in practice. Some of the benefits expected from administrative theorising and, especially, from developing typologies can be undermined by making them too elaborate or by losing sight of the intended practical benefits – that is, understanding how organisations work or should work. Furthermore, it should be noted that, in practice, it is by no means unusual to find combinations of various types of organisation present in well-established structures.

It is important to stress the value in any big organisation of developing a clear understanding of the basic concepts of authority and accountability. Authority usually relates to the right to require obedience to legitimate instructions given within the context of an organisation – and it should be noted that such authority only applies to instructions within the context of the organisation. It must be concerned with the work of the organisation and must not violate the laws, rules and conventions of the society. Accountability is the liability to answer for actions taken and it involves sanctions, including the possibility of punishment or dismissal if actions have not been properly taken. In formal organisation theory it is, of course, the task of senior managers to ensure that the organisation's work is properly analysed and allocated, and the senior managers are themselves accountable to shareholders, owners, governors or elected representatives for ensuring that these senior management tasks are effectively pursued. Consequently, in effective organisations, there is normally a clearly known arrangement, often including an organisation chart, to enable all within the organisation to appreciate their positions and their relationships to others in terms of authority and accountability.

17.2 Three basic types of organisation

At a very simple level three types of organisation are commonly found: line organisation, line and staff organisation, and functional organisation.

17.2.1   Line Organisation

A simple line organisation may consist of a number of levels of authority with variable numbers of positions at each level, often called the span of control, depending on the nature of the work involved. This type of structure is easily understandable because the manifestation of authority in the organisation is the giving of instructions, and the manifestation of accountability is the necessity to report. The span of control in such an organisation is the number of immediately junior officials over whom a superior exercises authority and who are directly accountable to him or her. To avoid confusion, it should be noted that the span of control is therefore quite different from the number of people through whom a superior official works – the span of control only relates to the number of persons directly accountable in a hierarchy of authority.

17.2.2   Line and staff organisation

A line and staff organisation exists when there is a requirement for a line manager to be advised by specialists on technical matters on which he could not expect to be an expert. These technical matters may involve particular management specialisms, perhaps relating to work study or information technology, or legal or financial advice. In such an organisation the line managers take all the operating decisions, though they may have to take into account the advice of staff specialists. In a pure line and staff organisation no staff member, however senior in the organisation, exercises authority over a line manager, and instead of levels of authority, staff specialists may be regarded as having levels of status – and these levels of status may confer comparable salary and physical working conditions, but such details are quite different from authority/accountability relationships. An example from a university context may be standard grades, salary and conditions of service for professors who are heads of academic departments with teaching and research responsibilities, and comparable arrangements for the heads of supporting services such as the university's registrar, treasurer or surveyor. In a large government organisation there may be comparable grades, salary scales and conditions of service for specialists such as lawyers, accountants or librarians. Where a staff function has significant importance, involving the employment of numerous specialists, the specialists may in turn be arranged in an auxiliary department with their own authority and accountability relationships, and with levels of technical authority comparable to levels in the – often parallel – line hierarchy. These simple examples are less clearly identifiable in actual organisations where staff in particular positions, such as managers, are expected to have a professional expertise they no longer practice.

17.2.3   Functional organisation

Functional organisations exist on a different basis from either line or line and staff organisations because within them operating authority and accountability are vested in specialist departments, intended to cooperate without a line of authority to ensure that the entire organisation is achieving its purpose(s). Because there is no unity of command there is no single source of problem resolution as there is in line or line and staff organisations. Nevertheless, functional organisations work well in relatively small businesses, especially those of a family type, where difficulties can be resolved on the basis of criteria quite different from formal organisation criteria. Elements of functional organisation could often be seen in British local government until about twenty years ago, because the town clerk was regarded as first among equals in relation to the other chief officers, and business proceeded on the basis of cooperation among colleagues. If serious disagreements arose they had to be resolved in council meetings or in committees of the council. There are also examples of functional organisation in universities where specialist officials have their own important departments that have to cooperate with academic departments as well as with each other, and if – or when – difficulties or disputes arise that cannot be easily resolved, they may be referred for resolution to the university senate or council or to their committees. Many of the working practices in these types of formal organisation are guided by commonsense rules or wisdom resulting from experience, and some examples of these rules are often referred to as classical organisation theory.

17.3   Classical organisation theory – organisation principles and their uses

Classical organisation theory, so named by Herbert A. Simon,[1] embraces the works of the founding fathers of the study of organisation. Some of the most important writings in this tradition include those of Luther Gulick and Lyndall Urwick, *Papers on the Science of Administration*,[2] Henri Fayol, *General and Industrial Management*,[3] Lyndall Urwick, *The Elements of Administration*[4] and F. W. Taylor, *The Principles of Scientific Management*.[5] Max Weber's writings on bureaucracy also fit within this approach and will receive special attention later in this chapter. The basis of these works is reflection by men of administrative experience, either because they were practising administrators of recognised ability or because they spent considerable time thinking about management practice.

Classical organisation theorists felt they were contributing to the development of a science of management. They were building their theories upon observation and/or practical experience of organisation structures, and developing and focusing attention upon what they thought or hoped were universally applicable principles. As Christopher Hodgkinson has said, these thinkers 'have provided analyses of organisational logic, diagnoses of a variety of organisation dysfunctions, and conceptual models or interpretative systems which have enhanced the knowledge base of administrative competence.'[6] Classical organisation theorists have also emphasised the importance of organisational efficiency, where efficiency is conceived as the cheapest way of accomplishing routine work. Keith Henderson encapsulated their approach well when he wrote: 'Lessons from practical experience and history were thought to be adequate guides [for their work] and the fundamental appeal was to common sense and basic values such as harmony, order and frugality.'[7]

Sir Arthur Helps, a very senior civil servant in the United Kingdom in the nineteenth century, and, more recently, the American scholar Herbert A. Simon, who was influenced by Helps, have drawn attention to a selection of the principles developed by classical thinkers, but have also indicated their limitations. Simon likened them to proverbs because: 'A fact about proverbs that greatly enhances their quotability is that they almost always occur in contradictory pairs. "Look before you leap!" but "He who hesitates is lost".'[8]

17.3.1   Principles of organisation

Four examples of the principles of organisation illustrate their practical, commonsense nature.

1. Administrative efficiency is increased by limiting the span of control at any point in an organisation hierarchy to a small number. A proper span of control should be small enough for the executive to be able to give sufficient personal attention to each. This is based on the idea that there is a psychological limit to the individual's span of attention.
2. Administrative efficiency is enhanced by keeping at a minimum the number of organisation levels through which a matter must pass before it is acted upon.

3. Administrative efficiency is increased if authority is delegated to the lowest possible level.
4. An efficient organisation should rely on individuals wherever possible. Consequently, boards should function in an advisory capacity only, not as administrative decision-making units. Committees should never be in a line of command, though they may be used for coordination.

17.3.2 Criticisms of classical organisation theorists

Numerous criticisms have been made of the achievements of classical organisation theorists, but four will be considered here.

1. As Simon in particular has said, the principles, like proverbs, can be seen as mutually contradictory. For example, the advantages of a limited span of control can be contradicted by the advantages of keeping to a minimum the number of organisational levels through which a matter must pass before it is acted upon. One can indicate other examples showing that many organisation principles occur in apparently contradictory pairs, and that the quest for scientific management does not always help in deciding which principle should apply in any given difficult situation. In practice, the size of an efficient span of control is often directly related to the amount of discretion involved in the work of subordinates or their experience and skill in their work.
2. Organisation principles largely disregard the human factor in organisations. If any organisation is to achieve its purpose(s) and encourage the cooperation of individuals, human factors, including aspects of informal organisation and the need for individuals to achieve satisfaction from their work, cannot be disregarded. This will be considered in Chapter 18, but it should, perhaps, be noted here that Frederick Taylor, one of the most important figures in the literature on scientific management, was not unaware of the dehumanising consequences of the rigid application of rules of scientific management.
3. Some of the most important and burdensome problems for managers involve dealing with conflict within their organisations, and the classical principles of organisation are of little help in such circumstances.
4. Formal organisation theory has a pro-management bias. The basis from which classical organisation theorists began their work was not the detached stance expected of an investigator, but thoughtful advice, sometimes including compendia or

guides, *for managers*. Good organisation practice, especially in complex public organisations, generally involves much more than this.

While management theorists were concerned to contribute to the development of scientific management, philosophers and specialists on government were considering the ways in which public power was exercised through government organisations. Martin Albrow has skilfully drawn attention to some of these writers in relation to bureaucracy. Towards the end of the nineteenth century Gaetano Mosca, for example, considered the role of the ruling class and emphasised the inevitability of minority rule, while Robert Michels, agreeing with Mosca about elites, drew attention to oligarchy and bureaucracy in political parties.

The most significant writer on bureaucracy, however, was Max Weber, the German sociologist, whose refined treatment incorporated an awareness of other writings with his own theorising and drew attention to some of the dangers implicit in highly developed bureaucratic systems.

17.4 Bureaucracy: its characteristics as seen by Max Weber

Although Max Weber wrote around the turn of the century, his work did not become widely known to the English-speaking world until the late 1940s with the publication of translations of his work by A.M. Henderson and Talcott Parsons (1947)[9] and by H.H. Gerth and C. Wright Mills (1948).[10] Moreover, like other classical theorists already mentioned, Weber's contribution to the literature was the result of scholarship and what is sometimes now called armchair theorising; it was not based on findings from empirical research.

For the purposes of this chapter Max Weber is important for two reasons: first, his exposition on authority and, second, his ideal-type of a form of organisation he called 'bureaucracy'. These will be considered in turn.

17.4.1   Weber on authority

Weber said: 'The foundation of all authority, and hence of all compliance with orders, is a belief in prestige, which operates to the advantage of the ruler or rulers.'[11] He observed that different forms of belief were associated with different authority structures and hence different organisational forms, and he expanded this by explaining three kinds of such beliefs.

1. In the first, obedience was justified because the person giving the order(s) had some sacred or other outstanding characteristic. This resulted in charismatic authority.
2. Second, a command might be obeyed out of reverence for old-established patterns of order. This was traditional authority.
3. Third, a person giving an order might be acting in accordance with his duties stipulated in a code of legal rules and regulations. This resulted in legal authority, which was rational in character.

In organisations that actually exist, and which tend to be more complex than Weber's pure examples, it should be noted that there may be mixtures or combinations of types of authority.

It is clear that different societies at different stages of development may be chosen to illustrate the practice of these different types of authority. In these various contexts a person could be said to have power if 'within a social relationship, his own will could be enforced despite resistance'.[12] It is in the context of modern liberal democracies, however, that legal-rational authority fits most easily, and it is within such political systems that the characteristics of Weber's ideal-type bureaucracy are most often expected to be seen in practice.

17.4.2 Weber on bureaucracy

While Weber is considered to be an outstandingly important writer on bureaucracy, it should be noted that he never actually defined it; instead he outlined the features of bureaucracy in its pure form, or as it existed in the world of ideas. There are generally thought to be six of these characteristics (the number varies according to which of Weber's writings is being used as the source – the arrangement here is taken from the references listed at the end of this chapter).

1. Regular activities required for the purposes of the organisation are distributed in a fixed way as official duties. This sometimes leads to problems of demarcation, especially where a particular task does not fit existing categories.
2. The organisation of offices follows the principle of hierarchy, that is each lower office is under the control and supervision of a higher one. This has important implications for accountability and authority. For example, authority can be delegated but accountability cannot, so that within a hierarchy an official is

not only accountable for his own actions but is also accountable for the actions of subordinates.

3. Operations are governed by a consistent system of abstract rules and consist of the application of the rules to particular cases. It should be noted that mastery of the rules, and how they may be applied, in any bureaucratic system gives power to the specialist in those rules; sometimes rules include scope for discretion and that involves a further increase in power. It is easy to see how bureaucrats become powerful and how potentially dangerous such power can be in a democratic political system.

4. The ideal official conducts his office in a spirit of formalistic impersonality, without hatred or passion, and hence without affection or enthusiasm. Consequently bureaucracies may adopt the practice of posting officials with particular enthusiasms or aversions to positions where it is hoped conflicts are minimised.

5. Employment in the bureaucratic organisation is based on technical qualifications and is protected against arbitrary dismissal. It constitutes a career. There is a system of promotions according to seniority or achievement, or both. Accordingly there are usually known qualifications for promotion as well as for selection.

6. Experience tends to show that the purely bureaucratic type of administrative organisation is, from a purely technical point of view, capable of attaining the highest degree of efficiency and is in this sense formally the most rational known means of carrying out imperative control of human beings.

Weber's analysis of bureaucracy was based on a functional approach, by which all elements in a social structure are considered in order to show how they contribute to the overall characteristics of the organisation. From this analysis he was able to present an ideal-type, a theoretical construct derived from the characteristics of known organisations.

17.5 Writers on the dysfunctions of bureaucracy

Weber was not concerned with informal elements in organisations or the dysfunctions of bureaucracy, the concern of later writers. Two of these discussed now as examples of quite different approaches are Michel Crozier and Harold Laski.

17.5.1   Michel Crozier

Michel Crozier wrote *The Bureaucratic Phenomenon* in the 1960s.[13] Unlike Weber and the classical organisation theorists, his book was the result not of armchair theorising but of empirical research, and it was dedicated to the structural explanation of behaviour in organisations, especially the inadequacies or dysfunctions that develop as a result of human characteristics. For our present purposes Crozier's work is important for two reasons: first, his hypothesis that a person has power over another if the second's behaviour is more predictable by the first than the first's behaviour is predictable by the second; and second, the attention Crozier drew to the significance of national character in administration. Crozier raised the question of whether the French bureaucratic organisations he studied might not be more French than they were bureaucratic: bureaucratic behaviour, as expounded by Crozier, was, he felt, endemic in French society.

17.5.2 Harold Laski

The other authoritative writer to be mentioned here is the British academic, Professor Harold Laski. Laski, unlike Weber, defined bureaucracy, and in an influential contribution to the *Encyclopaedia of the Social Sciences* his definition was that it is 'a system of government the control of which is so completely in the hands of officials that their power jeopardises the liberties of the ordinary citizens'.[14] Laski was also interested in measures to prevent bureaucracy as he had defined it. Indeed, his other writings showed how he went about this with enthusiasm, proposing measures of administrative reform that would redress dangers from the ruling class and ensure the survival of democratic government.

These two writers show how easy it has been for the popular use of the term bureaucracy to relate to what others might call its defects. As Geoffrey Roberts and Alistair Edwards put it in *A New Dictionary of Political Analysis*, in common usage 'the term refers to any set of governmental (or administrative) officials, possessed of certain traits of excessive formality, use of verbiage or jargon in communication, inflexibility of procedure, and insistence on the powers – and limitations – of their office.'[15]

The approach of formal organisation theorists still has practical uses, especially when considering how bureaucracy developed and what the advantages and disadvantages of it might be in the modern world. Good intentions and scientific approaches to management are not to be disregarded, but when it comes to practicalities it is also easy to be sympathetic to emphasis on the defects of bureaucracy. In a recent article Andrew Gumbel, writing about the problems of Venice following the fire in the opera house of La Fenice, said that digging up a street there requires thirty-seven signatures from twenty-four different offices from local through to national level. He added: 'It is no wonder nothing ever gets done.'[16]

It is important to bear these various perspectives on bureaucracy in mind when considering how it has developed and what its advantages and disadvantages are in the modern world.

17.6 Bureaucracy in Practice: Advantages and Disadvantages

This last section will offer comments on various aspects of formal organisation in public administration. Therefore it is probably wise to reiterate what was said when public administration was introduced in the previous chapter and when formal organisation was outlined at the beginning of this chapter.

Many of the problems and challenges of developing and sustaining formal organisations in order to enable them to achieve their objectives can be seen as much in business management as they can in public administration. In particular, bureaucracy as a type of organisation with well-known characteristics can exist, with advantage, in all types of organisation, whatever typology is used. This is partly because bureaucracy is associated with large-scale organisation. Big organisations tend to be bureaucratic because bureaucracies have relevant and easily understandable characteristics. They embody many of the principles of classical organisation theory, and they have the advantage that, in managing large-scale tasks, they tend to be more technically efficient than other types of organisation. Most government organisations tend to be big, and in the modern world they reflect the demand of people for large-scale services.

When Weber considered the causes of bureaucracy his first conclusion was that the remuneration of officials presupposed the development of a money economy. He did not imply, however, that a money economy was an essential cause of bureaucracy because such historic examples of developed and large-scale bureaucracies as the Roman Empire, the Roman Catholic Church and ancient Chinese dynasties depended on payment in kind. Therefore Weber concluded that a developed money economy was a *usual* precondition of bureaucratic administration, and even though the full development of a money economy was not an *indispensable* precondition of bureaucratisation, the maintenance of a bureaucracy depended on a constant income. The nearest Weber came to stating one cause more than any other for bureaucratic growth was when he observed that the proper soil for the bureaucratisation of an administration had always been the specific development of administrative tasks, in particular the introduction of taxation systems. He believed that bureaucratisation was caused more by internal development and the intensity with which administrative tasks were organised than by their extensive and quantitative increase.

Nevertheless, it is through examining the growth of administrative tasks that it is easiest to see the causes of bureaucracy. First, there are the activities a government is required to undertake, not just in modern times, but also as illustrated by examples from the past. In ancient Egypt, with a well developed bureaucratic state administration, technical economic factors led a demand for regulation of the waterways for the whole country. Regulation had to be done by large-scale organisation because of the huge area covered. This technical approach in turn created the bureaucratic mechanism of scribes and officials. Another example, from modern times, is the expansion of state activities into the welfare state. It is not sufficient, however, to say that size is the cause of bureaucracy in the modern state. The real cause may be found by adopting a more functional approach, for it is the social pressures, or will, which have demanded the new regulations, inspections or welfare provisions of twentieth-century government.

The second factor affecting size is the economy of manpower with which activities are administered. If a department or branch is well managed it is likely to have less staff than if it is badly managed. Consequently, if the popular conception of bureaucracy is used (which associates bureaucracy with 'red tape' and the imperfections of big organisations), bureaucracy can be reduced when services are reduced in quantity or increased in quality. As inefficiency mounts, the size of the bureaucracy and the cost of government tend to increase. As the size of government organisation increases, the difficulties of controlling it become greater, but again, it is social pressures which encourage organisation to become more efficient and better managed.

Weber also considered that a decisive reason for the development of bureaucracy was its purely technical superiority over any other form of organisation. 'The fully developed bureaucratic mechanism compares with other organisations exactly as does the machine with the non-mechanical modes of production.'[17] For example, its technical superiority includes precision, speed, unambiguity, knowledge of the files, continuity, discretion, unity, strict subordination, and reduction of friction and of material and personal costs. These in turn, however, may be seen as another example of the significance of social or political pressures, reflecting the will of society, since the demands for the technically superior methods come from society itself.

Once established, it is almost impossible to destroy bureaucracy, partly because it has so many features which can neither be stopped nor reversed. An example would be the training of officials for their specialised and methodically integrated functions. If the official stops working or if his work is seriously interrupted, chaos results. Untrained amateurs cannot easily take the place of bureaucrats. Moreover, bureaucracy is everywhere a late product of development. The more primitive a society, the less the bureaucracy, and in the advanced countries of contemporary Europe, the approval of bureaucracy by the people is reflected in the social approval a senior official receives.

It is not difficult to see how the alleged defects of bureaucracy arise from unsympathetic views of its consequences. As explained earlier, some of the defects are popularly referred to as red tape. They include over-devotion to precedent, remoteness from the people, lack of initiative and imagination by officials, ineffective organisation and waste of manpower, procrastination and unwillingness to take responsibility for decisions. Yet the reasons why some of these defects become apparent in the bureaucracies of public organisations are often to be found in the political system. For example, some of the qualities associated with democracy are the need to ensure that officials have the necessary legal and rational authority, that they are treating citizens equally with fairness and justice, and that any personal or private interests or enthusiasms do not have an influence in decision-making on behalf of the public interest.

Some of the features of what is increasingly known as the new public management may be seen as responses to the need to overcome the alleged defects of bureaucracy. Officials are increasingly given discretion to make decisions without prior reference to a hierarchical line going back, ultimately, to elected representatives. New organisations may be more functional or organic than their predecessors, and flexibilities are introduced to enable particular organisations to be less pure than the simple typologies listed earlier, and certainly much more flexible than some of the more sophisticated typologies not mentioned in this chapter. While these changes may be intended to have less bureaucratic defects, and, indeed, have less of the pure characteristics indicated by Weber, they may also bring new problems of authority and accountability, not only within particular organisations but also between officials and their organisations and the wider context of the political environment within which they work. Fashions in management techniques and systems come and go like fashions in other contexts, but their particular values include encouraging people to rethink their goals and objectives and how they are working towards achieving them. In the context of public administration in liberal democracies, however, special emphasis must also be given to the values and principles held by the people and the ways those qualities are reflected in the administrative systems and processes. Laski's vision of bureaucracy was a sinister one because he envisaged it powerful enough to jeopardise the liberty of individual citizens. Crozier's examination of power relationships within bureaucracy also revealed features not always welcome to impartial observers. In a liberal democracy it is the continuous responsibility of citizens to be interested in these matters and to ensure that formal organisations in public administration are consistent with their values and goals, and that when they are not, suitable corrective action is taken to reform them. It is during administrative innovation and reform, both of which are essential and continuing processes of public administration, that the principles of the classical organisation theorists often have such an important part to play. They may not have achieved universal applicability as part of a science of management or administration, but this should not mean that they are undervalued in the context of understanding how organisations work and how that work can be improved.

Notes

1. Herbert A. Simon, Donald W. Smithburg and Victor A. Thompson, *Public Administration* (New York: Alfred A. Knopf, 1950; New Brunswick, NJ: Transaction Publishers, 1991).
2. Luther Gulick and Lyndall Urwick, *Papers on the Science of Administration* (New York: Institute of Public Administration, 1937).
3. Henri Fayol, *General and Industrial Management* (London: Pitman, 1949).
4. Lyndall Urwick, *The Elements of Administration* (London: Pitman, 1943).
5. F. W. Taylor, *The Principles of Scientific Management* (New York: Harper & Bros, 1916).
6. Christopher Hodgkinson, *Towards a Philosophy of Administration* (Oxford: Blackwell, 1978), p. 26.
7. Keith Henderson, *Emerging Synthesis in American Public Administration* (London: Asia Publishing House, 1966), p. 16.
8. Herbert A. Simon, 'The proverbs of administration', *Public Administration Review*, vol. 6, 1946, pp. 53–67.
9. A. M. Henderson and Talcott Parsons (trans.), *Max Weber: The Theory of Social and Economic Organisation* (New York: Oxford University Press, 1947).
10. H. H. Gerth and C. Wright Mills (eds), *From Max Weber, Essays in Sociology* (London: Routledge & Kegan Paul, 1948).
11. Martin Albrow, *Bureaucracy* (London: Pall Mall, 1970), p. 40.
12. Ibid., p. 39.
13. Michel Crozier, *The Bureaucratic Phenomenon* (London: Tavistock, 1964).
14. Harold J. Laski, 'Bureaucracy', in *Encyclopaedia of the Social Sciences* (New York: Macmillan, 1930).
15. Geoffrey Roberts and Alistair Edwards, *A New Dictionary of Political Analysis* (Sevenoaks: Edward Arnold, 1991).
16. Andrew Gumbel, 'Bickering while Venice sinks', *The Independent*, 1 February 1996.
17. Gerth and Mills, *From Max Weber*, p. 214.

Questions

1. Consider the advantages and disadvantages of using the principles of formal organisation theory to structure and to reform public sector organisations within contemporary political systems.
2. What benefits may bureaucracy, as a type of organisation, have in modern government organisations? What are its dysfunctions and/or possible dangers and how may they be overcome?

18

Personnel management and informal organisation

According to Maurice Cuming in his standard textbook, personnel management 'is concerned with obtaining the best possible staff for an organisation and, having got them, looking after them so that they will want to stay and give of their best to their jobs.'[1] In one of the longest established American textbooks on this subject O. Glenn Stahl presents a similarly pithy definition when he says that personnel administration is 'the totality of concern with the human resources of organisation'.[2] These succinct, useful and carefully crafted definitions are both easily comprehensible and of considerable practical relevance. There are, however, other definitions that draw attention to some of the difficulties and wider implications of personnel management.

One of these more comprehensive approaches is the 'official' definition published by the Institute of Personnel Management in 1963 when the Institute celebrated its Golden Jubilee.

> Personnel management is a responsibility of all who manage people as well as being a description of the work of those who are employed as specialists. It is that part of management which is concerned with people at work and with their relationships within an enterprise. It applies not only to industry and commerce but to all fields of employment.
>
> Personnel management aims to achieve both efficiency and justice, neither of which can be pursued successfully without the other. It seeks to bring together and develop into an effective organisation the men and women who make up an enterprise, enabling each to make his own best contribution to its success both as an individual and as a member of a working group. It seeks to provide fair terms and conditions of employment and satisfying work for those employed.[3]

In this chapter the widest approach to public personnel management will be adopted. This implies three consequences.

1. It will not be viewed as a narrow specialism within management, or as a staff function that may be set aside because it is not a matter of daily importance to line managers. On the contrary, it is an aspect of management important to everyone in an organisation.
2. Personnel management involves an understanding of all aspects of organisation. Considered in its widest sense this includes not only the formal arrangements for personnel management (which are of great importance, are clearly evident and easily recognisable, and will be considered later in this chapter) but also informal aspects which permeate the whole organisation.
3. A wide approach also involves consideration of the impact of the political environment on various aspects of personnel management.

These features are very important for public personnel management within all political systems, though most examples will be taken from liberal democracies.

18.1 Informal organisation

In the previous chapter, formal organisation was defined as the pattern of behaviour and relationships that is deliberately planned for an institution. If that definition is accepted, then informal organisation may be defined, as it was by Chester I. Barnard in his classic work *The Functions of the Executive*, as 'the aggregate of the personal contacts and interactions and associated groupings of people'.[4] Informal organisation has two important effects:

1. 'it establishes certain attitudes, understandings, customs, habits and institutions; and
2. it creates the conditions under which formal organisation may arise.'[5]

Formal organisations, as Barnard also said, create and require informal organisations to sustain them.[6] It is simply not possible to understand how an organisation works, or, indeed, how to manage it properly, without appreciating how people work together, what their values are and how they communicate among themselves. As Herbert Simon has written: 'The term "informal organisation," refers to interpersonal relations in the organisation that affect decisions within it but either are omitted from the formal scheme or are not consistent with that scheme.'[7]

Any discussion about informal organisation must therefore consider such factors as the social norms and ideals, attitudes, understandings, customs and habits that exist within institutions because they are an indispensable part of understanding any system of cooperation. Good management depends on good communication within an organisation, but lines of communication are not the same as lines indicating relationships of authority and/or accountability. Moreover, modes of communication and language can be a crucial factor in achieving good communication and therefore facilitating effective management. Furthermore, the personality characteristics of individuals may be important when directing an organisation, as may the ways in which individuals behave in groups – for groups of individuals cannot be understood merely by trying to assess the sum of the characteristics of individual members. Two well-known examples from the literature on this sphere of management illustrate how important these factors are.

18.1.1   The Hawthorne study

A pioneering study of how individuals behave in organisations was carried out at the Hawthorne works of the Western Electric Company in the USA between 1927 and 1932. The first of the Hawthorne studies, the preliminary lighting experiments, considered the quality and quantity of illumination as a factor in the efficiency of employees. The experiments included increasing and decreasing the amount of light and considering how production was affected. While it was not surprising that production increased as the lighting level was increased, production did not fall when illumination was decreased – only when the lighting was *very* poor did the level of production actually decline.

Light, the researchers concluded, was only one factor affecting employee output, and it could not be usefully isolated and considered apart from other important variables. It seemed that the more attention the employees were receiving from the research studies, the more their production increased, leading the investigators to undertake a series of further studies.

These will not be considered in detail here, but they were designed to assess such factors as the effects of rest pauses, the nature of employee attitudes towards their work and the company, and the effects of different types of pay schemes. The results of the experiments were both somewhat surprising and somewhat confusing. As variables were adjusted there was a general upward trend in output, inducing the investigators to consider the possible relevance of psychological factors because it seemed necessary to focus on morale and the social situation the individuals were working in. An interview programme considered in depth the attitudes of individual workers on a large number of different topics, and found that they were not operating as isolated units: their attitudes were the result of their personal and work situations. A final study, known as the bank wiring room observation study, adopted a more sociological approach and found that the employees had their own codes of behaviour and rules of conduct, affecting levels of output. The employee group provided security and a sense of belonging for its members.

The influence of the Hawthorne experiments was considerable, especially as they drew attention to factors other than formal aspects of management. Some details were, however, later questioned, because they paid no attention to the influence of such wider variables as the role of trade unions within organisations and the economic environment of the time. It should also be noted that the experiments were undertaken during a period of very serious economic depression. There is a large literature on the Hawthorne experiments both by the investigators and their critics, but it is not possible to consider them in detail here. Two findings will, however, be reported further because they are of particular relevance for personnel management, for understanding aspects of communication, and for further discussion both within this chapter and for Chapter 20. These two findings are as follows.

First, there is the emphasis on the purpose of management, as expressed by F. J. Roethlisberger and William J. Dickson, in their monumental study of the Hawthorne experiments, *Management and the Worker*. After outlining how important it was to see an industrial organisation as a social system, they concluded:

> The function of management, stated in its most general terms, can be described as that of maintaining the social system of the industrial plant in a state of equilibrium such that the purposes of the enterprise are realised. To achieve this objective, management has two major functions:
>
> 1. The function of securing the common economic purpose of the total enterprise; and
> 2. The function of maintaining the equilibrium of the social organisation so that individuals through combining their services to this common purpose obtain personal satisfactions that make them willing to co-operate.[8]

It seems that the balance expressed here is not always sufficiently recognised, and when the balance between the two objectives is not properly appreciated malfunctions are very likely.

A second, and in some ways related, conclusion worth noting here is what Roethlisberger and Dickson call the 'logic of cost'. This arises from their observation that although the logic of cost is applied mostly to technical organisation, it is also relevant to human organisation where it is related to the term efficiency. They recorded that the word 'efficiency' is used 'in at least five different ways, two of which are rather vague and not clearly differentiated':

1. sometimes when talking about a machine it is used in a technical sense, as with the relation between output and input;
2. sometimes when talking about a manufacturing process or operation it is used to refer to relative unit cost;
3. sometimes when referring to a worker it is used to indicate a worker's production or output in relation to a certain standard of performance;
4. sometimes its reference becomes more vague and it is used as practically synonymous with 'logical coordination of function';
5. sometimes it is used in the sense of morale or social integration.[9]

In current usage the word efficiency may have even more meanings, so that it has almost become a word that should be defined every time it is used. One current use of the word in the public sector context seems particularly unfortunate because across-the-board financial cuts to promote 'efficiency savings' in public sector organisations now often result in setting aside the established purposes of an organisation, or result in the manipulation of objectives to the point where the equilibrium of the organisation is jeopardised. These comments will be considered further in Chapter 20.

18.1.2   Theory X and Theory Y

Apart from the example of the Hawthorne experiments, one other major contribution to the academic literature of management will be introduced here because of its relevance to personnel management. Douglas M. McGregor, in *The Human Side of Enterprise*, drew attention to underlying beliefs about the nature of man that influence managers to adopt one management strategy rather than another. He presented two examples of such beliefs which he called Theory X and Theory Y.[10] The central organisation principle of Theory X, which he regarded as the traditional view, is control and direction through the exercise of authority.

The three key features of Theory X are:

1. The average human being has an inherent dislike of work and will avoid it if he can.
2. Because of this human characteristic of dislike of work, most people must be coerced, controlled, directed and threatened with punishment to get them to put forth adequate effort toward the achievement of organisational objectives.
3. The average human being prefers to be directed, wishes to avoid responsibility, has relatively little ambition and wants security above all.

The central organisation principle of Theory Y is the integration of individual and organisational goals – the creation of conditions where staff can achieve their own goals best by directing their efforts towards the success of their organisation.

The five key features of Theory Y are:

1. Work is as natural as play or rest. Depending upon controllable conditions, it may be a source of satisfaction (and will be voluntarily performed) or a source of revulsion (and will be avoided if possible).
2. External control and the threat of punishment are not the only means for achieving effort – man will exercise self-direction and self-control in the service of objectives to which he is committed.
3. Personal satisfaction can be the direct product of effort directed towards organisational objectives.
4. Most people, under proper conditions, learn not only to accept but to seek responsibility – avoidance of responsibility, lack of ambition, and emphasis on security are generally consequences of experience, not inherent human characteristics.
5. The capacity to exercise creativity in solving problems is widely, not narrowly, distributed in the population – but under modern working conditions, the intellectual potential of the average person is only partially utilised.

McGregor himself stressed that these theories were intended to be examples of beliefs held by managers, and that other beliefs about the nature of man could be illustrated by other theories.

There are two important points to be made here about Theory X and Theory Y.

1. They are aptly chosen not because they were meant to be at opposite ends of a spectrum, but because, once described, it is easy to see the significance of beliefs about the nature of man in the everyday work of managing organisations.
2. It is easy to see their potential relevance in the context of certain recent developments in, say, new public management. For example, one of the arguments in favour of creating executive agencies at arm's length from government departments is that officials are feeling unsatisfied because of the constraints of accountability. Greater management freedoms are intended to give them more opportunities for personal satisfaction in a type of management system that politicians feel meets the contemporary public interest.

18.2 Personnel management: techniques and processes

As with other management contexts, the basic procedures relevant to the specialist skills of personnel management appear to have almost universal applicability. There are some differences of emphasis or detail between different areas, but the main features may be very similar in approach. A selection of eight of the most common elements will now be discussed.

First, personnel management involves job analysis and classification. A clear description of the work to be done is always important for the management of any organisation, not only because individuals need to know what their responsibilities are, but also because it is necessary for the recruitment of staff. In the public sector this is as important as elsewhere, though often with added significance: it is necessary to make these details known to satisfy governments and elected representatives that the highest standards of organisation and propriety apply. It is impossible both to achieve the highest standards of recruitment according to merit, with fair treatment for candidates from various backgrounds, and to ensure efficiency and economy in staffing, without an appropriate system for assessing and classifying jobs. Therefore, what may be matters of good personnel management practice become even more important when required to satisfy the demands of a democratic political environment.

Second, recruitment processes often involve personnel specialists because some selection procedures are now very sophisticated and specialised. In public administration in liberal democracies these processes are often conditioned by a stated philosophy applying known principles. For example, in the United Kingdom, civil service recruitment has to be done on the basis of selection on merit, by fair and open competition, with equality of opportunity throughout the process. These principles are explained in the Civil Service Commissioners' Recruitment Code, which has to be observed for all civil service appointments. At the level where the most able university graduates are appointed there is also provision for the participation of outsiders in the selection process, both because it is recognised that their wider experience is an asset and because the participation of such outsiders is thought to be an additional safeguard for the high standards and principles on which the recruitment procedures operate.

Third, once staff have been appointed, their careers are likely to be conditioned by known arrangements for promotions and transfers, recognising their accomplishments and using their abilities to the greatest advantage in the organisation's interest. Sometimes special features apply to staff movements in the public sector. For example, the frequency of transferring senior staff in the British civil service has been a topic for critical comment for many years, because it is often said that posting staff at intervals of one and a half to two years is not the most efficient use of staff resources. Critics argue that this means there is a waste of expertise and a perpetuation of the amateur approach in public administration. It should also be noted, however, that when staff in sensitive positions (e.g. tax inspectors) are moved at such frequent intervals the potential for corrupt practices and influence is greatly reduced. It is simply not worth the effort or expense to attempt to influence the judgement of a tax inspector who is likely to be moved to another post before favourable decisions can be made.

Fourth, it is generally recognised that there should be an established pay policy or philosophy. Broad general principles often include ensuring equal pay for equal work with salary gradations based on individual skills required for the job. Clearly, it is neither in the interest of taxpayers if employees are paid too much, nor is it in the public interest for pay to be so poor that good quality staff cannot be recruited, or that staff are unable to live on their pay or are unable to maintain lifestyles expected of their social group. Often public sector staff have to be paid on comparable lines to pay levels elsewhere in the economy, and procedures may be instituted to assess and ensure comparability. Also, it is not in the national interest for employees in vital services to strike, so arrangements may be made for pay review bodies to consider pay claims and to make binding decisions. Again, such provisions may be in addition to, and much more complex than, arrangements for business or private sector management.

Fifth, personnel management is responsible for the education and training of staff which may include providing courses to enable good staff to progress towards more senior positions on the basis of merit, experience and skills. Training may be provided through courses in departments, or in staff colleges and specialist institutes as many governments have their own civil service college or similar institutions. Courses may also be provided in non-specialist universities and training colleges. Training in the public sector also involves providing for new staff to work alongside experienced staff. This is a form of on-the-job training, but it is also a valuable means of socialisation because it includes more than learning about the technicalities and procedures of a job. Such socialisation is particularly beneficial from the perspectives of learning the organisation's values, its unwritten codes of conduct, how sensitive the working organisation is (or should be) to its political environment and the ethos of public service work.

Sixth, personnel management generally has a responsibility for maintaining relations with employee organisations and unions. These arrangements can differ in the public sector from those in other contexts because of the need to avoid disruption in essential services. In the United Kingdom, special consultative procedures were introduced after the First World War following recommendations from John H. Whitley, chairman of a sub-committee of the Cabinet Committee on Reconstruction. Although originally proposed as part of the postwar reconstruction programme for reforming relations with trades unions in industry, the recommendations were welcomed by public sector staff associations and were soon introduced with great benefit.[11] They presumed that employers and employees would be adequately organised and work together, so there were advantages in having well-run staff associations or unions. The arrangements, called Whitley Councils after their originator and introduced so long ago into United Kingdom government departments, have been copied by other institutions at home and abroad. They still exist in most British government departments and agencies, and at the highest level include the Council of Civil Service Unions as well as councils in departments and in their subordinate organisations. All consist of representatives of the employee side and of the management side. Their general purpose is internally to resolve difficulties about conditions of service and matters of dispute. In addition, they have been involved with many less significant social and welfare provisions.

Seventh, in most spheres of management the personnel function assumes responsibility for staff dismissals, ensuring they are procedurally correct and meet the requirements of the law. In practice, there may be fewer dismissals from government service than from jobs elsewhere because even where there are cuts or 'downsizing' reforms in the public sector, the overall organisations are so large that it may be possible to minimise the number of redundancies by means of transfers of staff or natural wastage. What in some circumstances may therefore appear as privileged arrangements against dismissal are in fact the benefits of working in a big bureaucracy. These arrangements and conditions of service must be taken into account when considering what seem to be relatively low pay levels.

Eighth, personnel management often involves a miscellaneous field of welfare and social activities. Welfare and sports facilities enable staff to meet for activities other than work to get to know each other, and therefore can stimulate feelings of belonging among staff as well as enable easier communications. There is a long history of enlightened industrialists providing facilities, in some cases housing and health services, to ensure that staff are safe and healthy and live satisfying lives. Marks and Spencer and other enlightened retailers are well known for their free chiropody and hair-stylist services for their staff. A recent small-scale example in this sphere in the United Kingdom is of an office relocated to an out-of-town site finding it financially possible and very beneficial to charter a lunch-time bus for its employees to visit a nearby shopping precinct.

These eight examples of common activities within personnel management could be elaborated and refined, and others could be added. Some activities become more, some less, important at different times. Together, they enable an organisation to function and to achieve its objectives, as well as compensating employees sufficiently well to ensure they wish to continue working for a particular employer.

It should be emphasised, though, that most functions mentioned may be seen as the responsibility of any manager, not just personnel specialists. All managers, as the Institute of Personnel Management definition made clear, have personnel responsibilities. It should be recognised, however, that in some areas techniques to measure and to improve the satisfactions or conditions of work in different parts of an organisation, or to compare different organisations, have been developed. One example is the development of sophisticated measurements of different types of staff turnover. These can benefit top management. Staff turnover rates are usually calculated by dividing the total number of separations in a given period by a measure of the average number of employees for the period and multiplying by 100. The result is an index of turnover useful for comparison with other organisations as well as within parts of one's own.

Thus a basic personnel management technique can draw attention to potential areas of dissatisfaction or different employment conditions among employees in different parts of an organisation. Sometimes all that emerges is a reflection on past recruitment policies or bulges in recruitment at different times (often resulting from changes in government policies or the initiation of new services). Broadly speaking, a healthy turnover rate should be sufficiently large to prevent stagnation in a particular service, though sufficiently small to reflect healthy working conditions. Of course, the cost of turnover may be higher in public personnel management than elsewhere if the methods of recruitment, selection and the placement and transfer of staff are more complex and expensive than elsewhere, perhaps because of democratic requirements or the need to achieve particularly high standards. It should not be overlooked that some of the distinctive features of personnel management in the public sector may be more expensive than elsewhere. As in other contexts, the influence of democratic principles can have additional costs as well as benefits. The last section of this chapter will therefore be concerned with some of the aspects of public personnel management, often conditioned by the political environment, that have not so far been discussed.

18.3 Public personnel management: institutions, procedures and ethos

Public personnel management policies and practices are often more amenable to pressures and influences from the political environment than other aspects of public administration. This is not to say that the pressures and influences are bad or wrong: it is to say that practice often differs from theory. The reasons for this are not always as widely recognised as managers might ideally wish. For example, in many countries the highest expectations of a pure merit system are modified either permanently or for limited periods and in limited areas of employment to ensure that special treatment or privileges are given to categories of citizens a nation may wish to recognise. In the United States and Canada, and in a number of other countries too, special privileges in civil service recruitment are given to citizens who have served their country in the armed forces, and in some cases this gives high priority to applicants who have been disabled. In some countries priorities are given to applicants who are bilingual or who come from particular minority groups. These privileges or priorities may be entirely acceptable as far as government and the people at large are concerned, but when implemented they may result in the appointment of applicants other than those who would have been appointed on strict grounds of merit and fairness. For example, it may mean that an economist is appointed to a particular position not because he or she is the best available economist but because he or she is the best available economist among applicants who are bilingual. (Bilingualism is not necessarily relevant to being a good economist.) Such constraints do not often apply outside the public sector. Similar constraints may relate to staff location or conditions of work. For perhaps entirely justifiable and acceptable reasons a department or branch may be located in a place chosen for political rather than purely management reasons. One reason might be to stimulate development or reduce unemployment in order to ensure a political advantage at an election. This may nevertheless introduce an element into personnel management quite different from its own pure criteria.

If this is so in the field of recruitment and location, it is often more evident in that of education and training. From time to time all governments impose cuts in financial provision, and when this occurs, departments have to make early economies in their running costs. An easy way to make economies is often to cut education and training provisions because the consequences of the cuts are sometimes less evident or are thought to be less damaging than cuts elsewhere. Nevertheless, in the long term there may be lasting and serious consequences. A former colleague of this author, responsible for training typing supervisors in an African country, found that economies and emergencies took away such supervisors as he had trained to a high level of competence. Their superior skills were needed for routine typing duties and they could not practise the supervisory skills they had acquired. He overcame the difficulty by giving a priority place on his course to a one-handed person who had the capacity to become an excellent supervisor but who could never be redeployed into typing duties.

It seems that in all countries training budgets and other aspects of personnel management vital to good organisation can be penalised when cuts are imposed. This dilutes the quality of personnel management and sometimes undermines it altogether. In some respects it reflects the low esteem in which personnel management is held in public administration. Generally it is not the most glamorous aspect of management and often the very best staff are reserved for what is thought to be more demanding or more urgent work. This in turn results in personnel management being less successful in protecting its resources or providing high quality services.

Sometimes attempts are made to enhance the status of personnel management by ensuring these disadvantages are avoided. One way to do this is to view personnel management as part of a larger appreciation of human resource management, where the key human resource, not just employees, is given a higher priority in the context of achieving the output objectives of an enterprise. In that way, it is hoped that personnel managers (as a distinct group within the profession of management) are given more recognition for the specialist advice they can give towards achieving plans and objectives. This may not imply that specialists in human resource management have anything more to offer than the best of personnel managers, but their higher status may give the personnel process more recognition for the important role it can play among all management specialisms. At its worst, however, the change in name may reflect a perception of staff as a resource to be used like other resources in order to achieve management objectives. Once the delicate balance of the purposes of an organisation is affected to the detriment of recognising the personal satisfactions sought by staff, as demonstrated in the lessons from the Hawthorne experiments, it may in turn have serious adverse affects on the achievement of *any* management function. This can apply in any management sphere, in both public and private sectors, and can be reflected in the morale of staff. Morale, in turn, can often be assessed in such measurable aspects as staff absenteeism, illness and a reduction in feelings of staff cohesiveness or *esprit de corps*.

Nevertheless, there may be distinct advantages for public personnel management over personnel management in other contexts. Surveys are often made of factors in job satisfaction among staff in particular areas of employment, and when these are undertaken it is rarely the case that pay or income is high on the list of factors of satisfaction. This is particularly evident in areas of the public sector. A good example of this was the research in the 1960s for the United Kingdom Fulton Committee on the Civil Service. In a survey of graduate entrants undertaken ten years after they had been recruited, the overwhelming attractions of working in the civil service were given as working with congenial colleagues, doing interesting and important work, being at the centre of things, the intellectual quality of the work, being 'in the know' and helping to shape policy. It is when qualities like these are given as the attractions of work in the public service in a liberal democracy that the ethos and importance of public service is seen to its best advantage. These attractions owe as much to the informal aspects of organisation as they do to the formal organisation structures, but the informal aspects of organisation can be fundamentally affected by frequent changes in the structures and procedures of formal organisations. Both formal and informal organisation must therefore be recognised as of importance if public sector organisations are to achieve their objectives in the context of providing public service(s) in the public interest.

Notes

1. Maurice W. Cuming, *The Theory and Practice of Personnel Management* (London: Heinemann, 1968), p. 1.
2. O. Glenn Stahl, *Public Personnel Administration* (New York: Harper &nd Row, 1936).
3. Cuming, *The Theory and Practice of Personnel Management*, quoted in the 1968 first edition. Modified in later editions but for the purposes of this chapter the earlier definition is more suitable.
4. Chester I. Barnard, *The Functions of the Executive* (Cambridge, Mass.: Harvard University Press, 1938), p. 115.
5. Ibid., p. 116.
6. Ibid., p. 120.
7. Herbert A. Simon, *Administrative Behaviour* (New York: Macmillan, 1955), p. 148.
8. F. J. Roethlisberger and William J. Dickson, *Management and the Worker* (Cambridge, Mass.: Harvard University Press, 1939), pp. 56–9.
9. Ibid., p. 563.
10. Douglas M. McGregor, *The Human Side of Enterprise* (New York, McGraw-Hill, 1960).
11. Cd. 8606 1917; Cd. 9002, 9085, 9099, 9153, 1918.

Questions

1. Explain the key functions of personnel management and how they may differ in the public sector compared with personnel management elsewhere.
2. In what ways may the informal features of organisation affect the achievements of the overall goals or purposes of a public administration institution? Suggest ways in which any possible dysfunctions may be remedied.

19

Decentralisation, devolution and deconcentration

One way of classifying constitutions is according to the method by which the powers of government are distributed between the government of the whole country and any other governments exercising authority over parts of the country. When this classification is used, constitutions may be referred to as 'federal' or 'unitary' (see Chapter 7).

Most countries have written constitutions, and all federal constitutions must have this basic document because there has to be a clearly formulated distinction between the powers that are to be exercised for the whole country and the powers to be exercised for parts of it. The important point to note is that in federal systems the legislature of the whole country has its powers and the legislatures of the states or provinces have their powers. In a unitary system, however, the legislature of the whole country is the most important law-making body. In the United Kingdom, for example, parliamentary sovereignty means that Parliament can create or abolish subordinate structures of government.

It is important to have a clear understanding of the nature of a country's constitution because, as has already been made clear, the management of public services has to operate in accordance with constitutional arrangements as well as with the law. In all countries the constraints of the law influence and condition the flexibilities of public sector management systems. These constraints, however, have special importance and are more clearly evident where there are written constitutions because they lay down the responsibilities of governmental structures within specified jurisdictions. The constraints are also more clearly evident where constitutional provisions are inflexible or difficult to change than where they are flexible or easy to change. In addition, codified legal systems present legal perspectives that in practice differ from legal systems based on common law. It follows that where constitutions are written and where they are more rigid, public administration practitioners and scholars have more contacts with lawyers, and often they are themselves qualified lawyers or have received legal training. This is because administrators have to be absolutely clear they have the powers to make particular decisions and are working in accordance with the law. In other constitutional systems public administrators and students of their activities have more to do with specialists in political science, sociology or management. Background considerations of constitutional provisions are particularly important in discussions of any form of decentralisation, and especially for that form of decentralisation known as local government.

19.1 Definitions of decentralisation, devolution and deconcentration

The concept of decentralisation refers to the delegation of decision-making within a political system, where delegation is seen as an administrative technique employed within unitary states or within the states, or provinces or regions, of a federal system. It is therefore important to note that decentralisation does not apply to the division of governmental powers defined in federal constitutions because any changes in them would be of a constitutional nature. Within unitary states or within the units of federal states, however, decentralisation encompasses two, often inter-related, practices. One of these is commonly known as devolution, which means that the authority to make decisions in some spheres of public policy is delegated by law to sub-national territorial assemblies, which are then called local governments. The other is deconcentration within the administrative system, involving the delegation of authority to make administrative decisions on behalf of central administration to public servants working away from the centre and responsible in varying degrees for government policy within their territories.

Unfortunately, the problems associated with understanding these terms are additionally complicated because they are not used consistently in the large literature on various aspects of decentralisation. For example, it is not uncommon to find references to democratic and bureaucratic decentralisation, though it is often easy to see that these terms in fact relate to what is more generally called devolution and deconcentration. Three examples of definitions of local government may help to make this clearer.

Professor S. E. Finer, in *A Dictionary of the Social Sciences*, defined local government as follows:

The government of restricted territories of a state in so far as it is carried out, under the general jurisdiction of the government of the whole territory, by authorities representative of their localities and enjoying a measure of discretion in the execution of their powers and duties.[1]

A United Nations definition says that the terms local government or local authority

> are used interchangeably (usually 'local government' refers to a system and 'local authority' to the unit) to refer to a political subdivision of a nation or (in a federal system) state which is constituted by law and has substantial control of local affairs, including the power to impose taxes. The governing body of such an entity is elected or otherwise locally selected.[2]

Professor W. A. Robson, one of the world's leading authorities on local government, presented possibly the most comprehensive definition in the *International Encyclopaedia of the Social Sciences*. He wrote:

> In general local government may be said to involve the conception of a territorial, non-sovereign community possessing the legal right and the necessary organisation to regulate its own affairs. This in turn presupposes the existence of a local authority with power to act independently of external control as well as the participation of the local community in the administration of its own affairs.[3]

These and other definitions are helpful because they have three key features in common.

1. Local governments are authorities subordinate to national governments or the governments of federal sub-units because they can be created or abolished by such superior forms of government, and they carry out many of the public services within a restricted geographical area.
2. They have organs all or most of which are elected, directly or indirectly, by the local citizens, and such elections give them authority to govern.
3. In practice, effective local government has a measure of autonomy normally including authority to raise at least a significant amount of its financial resources by local taxation.

Delegation of local decision-making to an official of central government is called deconcentration. Local offices of central government departments are easily identifiable as examples of this, but it should be noted that the degree of delegation of authority may be less than where there is a system of local government encompassing locally elected representatives. The disadvantages of deconcentration may include more red tape, a defect of bureaucracy, and less opportunity for citizens to play a part in the policy-making and procedures of government.

19.2 Advantages of local government: theoretical perspectives

A number of political theorists and philosophers have concerned themselves with the reasons for having local government. Five approaches which arise from their thoughts and writings will be considered here.

19.2.1 Impossible for central authorities to manage most local affairs

John Stuart Mill, whose *Considerations on Representative Government* was published in 1861, argued: 'It is but a small portion of the public business of a country which can be well done, or safely attempted, by the central authorities.' The functions of government include

> so great and various an aggregate of duties that, if only on the principle of division of labour, it is indispensable to share them between central and local authorities. Not only are separate executive officers required for purely local duties (an amount of separation which exists under all governments) but the popular control over those officers can only be advantageously exerted through a separate organisation.

He argued that where direct democracy could not be applied in practice (as it was in the past in the New England townships in the USA), 'recourse must generally be had to the plan of representative sub-Parliaments for local affairs.' He noted that this was so in England when he was writing, though the local government system then existing in England was incomplete and not systematic. Nevertheless, despite its deficiencies, he argued that as a result: 'In England there has always been more liberty, but worse organisation, while in other countries there is better organisation, but less liberty.'[4]

Although Mill argued in favour of locally elected representatives because that was the system with which he was familiar and which he thought was in the best interests of the liberty of citizens, it is possible to imagine that most of the advantages he saw for local government might be achieved by an enlightened form of local administration. Local *government* might not be essential in a democratic state, though delegation to some form of local *administration*, with good communications within the wider government organisation as well as with local people, might be essential. The really important criterion in a democratic state may be that decision-makers are aware of, and responsive to, local needs and local problems. While it may be necessary in a democracy to have locally elected officials or representative councils, specialists in local government argue that there is a close relationship between democratic decentralisation and a democratic political system. The election of local representatives is thought to be particularly valuable because it offers opportunities for greater participation by individuals in the business of government, and this helps to create a democratic climate of opinion. Consequently, although there is no generally agreed form for a democratic system of local government, local self-government is widely regarded as beneficial because it is a constituent part of the institutional provisions for democracy. As the lawyer Joshua Toulmin Smith rather pompously asserted in 1849:

> By institutions of local self-government alone is it possible that the interests of districts can be properly protected . . . Local self-government is the rock of our safety as a free state: the only absolute security for the maintenance of the fundamental laws and institutions of the land, on whose maintenance wholly depends our peace, prosperity and progress.[5]

19.2.2 A training ground for political leaders

An argument frequently heard to support local government is that it provides a valuable training ground for national legislators. Jeremy Bentham, for example, writing in 1830, said that a 'sub-legislature' constitutes 'a *nursery* for the supreme legislature; a school of appropriate aptitude, in all its branches for the business of legislature.'[6] Similarly, Professor Harold Laski believed: 'The case . . . for a strong system of local government in any state is clear almost beyond the needs of discussion' and argued: 'If members [of Parliament] were, before their candidature was legal, required to serve three years on a local body, they would gain the "feel" of institutions so necessary to success.'[7]

As Brian Smith has noted, a number of authoritative writers have stressed the importance of local government as a recruiting ground for members of parliament, and it is interesting to read that the psephologist, David Butler, found that in the 1964 United Kingdom general election, 50 per cent of Labour members of Parliament and 45 per cent of defeated Labour candidates had been councillors while 29 per cent of Conservative members of Parliament and 40 per cent of defeated Conservatives had similar experience. Professor W. J. M. Mackenzie produced statistics in 1954 showing this experience is not a peculiarly British phenomenon.[8]

While there is considerable debate about the value of such experience and the significance of the links between national and local politics, it is widely accepted that local government has an important role to play in a nation's democratic political experience. Between democratic decentralisation and a democratic political system there seems to be a close interdependence, and a crucial part is that local government provides a training ground for national legislatures and therefore has an important role in a democratic political culture.

19.2.3   Education of citizens

Of less importance for this chapter is the argument that local government constitutes a valuable opportunity for the political education of citizens. The classic formulation of this is again John Stuart Mill's *Representative Government*, where he recommended local government on the grounds that it 'provides extra opportunities for political participation, both in electing and being elected to local offices, for people who would have few chances to share personally in the conduct of the general affairs of the community.'[9] Hence it is argued that local government has an important role in the political socialisation of citizens.

19.2.4   More responsive to local persons

Local representative institutions are more responsive to local demands and control than other forms of decentralisation. Local government and its organisation is influenced, often on a daily basis, by local knowledge and information, it is more sensitive to local opinion and needs, its policies can be adapted to suit the requirements and characteristics of the locality, and it can be much more flexible, avoiding the rigidities of big organisations. It is much easier for locally elected bodies to be aware of local information and intelligence in influencing policies and decisions, and it provides opportunities for grievances to be aired and for wrongs to be remedied. These factors are of particular significance where communications are poor and where it is difficult to control in detail from a distance.

19.2.5   More efficient and economical

Fifth, it is argued that local government is often more efficient and economical than other forms of local administration because it takes advantage of voluntary service by councillors and by voluntary local organisations. Although local councillors in many countries are now paid for their work, the allowances they receive are often much less than they would earn from other forms of employment in return for the time they devote to their local government duties. In terms of using other organisations, most local authorities continue to harness local goodwill and the advantages of good citizenship. This is one aspect of local government illustrating why in recent years local authorities have been seen less as promoting particular services and more as enabling organisations, acting as media and stimulants for local provision of services.

What emerges from this discussion of the advantages of local government is that it enables decisions on a wide range of governmental functions to be made locally and as close to the people as possible, and it enables decisions not only to be made locally but by responsible persons with local information and local experience. This is thought to be necessary and appropriate in a democratic political culture because it is important for the political education and political participation of citizens. Local government also has a significant part to play in terms of the experience it provides for representatives of the people. It may also have a democratic role to play in influencing national government decisions between national elections. In addition, it may also facilitate good use of voluntary resources, and in this sense it is easy to justify local government as being economical and efficient. These aspects of the political environment, especially the implications of local democracy, have a significant effect on all local public administration, and it is examples of these phenomena in practice that will be considered next.

19.3   Delegation and communication

Delegation is the process of assigning duties and responsibilities to those who work for senior managers, giving them authority to carry out their responsibilities. Duties have first to be formally assigned, usually by processes that follow on from job analysis. Subordinates have to be given power to take necessary action on their own initiative, and obligations must be inculcated in subordinates to ensure an appropriate degree of loyalty and responsibility to the organisation. Necessary duties are thus carried out. This procedure often involves some features of informal organisation, especially the encouragement of feelings of belongingness, perhaps through an appreciation of the ethos of public service or loyalty to a particular service, whether it be a city or county in terms of local government, or a department or agency in the context of other forms of public service. In all discussion of delegation it should be remembered that management responsibility is not discontinued by the act of delegation, it is shared; authority can be delegated, but responsibility never can.

Delegation is an important concept in all aspects of decentralisation. It applies within organisations, as within the deconcentrated (and therefore local) offices of a central government department, within the departments of a central government, or within the departments of a local authority. It also applies between organisations, as when a central government department delegates authority to a local government or an agency or, indeed, any other organisation which is acting on its behalf. In one sense it is part of the directing of a service, but in another it may be inextricably linked to coordination and good communication.

The political and representational aspects of decentralisation have already been considered in the context of the discussion about the advantages of local government, but the practical aspects of decentralisation have not yet been sufficiently considered. At the formal level of designing an organisation structure these questions go back to the very earliest writings in the field of politics. Aristotle, for example, asked questions about the principles on which duties should be allocated. He said:

> We must . . . consider which matters need the attention of different local magistrates acting in different places, and which ought to be controlled by one central magistracy acting for the whole area . . . [and] whether to allocate duties on the basis of the subject to be handled, or on the class of persons concerned: e.g. should we have one officer for the whole subject of the maintenance of order, or a separate officer for the class of children and another for that of women?[10]

In practice, in modern times, other factors become at least as important. One of these is the size of an administrative service and the size of the country or population. A country like the Sudan, where by surface it may take seven days to travel from the north to the south, and where other forms of communication are often unreliable, could hardly continue its system of government without an appropriate form of delegation to enable local officials to take decisions on their own initiative. Similar considerations arise in a large developed country like Canada, for which a splendid example was provided by Dr J. M. Taggart in 1954.

Taggart recalled his own experience when, forty years previously, he was a junior officer in a small and junior service of the Canadian federal government, located in a remote area some 1,500 miles from Ottawa. When he took over in October he was given a book of instructions on how to get office supplies and such things. After studying the book for a while, he made out an order and sent it to Ottawa. Having recently come from employment with a large and well established commercial organisation, he expected that within ten days or two weeks, allowing mailing time to Ottawa, he would be receiving, by freight or express, the supplies ordered, and that he would then send someone to the local station to pick up the parcels. Instead of that, six weeks later things began to dribble in, some by mail, some by freight, some by express, in the strangest sort of combinations. Six or seven months later they were still dribbling in and nobody could say whether or not he had received all that he had ordered. As he did not have any clerical help and did not like clerical work himself, he gave up keeping an account of what had arrived. The most interesting part of the experience for Taggart was that in the following January, along with an assortment of non-perishables, there came a big bottle of ink. At that time the rules for ordering supplies were inflexible and did not permit discretion: officials were required to buy ink in quart bottles – it was considered inefficient to buy a five-cent bottle. When the quart bottle of ink arrived in January it was frozen. The bottle broke when the package was opened, and the ink fell out in a frozen block. That item had to be replaced, and by the time the next quart bottle of ink was received the following May, the weather had moderated. In the meantime he had purchased out of his own pocket a five-cent bottle of ink and it lasted him during the whole period. Then he began to wonder what efficiency there was in the business of central purchasing. Had appropriate authority been delegated, his fascinating vignette would never have been told and the Canadian public service supplies system may have remained proud of its economies and efficiencies of bulk purchasing and central ordering.[11]

Decentralisation permits flexibilities to enable local conditions and special cases to be considered individually, it sometimes results in reducing the paperwork involved in centralised operations, and it may increase staff satisfaction by giving lower-level officials the authority to make decisions themselves. Nevertheless, effective decentralisation may have to be introduced with appropriate constraints.

The first is an appreciation of responsibility in its widest context. If responsibility cannot be delegated (though management authority can), everyone in a public service organisation must be aware of what may be politically sensitive, and it is not surprising that grade for grade much more rewarding work is done in less sensitive areas than in areas of government where there is more political sensitivity. The more politically sensitive work is, the more likely provisions have to be made for account-ability to politicians and, therefore, to involve top management.

A second constraining factor may be administrative complexity. This may be evident in the need for speedy action, or the need to train personnel in special and highly skilled procedures – it is always easier to decentralise duties that do not have to be performed at great speed or that involve single uncomplicated functions. In these respects, and in others associated with decentralisation, the problem for top manage-ment is not so much deciding what to delegate, as deciding how to control (especially where the general interest of a department has to prevail over the more individual interests of decentralised units).

Third, one of the most important constraining factors on decentra-lisation is the need for good communications. Most basic textbooks on public administration deal with the importance of communication. Indeed, its importance is now sufficiently well recognised for it to have almost achieved the status of a specialist area within the study of politics. Communication is aptly defined by John M. Pfiffner and Robert V. Presthus as 'the process of transmitting cues in order to modify human behaviour'.[12] It does not have to be by word of mouth. A nod or a wink will often do, but in large-scale organisations new methods of commu-nication are now increasingly important, including the telephone, fax and e-mail – to give just a few examples. Good communication is also important for ensuring feelings of belongingness among staff and is therefore essential for motivating them. This may be achieved by many of the means mentioned, in passing, in Chapter 18, including: staff notices, a house journal, social and welfare clubs and associations, encouragement to use clear, meaningful language and, in a more formal context, well designed and effective channels of communication, so important in large and decentralised organisations. A personal example from a decentralised organisation illustrates this well.

About forty years ago I served in the Royal Air Force, in a specialised unit where one of the most important regular operations required the use of very large, specially printed forms used in psychometric testing to select officers. The unit had a standard means for ordering these forms which were delivered at intervals of about six months. In the normal course of events this ordering system worked well. During my time in the unit, however, the work increased, probably for reasons of international security though the details are now hazy in my memory and unimportant for this illustration. Because we ran out of forms regularly, and because the forms were classified 'confidential', and were so specialised, additional supplies had to be ordered by a sort of emergency procedure involving a despatch rider making a special delivery – a round trip of about seventy or eighty miles taking up to half a day. The reordering of these forms on an emergency basis became frequent at, say, monthly intervals during my time of service and I decided it was a misuse of resources to have them specially delivered so regularly. Instead I managed to increase the regular order and arrange for them to be delivered with other supplies in the normal way, but at monthly intervals instead of six-monthly intervals. After a relatively short time, perhaps a period of six to nine months, the demand for the forms declined significantly and the local stock built up. I tried by various means to reduce the order but the system of communication was unable to cope with the new instruction and the increased supply could not be stopped. As the forms were classified with a confidential security rating, they had to be stored in especially secure heavy steel cupboards. By the time I left the unit, an additional expensive heavy steel cupboard was being ordered to store the forms, simply because the supply could not be stopped. The story reveals not just poor communication for ordering supplies, but lack of appropriate control over the ordering of expensive steel cupboards.

19.4   The political environment

Any short series of introductory chapters on public administration must include some discussion about relationships between features of the political environment and management processes for providing public services. Various aspects of public administration may be used as illustration, but a discussion of decentralisation is as convenient as any, and has the additional advantage that it contributes to insights already provided on the way local government works. This last part of the chapter will therefore first consider further the constitutional significance of decentralisation and possible alternative institutional arrangements for providing certain services; second, it will consider the effects of interests and groups on decentralised organisations; and third, it will offer comments on what is sometimes termed 'closed politics' within the context of public organisations.

19.4.1   Constitutional arrangements affecting local government

First, some further comments on aspects of the constitutional arrangements affecting local government and possible alternative arrangements. As already observed, local government has a subordinate role in relation to central government in unitary political systems or, in federal political systems, in relation to the governments of the sub-units. Details of powers and responsibilities of local governments may be laid down in a constitution or in a specific statute or statutes. In all cases, however, local authorities are organs of government with powers and responsibilities that have been formally promulgated. In the United Kingdom, for example, the structures and responsibilities are to be found in Local Government Acts, though other Acts of Parliament, dealing with specific services may also give powers to existing local authorities. The most important feature to bear in mind is that British local authorities can only do what statutes say they can do, and all other possible activities are deemed *ultra vires* (beyond their powers). One consequence is that local authorities are very dependent on legal advice, for example to ensure that their actions are consistent with their powers, and when seeking new powers where they wish to undertake additional functions, as well as for day-to-day working arrangements. It is therefore not surprising that for constitutional reasons local officials have continuous contacts with officials in central government departments or with the officials in the state or provincial governments where they are located. Dame Evelyn Sharp discussed this in her book with special reference to the experience of the then Ministry of Housing and Local Government in the United Kingdom, but the patterns of working are similar in other countries. She stressed that the relationships of officials in her central government department with officials in local authorities, were

> in general, close and friendly. Officers of the Ministry know their opposite numbers in local government and are known to them. Many local government officers make it their business to know their way around the Ministry, whom to go to in order to find out how such and such a proposal is likely to fare, or why something seems to have stuck . . . Equally officers of the Ministry can turn to the officers of many local authorities for information, for help, for advice.

She perceptively added: 'The real exchange of information and points of view is mostly made in the more informal contacts.'[13] The important points she made are particularly evident in local government administration, but are no less significant where decentralisation is by means other than devolution. In all types of decentralised structure central-local relations are an important part of public sector management – though practice may vary from country to country or from time to time.

Finance is a second aspect of decentralisation of universal importance. One of the key elements of local government, mentioned above, is local autonomy, generally requiring local taxation. This explains why Saudi Arabia, for example, where government revenue is heavily dependent on receipts from the oil industry, has had hardly any success in developing a system of local government. Local administration it certainly has, but it is administration without participation by elected representatives. The reason seems to be that without provision for locally raised revenue there can be no effective local autonomy. Consequently there is no incentive for local participation. Experience tends to show that without an independent source of local finance there can be no effective local government, but such a bald statement conceals the complexity of the financial issues.

The issue of local finance in the modern world is by no means a black and white one. Few local authorities can manage without some support from central funding, but it is often difficult to decide how much should be granted from non-local sources and also how much autonomy should be permitted. In some cases central funding assists local authorities in maintaining services to some sort of national standard: poor authorities have to be helped or national standards are jeopardised. In some cases a delicate balance has to be achieved between preserving local autonomy while ensuring that local policies and ambitions do not undermine the achievement of national or provincial policies and objectives. Consequently ceilings may be put on the amount of local taxes that local authorities are permitted to raise, known in the United Kingdom as 'rate capping'. In addition, rules and procedures with controls and audits have to be laid down for decentralised bodies, whether devolved or deconcentrated, in order to ensure not only that proper standards are observed in financial matters, but also that propriety is maintained in the general public interest, as well as in the local interest.

Third, questions arise from time to time about delivering public services by means other than central government departments or decentralised administration. These stem from difficulties concerning the accountability of decentralised administration, or with constitutional arrangements or with financial provision for it. At their most fundamental, these problems may relate to philosophical or ideological discussions about the role of the state and the services it should provide for its citizens. Some large-scale services have to be provided even though they are uneconomic or seem to be more like commercial activities than public administration. New structures like public corporations may then be developed in the public sector to meet these needs, or agencies may be created with freedom from routine controls and detailed accountability. As its most extreme, an activity may be 'hived off' or privatised (i.e. sold), separating it entirely from the public sector. Where services continue in the public sphere, however, this does not exclude them from debates about the degree of autonomy that they should be permitted, how far democratic participation should be involved, and by what means and to what extent authority should be delegated.

19.4.2   Interest groups and local government

The relationship between requirements for efficient and effective management on the one hand and demands for democratic participation and control on the other is an essential feature of public administration in all democratic contexts. Therefore it is important to consider how this relationship fares in the case of officials dealing with groups and interests at national or local level. All such associations may feel they have legitimate contributions to make to the development of public policies, but dealing with them may require considerable management resources. Several years ago, research into local government in Birmingham showed there were just over four and a quarter thousand formal, voluntary, non-profit-making organisations at that time, and over one thousand five hundred were politically active.[14] This was a quite unexpectedly large number, and when it is recalled that such political activity had, in most cases, to be dealt with by council officials as part of their day-to-day regular duties (as well as involving elected representatives) it reveals the magnitude and time-consuming consequences of the political environment on the practice of public administration in a modern democracy. Further discussion of the constraints of the political environment will be included in Chapter 20.

19.4.3   Closed politics

One final aspect of contemporary public administration sometimes called 'closed politics,' may also be conveniently mentioned here.[15] The point is that all organisations, including government departments and local authorities, develop their own ways of doing things, have a working philosophy or departmental view, and often find themselves engaged in political activity to advance those interests or protect their positions. There is nothing sinister about this, and the political activity may be non-partisan, but it is a fact of life often beneficial in achieving the overall purposes of an organisation. Sir Brian Cubbon, for example, on one occasion said that if the uk Home Office had a departmental view it was that the prison population for the last thirty years had been too high. It followed that it was working to find ways of reducing it.[16] Where there is more decentralisation, there are more organisations to develop views and interests, and more activity is likely to develop between them to advance those views and interests. This, also, will receive further comment in Chapter 20.

Notes

1. S. E. Finer, 'Local government', in J. Gould and William L. Kolb (eds), *A Dictionary of the Social Sciences* (London: Tavistock, 1964).
2. United Nations, *Decentralisation for National and Local Development* (New York: United Nations, 1962).
3. William A. Robson, 'Local government', in *Encyclopaedia of the Social Sciences* Vol. 9 (New York: Macmillan, 1933).
4. John Stuart Mill, *Utilitarianism, Liberty and Representative Government* (London: Dent, 1910), Chapter 15.
5. Quoted by W. J. M. Mackenzie, *Theories of Local Government* Greater London Paper No. 2, London School of Economics and Political Science, 1961, pp. 10–11.
6. Ibid., p. 13.
7. Quoted by L. J. Sharpe, 'Theories of Local Goverment' and Brian C. Smith, 'The justification of local government', in Lionel D. Feldman and Michael D. Goldrick, *Politics and Government in Urban Canada* (Toronto: Macmillan, 1969) pp. 349 and 335.
8. Ibid.
9. J. S. Mill, *Representative Government*, Chapter 15, p. 348.
10. *The Politics of Aristotle* trans. Ernest Barker (Cambridge: Cambridge University Press, 1952), p. 196.
11. J. G. Taggart, 'Are central service agencies usually inefficient?', in J. E. Hodgetts and D. C. Corbett (eds), *Canadian Public Administration* (Toronto: Macmillan, 1960).
12. John M. Pfiffner and Robert V. Presthus, *Public Administration* (New York: Ronald, 1960), p. 134.
13. Evelyn Sharp, *The Ministry of Housing and Local Government* (London: George Allen & Unwin, 1969), pp. 31–2.
14. D. S. Morris and K. Newton, *Onymous Empire: Voluntary organisations in Birmingham Politics*, Discussion Paper No. 10, Series F, Birmingham Politics and Society, University of Birmingham, 1970.
15. Richard A. Chapman, *Leadership in the British Civil Service* (London: Croom Helm, 1984); and *Ethics in the British Civil Service* (London: Routledge, 1988).
16. Sir Brian Cubbon, 'The duty of the professional', in Richard A. Chapman (ed.), *Ethics in Public Service* (Edinburgh: Edinburgh University Press, 1993).

Questions

1. Explain the advantages and disadvantages of different forms of decentralisation.
2. How does the political environment affect the practice of public administration, with special reference to local government?

20

Administrative reform

Everyone, it seems, agrees that administrative reform is good. It is a 'hurrah' term, often used by politicians who wish to make changes for what they believe to be the better, and who are seeking support for their proposals or credit for their achievements. When used in relation to public administration practitioners it is often expected that they will be supportive and make positive contributions to reform processes or a reform agenda. As far as this chapter is concerned, however, it is a term which, perhaps more than any other, indicates the significance of the political environment within which public sector management is undertaken. It is important that any study of public administration appreciates the significance of this environment because of the values it embodies, the tendency for those values to change, and the links between administrative reform and other key concepts used frequently in public sector and other management contexts. The purpose of this chapter is therefore to consider administrative reform in general and how it relates to other important topics of contemporary relevance such as efficiency, accountability and openness in government.

20.1 Reform, change, evolution, development and innovation

As with other topics, it is important to have a clear idea of the meanings of terms being used. The need for clarity is not intended, however, to dominate the whole chapter. Below, somewhat assertively, are some definitions that may be helpful in starting subsequent discussion.

20.1.1 Definitions and features of administrative reform

Administrative reform is the process of making changes in administrative procedures within the public services because they have become out of line with the expectations of the social and political environment. The process is not necessarily one of development towards a clearly defined goal known in advance, but a complex matter of acceding to pressures, communicating and discussing ideas, stimulating comments from groups with potential interests, and making judgements within the administrative system about tactics and timing for the introduction of particular changes. This implies a number of differences between reform and other processes with which it may be closely related and/or with which it may overlap. Changes, however, may be introduced into an administrative system which do not result from tension between the administrative system and the expectations and values of the social and political environment. Changes may be neutral in comparison with administrative reforms (though the study of them might nevertheless provide valuable insights into administrative decision-making). Examples of such changes are to be seen in new procedures for taxation, minor transfers of functions between departments and the abolition of certain regulations or functions which relate to past lifestyles. Innovation may be part of administrative reform, as it has been in developing countries where administrative structures in the public sector have been created where none previously existed. Evolution may be another closely related process when it refers to structures or procedures in public administration that were at first simple but have become increasingly complicated and elaborate.

One of the essential features of administrative reform in public administration is the relationship of administrative changes to characteristics of, or pressures from, the broader social and political environment. In nineteenth-century Britain, for example, there was public concern about poor standards of public administration because of widespread corruption in the appointment of staff who were not competent or qualified for their positions. This led to the introduction of open competition and the creation in 1855 of a Civil Service Commission as a central department for civil service recruitment. By the 1990s, however, there had been considerable change in the social, political and educational conditions in the country as a whole, and a government with an ideological stance had been elected in 1979 to reduce to a minimum the scope of governmental activities. This has recently led to the abolition of the Civil Service Commission and the proposal to sell the Recruitment and Assessment Services agency which specialises in recruiting civil servants according to publicly known criteria. Both the creation of the Civil Service Commission and its abolition in 1991 may be regarded as administrative reforms because they were the results of complex social and political changes and pressures on the public administration system. Another example was the creation in the United Kingdom in 1968 of a Civil Service Department to enhance the status and improve the work of personnel management in the civil service. This had been recommended by the report of an important public inquiry in 1968 under the chairmanship of Lord Fulton. The report was widely welcomed at the time. In 1981, however, the Civil Service Department was abolished by the new government working in a quite different climate engendered by both its own values and beliefs about the role of government in modern society and by the economic and social attitudes of the time. Again, both the creation and later abolition of this department may be seen as reforms because they were intended changes widely discussed and accepted at the time, and were the consequences of policies advanced by properly elected and legitimate governments which had publicly stated their values and approach.

When considering the nature of administrative reform, it is also important to consider other factors including the origins of reform proposals, how they are accepted and how they are implemented. It is sometimes said that administrative reform is, in the end, a political process and some writers have seen reform proposals as waiting on political will. While there can be no doubt that it is, in part, political (involving politics within the political and administrative system as well as politics on a wider, national and/or partisan spectrum), it should also be considered as a management process, and any application of administrative reform must, therefore, allow for its political and administrative elements. The growth of more positive government in the nineteenth and twentieth centuries gave rise to questions about the relationship of management efficiency to the political goals and objectives of government. In early twentieth-century Britain this was expressed in conceptions of government in mechanistic terms, but in the mid- and late-twentieth century there was fundamental rethinking of the principles influencing the number and structures of major departments of state.

A great deal of emphasis has been placed by some reformers on making government more efficient and effective, but less attention has been paid to the meanings and consistent use of these terms in more recent writings of specialists in public administration. This serves to emphasise what Professor Gerald Caiden has called the underdeveloped nature and infancy of this aspect of the study of public administration.[1] This will be discussed briefly, later, in the context of efficency and effectiveness.

Furthermore, the management element in administrative reform is more than a question of formulating bold proposals for change and of working up strategies for reform. One important aspect of the art of administration is to be found in the judgements of individuals and groups about tactics and timing to ensure that agreed aims are achieved – deciding how and when changes should be introduced. This may be an important aspect of executive leadership in public administration and may be observed in two ways. First, appreciating the situation, assessing whether a consensus for change already exists, whether the opinions of important groups have had sufficient time to be formulated and expressed, and whether all interested parties have had an adequate hearing; second, establishing the manner in which proposed changes are introduced and deciding the right moment for proposals to gain the widest possible acceptance. This is sometimes done through committees – specialist committees consider particular problems, then further committees are created to gather together and assess the work of the specialist committees, reviewing and coordinating policy proposals. Professor Fred Riggs, in his studies of administrative reform in developing countries, has referred to this as 'the problem of dynamic balancing' in administrative reform. He has suggested that it is useful to think of all three branches of government as currently engaged in both political and administrative functions.[2] It follows that a balance of power is essential between them to enhance the administrative capabilities of government as well as to safeguard its political responsiveness.

20.1.2   Factors contributing to administrative reform

A number of factors contribute to the dynamics of administrative reform and five will be briefly discussed below.

The first factor is the practice and study of public administration. In some countries the relationship between practitioners and scholars is closer and has a more significant impact on administrative reform than in others. In most European countries the close and productive relationships of these two groups is helped by their mutual interests in the study of constitutional and administrative law and by the ease with which individuals are able to transfer between positions as academics and positions as practitioners. Indeed, it is noticeable that a number of the most prominent specialists in the public administration of West European countries hold joint positions in government administration and in universities or schools or institutes of public administration. The experience in the United Kingdom is different, however, because there have been virtually no comparable linked positions. A consequence is that British academics concerned with the study of public administration have generally been treated with scepticism by practitioners who tend to regard their comments as superficial, ill-informed and of little practical relevance. There are various possible explanations for this including the social and educational background of senior administrators, the lack of a written constitution and the way the study of public administration has developed within political science and the social sciences generally.

Second, there are contributions towards administrative reform from the world of intellectual ideas. Virtually all developed countries have encouraged intellectual groups in the fields of the social and political sciences through the creation of scholarly associations and societies, partisan think-tanks or independent institutes dedicated to the study of public policies and their implementation. In the United Kingdom these include the Royal Institute of Public Administration (from 1922 to 1992), the Fabian Society, research institutes associated with the three main political parties and *ad hoc* groups to study particular problems sponsored by organisations like the Joint University Council or the local authority associations. Comparable organisations in the United States would include the Brookings Institution and research institutes associated with the major universities. One example from France is the Centre for Administrative Research at the National Foundation of Political Science and one from Germany the Hochschule für Verwaltangswissenshaften, Speyer.

Third, major events have played a special part in the stimulation of administrative reform. Numerous examples can be traced to the consequences of coping with war. Major wars in Europe made long-term impacts on education programmes, on industrial relations (including the development of Whitleyism in the United Kingdom), on the reduction of corruption through improved staff recruitment procedures, on the development of new management techniques, and through the introduction of entirely new social welfare services associated with the growth of more positive government.

Fourth, political parties and the rise and decline of particular ideologies have been important. This is clear in some of the countries in Eastern Europe which, in recent years, have changed from being socialist regimes with the introduction of more democratic approaches to government. In Western democracies ideological factors stimulating administrative reform are often expressed by political parties in their election manifestos which, once a party has been elected to government, become the basis for reform programmes.

Fifth, and of particular importance in the context of this chapter, is the direction of administrative reform by officials. Often they play a key role because particular reform proposals originate from them. Officials tend to be best informed about the practical difficulties of reform proposals and their management implications, which sometimes include the importance of gaining a consensus among officials as well as with others involved in implementing them. Sometimes it is important to note that the bureaucrat's role in a democratic context is less in initiating change or producing their own original ideas than in making use of good ideas from wherever they happen to come. To do more may be to exceed the role of an official, especially if one accepts the basic characteristics of an ideal bureaucrat as outlined by Max Weber (see above); enthusiasm or ideological commitment in this context may encroach on the role of a politician. Nevertheless, there is a demanding and important role in administrative reform for administrators as managers of reform. This role has to be borne in mind when deciding qualities needed at the initial personnel selection stage as well as in subsequent socialisation and training. For example, officials appointed to positions dedicated to implementing administrative reform programmes must have a capacity for very hard work and a developed sense of public duty, implying that their personal interests must be subordinated to the public interest. They must be adept at recognising the political implications of proposed reforms and they need a fine sensitivity to the political environment. Sometimes they need to develop skills necessary for modifying or adapting reform proposals originating outside the political system. Their role in this is very important because to control the implementation of reform is often in practice to control its future direction and even, in some cases, the nature of a reform programme.

It should also be noted that while many pressures and incentives for administrative reform are exogenetic, originating beyond the administrative system, some may even originate from abroad. No country that has had economic difficulties and been helped by the International Monetary Fund can ignore its conditions for accepting such assistance, and no member of the European Union can disregard the decisions of its constituent organs. Consequently, pressures and incentives for change in this context can come from within the administrative system, from beyond it, from the national social or political environment or, sometimes, beyond that, from international organisations and influences.

20.2 Efficiency, effectiveness and economy

The nature of an administrative reform programme is to be found in what it sets out to achieve. Generally this is expressed in terms of achieving greater efficiency, effectiveness and economy in the provision of public services. Unfortunately, however, there is often a lack of clarity about the use of these terms and, like administrative reform, they have almost been put into the category of 'hurrah' words that now have little, if any, precise meaning. The example of the United Kingdom in the 1980s provides a useful lesson here – not so much a lesson in what and how something should be done as a warning about what might be avoided.

The new administrative culture of the 1980s included attempts to improve public sector management by making it more 'efficient', and also smaller by transferring activities away from it or, wherever possible, simply by government ceasing to provide services no longer thought necessary. The measures adopted were desired measures, approved by politicians for largely ideological reasons and presumably not disapproved of by the large number of voters who often benefited financially and who, at elections, returned the team of politicians from whom they hoped to continue to benefit. One of the main lessons of the British experience of the 1980s was that reform focuses on intentions as well as the methods to achieve them.

Two examples illustrate this approach. Universities in the United Kingdom are mainly funded by the government but in recent years funding arrangements have assumed an 'efficiency gain', or 'efficiency saving', of 1.5 per cent per year. The result is that a university is given 1.5 per cent less resources than is expected to be necessary and is meant to cope by being more efficient. The consequences are evident in overcrowded classes, inadequate library facilities, the introduction of teaching and examination measures to deal with 'mass education' and increased stress-related disorders among staff. Professor the Earl Russell commented in *The Independent* newspaper on 28 February 1991:

> If we take in more undergraduates without increasing the supply of books, the number of undergraduates who come to me and report that they cannot do their essays, because they cannot find the books, goes up. This appears to me to be inefficiency rather than efficiency.

A comparable scenario seems to have been featured in the recently much publicised 'mad cow disease'. It seems cows developed bovine spongiform encephelopathy (BSE) after being fed protein concentrate containing the ground-up remains of scrapie-diseased sheep. Some farmers have claimed ignorance of what the protein concentrate contained, but the manufacturers must have known, and even if the remains of sheep had not been diseased it seems odd to have fed protein to naturally herbivorous cows. Presumably it was done because it was an efficient form of manufactured cattle feed, less costly than traditional feed and therefore expected to result in cheaper meat for consumers and/or increased profits for farmers or the producers of cattle feed. Moreover, in order to reduce government regulations and their implementation through an appropriate number of officials in the meat hygiene service, regulations that should have eradicated the BSE problem after its identification were not applied with sufficient rigour. The practical consequences of policies intended to achieve greater efficiency have in fact led to serious health problems for animals and humans, a threat to a major UK exporting industry and secondary problems in the economy and to unemployment in a number of associated industries.

To anyone interested in the processes of reform, these two accounts may be seen as examples of difficulties arising from the lack of clarity in the use of popular concepts such as efficiency, effectiveness and economy in administrative reform. Sometimes efficiency and effectiveness are used in public administration discussions as if they were synonymous or, when linked together as they often are, as if they mean economical and convenient. Sometimes the more consistent approach of economists is adopted, and then efficiency is basically used to refer to the extent to which maximum output is achieved in relation to given costs or inputs, and effectiveness is used to refer to the extent to which overall goals are achieved. Students of public administration, however, may find it useful, particularly in discussions of administrative reform, to consider the ways in which these words are used so that misunderstandings are minimised. The following is one suggestion, based on literature referred to in previous chapters, especially the Hawthorne study as reported by F. J. Roethlisberger and William J. Dickson[3] and the classic text by Chester I. Barnard, *The Functions of the Executive*.[4]

Management activity is directed towards achieving two ends, goals and objectives. 'Goals' refers to the higher level of activity, which may be general in nature and the responsibility of the highest levels of management – for example, the elimination of substandard housing or the provision of a dental service. 'Objectives' refers to more specific and measurable activities, the responsibility of lower levels in the management hierarchy – for example, the processing of clearance schemes or providing for inspections of children's teeth in schools every year. Efficiency may be used to relate to one of these activities and effectiveness to the other. Effective may be reserved for the achievement of specific, measurable, desired ends – that is, objectives. Effective management can therefore be quantified, and the manager is concerned with using the available resources to achieve specified objectives. Efficiency may be reserved for the achievement of the ends set by the higher level of management, some of which may involve numerical targets and may therefore include quantifiable elements; however, because it will include human factors and take into account the unintended consequences of management activity, it will be mainly concerned with unquantifiable elements. For example, management objectives might be achieved at the cost of inhuman working conditions or in a manner inconsistent with other standards expected in society. Consequently, when the terms are used in this way, it may be possible for effective management to be inefficient or for effective action that is efficient in one society or at one time to be unacceptable and inefficient in another society or at a different time. Economy may then be introduced as a term concerned with the cost elements and the relationship of inputs to outputs.

Specialists in operational research have taken this a stage further to indicate ways in which degrees of effectiveness and economy can be measured. The degree of effectiveness is expressed as actual output divided by retrospective planned output (that is, the output expected to have been achieved given the actual input); this is generally one of the concerns of line managers. The degree of economy can be expressed as the actual input divided by the retrospective planned input (the input expected to have been needed to achieve the actual output); this is generally one of the concerns of chief finance officers and chief establishment officers in a government organisation.

The point being made here is really a consequence of the previous four chapters as much as an elaboration of a particular aspect of administrative reform. There is, of course, a need for terminological clarity in public administration as much as in any other aspect of the study of politics or of the other social sciences, but it is a matter of much more than that. Any discussion of administrative reform serves as a good opportunity to reconsider what the main purposes of an organisation are, how the purposes relate, how the organisation should be managed, how it should relate to environmental pressures both in the national society in which it is operating and to international pressures, and, above all, how it should relate to all aspects of the system of government of which it is a part. Nowhere is this more significant than in considerations of openness and accountability, and as these are topics which are often related to discussions of administrative reform, openness and accountability will be the last topic to be considered here.

20.3 Openness and accountability

Administrative reform is not only concerned with management outputs and with minimising costs. At least as much attention is given in the administrative reform programmes of democratic regimes to problems of openness and accountability in public administration because political accountability, and the political environment within which public sector management proceeds, have a continuous affect on so many aspects of it.

For the purposes of this present discussion, open government is a topic of considerable importance in a modern democratic political system, first because it refers to the ability of the public to hold the government fully accountable for its actions and to assess the validity of actions taken. Second, it refers to the rights of individual citizens in relation to information held about them in public organisations. Open government encompasses discussions about freedom of information, data protection, access to public records and the necessity in a healthy democracy for information about government activities to be publicly available. These topics are frequently discussed in terms of values and of the expectations of democratic government. There is no opportunity to cover properly the arguments for open government here. What is, however, worth noting is that the discussions do not always give much attention to the practical implications and applications of open government. In fact, open government has become one of the most important topics in the study and practice of public administration since the end of the Second World War.

In 1946 the General Assembly of the United Nations passed a resolution stating that 'Freedom of Information is a fundamental human right and is a touchstone for all the freedom to which the United Nations is consecrated.' This was followed in 1948 by the Universal Declaration of Human Rights which included an Article stating that 'Everyone has the right to freedom of opinion and expression; this right includes freedom to hold opinions without interference and to seek, receive and impart information and ideas through any media regardless of frontiers.' Then, in 1979, the Committee of Ministers of the Council of Europe agreed recommendations to member states giving detailed requirements for putting the widely agreed beliefs on open government into practice. These included ensuring access to information held by public authorities, making provisions for limiting access, and how requests should be dealt with. Since the passing of these resolutions the practical implications of access have been complicated because information is no longer stored simply on files in ways expected by writers on bureaucracy earlier in the century. Now, much information is held on computers and can be transmitted rapidly, and with little scope for control, by electronic means.

A great deal of personal information on individuals is held in the records of all public services. Citizens can be understandably concerned that the information is accurate and is being used only for purposes they accept as legitimate. Practical questions arise from the belief that all citizens should have access to this information. Providing access requires resources. Sometimes, in order to protect particular individuals, checks may have to be made to ensure that anyone requesting personal information about others has a right of access. These questions relating to the rights of individuals may require special procedures when collecting and storing information as well as when making provisions for access to it. Consequently, there are effects on day-to-day management practices concerning the proper storage of information and the development of acceptable arrangements for access. Some of these implications relating to personal information are as relevant in business or commercial management as they are in the public sector, and it is important to recognise the possible legitimacy of claims to access even where at first sight there may be a natural tendency to confidentiality. Other aspects of open government relate to rights of access to information of a less personal nature. Citizens may seek information about government policies and procedures that are of public importance, either at the present time or from the past, and in terms of democratic expectations it may be perfectly reasonable for them to be given such information. If citizens are to participate in government either directly or through representatives, and if there is to be the culture of openness that people generally feel should exist in a democracy, there must be effective two-way communication between those engaged in government and the people in whose interests democratic government is practised.

These considerations have important practical consequences and, from time to time, they lead to recommendations for administrative reform. They are important for relationships between officials and elected representatives. Sometimes officials may be answerable for the consequences of open government policies (as well as for the operational aspects of granting access to particular information). More often elected representatives are held to be accountable in the normal democratic ways, through parliamentary procedures or related processes of government. Roger Freeman, then a Minister in the UK government, recently said to a Parliamentary Select Committee that a spirit of openness makes for better decision-making because 'civil servants often have to take minor decisions on behalf of ministers in many different circumstances.'[5] Consequently a close and healthy relationship between ministers and officials in a democracy should start with the assumption that the public needs to be informed. Whatever the circumstances, the relationships between officials and politicians becomes important, and even when ministers are personally involved, ministerial responsibility for policies or particular decisions does not absolve officials in providing advice. This means that in public administration there are now important expectations for open government and, as a consequence, the day-to-day activities of officials have to bear these in mind. In some spheres, there are special activities in public sector management that simply do not exist in management elsewhere; in other spheres there may be more sensitivity in relation to individual citizens than would have to apply in other management contexts, or there may be special considerations with regard to the security aspects of work.

It is also important to note that in recent years there has been a growing demand in many countries for freedom of information legislation to enshrine the rights of individuals. Again, quite apart from the ideological or democratic implications, such reformist legislation has important administrative implications. A recent report has drawn attention to the experience of this form of legislation in Australia and New Zealand, and the Administrative Review Council in Australia noted that the Freedom of Information Act there

> had a marked impact on the way agencies make decisions and the way they record information . . . the FOI Act has focused decision makers' minds on the need to base decisions on relevant factors and to record the decision making process. The knowledge that decisions and processes are open to scrutiny, including under the FOI Act, imposes a constant discipline on the public sector.[6]

Sometimes demands for specific open-government reforms may appear like stages in progress towards an ideal democracy – an ultimate, if unexpressed, expectation where educated, reasonable and responsible citizens resolve their disagreements by political activity within an agreed framework of rules. Difficulties arise because both citizens and governments are not yet educated enough, reasonable enough, or responsible enough, to live in such conditions, and as with other aspects of public administration, it becomes the task of managers to keep the system of government operating in what always turn out to be much less than ideal conditions. That is why working in public administration so often requires good personal judgement and well developed political sensitivity.

This chapter has illustrated administrative reform not only as an important topic within the study of public administration, but also as a way of appreciating some of the essential qualities of management in the public sector in which difficulties and challenges more complex, more demanding and more satisfying than management in other contexts are encountered. Moreover, to a political scientist, public administration has the attraction of operating within a public service ethos. In a democracy this may be more evident than it is in other political systems because working for the public interest may bring its own rewards, different in quality from working for other sorts of interests or in other contexts.

Notes

1. Gerald E. Caiden, *Administrative Reform* (Chicago: Aldine, 1969).
2. Fred W. Riggs, *Administration in Developing Countries* (Boston, Mass.: Houghton Mifflin, 1964).
3. F. J. Roethlisberger and William J. Dickson, *Management and the Worker* (Cambridge, Mass.: Harvard University Press, 1939).
4. Chester I. Barnard, *The Functions of the Executive*, (Cambridge, Mass.: Harvard University Press, 1962).
5. Cm. 2290, *Open Government* (London: HMSO, 1993).
6. Select Committee on the Parliamentary Commissioner for Administration, Second Report, Session 1995–96, *Open Government* HC 84 (London: HMSO, 1996).

Questions

1. What factors contribute to administrative reform? What constraints apply to the implementatiom of reform proposals in the provision of public services?
2. What are the expectations for open government in liberal democracies? How do they affect the processes of management in public administration?

Section Four

Bibliography

Chapter 16 Public administration and public sector management

Barker, Anthony (ed.), *Quangos in Britain: Government and the Networks of Public Policy-Making* (London: Macmillan, 1982).

Chapman, Richard. A. and Dunsire, A. (eds), *Style in Administration (London: Allen & Unwin, 1971).*

Dunsire, A., *Administration: the Word and the Science* (London: Martin Robertson, 1973).

Elcock, H., *Change and Decay? Public Administration in the 1990s* (Harlow: Longman, 1991).

Greenwood, J. and Wilson, D., *Public Administration in Britain Today*, 2nd edn (London: Unwin Hyman, 1989).

Hood, C., *Beyond the Public Bureaucracy State? Public Administration in the 1990s* (London: London School of Economics, 1990).

Metcalfe, L. and Richards, S., *Improving Public Management*, 2nd edn (London: Sage, 1990).

O'Toole, B. J. and Jordan G. *Next Steps, Improving Management in Government?* (Aldershot: Dartmouth, 1995).

Plumptre, T., *Beyond the Bottom Line* (Halifax Nova Scotia: Institute for Research and Public Policy, 1988).

Riggs, F. W., *The Ecology of Public Administration* (London: Asia Publishing House, 1961).

Simon, H. A., Smithburg D. W. and Thompson, V. A., *Public Administration* (New York: Knopf, 1950; New Brunswick, NJ: Transaction Publishers, 1991).

Chapter 17 Organisation theory and bureaucracy

Albrow M., *Bureaucracy* (London: Pall Mall, 1970).

Bell, D., *The End of Ideology, On the Exhaustion of Political Ideas in the Fifties* (New York: Free Press, 1960).

Blau, P. M., *Bureaucracy in Modern Society* (New York: Random House, 1956).

Crozier, M., *The Bureaucratic Phenomenon* (London: Tavistock, 1964).

Fayol, H., *General and Industrial Management* (London: Pitman, 1949).

Gerth, H. H. and Wright Mills, C. (eds), *From Max Weber Essays in Sociology* (London: Routledge, 1948).

Gulick, L. and Urwick L., *Papers on the Science of Administration, Institute of Public Administration* (New York: Institute of Public Administration, 1937).

Henderson, A. M. and Parsons, T. (trans. and eds), *Max Weber: The Theory of Social and Economic Organisation* ((New York: Oxford University Press, 1947).

Henderson, K., *Emerging Synthesis in American Public Administration* (London: Asia Publishing House, 1966).

Taylor, F., *The Principles of Scientific Management* (Harper & Bros, 1916).

Urwick, L., *The Elements of Administration* (London: Pitman, 1943).

Wiggering, H. and Sandhovel, A., *European Environmental Advisory Council, Agenda 21 – Implementation Issues in the European Union* (The Hague: Kluwer Law International, 1996).

Chapter 18   **Personnel management and informal organisation**

Barnard, Chester I., *The Functions of the Executive* (Cambridge, Mass.: Harvard University Press, 1938).

Chapman, Richard A., *The Higher Civil Service in Britain* (London: Constable, 1970).

Chapman, Richard A., *Leadership in the British Civil Service* (London: Croom Helm, 1984).

Chapman, Richard A., *Ethics in the British Civil Service* (London: Routledge, 1988).

Chapman, Richard A. and Greenaway, J. R., *The Dynamics of Administrative Reform* (London: Croom Helm, 1980).

Cuming, Maurice W., *The Theory and Practice of Personnel Management* (London: Heinemann, 1968)

Curson, R., *Personnel Management* (London: Hodder & Stoughton, 1980).

McGregor, D. M., *The Professional Manager* (New York: McGraw-Hill, 1967).

Parris, H., *Staff Relations in the Civil Service: Fifty years of Whitleyism* (London: George Allen & Unwin, 1973).

Roethlisberger, F. J. and Dickson, W. J., *Management and the Worker* (Cambridge, Mass.: Harvard University Press, 1939).

Stahl. O. G., *Public Personnel Administration* (New York: Harper & Row, 1936).

Chapter 19   **Decentralization, devolution and deconcentration**

Chandler, J. A., *Public Policy-Making for Local Government* (London: Croom Helm, 1988).

Chapman, Richard A. (ed.), *Ethics in Public Service* (Edinburgh: Edinburgh University Press, 1993).

Elcock, H., *Local Government* (London: Methuen, 1982).

Gould, J. and Kolb, W. L. (eds), *A Dictionary of the Social Sciences* (London: Tavistock, 1964).

Mackenzie, W. J. M., 'Local government in Parliament', *Public Administration*, vol. 32, 1954, pp. 409–23.

Mackenzie, W. J. M., *Theories of Local Government* Greater London Paper No. 2, London School of Economics and Political Science, 1961.

Maddick, H., *Democracy, Decentralisation and Development* (London: Asia Publishing House, 1963).

Norton, A, *International Handbook of Local and Regional Government* (Aldershot: Edward Elgar, 1994).

Roberts, G. and Edwards, A., *A New Dictionary of Political Analysis* (Sevenoaks: Edward Arnold, 1991).

Sharpe, L. J., 'Theories and values of local government', *Political Studies*, vol. 18, 1970, pp. 153–74.

Smith, B. C., *Decentralisation: the Territorial Dimension of the State* (London: George Allen & Unwin, 1985).

Wheare, K. C., *Modern Constitutions* (Oxford: Oxford University Press, 1951).

Wilson, C. H., *Essays in Local Government* (Oxford, Blackwell, 1948).

Chapter 20 **Administrative reform**

Barker, E. (ed.), *The Politics of Aristotle* (Oxford: Oxford University Press, 1946).

Caiden, Gerald E., *Administrative Reform* (Chicago: Aldine, 1969).

Caiden, Gerald E. and Siedentopf, H. *Strategies of Administrative Reform* (Lexington, Mass.: Lexington Books, 1982).

Chapman, Richard A. and Greenaway J. R., *The Dynamics of Administrative Reform* (London: Croom Helm, 1980).

Chapman, Richard A. and Hunt, M. (eds), *Open Government* (London: Croom Helm, 1987).

Cm. 2290, *Open Government* (London: HMSO, 1993).

Riggs, F. W., *The Ecology of Public Administration* (London: Asia Publishing House, 1961).

Riggs, F. W., 'Administrative reform as a problem of dynamic balancing', *Philippine Journal of Public Administration* vol. 14, 1970, pp. 101–35.

Section Five

International Relations

Michael Sheehan

21

Approaches to the study of international relations

In the modern world it is impossible to understand the politics of any country without being able to place them in an international context. Domestic politics are profoundly influenced by political and economic forces originating beyond the borders of the state. In addition, the relationships between states and other international political actors are themselves a fascinating form of contemporary politics. International relations (IR) is concerned with how those national societies in turn relate to each other and interact to achieve national goals.

Increasingly, however, theorists of IR have argued that the relationships between states cannot truly be understood without understanding the internal workings of states and their populations. Nor can international relations be understood if its study is confined to interactions between states, for non-governmental organisations as well as intergovernmental bodies now play a crucial role in the workings of the international system.

In 1967 the American IR specialist Karl Deutsch wrote:

> An introduction to the study of international relations in our time is an introduction to the art and science of the survival of mankind. If civilisation is killed within the next 30 years, it will not be killed by famine or plague, but by foreign policy and international relations. We can cope with hunger and pestilence, but we cannot yet deal with the power of our own weapons and with our behaviour as nation-states.[1]

During the Cold War, focusing on the prudential question of the avoidance of war was seen by most IR theorists as the critical and central aspect of the study of the subject. Yet IR involves much more than just the pursuit of security in a narrow, military sense, it is also about security in the sense of quality of life. Aristotle's argument that 'the leading of a good and just life in the *polis*' was the proper objective of all political activity, applies as fully to international relations as it does to domestic politics. The way in which a society is organised involves class structures, economic systems, moral and ethical codes and the shaping force of history. All these help determine the shape of the political system and of society in general. The same is true for international relations. And in the same way, moral and political questions arise about whether the particular form of the international system promotes justice or economic well-being for more than a minority or the protection of human rights or the environment. Moral and ethical questions are central to the study of IR.

IR is particularly interested in generalisations and comparisons. Studying the outbreak of a particular war makes it possible to learn something about the reason why any war breaks out. IR attempts to identify the features common to particular phenomena or classes of event, for example war, peace, imperialism, levels of development, alliances, the balance of power.

21.1 Levels of analysis

International relations is an enormous field and inevitably obliges us to focus our attention on particular phenomena, regions or levels of analysis. There are certain areas of interest, such as war or the foreign policies of states, which can be analysed at different levels of scale. Doing so inevitably leads to different perspectives and often different conclusions, so the choice of scale is important.

Foreign policy is a good example of this. We can look at foreign policy at the level of the international system. This leads to questions like: How is a state's foreign policy shaped by the overall structure of the system, for example by its polarity, that is whether it is dominated by two major powers, by four or five, or whether power and influence is spread among a great number? Kenneth Waltz, among others, believes that this is the crucial feature.[2] Alternatively the system can be looked at in terms of its homogeneity, that is the extent to which it is composed of states of the same type which have similar objectives and a similar commitment to common values, reflected in international law, as suggested by Raymond Aron,[3] or by its geographical extent seen as crucial by Adam Watson,[4] or by the 'rules' of the system which were central to the analysis put forward by Hans Morgenthau.[5]

Or, we can look at it at the level of national foreign policy. What foreign policy objectives does a particular state have. What instruments does it have available to try and attain those objectives, for example diplomacy, military power, economic instruments, propaganda, the influence of allies, and so on? What environmental factors help shape its foreign policy? Are they geographical location, climate, shape, size, alliance membership, historical relations with neighbours?

What domestic factors influence its policy, such as the form of government and constitution, the population's size and education, population growth rates, economic performance, the role of public opinion and the media, the existence of national minorities, the influence of parties and pressure groups, and so on?

Or we can take it down to the level of individuals. How is policy affected, for example, by the role of leadership, by the personalities of leaders, by psychological factors, by the nature of the individual decision-making process, by the health of the leadership, and the political strength of leaders?[6]

The particular level of analysis chosen frames the kind of questions asked and therefore helps to determine the answers arrived at. Focusing on the level of the international system tends to emphasise long-term trends and the apparent continuities of international relations, for example imperialism, the balance of power, international law, attempts at international cooperation, cultural factors and the persistent recurrence of war. Concentrating on the national level emphasises the situational context, the distinctive features of states and peoples and their efforts to pursue policy in the face of other states with often conflicting interests. Focusing on the individual level emphasises that often it makes a very great difference who is in charge of a country's foreign policy at a particular period.

21.2   Early history of the subject

Although the study of IR can be traced back through particular writers for over 3,000 years, as a University subject IR dates only from the early part of the twentieth century. Prior to 1900 it is striking that many of the great thinkers who studied politics paid little or no attention to the question of relations between political entities. For example, Plato, Aristotle and Marx said nothing specific about the nature of relations between large communities. Often, however, a view of such relationships is implicit in their writings. However, it is possible to look at the works of historians such as the ancient Greek Thucydides, who in studying the origins and course of the Peloponnesian War between Athens and Sparta reflected upon the nature of relations between states. While from the mid-seventeenth century onwards the fascination with balance-of-power thinking did produce some systemic thinking about IR, for the most part speculation about relations between states was limited to studies of the problem of war, focused on by Machiavelli,

Hobbes and Kant, and international law, as in the works of Grotius and Oppenheim.

There was also recurrent speculation, however, about the possibilities for fruitful cooperation between states and schemes were proposed for the creation of international organisations able to resolve disputes and deter aggression between states.

The systematic study of international relations as a university subject dates only from 1919 and its original focus was very much upon the issue of the prevention of war. This was a reaction against the carnage of the First World War, 1914–18. War was seen as a disease to be cured or prevented. This was understandable in the circumstances, but it did have a constraining effect upon the growth in the study of the subject. It meant that many of the subjects which are now seen as central to the understanding of international relations, such as the nature and operation of the international economy, the problem of economic development, the crucial nature of the way we think about international political relationships, the question of nationalism and national self-determination and so on, were not given the attention they deserved. Nor, despite the fact that this was the era of the suffragettes and early steps towards female political emancipation, was the profoundly gendered nature of traditional thinking about IR apparent to those who studied and wrote about it in the 1919–39 period. The focus of attention was upon the causes of war and arms races, and upon the creation of institutional mechanisms such as international organisations which might inhibit or even abolish war.

21.3   Idealism and realism 1919–39

During the interwar period, 1919–39, the academic study of international relations was marked by a debate between two schools of thought subsequently characterised as 'Idealism' and 'Realism'. The names of these two schools of thought were both chosen by the 'realists', who used these unhelpful labels to give their own approach a greater credibility than that of their opponents. IR studies in the aftermath of the First World War were idealist. They focused upon the study of war and peace, with war seen as an evil to be eliminated. The emphasis was upon international law and upon normative or moral issues.

21.3.1   Idealism

The 'idealist' approach was based upon a number of implicit and explicit assumptions. It was assumed that human nature is essentially 'good' and altruistic and that people are therefore capable of mutual aid and collaboration. The fundamental human concern for the welfare of others would make progress possible. This was a reaffirmation of the Enlightenment, the eighteenth-century rationalist philosophers who believed in the possibility of continually improving civilisation. Bad human behaviour was seen as resulting not from people being inevitably evil, but from evil institutions and structural arrangements that motivated people to act selfishly and to harm others, including leading them to make war.

War was not seen as inevitable and its frequency could be reduced by eradicating the anarchical conditions that encouraged it. War and injustice were international problems that required collective or multilateral rather than national efforts to eliminate them. International society should therefore reorganise itself institutionally to eliminate the 'anarchy', or absence of world government, that makes problems such as war likely. This goal was felt to be realistic because history suggested that global change and cooperation are not only possible but are clearly part of the historical record.[7]

Idealists identified certain features of the international system, such as the existence of a flourishing arms trade, which, they believed, contributed to the outbreak of war. They therefore sought to constrain or eliminate these features. They looked back to examples in history of periods of international cooperation and sought to build upon these achievements. In particular they focused upon the absence of any world government able to control violence and uphold the law in the manner expected of national governments in the domestic context. They therefore strongly supported the new League of Nations, the forerunner of the current United Nations Organisation. In particular they promoted the League's 'collective security' approach to the problem of war and peace, under which all the League's members agreed to go to war in defence of any member attacked by another member-state.[8]

The idealists argued that there was nothing inevitable about war. If it was possible for populations to come together to form states because they believed that those states served their common purposes, then the same was true of the global population of states. They too were capable of recognising their common interests and cooperating or uniting in order to pursue those interests more effectively.

In particular there was an obvious logic in developing mechanisms for controlling or eliminating wars because, as the First World War had shown, such conflicts had disastrous consequences for all concerned. If war was used by states as a means of resolving disputes, then alternative, peaceful means of conflict resolution would have to be found.

Since the armed forces of states were seen as threatening by their neighbours and represented an economic burden for all states, disarmament should be pursued as a way of reducing tensions and freeing resources for more socially valuable purposes.

21.3.2 Realism

The 'realist' world-view was based on a very different set of assumptions. A reading of history was seen as teaching that people are by nature sinful and wicked. Of all Mankind's evil tendencies, none was more common, inevitable and dangerous than the instinctive lust for power and the desire to dominate others. Realists reflected the views of an era influenced by 'Darwinist' theories about the struggle for survival and Freudian psychology with its emphasis on the darker side of human nature. The dream of eradicating the instinct for power was felt to be naive and Utopian. Therefore international relations, as the seventeenth-century English philosopher Thomas Hobbes saw it, was a struggle for power, 'a war of all against all'.

In such an environment, it was argued, a state's primary obligation, overriding all others, was to promote 'the national interest' by acquiring power. The condition of 'international anarchy' makes necessary the acquisition of military capabilities sufficient to deter or defeat potential enemies. Economic development was less relevant to national security than military might and was important mainly as a means for acquiring national power and prestige. Allies might help a state protect itself, but their loyalty and reliability should not be assumed. Nor should reliance be placed in international organisations such as the League of Nations or upon international law. If all states sought to maximise power, stability would emerge through a balance of power system based upon the operation of alliances.

In the realist mind-set therefore, humanity was seen as permanently capable of evil and the world was a dangerous and essentially ungovernable environment. Governments should therefore continually prepare for the worst and ensure that their states always had sufficient weaponry and allies to protect themselves and their interests when the need arose.

During the interwar period European governments failed to pursue either realist or idealist policies consistently. A half-hearted commitment to idealism was seen in the disarmament negotiations of the period and the establishment of the League of Nations. These efforts were fatally undermined, however, by the persistence of a basically realist approach which can be seen in the harsh terms imposed on Germany by the terms of the Versailles Treaty, the failure of states to cooperate effectively for their mutual military and economic security, the unwillingness of the democracies to oppose Fascist aggression in Spain and elsewhere, and the lack of support given to the League of Nations in the crises of the 1930s.

Nevertheless realist theorists subsequently argued that the outbreak of the Second World War demonstrated the correctness of the realist perspective. Even after the end of the Second World War, the rapid emergence of the Cold War after 1945 left the realist world-view dominant in IR theory. The acceptance of realism was made easier by the large numbers of European IR scholars who had fled to Britain and America to escape the horrors of Fascism, and who not surprisingly brought with them a deeply pessimistic view of human nature. Key realist thinkers in this period were E. H. Carr, George Schwartzenberger and Hans Morgenthau the latter two both refugees from Hitler's Germany.

Realists argued that their world-view was not a simple reaction to 1930s Fascism (see Chapter 15), but had a long historical pedigree. They identified a number of classical thinkers who they included within the realist pantheon, notably Thucydides, Machiavelli and Hobbes.[9]

The main features of the realist outlook can be summarised as follows.

1. The state is the principle actor – non-state actors are unimportant. This made realists reluctant to accept the evolution of the international system after 1945. The number of actors in international relations is very large. Events may be influenced not only by the behaviour of states, that is national governments and the policy instruments at their disposal, but by a variety of other potential influencing forces. These may include, for example, inter-governmental organisations such as the European Union, NATO and the UN, non-governmental organisations such as Amnesty International and Greenpeace, revolutionary or terrorist groups such as the Palestine Liberation Organisation (PLO) and the IRA, large commercial entities such as Shell and the Ford Motor Company, global organisations such as the Roman Catholic Church, regional bodies such as the Nordic Council, political-cultural groups like the Commonwealth, economic groups such as the Organisation of Petroleum Exporting Countries (OPEC) and so on. While realists recognised the existence and occasional influence of such actors, they deemed them to be inconsequential compared to the overwhelming importance of state actors.

2. The state is a unitary actor, with a single decision-making elite. Again, this assumption flies in the face of most of the research

done on the issue in the past thirty years. Many studies of the governmental policy process point to the fragmented nature of decision-making. In many states a federal system (see Chapter 7) divides power and responsibility among different levels of government. Even within the national government there may be conflict over policy between executive and legislative branches and between organisations that make up the government such as the foreign ministry, defence ministry, home office and so on. The government may be a coalition of parties with different interests and policy agendas. Realists ignore these complexities and treat the state as having a clear and identifiable national interest pursued by a single-minded and stable government bureaucracy.

3. The state is a rational actor seeking to advance its own interest in foreign policy. Rationality in this context means that the key decision-makers in the state have complete information available about other states and international actors, are aware of all the possible policy options and can choose the option best suited to advance their state's national interests without being affected by personal or political bias. (In reality of course, the context in which decisions are taken involves all kinds of 'irrationalities'.)

4. The pursuit of 'power' (see Chapter 2) determines outcomes. Power has been defined as the ability to determine the outcome of events, made possible by the possession of high levels of capability in areas such as diplomatic influence, economic resources and especially military strength. Classical realism has at its core an account of human nature derived from the medieval Christian realism of St Augustine, which characterises human beings as having a lust for power which can be mitigated but can never be transcended.

5. National security issues are the most important. The agenda of potential issues and problems which statesmen could address is enormous. For realists those issues relating to defence and national security must be given priority over all others. Only when a state is militarily secure can it afford to devote time and attention to other issues. Realists do not accept the argument that a state's 'security' can in practice be destroyed by a variety of causes including economic failure, environmental catastrophe, social disintegration or other non-military factors.

6. Key aspects of the 'reality' of IR are seen as remaining fixed throughout history. For realists, while many things change in international relations such as technology or political ideologies, 'human nature' remains essentially fixed. Because of this, pat-

terns of human behaviour are recurrent over history and history therefore provides crucial lessons about how states ought to behave if they wish to achieve security.[10]

This bleak perspective was the dominant approach in university IR departments during the 1950s and 1960s. In the 1970s, however, realism was challenged by two alternative perspectives – liberal pluralism and globalism/Marxism (see Chapter 13).

21.4 Liberal pluralism and globalism/Marxism in the 1970s

21.4.1 Liberal pluralism

Liberal pluralism has four major assumptions.

First, non-state actors are more important than the realist school suggests and cannot simply be ignored.[11] Moreover, they can be independent actors in their own right. International organisations are not just arenas in which states compete. Other non-governmental organisations (NGOs), such as multinational corporations (MNCs), must also be seen as important because the world is marked by increasing *interdependence*. The metaphor which pluralists liked to use was the image of the 'web' of criss-crossing relationships.[12]

Second, the pluralists dispute with the realists on a number of issues. They argue that the state is *not* a unitary actor. There is not a single decision-maker. Rather the government is made up of bureaucracies, interest groups, individuals and other actors. These interact to produce policy. Policy is therefore the result of politics, of competition and coalition-building. It is the outcome of a complex process. A curious aspect of the study of politics in the 1940s was that the realist image of the state as rational actor became an article of faith in IR at a time when a very different pluralist image of the state was becoming the norm in political science (see Chapter 3).[13]

Pluralists disaggregate the state, breaking it down into its component parts. Thus they see no such simple thing as 'US foreign policy' – rather there is Pentagon foreign policy, White House foreign policy, State Department foreign policy, CIA foreign policy and so on. These may or may not be in any way in harmony. The overall foreign policy of a state is the outcome of the competition between these various alternative approaches. Pluralists see the state not as a hard shell, but as permeated by outside forces, sometimes producing outcomes which the central government would not wish.

Third, pluralists challenge the 'state-as-rational actor' view. Because they see policy as the outcome of a complex political bargaining process, it cannot be fully 'rational' in the sense of decisions being optimal choices between all available options. Rather, policy is chosen from a much more limited range of options – those that the government were actually aware of and those that were politically acceptable. They also lay great stress on problems caused by misperception in international relations. This can be caused by such factors as incomplete information, bias, the effects of stress on decision-makers, the difficulty of determining what is really important in the mass of available information, and uncertainty about cause and effect.

Pluralists believe that objectives such as the promotion of peace, justice and welfare are best pursued through international cooperation. Cooperation can consist of working together in international organisations, abiding by international law or adherence to prevailing moral norms. This is in contrast to the realist view which sees states as being in fundamental conflict, living in a dangerous anarchic environment in which the pursuit of national self-interest is the only rational course.[14]

Fourth, pluralists therefore see international relations as encompassing a much broader agenda than realists do. Unlike realists they do not see the world scene as being dominated by national security issues. Rather, economic and social issues are seen as often being at the forefront of foreign policy debates. Some realists have themselves accepted this broadening of the agenda of international relations. In 1975 Secretary of State Henry Kissinger (a realist) said:

> The problems of energy, resources, environment, pollution, the uses of space and the seas now rank with questions of military security, ideology and territorial rivalry which have traditionally made up the diplomatic agenda.

21.4.2 Globalism/Marxism

The debate between realism and pluralism dominated IR in North America. In Western Europe and the developing countries, a third perspective was also significant, though less influential – globalism/Marxism. This perspective is based on three major assumptions.

First, globalists, as the name suggests, take as their starting-point the global context in which IR takes place, though it is fair to say that some Realists and Pluralists also have this global perspective. The emphasis is upon the external, structural factors helping to determine foreign policy behaviour. Globalists also see it as crucial to interpret IR from a historical perspective. The past is seen as shaping the present. For many globalists (and not just those in the Marxist school), the central defining characteristic of the international system is that it is capitalist. A particular economic system which characterises the overwhelming majority of states, and therefore the international system as a whole, inevitably shapes the nature of the relationships between states and the structure of the system. The nature of capitalism, it is argued, implies that states are driven by economic, not just military, goals. It also means that the international system contains significant injustices in terms of the distribution and exploitation of global resources and that the existence of vast disparities in national wealth is an inevitable by-product of the economic system. Some benefit from this system, some do not. Globalists see capitalism as explaining the creation of states, not just their behaviour (see Chapter 12).

Second, globalists are interested in states, international organisa-tions, NGOs and so on as mechanisms of domination by which some states, classes or elites benefit from the capitalist system at the expense of others. Specifically they are concerned with the development and maintenance of dependency between the 'North' or developed indus-trialised states and the less developed 'South'. They argue that these states are backward not, as is suggested by liberal pluralists, because they are poorly integrated into the global capitalist system, but because they play an integral role in it as providers of cheap labour, raw materials and markets.

Third, globalists, even more than pluralists, emphasise the critical importance of economic factors. Realists by contrast subordinate eco-nomic factors to those of a political nature. Pluralists see them as of equal importance, but dependent on the issue in question. Although pluralists share the globalist focus on the importance of international political economy, they differ fundamentally in terms of explanation. Pluralists see policy outcomes as a result of complex interdependence and elaborate internal and international bargaining sequences. Plural-ists therefore stress the actual and potential international cooperation in the system and the importance of international institutions for the moderation and resolution of international disputes. Globalists see policy as the outcome of a country's predetermined place in the international capitalist system. The emphasis is therefore upon conflict in the system, and international organisations are seen as instruments of capitalist domination.

21.5 IR theory after the Cold War: challenges to Realism

In the period 1939–89 realism retained a dominant position in the study of international relations. It was challenged during the 1970s by pluralism and globalism, but re-emerged more vigorously in the 1980s as neo-realism.

This revival was partly the result of the publication of Kenneth Waltz's influential neo-realist text, *Theory of International Politics*,[16] and partly the result of the centrality of national security issues brought about by the outbreak of the 'Second Cold War', the period (essentially the first half of the 1980s) when superpower relations relapsed into hostile confrontation after the period of détente during the 1970s.

But realism and neo-realism were found wanting by the end of the Cold War. Realists did not predict the USSR's voluntary retreat from Empire, the deep disarmament reductions characteristic of the late 1980s and early 1990s, the democratic revolutions that swept the world or the surge of international cooperation, integration and change. Realists in general and neo-realists in particular paid little attention to developments within states. They were interested in relations between states, explained in terms of military competition. The changes within the Soviet Union under Gorbachev, which led to the end of the Cold War and the collapse of Communism in Europe, therefore took them completely by surprise. A theory which could neither predict nor explain such a fundamental event in modern history was clearly inadequate. The realists' generalisations appeared to fail when confronted by a radically new situation and also seemed ill-equipped to address the new issues dominating the post-Cold War international agenda, such as environmental problems, AIDS and the international drugs problem.[17]

Critics from all directions have called for a 'paradigm shift' in the study of international relations. Many argued that the idealist-pluralism which failed in the 1920s and 1930s was an idea whose time had finally come in the New World Order following the end of the Cold War.

This neo-idealism can be seen in the new emphasis given to the theory that democracy is a cause of peace. In the 1980s this thesis became prominent as a number of scholars, notably Michael Doyle, renewed interest in Kant's argument that the solution to world peace was the spread of 'republican' or democratic government. The Doyle thesis points to the fact that while democracies are no more or less warlike than other forms of government, democracies do not go to war with other democracies. Democracies fight dictatorships and military regimes, but not democracies. Therefore, as democracy becomes more universal as a form of government, international war should decline in proportion. Other ideas prominent in the interwar idealist era are also regaining prominence. Self-determination is back on the agenda again, and the state is on the defensive as a result of the growth of economic interdependence and globalisation. Devolution of power both upward and downward from the state level has become a feature of international politics in the 1990s. The idealist insistence that 'people matter' appears more convincing in the wake of the events in Eastern Europe in 1989–90.

Moreover, as the American President Woodrow Wilson predicted in the immediate aftermath of the First World War, but Realists deny, the motives of states *can* change as those of the USSR clearly did after 1985. Disarmament has moved from being a propaganda slogan to being recognised as a viable path to common security. The post-1985 disarmament by the superpowers would not have happened if international politics had operated in the way that realists insisted was inevitable – military confrontation between the dominant powers of the era. The economic underpinnings of international behaviour are now also receiving increasing attention from IR scholars. International political economy is arguably the fastest growing area of study within the general field of IR. In addition international organisations have been rediscovered as effective actors. Many states see their interests as best served by a partial pooling of sovereignty. Support for strengthening international law has grown visibly and human rights have become a much more important political issue than they were during the Cold War. In this sense it could be argued that morality has returned as an issue in statecraft, having long been marginalised by realism.

21.6   Post-Positivist approaches

From the 1980s onwards three further approaches emerged as important for the study of IR. Although they differ significantly they can all be described as 'post-positivist' or 'social constructivist'. The three approaches are critical theory, postmodernism and feminism.

21.6.1   Critical theory

Critical theory emerged from the Marxist 'Frankfurt School' in the 1930s, particularly with the work of Max Horkheimer and Theodore Adorno. It was only in the 1980s, however, that it became an important critique of prevailing theories of international relations. As far as its application to IR is concerned, the distinctive feature of critical theory is its commitment to human emancipation as the goal of both the study and practice of politics.

Much of traditional IR theory, particularly realism and liberal pluralism, can be termed 'problem-solving'. It essentially accepts the existing political and economic order and seeks merely to make it operate more effectively. Critical theory in contrast rejects the prevailing order and seeks to bring about radical change in order to eliminate as far as possible the constraints on human freedom by breaking with existing forms of injustice. It fundamentally challenges prevailing realist and liberal pluralist interpretations of such central concepts as security, development, justice and so on.

Unlike realists, critical theorists do not believe that a 'value-neutral' theory is possible. Whereas traditional theory tended to see the world as consisting of 'facts' waiting to be discovered, critical theorists argue that facts are socially produced outcomes of human action. The world is the product of human ideas and actions, and prevailing ideas and social conditions are, therefore, always capable of being altered by human actions.

The goal of critical theory is to bring international relations within the framework of the classical understanding of politics, the creation of a rational consensus between human beings which would allow progress towards a more humane and well ordered society. It attempts to do this by offering a critique of current institutions and practices, by stressing that they are time-bound rather than permanent features of political life, and by making individual human beings rather than states the object for which security in all its forms should be pursued.

21.6.2   Postmodernism

The postmodernist approach to international relations is not an easy one to define, though there are a number of theorists who are self-professed postmodernists. Postmodernists are suspicious of any theory or approach based on an assumption that it is possible to uncover 'truth'. Postmodernists are therefore suspicious of both critical theory and feminism because both assume that it is possible to determine foundations upon which to base moral judgements. Where postmodernism has made a useful contribution to thinking about international relations is in its emphasis upon the way in which knowledge and truth is in large part created by existing power relations rather than existing outside or beyond such relationships. Postmodernist analysis therefore focuses upon deconstructing assumptions and understandings in order to bring out alternative interpretations and thereby expose the way in which certain interpretations have been given preference in order to serve the purposes of the dominant groups in society. The postmodernist approach provides an effective critique for other theories of international relations.

21.6.3   Feminism

The basis of the feminist critique of IR theory is the argument that there is a fundamental difference between the way that men and women experience, and therefore see, the world. IR is perceived as having been overwhelmingly constructed by men working with models of human behaviour based on a purely male perspective. Because knowledge and theory are built on experience, by being so gender-biased IR has only drawn on a partial set of sources to build its models of 'reality' and its key concepts such as sovereignty, security, development and power.

Because women were absent from the classical texts of political theory, the discipline of IR is founded upon a gender-biased set of definitions and theories of knowledge. This has helped produce an academic field which places too much emphasis on the idea of war and international anarchy, and a tradition of foreign policy practice that emphasises competition and fear.

The use of the term 'gender' is important. It is not the biological or physical differences between males and females that are important, it is the social construction of 'masculinity' that is crucial. Gender in this context refers to the systematic social construction of masculinity and femininity, and its influence on the theory and practice of international relations.

The issues which have traditionally been given priority in international relations are those with which men have a particular affinity. Feminist IR scholars argue that gender bias does in fact crucially affect the way that the world is perceived, interpreted and organised, particularly when it concerns issues of 'international security'. Feminists therefore attempt to bring out the hidden assumptions about gender in IR and demonstrate that what scholars claim to be universal often turns out to be true only of males.

Given that most state leaders are male this may still be a reasonable reflection of reality, but it is important to study how the fact of them being male affects their views and the decision-making in which they take part. The broad term 'feminist' disguises the fact that there is a wide variety of different approaches within the feminist school. These range from 'essentialists' to liberals. Essentialists believe that the differences between genders are not just the result of social constructions and cultural indoctrination, but that there is in fact a core biological essence to being male or female which is particularly strongly reflected in different attitudes towards independence and connection. They argue, therefore, that an international system based on feminist principles would place more emphasis on the interdependence of states than on their autonomy, would give human rights priority over sovereignty and would seek foundations for stable peace in the minds of women rather than of men.

'Liberal feminists' in contrast see the 'essential' differences between male and female as being trivial and seek merely to gain equality of opportunity for women within the current international system. They criticise the current exclusion of women from positions of power within international relations, but do not believe that including women would fundamentally change the nature of the international system.

Women theorists, even when they have little else in common, offer similar definitions of power which differ substantially from the realist understanding of power as domination. Hannah Arendt, for example, defines power as the human ability to act in concert or to take action in connection with others who share similar concerns. Feminist scholars portray power as a relationship of mutual enablement. Thinking about power in this multidimensional sense might help us think more constructively about the potential for cooperation and not simply about conflict in international relations.

Scholars of international relations are still seeking a convincing overall theory of the subject. It may be that such a theory is not even possible. The reality at present is that no such theory exists, only a number of partial theories, each with their own strengths and weaknesses. Yet in many ways such theoretical pluralism has a virtue of its own.

How states and other international actors conduct their relations with one another is to a large extent a reflection of prevailing national and international attitudes, norms and values. These will change over time in the way that, for example, attitudes towards slavery and imperialism have changed in the past two hundred years. The nature of the 'reality' being studied is therefore not constant and the study of the subject must naturally evolve to reflect altered perceptions, indeed may even play a part in bringing about those changes of perceptions. Theoretical pluralism is valuable in that it reduces the danger that the study of the subject will become locked into a misleading reading of international reality.

Notes

1. K. Deutsch, *The Analysis of International Relations* (Englewood Cliffs, NJ: Prentice Hall, 1968), p. v.
2. K. Waltz, *Theory of International Politics* (New York: McGraw-Hill, 1979).
3. R. Aron, *Peace and War* (London: Weidenfeld & Nicolson, 1966).
4. A. Watson, *The Evolution of International Society* (London: Routledge, 1992).
5. H. Morgenthau, *Politics Among Nations* 5th edn (New York: Knopf, 1978).
6. B. Russett and H. Starr, *World Politics: The Menu for Choice* (San Francisco: W. H. Freeman, 1981), pp. 294–324.
7. For a useful survey see, T. Knutsen, *A History of International Relations Theory* (Manchester: Manchester University Press, 1992).
8. F. Parkinson, *The Philosophy of International Relations* (London: Sage, 1977).
9. J. A. Vasquez, *Classics of International Relations* 2nd edn (Englewood Cliffs, NJ: Prentice Hall, 1990), pp. 16–39.
10. H. Morgenthau, *Politics Among Nations* 5th edn (New York: Knopf, 1978).
11. A key early example of this interpretation was given in R. O. Keohane and J. Nye, *Transnational Relations and World Politics* (Princeton, NJ: Princeton University Press, 1971).
12. J. W. Burton, *World Society* (Cambridge: Cambridge University Press, 1972), pp. 35–45.
13. R. Little, 'The growing relevence of pluralism', in S. Smith, K. Booth and M. Zalewski (eds), *International Theory: Positivism and Beyond* (Cambridge: Cambridge University Press, 1996), p. 74.
14. M. Zacher and R. Matthew, 'Liberal international theory: common threads, divergent strands', in C. Kegley Jr (ed.), *Controversies in International Relations Theory* (New York: St Martin's Press, 1995), p. 117.
15. I. Wallenstein, 'The rise and future demise of the world capitalist system', in R. Little and M Smith (eds), *Perspectives on World Politics*, 2nd edn (London: Routledge, 1991).
16. K. Waltz, *Theory of International Politics* (New York: McGraw-Hill, 1979).
17. For a survey of the new agenda see, W. C. Olson (ed.), *Theory and Practice of International Relations*, 9th edn (London: Prentice Hall, 1994).

Questions

1. What are the main principles of the realist approach to international relations and how do they differ from those of the pluralist approach?
2. How do post-positivist approaches to International Relations differ from earlier approaches?

22

The structure of the global system

Planet Earth is currently divided politically into nearly 200 states. The most striking feature of the international system is that it is apparently anarchic – there is no sovereign authority able to make rules and enforce them in the way that the legislative and executive branches of government do at the state level. The anarchy is not in fact complete – there is a body of international law which most states obey most of the time and there are supranational bodies which have authority over the state in certain policy domains. Nor does the existence of the international anarchy rule out international cooperation, shared international norms or explicit rules of behaviour. Nevertheless the international anarchy is in many ways the defining characteristic and central problem of the state system.[1]

22.1 The state as international actor

Despite the emergence of trends threatening its authority, the state remains at this point in history the key actor in international relations. Sovereignty and territoriality provide the state with major advantages over non-state actors in the international environment.

The state is a geographically bounded entity governed by a central authority that has the ability to make laws, rules and decisions and to enforce them within its own boundaries (see Chapter 3). A state is also a legal entity recognised under international law as the fundamental decision-making unit of the international legal system. Whether they are citizens of that particular state or not, the inhabitants of a state are subject to its laws.

In contrast to the state, a 'nation' need not be either geographically bounded or legally defined. A nation is a collectivity whose people view themselves as being components of a distinct cultural or political entity (see Chapter 12).

Human beings have always formed themselves into groups, a process intimately linked with the act of identification. Human individuals tend to identify with groups, and to give their loyalty to them. They will act to maintain the character, security and survival of such groups.[2] For the most part this process can be seen in a positive light since it helps bond the people of a collectivity so that group norms can operate which maintain order, and enables a sense of solidarity to emerge, encouraging people to give sympathy and help to members of the community who suffer misfortune. There is also, however, a negative side. The act of identifying with particular groups has the effect of distancing people from those who are not included in their own groups. It creates insiders and outsiders.

Nations consist of groupings of people who consider themselves to be ethnically, culturally or linguistically related in a way that defines their similarities to those who share that particular identification and distinguishes from those who do not. The very features that unite the people of one group or nation divides them from others. This creates the danger that if the feelings of nationalism or particularism are very strongly held, foreigners who cannot share this loyalty will be looked upon with suspicion or even hatred. Nationalism and patriotism are positive forces to the extent that they enable an identification and sympathy with fellow citizens. They are negative forces to the extent that they raise boundaries, making it difficult to extend the same sympathy to the rest of the world's population or to particular sections of it.

Prior to the nineteenth century, the nation-state in its modern form was not seen as the normal or appropriate level for peoples to organise themselves. Historically, a variety of alternative forms of organisation were more common, such as sub-national states as in ancient Greece and medieval Italy, Germany and Spain, as well as in India and China during various periods. At the other extreme were multi-national Empires such as the Roman Empire which survived for several centuries and the Byzantine Empire which lasted for a thousand years, both leaving a lasting legacy in Europe.[3] In addition, there were important non-state focuses of international loyalty such as Christendom and Islam. Since the late eighteenth century, 'nationalism' has been the main spiritual and political force cementing all other elements of statehood and the so-called 'nation-state' has become the fundamental unit of the international system. Despite their common association, however, the two concepts of 'state' and 'nation' are quite distinct and in reality the genuine nation-state, the state whose borders are identical to those of the nation, is a very rare phenomenon indeed.

The term 'nation-state' reflects the growing convergence in the twentieth century between the two terms. Prior to the eighteenth century nations were seen as cultural entities and there was no suggestion that a relationship existed between such communities and the sovereign state. It was during the nineteenth and twentieth centuries that the state became nationalised. Countries are now commonly referred to as nation-states even though in most instances they are not. In Africa, for example, most states have borders which simply reflect the old colonial boundaries and bear no relation to the ethnic or linguistic features of the populations through which they run. Such states are not nation-states. In most cases the governments of these new entities have sought to use symbols to attempt to create a sense of identification with the new collectivity – to create a Kenyan or Nigerian 'nation' for example. In a general sense the common unifying factor is 'culture'. Culture can be defined as 'any group's distinct collective means of interpreting and interacting with the world and each other in a given environment'.[4] Many factors can help to reinforce a common national identification, for example language (Portugal, Italy), religion (Israel, Pakistan), or geography (Iceland, Australia). For most countries, numerous factors apply.

In practice so-called nation-states come in four important varieties.

1. *The classic nation-state.* An example of this is Japan, where the boundaries of state and nation are identical. The state is a political expression of the nation and the bonds between the two are extremely strong.

2. *The state-nation.* In contrast to this is the idea of the 'state-nation'. This emerges when the state acts so as to create a sense of nationhood where none previously existed, as was the case of most African states after independence. Governments have deemed this necessary when the racial, linguistic, religious or geographical background to the state does not itself provide any obvious basis for group identification. Few states actually fulfil the criteria of 'nation-state'. In the mid-1980s only one-third of the world's states were homogenous in the sense that 90 per cent or more of their populations belonged to a single ethnic group.[5]

3. *The part-nation state.* There are a number of examples of another variant, the part-nation state. In this case a state's population may be almost entirely composed of members of a single nation, but the state is not the only one composed of this nation. For example, both Austria and Germany are German nation-states. North and South Korea similarly are both Korean nation-states. This situation can produce political pressures to unite the nation in a single state, or conversely can trigger an integrative process as the government attempts to legitimise its own state. Germany

saw examples of both processes in the three decades prior to reunification in 1991. The German Democratic Republic (East Germany) sought to build up a distinctive identity, notably through heavy subsidies for the 'national' sporting teams. This effort was ultimately unsuccessful and the GDR disappeared when it was absorbed into the German Federal Republic (West Germany) which had always been committed to the goal of reunification of the two Germanies.

4. *The multinational state.* The fourth category is the multinational state, where a state contains two or more complete nations within its boundaries. Britain, Canada and the former Soviet Union are examples of this type of state. How strong the pressures for separate statehood are within these states will depend on how successful the political system is in accommodating the pressures created by a strong sense of national identity among the component nations.[6]

A final, critical aspect of statehood in the contemporary system is the concept of sovereignty. For some, sovereignty is simply the fundamental legal basis of international society. For others it is an obsolete concept and is to blame for many of the problems of the modern world. Certainly sovereignty expresses an important political reality, but in the contemporary system it is far from being an absolute reality.

Sovereignty means supreme authority which recognises no superior and beyond which there is no legal appeal. Internal and external sovereignty were two of the key principles of modern international relations which emerged as a result of the 1648 Treaty of Westphalia. Internal sovereignty is the pre-eminence of the government against the claims of other centres of power within the state, while the associated principle of external sovereignty means independence from power centres outside the state. Theoretically, sovereign governments are in full control both of domestic and foreign policy, though in reality this is not always the case. Czechoslovakia's sovereignty was compromised through its domination by the Soviet Union between 1968 and 1989, while Panama's sovereignty is circumscribed by its domination by the United States. Moreover some states, such as those which belong to the European Union, have voluntarily limited their sovereignty in certain areas 'Sovereignty is now more of a concept than a reality.'[7]

The concept of sovereignty is important because it is the foundation of the conception of the state system as being an international anarchy. The assumption that the international system is essentially anarchic underpins most theorising about international relations. Indeed, both the realist and neo-realist schools attempted systematically to explain all the important behavioural characteristics of international relations, particularly the inevitability of balances of power in terms of the effects of the international anarchy.[8]

Despite the dominance of the nation-state idea in international relations for two centuries, its utility has come to be increasingly questioned. Some groups see the nation-state as the cause of war. Because ethnic population distribution does not always follow political borders, substantial ethnic minorities exist in many states. In a world of 'nation-states' such groups often feel that their human and political rights are not fully catered for by the dominant group. This can lead to violent secessionist movements or to irredentist foreign policies as existing states attempt to expand their borders to embrace ethnic groups separated by existing borders.[9] Other critics of the state argue that processes of 'globalisation' are rendering the state increasingly obsolescent.

22.2 Globalisation

During the 1970s and 1980s increasing attention was drawn to trends of internationalisation and interdependence. The states of the world were being drawn, to varying degrees, into a steadily more complex set of interrelationships in military, political, economic, technological, cultural and other fields. The states remained essentially distinct entities, but their interconnections were rapidly multiplying.

These trends were most notable in the economic realm and particularly in relations between the developed states. Growing interdependence meant growing sensitivity, in many cases vulnerability, to events taking place around the globe. Many of these changes appeared to threaten the place of the state as the central actor in international relations.

The most significant challenges to the state as international actor can be seen as falling into five categories – economic interdependence, advances in military technologies, transnational movements, international organisations and internal fragmentation.

22.2.1 Economic interdependence

Interdependence means 'interconnectedness between nations and other actors in the international political economy conditioned by trade, aid, finance and investment.'[10]

Economic interdependence has seen historical policies of economic self-sufficiency abandoned in favour of a global trading regime that allows market forces to identify low-cost producers of products in demand. Goods and services may be obtained more cheaply elsewhere than they can be produced domestically. Moreover, few finished products are nowadays manufactured in a single country. The Ford Motor Company, for example, produces vehicles manufactured from components from twenty different countries. While the impact of economic interdependence is crucial, however, it is important to remember that the interaction between the international economy and international politics is a two-way process. The political system shapes the economic system and political concerns often shape economic policy.[11]

Economic globalisation implies 'the existence of a unified global economy which has a dynamic beyond the interaction of separate domestic economies'.[12] It is in this category that the statistical evidence for the globalisation effect is most convincing. For example, foreign direct investment grew at twice the rate of Gross Domestic Product for the OECD countries (the leading developed countries) during the 1960s. During the 1980s it grew at four times the speed of GNP growth.[13] More than half of the world's goods and services are now produced as a result of commercial firms operating on a global scale.[14]

The image of the economic globalisation process is of multinational corporations that have become placeless networks of economic power. MNCs are seen as being able to hold governments to ransom through their ability to move capital easily between regions and base activities where labour and other costs are lowest. Yet the image of globalisation affecting all areas of economic activity is an illusion. Certainly for a limited number of major companies there are elements of their economic activity that are significantly globalised, for example product design, finance and advertising, but production itself is still largely national or regional.

In the developing world globalisation effects have been significantly different to those experienced in the developed states. Rather than benefiting, many developing countries have been impoverished by becoming part of the global economy. From a developing world perspective, globalisation is nothing new, just another form of neo-colonialism. The penetration of national economies by powerful outside forces is something that these states have long been familiar with, but globalisation has not yet fully affected the majority of developing nations.

Even in the developed world the record is mixed. Multinational corporations have not broken with their national roots entirely, and the influence of historical links remains strong. Only around 2 per cent of the membership of the boards of major American corporations are not citizens of the United States.[15] While production is managed on a global scale by some corporations, this remains the exception. For most economic indicators, the origins remain national rather than global.

22.2.2 Advances in military technology

Similarly, military developments threaten the future of the nation-state. Nuclear weapons mean that not even the most powerful state on Earth can provide an absolute guarantee of security for its citizens. Even modern conventional weapons are now enormously more powerful than those used during the Second World War. The protection of its citizens is one of the central purposes of the state. Developments threatening states' ability to perform this role effectively thereby threaten the utility of the state as a form of political organisation.

The effects of globalisation have not gone unopposed. Much of the international violence since the end of the Cold War can be put down to a revival of ethnic and national 'ideologies', to some extent a reaction against the unifying pressures of globalisation. The Soviet Union, Yugoslavia, Georgia and Czechoslovakia have all fragmented since 1990, all but the latter doing so violently. This suggests that local identities retain a powerful loyalty that has not yet been smothered by globalisation and, indeed, may be reinvigorated by it.

The growth of 'identity politics' as a reaction to globalisation is one of the key factors that explain the security paradox of the era. The past few decades have seen a marked fall in the incidence of interstate war, i.e. war between legally constituted state actors in the international system. Since 1945 most wars have not been of this type: they have been civil wars, often with some external intervention.

22.2.3 Cultural globalisation

Globalisation can be seen as a process by which the human race is progressively incorporated into a single global society. In this respect there is a marked similarity between ideas of globalisation and of Westernisation. Globalisation can be seen in terms of modernity, as an aspect of the breakdown of traditional societies and the spread of key Western cultural concepts and forms of political organisation.

The spread of liberal democracy and capitalism since the end of the Cold War can be seen as examples of a more general phenomenon, the spread of ideas. In addition, there is another aspect of globalisation which relates to the increasing tendency for issues to be perceived as being global in scope and therefore requiring policy responses that act at the global level. In the latter category can be placed issues such as the environmental effects of global warming and the management of international regimes that form part of the 'global commons' such as the deep oceans and outer space. There is also a cluster of issues which, while not global in the same sense as the above, are nevertheless transboundary in their effects and which require responses operating at a global rather than a national level. Issues that fall into this category include the control of certain pandemic diseases such as AIDS, large-scale pollution problems such as those caused by acid rain and the build-up of atmospheric CFCs.

The state is also being challenged by the emergence of transnational movements and belief-systems. Though many have compromised with nationalism to some extent, religion and ideology continue to have an appeal, often crossing national boundaries. This feature can be seen not just in terms of developments which might seem threatening. Where religious faith or ideological commitment mean that an individual cannot give her or his undivided loyalty to a state, national security can be threatened. Certainly if this feeling is held by a large proportion of the population the state will feel genuinely menaced. In a more benign way the same forces can be seen at work in phenomena such as the international environmental movement. Again, this calls upon individuals to give their loyalties to ideals that cross boundaries, and to consider seeing their own state as being 'in the wrong' on key issues.

22.2.4   International organisations

International organisations challenge the state to the extent that they embody supranational objectives or carry the authority to impose policies upon states. The European Union is an example of the former, the International Monetary Fund (IMF) an example of the latter. Many of these organisations, such as the IMF, are intergovernmental bodies which are instruments of national purpose. They pose no fundamental threat to the concept of the state as such. Other bodies such as the European Union are a different matter. The EU's commitment to an 'ever closer union' is a long-term threat to the sovereignty of the states who are members.

Many of these trends have gone so far that commentators no longer feel that the terms 'transnational' or 'interdependence' really describe the phenomenon and they prefer the term 'globalisation'. Globalisation refers to processes in which social relations are increasingly unaffected by the traditional constraints of distance and international borders (see Chapter 5). What this means is a vision of the world where human social activities are decreasingly governed by the existence of national borders. It does not mean that these borders are no longer of any significance, but rather that they are far less so and that the world is increasingly becoming a relatively borderless social sphere.

This process is not a uniform one. The degree of interconnectedness and the impact of globalising trends are far more evident in the developed world than among the poorer developing states. Efforts to strengthen the power of the national state are most evident in the developing world, where sovereignty and independence are in many cases comparatively recent achievements and are therefore vigorously defended.

Examples of the networks of flows created by globalisation can be seen in many areas of activity. A familiar one is the products of the revolution in communications technology. The World Wide Web, e-mail, fax and satellite-linked telephone communications have produced a world where telecommunications are unaffected by the existence of international borders.

Another aspect which has received considerable attention in the past decade is the ecological question. The problems associated with rapid environmental change and the damaging impact of human activities on the natural ecology are issues which at least require regional rather than national responses, but which in many cases, such as the problem of global warming, require a response at the global level if they are to have any possibility of success.

As noted already, both the economic and military realms show clear evidence of globalising trends. Manufacturing is increasingly spread across many countries, while the international financial and stock markets have become borderless markets operating twenty-four hours a day and posing enormous problems for states attempting to maintain control over key areas of their national economies. Similarly in a world monitored from orbiting satellites and menaced by intercontinental ballistic missiles, the military leaderships in major states such as the USA view the world as a single strategic domain.

The globalisation of trade, security and communications has itself contributed to the globalisation of political and ethical norms. Democracy and human rights are no longer aspirations for the populations of the developed 'European' nations, but are shared by those of most societies. Overall there is a global awareness of these political, economic, environmental and social issues not present a generation ago. The global human rights movement expresses the belief that all human beings, in every society without exception, are entitled to the same basic rights simply by virtue of being human.[16]

Globalisation is a critical development for the study of international relations. IR theory has long been based upon the concepts of 'Sovereignty' and 'international anarchy'. Globalisation casts doubt over the future validity of these concepts and weakens their current claims. Sovereignty, whatever its continuing centrality in partisan debate, no longer retains the meaning that it had fifty years ago. The concept is premised upon a bounded, territorial state system, increasingly threatened by social and technological change.

This poses questions for the issue of international governance. Many of the processes described above are responsive to democratic controls or oversight at the national level, but this is not the case at the global level. The so-called 'marketisation of governance' and the rise of technocratic government by bodies such as the IMF pose questions of democratic control which have yet to be effectively addressed. Finding new forms of democracy to address these developments is an important task for political scientists.

It is also possible to speak of the globalisation of democracy. Democratisation in the past twenty-five years has been profoundly influenced by external forces, both in terms of the spread of ideas and in terms of political pressures exerted by external powers. Democratisation has been helped in many cases by factors such as the human rights conditions attached to offers of aid by developed democratic states.[17]

Yet the political pressures produced by economic globalisation do not operate in a single direction. The structural adjustment policies which Western-dominated international economic institutions such as the IMF have imposed on many states in the post-Communist and developing states (the former 'second' and 'third' worlds), have put enormous strains upon the processes of democratic transition and consolidation. In states such as Russia, the West has accepted reversals of democratic progress in the hope that a more authoritarian democracy will survive the unpopularity produced by a painful economic transition to late twentieth-century capitalism. In doing so the West has accepted that while democracy may be triumphant world-wide, it can take many different forms.

22.3 Influence distribution

Perhaps the most critical systemic characteristic of international relations is the way influence is distributed in the system. Power can be understood as the ability to influence outcomes (see Chapters 2 and 21). The physical components of a state's 'power', its natural resources, population, economic strength, military capabilities and so on, contribute to the ability of a government to affect international outcomes so that they meet the national or governmental interests of that particular regime.

States can exercise influence with a variety of instruments, most notably military and economic ones. The latter is most effective and influential outside of crisis situations. It enables one state to exert pressure on another for various purposes. In crises where security issues are involved, the military component of national power may come to the fore because it is seen as a way of rapidly and decisively effecting outcomes in a particular direction.

One traditional way of analysing international relations has been in terms of the distribution of military power between the leading state actors in the system. There are differing theories about the significance of power distribution. For example, balance-of-power theorists see equilibrium as an ideal situation. States will react to the efforts of others to alter the prevailing distribution of power and in doing so will create a certain level of international stability. One major debate between balance-of-power theorists in IR has been on the issue of whether bipolarity or multipolarity produces greater international stability, that is whether a system dominated by two 'superpowers' is more stable than one in which there are more than five great powers.

Kenneth Waltz makes the case for bipolarity. He argues that where there are no peripheries, as in the case with only two world powers because both are involved everywhere, there is a solid and determinate balance. Competition is intensive, as well as extensive, since each power is concerned about even minor changes to the balance of power. There is a tendency for the states in the system to develop schemes for coping with recurrent crises. With preponderant power, minor shifts in the power balance will not be decisive. Both states are already so powerful that a minor change makes no real difference.

Critics have argued, however, that with recurring crises and constant contact the danger of war is always very high. Supporters of multipolarity argue that there will be greater opportunities for interaction in a multipolar world, which increases the prospects of international cooperation. With mulitipolarity, cross-cutting loyalties will exist. A state that is an opponent on one issue might be an ally on another. Not every issue will be perceived as a zero-sum game in which one country's gain must mean another country's loss. Multipolarity diminishes the amount of attention paid to other states and conflict situations. By thus limiting preoccupation with any one conflict, the total amount of violence may be reduced. A multipolar system will also hold down the arms race. Not every increase in power by other states will be seen as directed against oneself, but may be seen as a reaction to one of the many other states in the system. Multipolarity also provides mediators who can help resolve conflicts.

Those who favour a balance-of-power system tend to support multipolarity as a necessary prerequisite for its successful operation. There must be an opportunity to shift alliances so that threats to the peace can be blocked by new constellations of power. Historical studies indicate that what might be called 'unipolar' systems where there is one overwhelmingly dominant power are the most stable. Bipolar systems tend to have less frequent though more prolonged wars. Multipolar systems produce more violence, more countries at war and more casualties. Yet since the emergence of the modern state system in the seventeenth century, the states within the system have strongly resisted attempts to move towards a unipolar system.

In this characterisation of the system, 'polarity' is defined overwhelmingly in military terms. In the contemporary international environment, however, there is no longer one basic structure that dominates the international system, for power and influence are no longer solely related to military strength. The structure of global power has become disaggregated to such an extent that there are almost as many hierarchical structures as there are issues.

For example:

1. The USA dominates at the strategic nuclear level, with Russia remaining important. There are another three declared nuclear weapon states, Britain, China and France, but America and Russia remain overwhelmingly important. Their nuclear weapons arsenals dwarf those of the other three states. Yet although Russia maintains the same number of strategic nuclear weapons as the United States, the latter retains a superiority in terms of the quality and reliability of the nuclear systems it has available. Paradoxically, this overwhelming superiority is virtually worthless since the weapons exist only to deter attacks on each state by the other, attacks which none of the nuclear states have any desire to launch. Both states are currently in the process of dramatically reducing their nuclear weapons stockpiles.

2. The USA/EU/Japan dominate the international economic system. In terms of global trade and economic activity the key actors are not the same as in the strategic military sphere. Russia is not a key player, whereas Japan, which is not a key military power, is a crucial actor on the economic scene. Militarily the European Union is of little or no significance at present, but it plays a central role in the international economy.

3. In energy questions OPEC and OAPEC members are crucial. The Arab states are not crucial actors in a global military sense or in terms of the general international economy, but the vital position of the states comprising the Organisation of Arab Petroleum

Exporting Countries gives them a powerful influence which they would not otherwise have.

Foreign policy-makers therefore face a bewildering array of hierarchies at both the global and regional level. Useful allies on some issues can become unhelpful opponents on others. For example, Britain and the United States work closely together as military allies within NATO, but found themselves on opposite sides of bitter disputes over trade during the GATT negotiations between the European Union and the United States.

Consensus in the international environment is challenged by conflict between ideas of order and of change. There is a constant struggle between those who demand change and those who see their interests as best preserved by the maintenance of the status quo. These ideas sometimes seem mutually exclusive. For some states almost any change is seen as being subversive of order; others see the institutions of international society as designed to favour certain states, or types of states, to the permanent exclusion of others. Changing aspects of the system to suit one's own interests in the midst of an environment full of other states attempting to defend and promote their own interests is the task of foreign policy.

Notes

1. R. J. Leiber, *No Common Power: Understanding International Relations*, 3rd edn (New York: HarperCollins, 1995), pp. 3–14.
2. B. Russett and H. Starr, *World Politics: The Menu for Choice* (San Francisco: W. H. Freeman, 1981), p. 43.
3. An excellent introduction to the state forms and state systems which preceded the modern era is Adam Watson, *The Evolution of International Society* (London: Routledge, 1992).
4. W. Nester, *International Relations: Geopolitical and Geoeconomic Conflict and Cooperation* (New York: HarperCollins, 1995).
5. Ibid., p. 69.
6. B. Buzan, *People, States and Fear*, 2nd edn (Boulder, Colo.: Lynne Rienner, 1991), pp. 69–82.
7. Nester, *International Relations* p. 3.
8. M. Sheehan, *The Balance of Power: History and Theory* (London: Routledge, 1996).
9. W. S. Jones, *The Logic of International Relations*, 7th edn (New York: Harper Collins, 1991), pp. 382–88.
10. D. Balaam and M. Veseth, *Introduction to International Political Economy* (Upper Saddle River, NJ: Prentice-Hall, 1996).
11. J. E. Spero, *The Politics of International Economic Relations*, 4th edn (London: Unwin Hyman, 1990), p. 4.
12. C. Bretherton, 'Introduction', in C. Bretherton and G. Ponton, (eds), *Global Politics* (Oxford: Blackwell, 1996), p. 6.

13. J. Howells and M. Wood, 'The global dynamics of production and technology: new challenges', in U. Muldur and R. Petrella (eds), *The European Community and the Globalisation of Technology and the Economy: Final Report*, EUR 15150 EN (Brussels: Commission of the European Communities, 1994), p. 4.

14. J. Stopford and S. Strange, *Rival States, Rival Firms: Competition for World Market Shares* (Cambridge: Cambridge University Press, 1991), p. 4.

15. M. Svetlicic, 'Challenges of globalisation and regionalisation in the world economy', *Global Society*, vol. 10, no. 2, 1996, p. 111.

16. S. Brown, *New Forces, Old Forces and the Future of World Politics* (New York: Harper Collins, 1995), p. 217.

17. W. Oguyi et al., *Democratic Theory and Practice in Africa* (London: Curry, 1988).

Questions

1. Discuss, using examples, the differences between a 'nation' and a 'state'.
2. What do you understand by the term 'globalisation'? How important is it for understanding contemporary international relations?

23

Foreign policy analysis

Because states are still currently the most important actors on the international stage, the processes by which they choose and execute their foreign policies remains an important part of the study of international relations. Foreign policy occurs at the meeting point of the state and its international environment, where influences arising in the international environment become influences in the domestic arena and where domestic politics produces outputs with an impact on external relations. It is what many people understand by the phrase 'international relations', that is political relations between the states of the world. In the modern world, however, things are not so clear-cut. The processes referred to as globalisation imply that it is no longer possible to speak of a clear distinction between foreign and domestic government policy.

23.1 Meaning of foreign policy

For some commentators the term 'foreign policy' refers to a clear set of attitudes towards the international environment and a vision of one's country's place in the world. This outlook assumes the existence of guiding principles which determine or at least significantly shape decisions on particular policy issues. This is what General de Gaulle meant when he accused the French Fourth Republic of not having a foreign policy. He did not mean that it had no relations with the outside world, rather he implied that those relations were not guided by a sense of what France's overarching aims in international politics should be.[1]

An alternative view sees foreign policy as simply the policies of governments obliged to react to external events. As a former British Foreign Secretary put it, 'foreign policy is just one damn thing after another', a view which sees governments as essentially concerned with domestic issues, but forced to react to events in the external environment.

Those who hold the first perspective tend to emphasise issues of war and peace and see foreign policy as involving the skilful use of a state's policy instruments – particularly diplomacy and military power – to help shape the international environment in ways that favour one's own state. Those who take the latter view see war and the use of military force as being rather exceptional events. They view international relations as a field of activity, a complex web of interactions in which all states are sensitive to each other to a greater or lesser extent. Much greater emphasis is placed upon trading relationships and the direction of the international economy. Policy issues relating to investments, aid, human rights, cultural policies and immigration are seen as highly important.

Because the Gaullist view focuses on a limited number of key issues and actors, it is easier to discern continuity and coherence in the pattern of international relations when military security is the point of reference. The broader interpretation sees a much larger number of groups influencing policy across a vast range of issues and the emphasis is far more upon compromise, accommodation and, to some extent, incoherence.

23.2 Nature of foreign policy

Foreign policy is closely interrelated with domestic policy, but it differs from the latter in one critical respect. As Northedge noted, 'domestic politics is social control through law, foreign policy is the use of political influence in order to induce other states to exercise their law-making power in a manner desired by the state concerned.'[2]

Foreign policy actors cannot rely on the authority structures of the state to ensure compliance with their wishes as can governments once their domestic policy becomes law. An Act of Parliament automatically obliges citizens of Britain to obey the new law. Foreign governments and citizens cannot simply be ordered in this way. They must be convinced, bribed or threatened to induce compliance. In international relations there is no settled constitutional order that a government can use to implement its policies. Foreign policies are executed through negotiation, persuasion, compromise or coercion and other states will cooperate only to the extent that their own interests or value systems dictate. In the same way that authority cannot be relied upon, the common ties of culture and history are usually absent. Those who implement foreign policy are dealing with issues on which their knowledge is inevitably more limited than is true of domestic issues and where their ability to control events is severely constrained, if indeed it exists at all.

James Rosenau has described this attempt to modify behaviour across national boundaries as perhaps the purest of all political acts. It requires a degree of manipulation of symbols that is unmatched in any other political situation. Northedge captures this fragility by suggesting that foreign policy bears the same relationship to the certainty of domestic policy that gliding does to power-driven flight or sailing a dinghy does to driving a motorboat.[3]

One difficulty produced by this complexity is that politicians attempting to understand other countries' political systems, with which they have no direct experience, will resort to analogies from domestic politics. Such analogies can be highly misleading. All politicians are culture-bound to some extent. Other societies have different historic cultures and traditions and it is a mistake to simply regard them as unnatural deviations from one's own.

Foreign and domestic policy do not exist in separate compartments. They are related products of the same leadership and domestic political system and will reflect similar purposes. Moreover, both foreign and domestic policy are conditioned by the same ideologies and cultural factors.

In addition it is a truism that foreign and domestic policies must be mutually supporting if they are to be successful. Sweden, for example, has long counted social spending as part of its defence efforts on the grounds that no country can be successfully defended if its population does not believe that it is a society worth protecting. Similarly, in an era of globalisation states seeking to generate employment cannot rely simply on national macroeconomic policies, they must work with other governments to create a favourable international environment. British interest rates are influenced as much by the actions of the German government as they are by the British.

In certain parts of the world the processes of globalisation and regional integration significantly soften the boundaries between domestic and foreign policy. Although there are important variations in the belief systems and value systems of states, globalisation has acted to create a growing similarity in perspectives on certain issues such as human rights. This does not apply to all states but influences an increasingly large proportion. In areas where regional integration or cooperation has become the norm, these pressures are particularly strong. Member states of the European Union are powerfully influenced by emergent common 'European' values, laws and policies.

Foreign policy analysis can be seen as a single process with the borders of states not being a fundamental divide. There is no sharp division between domestic and foreign policy and the flow of policy is a continuous process whereby domestic controversy complicates external relations and foreign actions feed back into national politics. In practice it is not always easy to draw a clear distinction between domestic politics and foreign policy – many important issues have crucial implications in both domains. For example, defence spending is clearly related to prevailing perceptions of international insecurity, but it will also be profoundly influenced by domestic political and economic considerations.

In almost all democratic states there is a widely held belief that foreign policy issues should be addressed in a somewhat different manner to domestic issues. There is a greater tendency to seek bipartisan agreement on issues and where possible it is felt that continuity should be ensured even when governments change.

There are a number of reasons why this is the case. In external relations a government speaks for the nation, or state, to the outside world. Attempts to undermine their policies in this area therefore affect not only the domestic credibility of a government, but also the international standing of the country itself. Oppositions are therefore more cautious on such issues, not wishing to be perceived as in some way disloyal or unpatriotic. It is also the case that many of the issues at stake in foreign policy relate strongly to perceptions that are fundamental to the very idea of a nation-state. National survival, either in a physical sense or in a less tangible cultural sense, is clearly affected by issues concerned with protection of the national territory and population from foreign threats and invasion and the control of boundaries to limit immigration and the importation of foreign goods or cultural influences. These kinds of questions may be deemed too fundamental to a population's national self-perception for them to be thought appropriate subjects for partisan debate and factional strife, though unless a state is ethnically and culturally homogeneous, domestic politics is likely to be influenced by differing internal perceptions of what constitutes the 'national' interest.

For these very reasons it has been traditional for foreign policy to be seen as largely a function of the executive branch of government. Hobbes argued that the right of making war and peace had to remain in the hands of the sovereign.[4] Even Locke, the great exponent of balanced constitutions, believed that foreign policy should remain the prerogative of the executive branch of government.

The external environment imposes other constraints. When governments conclude an international agreement or treaty, it is between states not governments. A treaty signed by the German government is deemed to commit Germany as a state, not just the Christian Democrat or Social Democrat government which has signed it. States would not conclude major agreements if they felt that they would be reversed every time the government changed in their partner's country. Thus the international community imposes an expectation that international agreements will outlive any particular signatory government, and governments often seek consensus with the opposition on these issues for that very reason. France and the United States have habitually sought consensus on major security policies in this way.

23.3 Major factors influencing policy

All international actors in theory have a vast range of objectives which they could choose to pursue. These will vary in terms of the scope, intensity and time period in which they are pursued and the resources which are allocated in an attempt to achieve them. Objectives are the 'ends' of foreign policy, though in practice such ends are merely the means to further ends. When Britain achieved its goal of joining the then European Economic Community in 1973, this was as a means of pursuing the additional goals of improving its economic performance and increasing its diplomatic influence.

Objectives can be categorised in a number of ways, for example short-term and long-term goals. Wendzel distinguishes between three types of objective: fundamental, middle-range and immediate.[5] A fundamental objective is the kind for which a state might be expected to make the maximum effort to achieve – the obvious fundamental objective is national survival. This can comprise two elements: the physical survival of the population, and the continuation of the effective sovereignty and political independence of the state, that is its ability to make independent decisions about domestic and foreign policy.

A second fundamental objective might be the defence of the territorial integrity of the state. States can lose territory and survive, as Finland did in 1940 and Japan in 1945, but states are usually highly sensitive to such losses which they may see as threatening their viability as a state. In 1938 Czechoslovakia was forced to give its western terrritories, the Sudentenland, to Germany. This cost Czechoslovakia its mountainous western border and the Maginot line style defences that had been constructed there. Without this area, the Czech government considered Czechoslovakia effectively undefendable and it was annexed by Hitler's Third Reich in 1939 without a fight.

A third objective often seen as fundamental is the protection of a country's belief system or ideology.

Although such fundamental objectives might be seen as the easiest to identify, a government may still experience difficulty in deciding what constitutes its fundamental goals. If it is a member of an alliance, for example, 'survival' might arguably encompass the survival of allies, not just oneself, as was the case with the NATO allies during the Cold War. In addition definitions of 'oneself' may change over time. At the start of the twentieth century Britain was committed to the defence of its Empire as a fundamental goal. By the middle of the century this was no longer the case and Britain was decolonising.

In the middle-range category can be placed political, material, ideological and prestige objectives. An example of a political objective would be an arms control agreement designed to endure for a number of years, such as the nuclear non-proliferation treaty. Material objectives are those that relate to economic growth and development, for example the creation of the European Economic Community in 1957 or the pursuit of IMF loans by the developing countries.

Ideological objectives relate to the spreading of a belief or value system. Examples include the foreign policy of the infant French republic after 1792, and that of Iran after the overthrow of the Shah in 1979. When President Wilson took the USA into the First World War, 'to make the world safe for democracy', he was pursuing an ideological objective.

Prestige is a very important consideration to statesmen. The British and French 'independent' nuclear deterrents exist primarily to enhance the prestige of those states. Prestige is increasingly measured in terms of levels of industrial development and scientific expertise and is reflected in the space programmes of France and India for example. In crises an important political skill is the ability to achieve objectives without seeming to humiliate the adversary.

Immediate objectives are those specific policies which are seen as appropriate for achieving other goals. Thus if a state's survival is seen as being threatened by poor economic performance, improving that performance will become a middle-range objective. The specific policy to bring this about may be the signing of a trade agreement.

The choice of a state's objectives is influenced by a wide range of factors, five important ones being as follows:

1. Domestic politics play a significant role, the importance of which varies according to the political structure of the state. It is influenced by such factors as the degree of bipartisanship traditional in the political system, the strength of party dogma and the influence of sectional interest groups such as farmers and big business. The needs of the political leadership will be relevant. It is not unknown for a goverment to play up an overseas crisis in order to divert attention from its domestic failures. In a democ-

racy it will be affected by the need to maintain support from the legislature or from the other coalition partners in the government. It may also be influenced by positions adopted by the print and electronic media. It can also be shaped by electoral cycles – difficult decisions may be postponed until after an election, while policies may be followed that are not truly in the national interest but are likely to win votes from particular ethnic groups within the electorate.

2. Public opinion is less influential on foreign policy than it is on domestic. The background political culture will be influential in helping to define the boundaries of what is acceptable policy, but on specific issues, populations tend to feel less involved and less knowledgeable on foreign policy issues than they do on domestic ones. This is a situation which most governments seek to maintain by denying their populations much of the information needed for informed assessment. The excessive secrecy surrounding foreign policy and the generally inadequate constitutional controls over it mean that public opinion asserts itself only sporadically.

3. Administrative influences tend to be more potent. In the modern world almost all government departments contribute to foreign policy-making to a greater or lesser extent. In the United States, for example, there are twenty-eight government departments, agencies and bureaux which have specific responsibilities in foreign affairs. Generally speaking, administrative influences work by limiting policy alternatives and tending to produce policies which represent the lowest common denominator of bureaucratic interest.

4. The international system, the external environment itself, acts as a source of both objectives and constraints. The constraints are in terms of alliance and treaty commitments, security threats of various kinds and the workings of the international economy. Systemic variables operate particularly strongly on the smaller and economically weaker states in the global system, who are relatively more dependent on the external environment for their economic well-being and political and military security.

5. The past acts both as a useful guide and as a major constraint. Some states have adhered to patterns of behavior over long periods. British governments over several centuries have shown a concern to keep the Low Countries out of the control of a major power and have shown a more general inclination to support the maintenance of a balance of power on the European continent.

    Yet the past can also be a constraint. The options for decision-makers may be limited by the past actions of their government or state. Commitments may have been made that are hard to break. In addition a country's historical experience influences the content of its leaders' perceptions. The Russian obsession with security is in large part a reflection of Russia's experience in having suffered three devastating foreign invasions in the past two centuries. Similarly China's tragic experiences at the hands of the imperialist Western powers in the nineteenth and early twentieth centuries continues to exercise an influence on Chinese attitudes to international issues.

Although all kinds of factors influence the choice of a particular policy, once a policy has been adopted it may prove very hard to alter or abandon. Incoming governments 'inherit' many policies and may continue them without examining whether or not they continue to be effective. In addition, once a policy has been adopted those decision-makers responsible for its formulation and implementation have a vested interest in its success. Therefore they prefer existing policy to succeed rather than to consider other options. In addition, implementation of any policy involves commitment of some of the state's resources for its success. It may not be politically easy to abandon this investment or to rearrange the allocation of resources. Implementing policy also involves committing some of a state's prestige, which can be considered a resource.

When these factors are added to the fact that all governments prefer there to be a degree of stability and predictability in foreign policy it is not surprising that foreign policy tends to be characterised by incrementalism. Policy emerges largely as modifications to existing policy.

23.4 Instruments of foreign policy

In seeking to influence the behaviour of other states, governments have a number of traditional policy tools at their disposal, of which the three most important are diplomacy, economic leverage and military power.

23.4.1 Diplomacy

Diplomacy is the management of international relations by negotiation. It seeks to unite differing interests, or at least to make them compatible, and to enable some interests to prevail peacefully over others. It is most suited to cooperative undertakings such as economic exchanges and alliances, but it is also central to efforts to avoid war and to end wars once they have begun.

Diplomacy can be seen as having four key functions.[6]

1. It facilitates communications between political leaders and other entities in international relations.
2. It makes possible the negotiation of agreements when the differing interests of states are perceived to overlap.
3. It enables the gathering of intelligence or information about other countries. A state's foreign policy can be no better than the information on which it is based.
4. It reduces the effects of clashes of interest in international relations.

Although advances in communications technology in the past half century have clearly affected the practice of diplomacy, the traditional values of diplomacy are still largely valid. Conflicts of interest, actual, apparent or potential, are the central reality of international politics, and diplomacy is the technique for accommodating such interests. It can be seen as involving two stages: determining the facts of the disagreement, and then formulating the terms of a settlement.

The development of modern communications has not altered the diplomat's role in this respect. There is more to communication than simply the exchange of messages. Meaning depends upon context. Messages have to be understood and interpreted. The significance of a message may lie as much in what it leaves out as what it includes. Diplomats are specialists in detecting and conveying such messages. The function of a diplomat is not to formulate his or her government's goals, but to explain them abroad and attempt to persuade others to adjust their own policies to conform with those objectives.

In the modern era, a great deal of diplomacy is concerned with issues that do not involve conflict in the sense of fundamental clashes of interests. Rather they relate to the need to coordinate and regulate an increasingly complex international system for the mutual benefit of all its members, for example in terms of trade or communication agreements. In addition states cooperate in order to address a range of problems for which a purely national response would be inappropriate. Efforts to coordinate international action to protect the Earth's deteriorating environment fall into this category.

While some novel developments may have appeared to overshadow traditional diplomacy, this is a misleading impression. For example, the age of the jet airliner has led to a great increase in 'summit' diplomacy, where heads of government meet directly to resolve international issues. Summits can help establish a personal relationship between leaders and can energise a bureaucracy, but for a summit to be success-ful the ground must be carefully prepared beforehand.[7] It is still patient, traditional diplomacy that brings the sides close enough together to a point at which a final summit can wrap up the details and produce an agreement. The vast increase in the number of states since 1945, the growing importance of economic diplomacy, the trends towards inter-dependence and globalisation, and the security dangers produced by the Cold War and nuclear weapons have led to the characterisation of the past half century as 'the era of negotiations.'

23.4.2 Economic leverage

The economic instrument can be defined as any economic capacity or technique which is explicitly used in an attempt to achieve foreign policy objectives. In theory almost every facet of economic activity could be employed in this way, but in reality the options are far more constrained. Many states are simply too poor and weak to use economic resources as a positive tool of policy. Even for wealthy, more powerful states, domestic pressures, international treaty obligations and the workings of the international economy may constrain the ability to use economic techniques.

The options open to states fall into a number of categories.

1. The first is financial techniques. States can attempt to put pressure upon other governments through the reduction, sus-pension or cancellation of aid or of credit facilities. Governments may freeze or confiscate bank or other assets of the foreign power held on their territory. They may impose a ban on interest payments or capital movements and may refuse to reschedule debt repayments.
2. States may also use commercial pressures such as the imposition of quotas on imports and exports, restrictions on licences, im-port–export embargoes, discriminatory tariff policies, the sus-pension or outright cancellation of trade agreements and joint projects, the banning of technology exports or the blacklisting of firms which trade with the target state.
3. In addition measures may be adopted with an impact on the target state's membership of international economic organisa-tions such as the IMF or World Bank. Governments of other states may veto (or threaten to veto) the target state's membership of the organisation, or vote for its suspension or expulsion from that body. They may be able to block the granting of loans or to oblige the organisation to move its headquarters or regional office away from the target state.

There are thus a wide range of economic activities which can be manipulated for foreign policy purposes. In the past thirty years, however, such economic sanctions have proved to be far more difficult to implement successfully than was thought to be the case in the years immediately after the Second World War, when a series of American successes created an exaggerated image of their usefulness.

There are a number of reasons why economic sanctions are difficult to make work in practice. In the first place threats to impose economic deprivation and hardship can create intense hostility in the target state. The population's resentment may make them more rather than less willing to endure continuing hardship. It becomes a patriotic duty not to submit to foreign pressure. The peoples of Iran and Iraq reacted to the pressure of US-led sanctions in this way in the 1980s and 1990s. Sometimes the population learns to adapt to the difficulties. Improvisation and innovation occur and economic restructuring in time reduces reliance upon imported materials. This pattern was seen in the sanctions imposed upon Rhodesia in the 1960s and Serbia in the 1990s.

In any case some states have relatively diversified economies and are difficult to pressurise economically without doing as much or more harm to one's own state. Where states have large diversified economies interruption of economic activities may produce dislocation, though not at a level sufficiently critical to produce the desired policy change. Even where a state is vulnerable it will make every effort to defeat the sanctions. Unless the sanctions regime is universal and vigorously enforced it is usually possible for a target state to find alternative sources of supply and alternative markets. Substitutes can be found for many products.

The economic weapon when it is effective at all, is a slow-acting instrument. It is often resorted to as an alternative to the use of military force in order to minimise human suffering, but it may itself produce effects that are far from morally neutral. The economic sanctions imposed on South Africa during the 1970s and 1980s were intended to influence the white ruling elite, yet their impact fell primarily on the majority black population that the sanctions were designed to help. Similarly, during the 1990s the United Nations imposed economic sanctions on Iraq designed to influence government policy. The sanctions caused tremendous suffering for ordinary Iraqi citizens who had no democratic way of influencing their government and led directly to the deaths of thousands of Iraqi children without significantly harming the lifestyles of the ruling elite. Economic pressure is not normally effective when it is the only pressure being applied, but is a valuable tool when used in conjunction with other pressures and inducements. The fact that it is resorted to so frequently despite its largely unimpressive record is explained by two factors.

1. States often wish to be seen to be doing something, possibly in response to public or international pressure, when in reality they are largely indifferent to the issue. Sanctions allow them to 'take action' in a way that will have little real impact.
2. Where the issues at stake genuinely are crucial, states often resort to economic sanctions as a way to avoid using the alternative of military power.

23.4.3 Military power

Military power is an important foreign policy instrument. It can be used to back up threats, to demonstrate strength ('showing the flag'), to intervene in, if not to actually instigate, international or civil war, to support allied or client states and to subjugate foreign populations. It is a contributor to national prestige and a shield behind which other policy instruments can come into play.[8]

This is to see military power and war in a Clausewitzian sense. The nineteenth-century Prussian strategist, Karl von Clausewitz, was the first to argue systematically that war should be seen and employed as a rational tool of policy in the same way as diplomacy and economic strength.[9] But military power, as Knorr points out, is 'the power to destroy and kill, or to occupy and control and hence to coerce'.[10] It is a tool that democratic governments have become reluctant to employ unless they believe that all possible alternatives have been exhausted.

In the 1970s, and to some extent in the 1990s, it was fashionable to argue that military power no longer served its traditional purpose. The scholars who argued this, however, came from North America and Western Europe, two areas unusually free of large-scale international violence since 1945. Critics of the military instrument pointed to the uselessness of weapons of mass destruction such as nuclear weapons and the failure of Western military force in Suez, Vietnam and Somalia and of Soviet failure in Afghanistan. Moreover war has become a more risky option. Some 80 per cent of the wars fought between 1815 and 1910 were won by the side which started the war. But between 1910 and 1965, 60 per cent of the wars fought were lost by the side which initiated them. More generally, foreign policy objectives have become more varied and intangible than before. The emphasis is less on territorial expansion and more upon improving trade, gaining allies, influencing international opinion and protecting the environment.

Outside the security communities in North America and Western Europe, however, war, particularly civil war with outside intervention, has been far more prevalent. There have been several examples in Africa and Asia, notably the Gulf Wars, Angola, Mozambique, Cambodia, Vietnam and Ethiopia.

One can distinguish between the concepts of military power and military force. The former depends on the latter, but is conceptually quite different. Thomas Schelling[11] defines it as the difference between taking what you want and making someone give it to you, between conquest and blackmail. The possession of military power allows a state to achieve certain foreign policy objectives without resorting to the use of military force. Military force is the actual use of instruments of violence to gain one's objectives. It achieves the objective by hurting the opponent. Military power, on the other hand, is rooted in psychology: it is the attainment of objectives by the exploitation of the opponent's fear of being hurt.

To an extent, therefore, the use of military force represents the breakdown of military power. A truly powerful state should not have constantly to demonstrate its power. The threat, either implicit or explicit, to do so should be enough to achieve its objectives.

Military power often forms an important backdrop to negotiations. Schelling correctly defines war as a bargaining process, a kind of 'vicious diplomacy'.[12] This suggests that war, far from signifying the end of diplomacy, is a part of diplomacy itself. The terms 'coercive diplomacy' and 'compellance' have been developed to describe the use of military force for diplomatic purposes, where the object of fighting is to make the opponent behave rather than to defeat him. It was this idea that lay behind the strategic bombing of the Second World War and the nuclear attacks on Hiroshima and Nagasaki. Real effectiveness in the military instrument lies in a state that possesses it being able to make other states behave in a desired way without continual recourse to the use of force.

States acquire military power as a means to achieve security. It can contribute to security in a number of ways, both in terms of support of one's own foreign policy and that of one's allies. Although military strength is crucial, it also represents a worry for governments, particularly democratic ones. Military power has to be acquired through spending which is unpopular and has to be at the expense of government spending on other, perhaps more socially useful, purposes. Moreover, for many societies the military represents a threat to the regime itself. Many states are military regimes and others live in fear of a military coup (see Chapter 4). A society that exploits military power too frequently risks becoming militarised itself and joining the ranks of the military regimes.

Foreign policy is 'the output of the state into the global system'.[13] It is the efforts by governments to affect events in the world beyond their sovereign territory, to pursue objectives and to influence the behaviour of states and other political actors in the international system. States attempt to exercise this influence by utilising their military, diplomatic and economic resources, either singly or, more usually, in combination. In terms of the study of politics, foreign policy analysis is particularly interesting because, both as a process and as an output, it occurs at the interface between domestic politics and international relations.

States therefore act in an international environment that constrains them as much as it presents opportunities. Governments have a number of policy instruments which they can employ to achieve their purposes, but the combination of instruments that is appropriate will vary from one situation to another.

Notes

1. W. Wallace, *Foreign Policy and the Political Process* (London: Macmillan, 1971), p. 11.
2. F. S. Northedge (ed.), *The Foreign Policies of the Powers* (London: Faber and Faber, 1968), p. 11.
3. Ibid., p. 11.
4. T. Hobbes, *Leviathan* (Oxford: Blackwell, 1960), chapter 18, p. 117.
5. R. L. Wendzel, *International Relations: A Policymaker Focus* (New York: Wiley, 1977), pp. 44–7.
6. H. Bull, *The Anarchical Society* (London: Macmillan, 1979), pp. 170–1.
7. G. R. Berridge, *International Politics: States, Power and Conflict Since 1945*, 2nd edn (Hemel Hempstead: Harvester Wheatsheaf, 1992), pp. 192–5.
8. J. Garnett, 'The role of military power', in J. Baylis et al., *Contemporary Strategic Thought* (London: Croom Helm, 1975), p. 51.
9. K. von Clausewitz, *On War* (New York: Random House, 1943).
10. K. Knorr, 'The international purposes of military power', in J. Garnett (ed.), *Theories of Peace and Security: A Reader in Contemporary Strategic Thought* (London: Macmillan, 1970), p. 50.
11. T. Schelling, *Arms and Influence* (New Haven, Conn.: Yale University Press, 1966), pp. 2–3.
12. Ibid., p. 2.
13. B. Russett and H. Starr, *World Politics: The Menu for Choice* (San Francisco: W. H. Freeman, 1981), p. 188.

Questions

1. What are the main factors shaping a state's foreign policy objectives?
2. Discuss the problems involved in using either military power or economic capability as an instrument of foreign policy.

24

International security

The issue of international security has always been central to the study of international relations. For some writers indeed it is the essence of IR, the issue on which study should be focused to the exclusion of other matters such as the workings of the international economy. Certainly it is the aspect of the study of IR which has given it its distinctive flavour, and it continues to be a central issue, even while perspectives on the nature of security have been changing.

24.1 The meaning of security

Although security has always been a central concept in IR, until recently it was one which few scholars attempted to define.[1] There is a general acceptance that it implies freedom from threats to core values, but there is disagreement about what those values should be. There is also disagreement about whether the focus for security should be at the level of the individual, the state or the international community.

From 1945 to 1980 security was interpreted in a rather crude manner to mean simply the military security of the state. Security policy was characterised as 'the result of rational assessment, by knowledgeable analysts, of a universe of potential threats, of varying risk, to which a country might be subjected'.[2] Similarly, the variety of potential threats tended in practice to be reduced simply to external military threats.

Yet there is no reason why the understanding of security should be limited in this way. The state is simply the means to an end, the pursuit of the good life for its people – not an end in itself. Historically, states come and go. East Germany, South Vietnam and Czechoslovakia have disappeared in recent decades. The existence of some states remains controversial for their 'citizens' as it does for Chechens in Russia and Irish nationalists in Ulster. Some states, dictatorships for example, are the main 'security' threat to their own people.

Nor is it always self-evident that external military threats are the obvious meaning of security. In countries like Switzerland and Denmark the threat to security may be seen more in terms of job security than military security. In countries like Estonia the problem is 'societal' security, the fact that nearly half of the Estonian population are Russians. In parts of Africa the nearest clean drinking water supply is half a day's walk distant and has to be transported on foot. The 'battle' against hunger, thirst and disease are the 'security' realities, not a nebulous external military threat.

Clearly, then, security can be defined in many different ways and the way we choose to define it has important implications for which issues and problems governments choose to give priority to. Three definitions will help to make this clear.

> A nation is secure to the extent to which it is not in danger of having to sacrifice core values if it wishes to avoid war, and is able, if challenged, to maintain them by victory in such a war.[3]

This is a very traditional interpretation, which focuses purely on the military aspect.

> Security, in any objective sense, measures the absence of threats to acquired values and in a subjective sense, the absence of fear that such values will be attacked.[4]

This is an improvement on the previous definition because it captures the idea that what a nation chooses to consider vitally important is up to it and may well differ in important ways between countries.

> Stable security can only be achieved by people or groups if they do not deprive others of it; this can be achieved if security is conceived of as a process of emancipation.[5]

The crucial point being made in this definition is the relationship between security and the *telos* defined by Aristotle. All political activity, at whatever level it occurs should have as its goal human emancipation – that is, the creation of a better life for ordinary human beings. The search for security is part of this effort, but to be truly successful it is therefore necessary that one community does not purchase its security at the expense of another's. It was the recognition of this requirement by the Soviet leader Mikhail Gorbachev that led him to bring about the end of the Cold War in the late 1980s.

The acceptance of a broader conception of security in modern international relations has meant that it is no longer a question of 'what is security?', but rather questions of, 'security for whom?', 'security for which values?', 'how much security?', 'security from what threats?', 'by what means?' and 'at what cost?', which have become the central.

24.2 The broader security agenda

'Security', like all political ideas, is a socially constructed concept. Thus its meaning can and does change over time. In the current era the use of the concept has been changing in a number of ways in response to changes in the international environment.

As early as 1980, the United Nations-sponsored Brandt Commission in its Report on world poverty, *North–South: A Programme for Survival*, called for 'a new concept of security that would transcend the narrow notions of military defence and look more towards the logic of a broader interdependence'.[6] It was a suggestion that was taken up in an influential book by the British IR scholar Barry Buzan, who argued that security could be thought of under two headings.

The first was the appropriate level of analysis – should it be the traditional focus on the state, or should it concentrate either at the level of the individual human being or perhaps at the level of the international or global community?

The second category for Buzan concerned the domain in which the security threats were perceived. He identified five such areas: military, political, economic, societal and environmental. He defined these as follows:

1. Military security 'concerns the two-level interplay of the armed offensive and defensive capabilities of states and states' perceptions of each other's intentions'.
2. Political security concerns 'the organisational stability of states, systems of government and the ideologies that give them legitimacy'.
3. Economic security concerns 'access to the resources, finance and markets necessary to sustain acceptable levels of welfare and state power'.
4. Societal security concerns 'the sustainability, within acceptable conditions for evolution, of traditional patterns of language, culture and religious and national identity and custom'.
5. Environmental security concerns 'the maintenance of the local and the planetary biosphere as the essential support system on which all other human enterprises depend'.

Buzan argued that the 'rising density' of the international system was producing new realities. By density he meant the frequency and complexity of the networks of interaction that tie the international system together,[7] in other words the effects of the ongoing processes of interdependence and globalisation. Examples of this were the capacity for planet-wide destruction represented by nuclear weapons, the global circulation of political ideas and the fact that many issues are now discussed in a planetary forum (the United Nations). The increasingly global network of economic production, trade and finance and the manner in which the activities of humanity are affecting the natural environment create common problems and the necessity for collective action to solve them.

24.3 Military security

Traditionally, international relations has discussed military security in terms of the 'security dilemma' facing states: that is to say, states exist in an international system without a world government. They must therefore look to themselves to defend their own people and territory against injury and attack. To do this they acquire armed forces which seem threatening to the other states in the system, who therefore strengthen their own armed forces. This makes the first state feel insecure and so on. States attempt to purchase security at the expense of the security of other states.

Yet it is not quite that simple. Historically states have not come into existence and then sought military power to protect themselves. On the contrary, the state was essentially created through warfare in the interests of the ruling classes of the day. War in that sense has historically been the health of the state. Moreover, while states tend to speak of their armed forces as if they were purely for defence, this is actually a role they rarely play. States actually maintain armed forces for a wide variety of reasons. In many states their role is to control the domestic population rather than to deter outsiders, while in many developed states their purpose is normally to support the foreign policy of the state.

States employ the military instrument for a variety of purposes. One of these is deterrence. Deterrence is the prevention of the use by another state of its military instrument by posing a contingent threat against it. Dr Henry Kissinger defined deterrence as 'the ability to prevent certain threats or actions from being carried out by posing an equivalent or greater threat'. The most obvious example of such a strategy was the Cold War nuclear 'balance of terror' between the

United States and the Soviet Union, in which both sides threatened the other with a genocidal nuclear retaliation if the other should launch a nuclear first-strike against it. Conventional armed forces may also act as an effective deterrent against attack.

Should deterrence fail, a state may be obliged to defend itself against attack. A state may also feel that it must possess armed forces capable not only of protecting itself, but also of rendering aid to important allies whose downfall would be detrimental to its own security.

Outside of full-scale war, armed forces may be used for other functions. They can be used as an instrument of coercion, as for example when China attacked Vietnam in 1979 in an attempt to force her to withdraw from Cambodia, or when the United States invaded Grenada in 1983 to overthrow a government of which it disapproved.

24.4 Environmental security

Environmental security is a good example of the way that the broadened security agenda has operated. The concept has been called the 'ultimate security' issue.[8] The collapse of the global environment would in turn produce a collapse of human civilisation, since the environment is the lifeboat for all Planet Earth's inhabitants.

A wide range of problems are seen as falling within the environmental security agenda. The first category would be issues related to the disruption of the regional and planetary ecosystems. These include climate change, deforestation, loss of biodiversity, desertification and other types of erosion, depletion of the ozone layer and various kinds of pollution. A second cluster of issues are those relating to energy shortages, for example depletion of natural resources such as fossil fuels and forests. To this can be added the difficulties arising from the transportation of certain energy forms (nuclear material and oil), and pollution problems related to production and storage.

The third group of problems are those that overlap with the 'development' category such as the general problem of rapid population growth threatening to overload the Earth's 'carrying capacity'. This in turn is a major factor in producing epidemics of dangerous diseases. Finally, shortages of food produced by overconsumption of scarce resources and the loss of fertile soils and water resources are included in this category.

In theory environmental security threats can be either natural or man-made. A volcanic explosion such as that which devastated the island of Montserrat in 1997 is clearly a massive security threat to a population, as would be an earthquake or other natural disaster.

National governments do in practice plan and operate against such dangers where they are to some extent predictable. The international community also coordinates certain activities to try and reduce the death and destruction caused by such events, for example through satellite monitoring of weather patterns and the exchange of data on earthquake activity and tsunamis (tidal waves) in the Pacific region.

In practice, however, most of the focus of environmental security is on the effects of humanity's impact upon the environment, for example in the build-up of 'greenhouse' gases in the atmosphere and the destruction of the Earth's protective ozone layer. The underlying assumption behind environmental security is the belief that humanity is living beyond the 'carrying capacity' of planet Earth. Carrying capacity can be defined as 'the total patterns of consumption that the Earth's natural systems can support without undergoing degradation'.

Although there are certain issues where there is a general awareness and concern regarding environmental security, such as the reduction of the ozone layer and the problem of global warming, there are many issues where the attitudes of states varies widely. Some states are more concerned about certain issues than other states and therefore tend to take the lead role in the diplomacy surrounding them.[9]

For example, Australia took the lead in creating an international environmental regime for Antarctica as did Sweden in attempts to create an international legal regime to prevent transboundary pollution through 'acid rain'. Sometimes it may not be a state which plays this role but rather a non-governmental organisation (NGO). For example, it was Greenpeace which played the lead role in the efforts to preserve the declining numbers of whales in the world's oceans.

Environmental security issues are 'federative', that is the complexity and sensitivity of ecosystems means that they can be disturbed by hitting even a single aspect, the effects of which cannot be contained within the borders of a single state. This turns specific ecosystems into regional environmental security complexes and implies that the international community must be forced to take concerted international action at either the global or the regional level to deal with the problem.

24.5 The problem of war

Alongside the threat of massive environmental collapse, the problem of war exists as the gravest security threat that many human populations have to face. But war has proved to be a daunting problem to overcome, for while most states claim to desire only peace, in practice they maintain armed forces not simply to protect themselves but in order to pursue their foreign policy goals. Their willingness to use force in pursuit of their objectives and the knowledge that other governments share this outlook produce the possibility of international war.

Hedley Bull defines war as 'organised violence carried on by political units against each other'.[10] War must involve organised violence that aims to kill members of another group, not simply to do them harm, otherwise war becomes synonymous with force. War involves large-scale collective violence, it is not merely conflict. Baruch's 1947 phrase 'Cold War' is misleading in this respect. Although all states have conflicts of interest these do not usually lead to war. Indeed war remains a relatively infrequent event in the history of most nation-states. Singer and Small assert that there were only 118 international wars between 1816 and 1980.[11]

Although images of certain wars such as the First World War are of states sliding unwillingly or accidentally into war, this is misleading. There is no such thing as an accidental war. States choose to go to war, and they do so because the governing elite believe that their goals are better served by going to war than by remaining at peace. 'War is not random violence, but focussed and directed. It reflects, no matter how irrational its overall impact or the chaos of immediate battle, some rational purpose for which it was initiated.'[12]

International society does not permit states to go to war for just any reason. It identifies legitimate reasons for war. Because war is not random violence, the presence of war in international relations does not in itself mean that there is an absence of order. War is itself a part of the current international order. The key questions traditionally associated with war are those which Hedley Bull noted: How does international society make war? When is war legitimate or not? What are the rules of legal behaviour associated with warfare?

Bull was working within the realist framework of IR thinking and therefore accepted war as being a natural and inevitable part of inter-state relations and a result of a warlike tendency within man. However, the warlike 'nature' of man appears to be something he learns from society rather than a part of his genetic inheritance.

The anthropologist Margaret Mead argued that war is an invention, like writing, cooking, marriage or trial by jury. It forms part of the knowledge which is derived from the cultural inheritance of a group. There have been isolated societies discovered in the past 200 years who have no conception of war. Since not all societies are aware of the invention it is clearly not inherent in human nature. More importantly Mead argued that to eliminate war, it would be necessary to develop a different way of handling the situations that a society deals with by going to war.[13]

War appears to be an attractive option for states under certain conditions because it is an escape from the pressures of compromise. It allows them to try to impose their preferred outcome in a situation upon others. When war is looked at in this way it becomes simply the use of force to achieve political objectives. Much of the attention IR scholars have given to the study of war in this century, however, results from the suspicion that war is not simply a rational political act.

Nevertheless, in the context of international politics war has acquired a certain legitimacy. International law recognises the legitimacy of warfare that is fought in self-defence. For the international system war serves as a brutal method of resolving disputes that cannot be settled through compromise.

24.6 Peace and security

Although international relations is sometimes characterised as a choice between war and peace and while studies of war are innumerable, far less attention has been paid to the question of peace. What exactly is the 'peace' that all states claim to seek, and how might it best be achieved?

IR theory assumes that states will not resort to war

> if there are more efficient, less costly and more legitimate ways of achieving their objectives. Empirical research indicates that peaceful periods are ones in which there has been a rich global institutional context in which major states have consciously attempted to establish rules for the conduct of relations and implement practices and institutions for resolving disputes.[14]

Peace, like war is the result of human decisions. How well a peace settlement is constructed will determine how long the subsequent period of peace is likely to last. A settlement like Vienna in 1815 produced nearly half a century of peace, while the Versailles agreements of 1919 led to a period of instability and great power war twenty years later. A poor peace can throw away the efforts of a successful war.

Peter Wallenstein argues that what distinguishes a period of peace between the major powers is that they have developed a set of informal rules to guide their relations. The effect of these is to prevent wars between the most powerful states and to lessen the frequency of the clashes between the major and minor powers.[15]

These policies focus upon what appears to be the major difference between peaceful and warlike periods. In warlike periods the great powers attempt to resolve their conflicts of interest unilaterally. They try to impose their own preferred solutions to the problems of the day. In peaceful periods the great powers are inclined to cooperate, to seek compromises with the other key states in the system. To facilitate this, they establish recognised procedures and international institutions which make such cooperation easier. On the basis of studies by Wallenstein (1984), Kegley and Raymond (1982, 1984, 1986, 1990) and Vayrynen (1983)[16] the following three factors seem to be associated with peace:

1. In peaceful periods rules of the game have been created and norms are not unilaterally abandoned.
2. The system as a whole restrains actors by offering them practices other than power politics for the resolution of issues. Such practices as buffer states, compensation and concerts of power permitting states to deal with territorial issues have been implemented.
3. Issues involving severe threats to territory, especially to the core territory of major states, and certain life-and-death issues are kept off the agenda through the creation of a tolerable status quo and the avoidance of messianism. The onset of war comes only after actors have failed to resolve the issue by following the non-violent practices and systematic rules presented as the most legitimate.

It is clear that at certain periods the states within international systems have been able to live in peace for considerable periods. Such periods are characterised by a reduction of the importance of the military instrument in relations between states. It may also be characterised by a reduction in the scale of armaments possessed by the major states. They achieve this goal by pursuing a partial disarmament strategy.

Disarmament is an approach to peace with a long history.

1. Its most radical form is general and complete disarmament (GCD). This requires the elimination of all weapons, but a problem is that almost anything could be used as a weapon. If all technology was frozen to solve this problem humanity would have to give up all its industrial technology, including not just nuclear power plants and aircraft, but all the medical advances of the past century. It would still leave the problem that, even if

weapons were abolished, the knowledge of how to make them would still exist. Alternatively, states may opt for partial disarmament. This may take the form either of a limited reduction in all classes of weapons, or alternatively. the partial or complete elimination of one particular category of weaponry, such as chemical weapons.

2. It is possible to distinguish between qualitative and quantitative disarmament. Qualitative disarmament attempts to identify weapons which are 'offensive' and eliminate them. This approach was tried unsuccessfully at the 1932 Geneva Disarmament Conference.

3. The alternative is quantitative disarmament. This would involve reducing numbers of one or more types of weapons or agreeing to preserve a particular fixed ratio of forces. The ratio approach was tried at the 1921 Washington Naval Conference. It was reasonably successful although Japan was unhappy at its allocation. The agreement also had the unintended effect of tending to channel competition into non-regulated fields.

4. Because of a perception that the interwar disarmament efforts had not produced the hoped for results, the late 1950s saw a new approach which came to be called 'arms control'.[17] It was based on the assumption that there could be military cooperation even between adversaries or potential enemies. Even the bitterest enemies have some interests in common such as preventing actions which could start genuinely unintended wars. This was obviously particularly true in the case of nuclear weapons.

    Arms control encompassed a wide variety of approaches designed to reduce the likelihood of war and the costs of being prepared for it in peacetime. Arms control focuses on stability and restraint. It can lead to weapons reductions, though it need not necessarily do so. Its goals are being achieved so long as restraint of some kind is being exercised with regard to weapons acquisition or deployment and stability is being maintained.

24.7 Gender and security

In looking at the issue of international security and the relationship between military security and environmental, economic and societal security as well as the relationship between security and justice, a particularly useful approach is to focus on the question of gender and IR.

Feminists have long argued that, as the UNESCO motto puts it, 'wars begin in the minds of men', that war is a peculiarly masculine activity and that studying the effects of gender on IR generally and security in particular is the solution to the problem of war.

In addition, they argue that male political leaders have historically chosen to define 'security' in purely military terms. This has diverted concern away from other areas such as the systemic insecurity represented by 'structural violence'.[18] Structural violence refers to reduced life expectancy as a consequence of oppressive political and economic structures, for example the much higher levels of infant mortality that are associated with poor women who do not have access to adequate health care facilities. Structural violence is particularly marked in its impact upon women and other subordinated groups and 'when we ignore this fact, we ignore the security of the majority of the planet's occupants'.[19] In addition, while on average 1 million people a year die from war killings, some 19 million die from preventable diseases associated with poverty.

This picture of relative human losses is particularly striking because of the resources being consumed by global preparations for war. The cost of twenty American Patriot missiles would purchase enough vaccine to inoculate the entire female population of Africa against tetanus. The opportunity costs of defence spending are therefore profound.

Feminists argue that for most women 'security' means very different things from the meanings given to it by men. Moreover, war has increasingly become an activity that involves women rather than men. In the First World War 80 per cent of casualties were soldiers; by the Second World War, 50 per cent of the casualties were civilians, a proportion that had risen to 80 per cent by the time of the Vietnam War. In the wars of the 1990s, the ratio was around 90 per cent civilian casualties, with most of them being women and children. In 1994 the Save the Children Fund reported that in the previous decade 1.5 million children had died and a further 4 million had been seriously injured in wars. It is therefore no longer appropriate to speak of war as if it were primarily an adult male sphere.

The same pattern can be seen in the area of environmental security. Gender divisions are identifiable in terms of who has access to what resources, what they are used for and who suffers most from environmental degradation. World-wide women suffer far more from the effects of environmental degradation than do men. As the main providers of food for the planet's population the workload of women increases when water, food and fuel resources are scarce. As the least well fed they suffer most from starvation and malnutrition. As the poorest they are least able to find adequate health care or to move away from environmental threats.

As Peterson and Runyan point out, women are the main food producers in most areas of the developing world. As their land is lost to corporate farms and water resources are increasingly polluted, rural women have to travel further and further in search of clean water. Similarly as forests are destroyed, they must travel further in search of the firewood they need to cook and to boil water to make it safe to drink.[20]

When such resources become scarce the possibility of practising sound ecological farming is reduced. Female subsistence farmers are forced to cultivate the same plots of land over and over again rather than rotating crops. If their families are forced away to seek fuel and water this is likely to push them onto untouched but marginal land with very sensitive ecosystems. Although half the population of Planet Earth are women they own only 1 per cent of the land.[21]

Feminists have also been at the forefront of the debate on security and global poverty. Clearly no one can be considered to have security if they are dying in abject poverty. Yet the facts of global poverty are shocking. More than one-fifth of the entire human race, 1.3 billion people, live in absolute poverty, lacking access to the most basic necessities such as food and clean drinking water. One third of the world's children are under-nourished and 12.2 million die before the age of five, 95 per cent of them from poverty-related illnesses. Half the world's population lacks regular access to the most essential drugs.

Yet all of these tragedies are preventable. The United Nations Development Programme estimates that an additional $30 billion in development aid over the next ten years would be enough to meet the basic nutritional, health, sanitation and education needs of the 1.3 billion people living in absolute poverty. Although $30 billion sounds like a lot of money, in reality it is not. It is only 5 per cent of annual global defence spending . Ending absolute poverty on this planet would cost just three weeks' defence spending.

24.8 Security communities

The security dilemma which drives states to acquire military forces to deter and use against each other is a fundamental obstacle to disarmament or the freeing of resources to address issues such as global poverty, but it has proved possible for certain groups of states to overcome this situation and create communities of states between whom the possibility of war is reduced effectively to zero.

In a famous study in the 1950s, the American Karl Deutsch examined this phenomenon and described such groups of states as 'security communities'.[22] Deutsch was interested in the age-old problem of the elimination of war. The way in which the study tried to do this was to investigate the problem of building a wider political community. If we knew why certain groups have permanantly ceased fighting wars against each other, we might learn how this achievement might be extended over larger and larger areas of the globe.

He defined a security community as 'one in which there is real reassurance that the members of the community will not fight each other physically, but will settle their disputes in some other way.' A 'pluralistic security community' was one composed of autonomous independent states. Western Europe is an example of such a community, as is North America. According to Deutsch, the key factors in achieving a successful security community were, first, a high correlation of certain shared values such as democracy, social market economies and respect for the rule of law, and second, a growing degree of mutual understanding, solidarity and responsiveness among the states that made up the political community.

The vital engine of this process was not military integration but rather economic integration coupled with pluralistic political systems, both domestically and in terms of relations with the other states in the community. For a security community to exist states must be prepared to compromise and cooperate on a daily basis.

24.9 Conclusion

Security is a state of affairs sought by states. Military security is an important component of this since war brings about a reduction in virtually all categories of security. However, there is much more to security than simply the military element and true security requires governments to address such goals as social and economic justice, the protection of the supportive regional and planetary ecosystem, and political freedoms.

Notes

1. P. Brock and M. Berkowitz, 'The emerging field of national security', *World Politics*, vol. 19, 1966, p. 124.
2. R. Lipschutz, 'On Security', in Lipschutz (ed.), *On Security* (New York: Columbia University Press, 1995), p. 6.

3. Walter Lippman, quoted in J. Baylis, 'International security in the post Cold-War era', in J. Baylis and S. Smith (eds), *The Globalisation of World Politics* (Oxford: Oxford University Press, 1997), p. 195.
4. Arnold Wolfers, 'National security as an ambiguous symbol', *Political Science Quarterly* Vol. 67, 1952, p. 485.
5. K. Booth and N. Wheeler, quoted in Baylis, 'International security, p. 195.
6. *North-South: A Programme for Survival*, Report of the Brandt Commission (London: Pan, 1980).
7. B. Buzan, 'Is international security possible?', in K. Booth (ed.), *New Thinking about Strategy and International Security* (London: Harper Collins, 1991), p. 41.
8. N. Myers, *Ultimate Security: The Environmental Basis of Political Stability* (New York: W. W. Norton, 1993).
9. G. Porter and J. Brown, *Global Environmental Politics* (Boulder, Colo.: Westview Press, 1991).
10. H. Bull, *The Anarchical Society* (London: Macmillan, 1977), p. 184.
11. M. Small and J. David Singer, *Resort to Arms: International and Civil Wars, 1816–1980* (Beverly Hills, Calif.: Sage, 1982), p. 78.
12. J. A. Vasquez, *The War Puzzle* (Cambridge: Cambridge University Press, 1993), p. 25.
13. M. Mead, 'Warfare is only an invention – not a biological necessity', *Asia*, vol. 40, 1940, pp. 402–5.
14. Vasquez, *The War Puzzle*, p. 264
15. P. Wallenstein, 'Universalism vs particularism: on the limits of major power order', *Journal of Peace Research*, vol. 21 1984, p. 246.
16. Charles W. Kegley and Gregory Raymond,'Alliance norms and war: a new piece of an old puzzle', *International Studies Quarterly*, vol. 26, 1982, pp. 572–95. Charles W. Kegley and Gregory Raymond, 'Alliance norms and the management of interstate disputes', in J. D. Singer and Richard Stolle (eds), *Quantitative Indicators in World Politics* (New York: Praeger, 1984), pp. 199–200. Charles W. Kegley and Gregory Raymond, 'Normative constraint on the use of force short of war', *Journal of Peace Research*, vol. 23, 1986, pp. 213–27. Charles W. Kegley and Gregory Raymond, *When Trust Breaks Down: Alliance Norms and World Politics* (Colombia: Univesity of South Carolina Press, 1990). Raimo Varynen, 'Economic cycles, power transitions, political management and wars between major powers', *International Studies Quarterly*, vol. 27, 1983, pp. 389–418. See Vasquez, p. 278.
17. For a detailed study see M. Sheehan, *Arms Control: Theory and Practice* (Oxford: Blackwells, 1988).
18. S. Dalby, 'Security, modernity, ecology: the dilemmas of post-Cold War security discourse', *Alternatives*, vol. 17, 1992, pp. 95–133.
19. V. Spike Peterson and A. S. Runyan, *Global Gender Issues* (Boulder, Colo.: Westview Press, 1993), p. 36.
20. G. Sen and C. Grown, *Development, Crises and Alternative Vision: Third World Women's Perspectives* (New York: Monthly Review Press,1987), pp. 44–52.
21. Peterson and Runyan, *Global Gender Issues*, p. 108.
22. K. Deutsch et al., *Political Community and the North Atlantic Area* (Princeton, NJ: Princeton University Press, 1957).

Questions

1. What is meant by the 'broader security agenda'?
2. Is war an inevitable feature of international relations?

25

International society

25.1 Introduction

Despite the obsessive focus on military security characteristic of much writing on international relations, much if not most of the activity in international relations concerns matters where the threat of war is not present. In addition, whereas the Hobbesian image of international relations is of an anarchy akin to 'nature red in tooth and claw', an alternative conception sees international relations as largely comprising commercial and political cooperation. This latter perspective sees the states and international institutions of the world as forming an 'international society'.[1]

This image of world politics, which can be called 'rationalist',[2] accepts that the international system is a global anarchy, but believes that 'the sense of belonging to the community of humankind, has left its civilising mark upon the state and international relations'. Thus according to Adam Watson:

> A strong case can be made out, on the evidence of past systems as well as the present one, that the regulatory rules and institutions of a system usually, and perhaps inexorably, develop to the point where the members become conscious of common values and the system becomes an international society.

The idea of international society is at least as old as the writings of Grotius in the seventeenth century.

During the 1980s the British Prime Minister Margaret Thatcher once declared that there is no such thing as society. In the national context of which she was speaking she was clearly incorrect. But could the same not be said more realistically about the idea of international society? The world appears to be far too large and its peoples too diverse for the concept of society to be accurately applied. Many of the elements usually associated with the idea of society are absent or extremely weak. Common traditions, common values and a sense of ethnic or other kinship are all absent. In addition, as Aron noted, the shadow of conflict and war hangs over the states in the system.

This is obvious, however, only if the comparison being made is with small-scale societies such as villages. In modern states, particularly the large, heavily populated industrialised states, the difference is less clear. Societies like modern India, Malaysia, the United States, Russia and the many multicultural states of the European Union are characterised by major variations in culture, religion, race, colour, language and so on.[3]

Luard therefore argues that while societies in many states are becoming less and less traditional, the opposite is true at the international level which is starting to take on some of the characteristics of a society. 'If not integrated', he says, it is 'at least interdependent and interrelated'.[4] The process of globalisation has played a crucial role in this development.

In practice, community does exist at the international level and the behaviour of states and other actors is crucially shaped by this reality. It is a mistake, however, to assume that all states are basically the same, or that the same 'rules' of international relations operate for all states everywhere. The geographical, political and security environment in which states exist is not the same everywhere. Therefore some states will operate in an environment overwhelmingly conditioned by 'societal' factors, such as the member states of the European Union, while others will operate in a region where societal features are much less strong, such as North–East Asia.

25.2 Theorists of international society

25.2.1 Grotius

The ideas put forward by Grotius about international cooperation, Seyom Brown has argued, have been added to little by twentieth-century IR.[5] For Grotius writing in the seventeenth century, an essential characteristic of human nature was sociability, the desire for a peaceful life that led humans to form communities of law and order and which helped lead to the creation of the states characteristic of the modern era. The order of these states is essentially based upon the ideas of 'live and let live' and respect for each other's territorial jurisdiction.

The Grotian tradition sees international relations as taking place within an international society in which states 'are bound not only by rules of prudence or expediency but also by imperatives of morality and law.'[6] It is a 'constitutional' approach to the study of international relations because of the emphasis it places on rules and law. The Grotian tradition has been distinguished from that based upon Hobbesian or realist assumptions, which deny that common values, rules and institutions bind states together in a society, and argue that international relations is a 'state of war' and 'an anarchy whose social elements are negligible'.[7]

Grotius accepted that the world is composed of sovereign states, but denied that the world is necessarily disorderly or conflictual. He differs from the classical tradition because he asserted that states, like people, are basically sociable, and he argued that through the reciprocity of mutual needs 'a great society of states' develops, characterised by common laws and customs. States abide by these rules out of long-term, enlightened self-interest.

25.2.2   Bull

Hedley Bull, like Grotius, defined the *problematique* or *raison d'être* of international relations in terms of the phenomenon of war and the conditions of peace and order, and was more concerned with the question of order. According to Bull international law, the balance of power, great power management and war are the common institutions of international society. Mutual respect for the territorial integrity and independence of states, and belief in the sanctity of agreements and in certain limitations on the use of force constitute the common interests of its members. These common interests in turn reflect the desire of states to maintain their independence.

Bull was not centrally concerned with the state and power but rather with the idea of international society. He criticised the way that earlier writers such as E. H. Carr jettisoned the idea of international society, and said: 'This is the idea with which a new analysis of the problem of International Relations should now begin.' By society he meant common interests and values, common rules and institutions.

According to Bull:

> A *society of states* (or international society) exists when a group of states, conscious of certain common interests and common values, form a society in the sense that they conceive themselves to be bound by a common set of rules in their relations with one another, and share in the working of common institutions.[8]

He argued that naked power is not the only reason why rules are obeyed in a state or in the international system.

Bull stressed the emergence of a universal international society, previously dominated by Western States, then by states which accepted Western values, and now embracing non-Western values. This raised the question of whether you could have an international society without shared values. Bull thought 'yes – as long as there are still common interests'. Bull interposed the idea of international society between, on the one hand, the Hobbesian rejection of the idea of a society of states (because states existed together in a state of nature that was a state of war) and, on the other hand, a Kantian view of a cosmopolitan or world society of individuals.

Hobbes' assertion that the notions of right and wrong had no place in the international state of nature was observably untrue. States recognised the existence and authority of legal and moral rules, they criticised each other's conduct in terms of them, and they showed their attention to them even in the breach by making excuses for their infraction.

Bull agreed with Grotius's view that international society cannot survive if it is prepared to tolerate resort to war for any purpose whatever. Bull thought that order existed, was part of the historical record of international relations and could be identified in contemporary world politics. Order had roots in the actual practice of states and not just in ideas about their relations. That it might be a precarious and imperfect order did not mean that it did not exist. The evidence for its existence lay in the common interest of all states in the achievement of the elementary goals of social life, in the rules that they established to that end and in their participation in common institutions – conceived in the anthropological sense as recurrent patterns of activity.

States prefer order and obedience to international law whenever possible. Foreign policy operates in an uncertain environment in which governments must constantly take decisions on the basis of less information than they would ideally like to have available. Any features which add order or predictability to this environment are therefore welcomed. States will normally adhere to orderly and lawful behaviour because they want other states in the system to do the same. They create common institutions both in the sense of structures like the International Court of Justice and the United Nations Organisation, and also in the sense of patterns of reciprocal orderly behaviour, such as the privileges given to diplomatic representatives, which states adhere to.

International society is obviously very different from national societies. It is not simply that power is very decentralised, it is also very concentrated. Military and economic power are dominated by a fairly small number of key states. In addition, the relationships between the various institutions that comprise international society are far looser than is true at the national or local level. The relationship between them is also less clear than is true in a traditional society. Thirdly, and most notably, international society lacks a well-developed sense of solidarity, the sense in which a member of a society feels a primary loyalty to it and feels a sense of belonging to it.[9] Evan Luard argues that international society also lacks an acceptance of the legitimacy of the existing social order comparable to national society and that it has no common value system, a feature that is often held to be an essential element of a stable social order.

25.3 International cooperation

The commonly held view in IR literature that the international system is essentially 'anarchic' is extremely misleading. It implies that because there is no world government, states are absolutely sovereign and that there are no significant external institutional constraints upon their behaviour. This is in fact very far from being the case. All states are bound up in a complex web of interrelationships and organisational memberships which profoundly affect their international behaviour. There are a wide range of international organisations which exist in order to facilitate international cooperation. Many of these are highly institutionalised, with permanent secretariats, specialist bodies and often formal assemblies. One of these organisations, the United Nations, includes virtually every state on Earth as a member and in addition has a vast number of non-governmental organisations with observer status, ranging from political groups such as Amnesty International to religious groups such as the Franciscan Order.

While all states in the international system subscribe to a basic minimum degree of cooperation involving mutual respect for each other's sovereignty and territory, international society embraces groups of states that have agreed to be constrained by more demanding rules of interaction in pursuit of common interests. These types of cooperation have been growing in number and scope since 1945 under the impact of growing material interdependence and globalisation, particularly in the realms of trade, communications and protection of the environment.[10]

Whether such increasing cooperation signals 'the end of anarchy' or not is a moot point. Some forms of cooperation, such as the rolling integration project of the states belonging to the European Union, signal the end of complete formal sovereignty for those states. Yet many forms of international cooperation are a product of the international anarchy rather than an alternative to it. Military alliances would fall into this category. They help constitute the international anarchy based on a balance-of-power logic. Even groups such as the EU can be seen as a reflection of anarchy to the extent that their development is motivated by a desire to compete economically against sovereign states such as Japan and the United States.[11]

Nevertheless, the degree of international cooperation is now such that Berridge, for example, speaks of the existence of a 'constitution' of world politics, composed of common interests being reflected in agreed rules of international procedure and institutions, including both formal bodies such as the United Nations and traditional forms of behaviour such as diplomacy and acceptance of international law.[12]

25.4 International law

International law is of a special kind. It does not come from the enactments of a body with the authority to make law (like Parliament), nor normally from the judgement of a court. It is constituted by agreement among states on the rules, principals and conventions which they will observe in their mutual relations. It may be formalised in a treaty and treaties may be buttressed by national enactments, or agreements may be of an informal, 'tacit' nature.

As its name suggests international law is (or was initially) the law operating 'among nations' or states. Even today states remain the main focus of international law though there are other actors (MNCs, international organisations, NGOs etc) and there always have been.

25.4.1 Positive law and natural law

According to the strict doctrine of legal positivism, states are not bound by any law to which they have not consented. There are, however, problems associated with positivism. For example, can a state arbitrarily withdraw its consent and break obligations to which it had been thought bound? Treaties usually include a clause allowing states to withdraw from the agreement, but oblige them to give a minimum period of notice of their intention to do so. General international law has held that in some cases it is applicable to states merely by virtue of their being members of the international community. For example, new states are considered bound by the existing international law. This is a view strongly held by the conservative Anglo-Saxon states.

More controversially, the example of practice over the past twenty years has led to the emergence of a view that if the overwhelming majority of the world's governments become party to an agreement over a long period, then it becomes binding even upon these states that have not signed. Essentially the argument is that a minority of governments may not frustrate the wishes of those who speak for the overwhelming majority of humanity. If this perspective became an explicit feature of international law it would have major implications for the concept of national sovereignty.

The natural law tradition in international law was based on a set of Roman principles derived from the ability of human beings to reason. Grotius modernised natural law by basing it on secular rationalism. The Roman concept evolved as a body of law for managing Rome's relations with other states and peoples. The Roman Cicero defined natural law as 'right reason in agreement with nature of universal application, unchanging and everlasting'.[13] Later theorists, such as Suarez in the sixteenth century, added that natural law was based upon custom.

There are problems when positivism and natural law diverge, for example in the area of human rights where positivism has emphasised the right of a sovereign state to do what it likes within its sovereign territory while natural law stresses the rights of the individual. The positivistic theory led the International Court to rule in favour of South Africa during the 1966 UN South-West Africa case.[14] In international law the failure definitely to resolve the dispute over positivism and natural law has meant that there is no universal agreement over what are the formal sources of such law.

25.4.2 Customary law

The sources of international law include customary law. This is based on the effect of the practice of a number of states with regard to a particular type of legal problem or situation. That is, what do states actually do when faced with a particular type of problem? But state responses may not always be consistent – in this case there is the question of how far do they establish norms?

Customary law evolves over time. A number of aspects of a practice may contribute to its eventual acceptance as customary law.

1. *Evidence*. Evidence of a state's practice may come from diplomatic correspondence, press releases, policy statements, legislation from that state's higher courts and the actual record of the state's behaviour in similar cases.
2. *Duration*. The longer a practice has been followed the more likely it is to be accepted as customary law.
3. *Consistency*. Even a short duration might suffice if the practice demonstrates uniformity and consistency among states. Consis-

tency implies that there should not be contradictions or discrepancies between states between one relevant instance and another.

4. *Generality*. This relates to whether the practice is widespread among a majority of states. A state which objects to a practice from the outset and objects persistently thereafter may be deemed not to be bound by that aspect of international law.

25.4.3 Rules of international law

The 'rules' of international law are a framework which has developed over centuries and which is still developing. A core of rules of international law laying down rights and duties of states in relation to each other developed in the sixteenth and seventeenth centuries. They were securely established by the Treaty of Westphalia in 1648. Westphalia codified a system based on the territorial state. Because the system revolved around the state, the rules of the system were those favouring the continuing existence of the state. The system evolved around the following ideas:

1. *National sovereignty*. The notion of national sovereignty asserted that the state was the highest form of political body. Within its borders it had complete autonomy and control. There was no higher form of authority such as those represented by the Pope and the Holy Roman Emperor during the European Middle Ages.
2. *Non-intervention*. Non-intervention was related to sovereignty. Because the state was sovereign states had no legal right to interfere in the domestic affairs of other states, for example by intervening in civil wars or supporting political parties or co-religionists. Although frequently breached over the next three centuries, this has remained a fundamental principle of modern international law.
3. *National loyalty*. National loyalty implied a loyalty to one's own state above all. In an era marked by religious warfare, this precept was particularly aimed at Catholics or Protestants who might wish to accord loyalty to co-religionists or countries governed by leaders sharing their religious beliefs rather than to their own state. A similar loyalty issue arose in the twentieth century during the era of communist states.

On this basis in the eighteenth century and more importantly the nineteenth and twentieth centuries was built an imposing edifice consisting of thousands of treaties, hundreds of decisions of international tribunals and innumerable decisions of domestic courts. Although the elements of continuity in the system are marked, the system is evolutionary. The great peace settlements, especially Vienna 1815 and Versailles 1919, marked major steps in the developing codification of the rules and norms governing behaviour between states.

25.5 Enforcement of international law

Each nation is bound only by those rules of international law to which it has consented. The main instrumentality by which international law is created is the international treaty, leading many political jurists to argue that it is only obeyed when it suits the interests of states to do so. Dickinson described it being 'as fragile as a cobweb stretched before the mouth of a cannon'.

It is not true, however, that international politics is one long brawl with the strong coming out on top. International law is *surprisingly effective*. In fact, during the 400 years or so of its existence, international law has in most cases been closely observed. Why is this the case?

Morgenthau puts it down to power politics. He argues:

> The small must look for the protection of their rights to the assistance of powerful friends. Whether such assistance will be forthcoming or not is a matter not of international law but of national interest as conceived by the nations . . . in other words whether or not an attempts to enforce international law will be made, and whether it will be successful will not depend on the justice of the case, but on the considerations of power politics . . .[15]

Yet most international law is effective without compulsion being needed. The reason for this is simply that it is in the interest of all nations to honour their obligations under international law. While states may obey a great deal of international law because they do not see it as especially important, they also usually obey it even when their interests are adversely affected. This is true for the same reason that it is at the domestic level. As Henkin points out:

> Law is generally not designed to keep individuals from doing what they are eager to do. Much of law, and the most successful part, is a codification of existing mores, of how people behave and feel they ought to behave.[16]

K. J. Holsti gives five reasons why states invariably obey international law:

1.   self-advantage;
2.   habit;
3.   prestige;
4.   fear of reprisal;
5.   a desire for stability and predictability in foreign policy.[17]

For example, a state will not infringe the rights of foreign diplomats on its own territory because that would only lead to reprisals against its own diplomats. For the same reason it will not renege on its commercial commitments and will expect other states to live up to theirs. Breaking international laws may bring short-term advantages but has long-term drawbacks. A state that gains a reputation for breaking treaties will find it hard to conduct diplomacy and will suffer a loss of prestige. In addition, other states are likely to retaliate. They may thereafter oppose the continuation or limit the implementation of other treaties which the original treaty-breaker has no wish to see threatened.

All governments desire some stability and predictability in IR. Orderly policy-making would be impossible if chaos was the usual state of affairs. Law observance for many types of transaction becomes so routine that policy-makers would consider alternatives only in great conflicts or emergencies. If an issue is believed to be of vital importance, however, the likelihood that a government will yield to a legal or ethical principle is minimal unless other and more powerful states are determined to enforce compliance, and this is rare unless substantial political or other reasons go together with the principle in question.

The small must look for the protection of their rights to the assistance of powerful friends. Whether such assistance is forthcoming is a matter not simply of international law but of national interest. Thus on some occasions, whether or not international law is enforced will depend not on the justice of the case, but on the considerations of power politics.

International law contributes to international order by stating the basic rules of coexistence among states – but only if it is based upon the way states normally behave towards each other anyway. International law cannot by itself be a factor for strengthening world order or peace.

Since 1945 international law seems to have moved away from strict positivism. Individual human beings are now seen as subjects of international law. This can be seen for example in the Nuremberg and Hague war crimes trials and in human rights issues during the 1990s, for example Iraq and the Kurdish minority after the 1991 Gulf War. It can also be seen in the 1950 European Convention on Human Rights. International Law now effects many non-state actors – IGOs,

NGOs, MNCs and so on. Also since 1945 there has been a huge growth in international law covering economic, social, communication and environmental matters rather than just political and strategic affairs.

25.6 International economic relations

One of the factors helping to sustain the current international society not existing prior to the middle years of the twentieth century is the extremely complex and integrated system of international trade and finance. The pattern of behaviour in the international economic system mirrors to a considerable extent that of the international political system itself and, as Spero has pointed out, can likewise be seen as an example of 'the management of conflict and cooperation in the absence of government'.[18] As with international politics the pattern of behaviour in international economics embraces everything from outright conflict to absolute cooperation, but unlike the political field it is always characterised by the density of the linkages created by trading and capital flows.

The current international economic order was laid upon foundations built during the second half of the 1940s. The Great Depression of the 1930s, which had devastatated the world's economies, was the result of fundamental flaws in the workings of the international capitalist system. In particular, lacking any international coordinating bodies, the system encouraged what has been called 'beggar thy neighbour'[19] foreign economic policies in which a combination of protectionism and ferocious competition led to simultaneous economic collapse in the 1930s. The result was a series of diplomatic initiatives during the 1940s which created the International Monetary Fund (1944) and the General Agreement on Tariffs and Trade (1947).

GATT consisted of a legally binding set of rules for the conduct of trade between its member states, designed to minimise the obstacles to free trade between countries. When a state's trade policies were found to be in breach of GATT rules there was a clear set of procedures for dealing with the issue in a way that minimised restrictions on trade. Between the late 1940s and the early 1990s, the numbers of states that were members of GATT rose from twenty-three to one hundred. Partly as a result of the GATT regime, world exports rose twentyfold in value and ninefold in volume in the period from 1950 to 1990.[20]

In assessing the contribution of the international economic system to international society two points need to be borne in mind. The first is that the system itself is characterised by conflict as well as cooperation, as is true in any society. The end of the artificial bonds of unity imposed by the Cold War and the rise of Japan and the European Union as trading rivals to the United States has created major tensions in the unity characteristic of the leading Western states.

Secondly, the international economic system is not in any sense homogeneous. There are massive differences in the relationships between different groups of states in the system. For example, the traditional 'West', which embraces Japan, North America and Western Europe, has economies which are highly developed, wealthy and linked in a dense system of economic interactions. In contrast many 'developing' states are poor, weakly developed, have only shallow links with other similar economies in their geographical regions and are effectively dependent upon the more developed states within the system. They have virtually no influence over the key international economic institutions, yet are the most likely to have to implement policies imposed by those institutions.

The growing pressures of globalisation have encouraged states in many parts of the world to pursue a regional solution to their economic and political problems. This is most evident with the European Union in Western Europe, but the same phenomenon can be seen in many other parts of the world, for example with the Association of South-East Asian Nations (ASEAN) and the Economic Community of West African States (ECOWAS).

25.7 International organisation

The difficulties associated with international law are related to the absence of sovereign international institutions under the condition of international anarchy. International anarchy, however, is no longer absolute. A growing number of international organisations are emerging, in rare cases having authority over states in certain areas. Archer defines an international organisation as 'a formal, continuous structure established by agreement between members (governmental and/or non-governmental) from two or more sovereign states with the aim of pursuing the common interests of the membership.'[21]

There has been a steady growth in the number of both inter-governmental organisations (IGOs) and non-governmental organisations, (NGOS). There are at present more than 300 IGOs and over 2,000 NGOS.[22] They can be divided into global and regional organisations, for example the United Nations and North Atlantic Treaty Organisation respectively. These in turn can be subdivided in terms of whether, like the UN, they are multipurpose or, like its functional bodies (the International Court of Justice or the International Civil Aviation Organisation) they have a single area of responsibility. Regional organisations can be differentiated in terms of the extent to which they pursue integration (the European Union) or simply attempt cooperation in certain fields (Organisation of American States, Association of South-East Asian Nations).

The United Nations consists of a family of international organisations covering a number of fields of international cooperation. Each of these bodies varies in terms of objectives. They include the six permanent organs of the United Nations itself and a wide range of specialised agencies and commissions. Examples include the World Health Organisation, the Food and Agricultural Organisation, the Universal Postal Union, the International Labour Organisation, the International Atomic Energy Agency, the United Nations High Commission for Refugees and the Disaster Relief Office.[23]

Although it is active in a vast number of fields, impressions of the effectiveness of the UN are often based upon its efforts regarding the maintenance of international peace and security. Despite perceptions of failure in Somalia and Bosnia during the 1990s, the UN record is historically impressive. Between 1945 and 1993 the UN sent twenty-two peacekeeping missions, alleviated half of all the disputes brought before it and resolved a quarter of them.[24]

25.8 Conclusion

International society is notably complex and diverse. It includes a vast range of complicated subordinate societies and embraces a wide variety of functional organisations. It is also marked by its decentralised nature and by huge disparities in the wealth and influence of the bodies which compose it. There are also major differences in the value and belief systems held by individual cultures and states. Nevertheless, the process of globalisation is increasingly reinforcing the sense in which there is an international society, not simply an overlapping web of cooperating but essentially distinct and self-contained political systems. The existence of global processes and global problems is generating increasing demands for new forms of international governance with which to maintain order in this complex system.

Notes

1. R. Aron, *Peace and War* (London: Weidenfeld & Nicholson, 1966), p. 6.
2. A. Linklater, 'Rationalism', in S. Burchill (ed.), *Theories of International Relations* (London: Macmillan,), pp. 93–118.

3. Ibid., p. 94.
4. E. Luard, *International Society* (London: Macmillan, 1990), pp. 1–2.
5. S. Brown, *International Relations in a Changing Global System* (Boulder, Colo.: Westview Press, 1992), p. 29.
6. H. Bull, *The Anarchical Society* (London: Macmillan, 1977), p. 27.
7. M. Wight, 'Western values in international relations', in H. Butterfield and M. Wight, *Diplomatic Investigations* (London: Unwin, 1966), p. 92.
8. Bull, *The Anarchical Society* (London: Macmillan, 1977), p. 13.
9. Luard, *International Society* p. 7.
10. Brown, *International Relations in a Changing Global System* p. 30.
11. Ibid., pp. 32–3.
12. G. R. Berridge, *International Politics: States, Power and Conflict Since 1945,* 2nd edn (Hemel Hempstead: Harvester Wheatsheaf, 1992), p. 155.
13. F. Parkinson, *The Philosophy of International Relations* (London: Sage, 1977), p. 12.
14. R. L. Leiber, *No Common Power: Understanding International Relations*, 3rd edn (New York: Harper Collins, 1995), p. 290.
15. H. Morgenthau, *Politics Among Nations*, 5th edn (New York: Knopf, 1978).
16. L. Henkin, *How Nations Behave: Law and Foreign Policy*, 2nd edn (New York: Columbia University Press, 1979), p. 93.
17. K. J. Holsti, *International Politics: A Framework for Analysis,* 2nd edn (London: Prentice-Hall, 1974), p. 418.
18. J. E. Spero, *The Politics of International Economic Relations*, 4th edn (London: St. Martin's Press, 1990), p. 10.
19. R. Walters and D. Blake, *The Politics of Global Economic Relations,* 4th edn (Englewood Cliffs, NJ: Prentice-Hall, 1992), p. 13.
20. Ibid., p. 16.
21. D. Zeigler, *War, Peace and International Politics,* 4th edn (Glenview, Ill.: Scott Foresman, 1987), pp. 156–9.
22. C. Archer, *International Organisation*, 2nd edn (London: Routledge, 1992), p. 37.
23. R. Ofeogbu, *Foundation Course in International Relations for African Universities* (London: Allen & Unwin, 1980), p. 197.
24. W. Nester, *International Relations: Geopolitical and Geoeconomic Conflict and Cooperation* (New York: Harper Collins, 1995), p. 174.

Questions

1. Why do states obey international law?
2. Why are international organisations important actors in world politics?

Section Five

Bibliography

Chapter 21 **Approaches to the study of international relations**

Ashley, R., 'The poverty of neorealism', *International Organisation*, vol. 38, no. 2, 1984, pp. 225–86.

Baylis, J., and Smith, S. (eds), *The Globalisation of World Politics* (Oxford: Oxford University Press, 1997).

Brown, C., *International Relations Theory: New Normative Approaches* (New York: Wheatsheaf, 1992).

Brown, S., 'Feminism, international theory and international relations of gender inequality', *Millennium*, vol. 17, 1988, pp. 461–76.

Burchill, S. and Linklater, A., *Theories of International Relations* (London: St. Martin's Press, 1996).

Dougherty, J. R. and Pfaltzgraff, R. Jnr (eds), *Contending Theories of International Relations*, 3rd edn (New York: HarperCollins, 1990).

Gabriel, J. M., *Worldviews and Theories of International Relations* (London: St. Martins Press, 1994).

Grant, R. and Newland, K. (eds), *Gender in International Relations* (Milton Keynes and Buckingham: Open University Press, 1991).

Hoffman, M., 'Critical theory and the inter-paradigm debate', *Millennium: Journal of International Studies*, vol. 16, no 2, 1987, pp. 231–49.

Holsti, K. J., *International Politics: A Framework for Analysis*, 5th edn (Englewood Cliffs, NJ Prentice Hall, 1988).

Holsti, K. J., 'Mirror, mirror on the wall which are the fairest theories of all?', *International Studies Quarterly*, vol. 33, no. 3, 1989, pp. 255–61.

Keohane, R. O., (ed.) *Neorealism and its Critics* (New York: Columbia University Press, 1986).

Knutsen, T., *A History of International Relations Theory* (Manchester: Manchester University Press, 1992).

Lieber, R., *No Common Power: Understanding International Relations*, 3rd edn (New York: Harper Collins, 1995).

Linklater, A., *Beyond Realism and Marxism: Critical Theory and International Relations*, (London: Macmillan,1990).

Linklater. A., 'The question of the next stage in international relations theory: a critical-theoretical point of view', *Millennium: Journal of International Studies*, vol. 21, no. 1, 1992, pp. 77–98.

Little, R. and Smith, M., *Perspectives on World Politics*, 2nd edn (London: Routledge, 1991).

Nye, J., 'Neorealism and neoliberalism', *World Politics*, vol. 40, no. 2, 1988, pp. 235–51.

Olson, W. and Groom, A. J. R., *International Relations Then and Now* (London: HarperCollins, 1991).

Parkinson, F., *The Philosophy of International Relations* (London: Sage, 1977).

Peterson, V. Spike and Runyan, S., *Global Gender Issues*, (Boulder, Colo.: Westview Press, 1993).

Reynolds, C., *The World of States: An Introduction to Explanation and Theory* (London: Edward Elgar, 1992).

Runyan, S., *Global Gender Issues* (Boulder, Colo.: Westview Press, 1993).

Sjolander, C. T. and Cox, W., *Beyond Positivism: Critical Reflections on International Relations* (Boulder, Colo.: Lynne Rienner, 1994).

Smith, S., Booth, K. and Zalewski, M., *International Theory: Positivism and Beyond* (Cambridge: Cambridge University Press, 1996).

Thompson, K. W., *Masters of International Thought* (Baton Rouge, La.: Louisiana State University Press, 1980).

Tickner, J. A., *Gender in International Relations: Feminist Perspectives on Achieving Global Security* (New York: Columbia University Press, 1992).

Viotti, P. and Kaupi, M., *International Relations Theory* 2nd edn (New York: Macmillan, 1993).

Waltz, K., *Man, the State and War* (New York: Columbia University Press, 1959).

Chapter 22 **The structure of the global system**

Axford, B., *The Global System* (Cambridge: Polity Press, 1995).

Balaam, D. and Veseth, M., *Introduction to International Political Economy* (Upper Saddle River, NJ: Prentice Hall, 1996).

Berridge, G. R., *International Politics*, 2nd edn (Brighton: Harvester Wheatsheaf, 1992).

Bretherton, C. and Ponton, G., (eds), *Global Politics: An Introduction* (Oxford: Blackwell, 1996).

Brown, S., *New Forces, Old Forces and the Future of International Politics* (New York: Harper Collins, 1995).

Gellner, E., *Nations and Nationalism* (Ithaca, NY: Cornell University Press, 1983).

Gilpin, R., *The Political Economy of International Relations* (Princeton, NJ: Princeton University Press, 1987).

Graham, K, (ed.), *The Planetary Interest* (London: UCL Press, 1998).

Holland, S., *The Global Economy* (London, Weidenfeld & Nicholson, 1987).

Jones, W. S., *The Logic of International Relations* 8th edn (New York: Addison Wesley, 1997).

Kegley, C. W. and Wittkopf, E. R., *World Politics: Trend and Transformation*, 6th edn, (London: Macmillan, 1997).

Keohane, R. O., *After Hegemony: Cooperation and Discord in the World Political Economy* (Princeton, NJ Princeton University Press, 1984).

Kofman, E., *Globalisation: Theory and Practice* (London: Pinter, 1996).

McGrew, A. and Lewis, P. et al. *Global Politics* (Cambridge: Polity Press, 1992).

Mansbach, R., *The Global Puzzle: Issues and Actors in World Politics*, 2nd edn (New York: Houghton Mifflin, 1997).

Nester, W., *International Relations: Geopolitical and Geoeconomic Conflict and Cooperation* (New York, HarperCollins, 1995).

Northedge, F. S., *The International Political System* (London: Faber, 1976).

Olson, W., *Theory and Practice of International Relations*, 9th edn (Englewood Cliffs, NJ: Prentice Hall, 1994).

Rosenau, J., *The United Nations in a Turbulent World* (Boulder, Colo.: Lynne Rienner, 1992).

Russett, B. and Starr, H., *World Politics: The Menu for Choice*, 5th edn (London: Macmillan, 1995).

Seligson, M. and Passe-Smith, J., (eds), *Development and Underdevelopment: The Political Economy of Inequality* (Boulder, Colo.: Lynne Rienner, 1993).

Sheehan, M., *The Balance of Power: History and Theory* (London: Routledge, 1996).

Spero, J. E., *The Politics of International Relations*, 4th edn (London: Unwin Hyman, 1990).

Spyby, T., *Globalisation and World Society* (Cambridge: Polity Press, 1995).

Walters, R. and Blake, D., *The Politics of Global Economic Relations*, 4th edn (Englewood Cliffs, NJ: Prentice Hall, 1992).

Weiss, T. and Gordenker, L., (eds), *NGO's, the UN and Global Governance* (Boulder, Colo.: Lynne Rienner, 1996).

Chapter 23 **Foreign policy analysis**

Allison, G., *Essence of Decision: Explaining the Cuban Missile Crisis* (Glenview, Ill.: Scott Foresman, 1971).

Arbatov, A., 'Russia's foreign policy alternatives', *International Security*, vol. 18, 1993, pp. 5–43.

Bahgat, K., ed.), *How Foreign Policy Decisions are Made in the Third World* (Boulder, Colo.: Westview Press, 1986).

Baldwin, D., *Economic Statecraft* (Princeton, NJ: Princeton University Press, 1985).

Caporaso, J., Hermann, C. and Kegley, C., 'The comparative study of foreign policy: perspectives on the future', *International Studies Notes*, vol 13, (1987), pp. 32–46.

Checkel, J., 'Ideas, institutions and the Gorbachev foreign policy revolution', *World Politics,*, vol. 45, 1992–3, pp. 271–300.

De Ruyt, J., *European Political Cooperation: Towards a Unified European Foreign Policy* (Washington, DC: Atlantic Council of the United States, 1989).

Doxey, M., 'International sanctions', in Haglund, D. and Hawes, M. (eds), *World Politics: Power, Interdependence and Dependence* (Toronto: Harcourt Brace Jovanovich, 1990), pp. 242–261

Gates, R. M., 'The CIA and Foreign Policy', *Foreign Affairs*, vol. 66, 1987/8, pp. 215–30.

Geller, D., *Domestic Factors in Foreign Policy* (Cambridge, Mass.: Schenkman, 1985).

Gerner, D., 'Foreign policy analysis: exilerating eclecticism, intriguing enigmas', *International Studies Notes*, vol. 17, 1992, pp. 4–19.

Gordon, P. H., 'Europe's uncommon foreign policy', *International Security*, vol. 22, no. 3, 1997/8, pp. 74–100.

Hagen, J., *Political Opposition and Foreign Policy in Comparative Perspective* (Boulder, Colo.: Lynne Rienner, 1994).

Hastedt, G., *American Foreign Policy: Past, Present, Future* (Englewood Cliffs, NJ: Prentice Hall, 1988).

Hellmann, G., 'Goodbye Bismarck? The foreign policy of contemporary Germany', *Mershon International Studies Review*, vol. 40, no. 1, 1996, pp. 1–40.

Hermann, C., 'Changing course: when governments choose to redirect foreign policy', *International Studies Quarterly*, vol. 34, 1990, pp. 3–22.

Hermann, M. and Hermann, C., 'Who makes foreign policy decisions and how: an empirical enquiry', *International Studies Quarterly* vol. 33, 1989, pp. 316–88.

Hilsman, R., *The Politics of Defense and Foreign Policy:Conceptual Models and Bureaucratic Politics* (Englewood Cliffs, NJ:, Prentice Hall, 1987).

Hindell, K., 'The influence of the media on foreign policy', *International Relations*, vol. XII, 1995, pp. 73–82.

Hudson, V. and Vore, C., 'Foreign policy analysis yesterday, today and tommorow', *Mershon International Studies Review*, vol. 39, no. 2, 1995, pp. 209–38.

Lindsay, J., 'Trade sanctions as policy instruments: a re-examination', *International Studies Quarterly*, vol. 30, June 1986.

Lindsay, J., *Congress and the Politics of US Foreign Policy* (Baltimore, Md: Johns Hopkins University Press, 1994).

McFaul, M., 'A precarious peace: domestic politics in the making of Russian foreign policy', *International Security*, vol. 22, 1997/8, pp. 101–37.

Macridis, R., *Foreign Policy in World Politics*, 7th edn (Englewood Cliffs, NJ:, Prentice Hall, 1989).

Shearman, P., ed., *Russian Foreign Policy Since 1990*, (Boulder, Colo.: Westview Colo: Press, 1995).

Shih, C. Y., *China's Just World: The Morality of Chinese Foreign Policy* (Boulder, Colo.: Lynne Rienner, 1993).

Singer, E. and Hudson, V., (eds), *Political Psychology and Foreign Policy* (Boulder, Colo.: Westview Press, 1992).

Talbott, S., 'Globalisation and diplomacy: a practioners perspective', *Foreign Policy*, Fall 1997, pp. 69–83.

Wallace, W., *Foreign Policy and the Political Process* (London: Macmillan, 1971).

Wiarda, H., *Foreign Policy Without Illusion: How Foreign Policy Works and Fails to Work in the United States* (New York: Scott Foresman/Little, Brown, 1990).

Chapter 24   **International security.**

Blainey, G., *The Causes of War* (London: Allen & Unwin, 1983).

Booth, K., 'Security and emancipation', *Review of International Studies*, vol. 17, 1991, pp. 313–26.

Brown, S., *The Causes and Prevention of War*, 2nd edn (New York: St. Martin's Press, 1994).

Buzan, B., *An Introduction to Strategic Studies: Military Technology and International Relations* (London: Macmillan, 1987).

Buzan, B., *People, States and Fear*, 2nd edn (Hemel Hempstead: Harvester Wheatsheaf, 1991).

Craig, G. and George, A., *Force and Statecraft*, 2nd edn (Oxford: Oxford University Press, 1990).

Dalby, S., 'The politics of environmental security', in J. Kakonen, (ed.) *Green Security or Militarised Environment?* (Aldershot: Dartmouth, 1994), pp. 25–53.

Deudney, D., 'The case against linking environmental degradation and national security', *Millennium*, vol. 19, 1990, pp. 461–76.

Deudney, D. and Matthews, R. (eds), *Contested Grounds: Security and Conflict in the New Environmental Politics* (Albany, NY: State University of New York Press, 1996).

Gaddis, J. L., 'The long peace: elements of stability in the postwar international system', *International Security*, vol. 10, 1986, pp. 99–142.

Galtung, J., 'Violence, peace and peace research', *Journal of Peace Research*, vol. 6, 1969, pp. 167–91.

George, A., (ed.), *Avoiding War: Problems of Crisis Management* (Boulder, Colo.: Westview Press, 1991).

Gilpin, M., *War and Change in World Politics* (Cambridge: Cambridge University Press, 1981).

Grant, R., 'The quagmire of gender and international security', in V. Spike Peterson (ed.), *Gendered States* (Boulder, Colo.: Lynne Rienner, 1992), pp. 83–98.

Howard, M., *Clausewitz* (Oxford: Oxford University Press, 1983).

James, A., *Peacekeeping in International Politics* (New York: St. Martin's Press, 1990).

Kaysen, K., 'Is war obsolete?', *International Security*, vol. 14, 1990, pp. 42–64.

Klare, M. T. and Thomas, D. C. (eds), *World Security: Challenges for a New Century* (New York: St. Martins Press, 1994).

Kolodziej, E., 'What is security and security studies? Lessons from the Cold War', *Arms Control*, vol. 13, 1992, pp. 1–31.

Krause, K. and Williams, M. (eds), *Critical Security Studies* (London: UCL Press, 1997).

Mathews, J. T., 'Redefining security', *Foreign Affairs*, vol. 68, 1989, pp. 162–7.

Mische, P., 'Ecological security and the need to reconceptualise sovereignty', *Alternatives*, vol. 14, 1989, pp. 389–427.

Moran, T., 'International economics and national security', *Foreign Affairs*, vol. 1990–1, 68, pp. 74–90.

Murray, D. and Viotti, P., *The Defence Policies of Nations*, 3rd edn (Baltimore and London: Johns Hopkins University Press, 1994).

Myers, N., *Ultimate Security: The Environmental Basis of Political Stability* (New York: N. W. Norton, 1993).

Reardon, B., *Women and Peace: Feminist Visions of Global Security* (Albany, NY: State University of New York Press, 1993).

Sheehan, M., *The Arms Race* (Oxford: Martin Robertson, 1983).

Stoett, P., 'The environmental enlightenment: security analysis meetes ecology', *Coexistence*, vol. 31, 1994, pp. 127–47.

Vasquez, J., *The War Puzzle* (Cambridge: Cambridge University Press, 1993).

Waltzer, M., *Just and Unjust Wars*, 2nd edn (New York: Basic Books, 1992).

Weltman, J., *World Politics and the Evolution of War* (Baltimore: Johns Hopkins University Press, 1994).

Chapter 25 **International society**

Akehurst, M., *A Modern Introduction to International Law*, 6th edn, (London: Unwin Hyman, 1987).

Archer, C., *International Organisations*, 2nd edn (London: Routledge, 1992).

Archer, C. and Butler, F., *The European Union: Structure and Process*, 2nd edn (London: Pinter, 1996).

Bennett, A. LeRoy, *International Organisations: Principles and Issues*, 5th edn, (Englewood Cliffs, NJ: Prentice-Hall, 1991).

Bull, H., *The Anarchical Society* (London: Macmillan, 1977).

Burton, J., *World Society* (Cambridge: Cambridge University Press, 1972).

Claude, I., *Swords into Ploughshares*, 3rd edn (London: University of London Press, 1964).

Dell, D., *The Politics of Economic Interdependence* (London: Macmillan, 1987).

Deutsch, K. and Hoffman, S. (eds), *The Relevance of International Law* (Garden City, NY: Doubleday-Anchor, 1971).

Diehl, P., (ed.), *The Politics of Global Governance: International Organisations in an Interdependent World* (Boulder, Colo.: Lynne Rienner, 1996).

Ekins, P., *A New World Order: Grassroots Movements for International Change* (London: Routledge, 1991).

Fawn, R. and Larkins, J. (eds), *International Society after the Cold War* (London: Macmillan, 1996).

Feld, W. and Jordan, R. with Hurwitz, L., *International Organisations: A Comparative Approach*, 2nd edn (New York: Praeger, 1988).

Hoffman, S., 'International society', in J. B. Miller and R. J. Vincent, (eds), *Order and Violence: Hedley Bull and International Relations* (Oxford: Clarendon Press, 1990).

Hurrell, A., 'International society and the study of regimes: a reflective approach', in V. Rittberger (ed.), *Regime Theory and International Relations* (Oxford: Clarendon Press, 1993), pp. 49–72.

Jacobson, H., *Networks of Interdependence: International Organisations and the Global Political System* (New York: Knopf, 1984).

Keohane, R. O., *Power and Interdependence* (Boston, Mass.: Little Brown, 1977).

Krasner, S., (ed.), *International Regimes* (Ithaca, NY: Cornell University Press, 1983).

Luard, E., *The United Nations* (London: Macmillan, 1979).

Luard, E., *International Society* (London: Macmillan, 1990).

Mansbach, R., Ferguson, Y. and Lampert, D., *The Web of World Politics* (New York: Prentice-Hall, 1976).

Mearsheimer, J., 'The false promise of international institutions', *International Security*, vol. 19, no. 3, 1995, pp. 5–49.

Onuf, N. G., (ed.), *Law-Making in the Global Community* (Durham, NC: North Carolina Academic Press, 1982).

Urwin, D., *The Community of Europe* (Harlow: Longman, 1991).

Watson, A., *The Evolution of International Society* (London: Routledge, 1992).

Wendt, A., 'Anarchy is what states make of it: a social costruction of power politics', *International Organisation*, vol. 46, no. 2, 1992, pp. 391–425.

Young, O., *International Cooperation* (Ithaca, NY: Cornell University Press, 1989).

Index